ENCOUNTERING RELIGIOUS PLURALISM

The Challenge
to Christian
Faith &
Mission

HAROLD NETLAND

InterVarsity Press
Downers Grove, Illinois

Apollos
Leicester, England

InterVarsity Press USA
P.O. Box 1400, Downers Grove, IL 60515-1426, USA
World Wide Web: www.ivpress.com
E-mail: mail@ivpress.com

APOLLOS (an imprint of Inter-Varsity Press, England)
38 De Montfort Street, Leicester LE1 7GP, England
World Wide Web: www.ivpbooks.com
E-mail: ivp@uccf.org.uk

InterVarsity Press® U.S.A. is the book-publishing division of InterVarsity Christian Fellowship/USA®, a student movement active on campus at hundreds of universities, colleges and schools of nursing in the United States of America, and a member movement of the International Fellowship of Evangelical Students. For information about local and regional activities, write Public Relations Dept., InterVarsity Christian Fellowship/USA, 6400 Schroeder Rd., P.O. Box 7895, Madison, WI 53707-7895.

All Scripture quotations, unless otherwise indicated, are taken from the Holy Bible, New International Version®. NIV®. Copyright ©1973, 1978, 1984 by International Bible Society. Used by permission of Zondervan Publishing House. Distributed in the U.K. by permission of Hodder and Stoughton Ltd. All rights reserved. "NIV" is a registered trademark of International Bible Society. UK trademark number 1448790.

Cover illustration: Roberta Polfus

USA ISBN 0-8308-1552-X
UK ISBN 0-85111-488-1

Printed in the United States of America ∞

Library of Congress Cataloging-in-Publication Data

Netland, Harold A., 1955-
  Encountering religious pluralism : the challenge to Christian faith and mission / Harold
A. Netland.
   p. cm.
  Includes bibliographical references and index.
  ISBN 0-8308-1552-X (pbk. : alk. paper)
   1. Theology of religions (Christian theology) 2. Evangelicalism. 3. Hick, John. I. Title.
BT83.85 .N48 2001
261.2—dc21
                                                                                                  2001024840

British Library Cataloguing in Publication Data

A catalogue record for this book is available from the British Library.

25 24 23 22 21 20 19 18 17 16 15 14 13 12 11 10 9 8 7 6 5 4 3 2 1
22 21 20 19 18 17 16 15 14 13 12 11 10 09 08 07 06 05 04 03 02 01

For Ruth

CONTENTS

Introduction

The religious landscape of Europe and North America has been undergoing rapid and profound changes over the past half century. The historical ties between the West and Christianity are clear enough—so much so, in fact, that in the eyes of many Christianity is little more than the religious dimension of Western culture. Whatever the case in the past, however, there is little question that the traditional links between Christianity and Western culture have been loosened considerably, through both the diminishing cultural significance of Christianity and the growing impact of non-Christian (especially Asian) religious traditions in the West.

Secularization, globalization and the sweeping demographic changes brought about by immigration have produced an unprecedented degree of diversity. Ethnic, cultural and especially religious diversity are most apparent in modern urban centers of the West. Driving through the congested streets of Los Angeles, Boston, Vancouver or Toronto, one passes by restaurants and specialty stores representing a bewildering variety of ethnic communities. But diversity goes much deeper than merely ethnic foods and music, for our societies are also marked by striking differences in basic values, lifestyles, worldviews and religious commitments. We live and work alongside atheistic naturalists, Wiccans, Muslims, New Agers and Sikhs. In school our children form friendships with Hindus, Buddhists, Jains, neo-pagans and Scientologists.

In the United States one of the more significant factors behind these changes was the 1965 immigration law. Not only did this law allow for increased numbers of immigrants but also it enabled groups that had previously been carefully restricted or even excluded, such as the Chinese and Japanese, to immigrate on the same terms as Europeans. Almost 40 percent of the new immigrants were from Asia, with millions bringing their Hindu, Muslim, Buddhist, Jain or Zoroastrian traditions and commitments with them. Reliable statistics are notoriously difficult to come by, but Diana Eck, chair of the Pluralism Project at Harvard University, reports that there are an estimated 5.5 million Muslims in the United States (almost as many Muslims as American Jews, estimated at 5.9 million), roughly 1.3 million Hindus, and about six hundred thousand Buddhists (although, as Eck points out, this last figure probably does not include native-born American meditators identifying themselves as Buddhist).[1] Driven by both immigration and conver-

---

[1] Diana Eck, "America's New Religious Landscape," in *Religion and Ethics Newsweekly: Viewer's Guide* (New York: Thirteen-WNET, 1998), p. 2.

sion, Islam is arguably the fastest-growing religion in the United States, with the *Chicago Tribune* reporting in 1997 that there are now more Muslims than Jews in metropolitan Chicago.[2]

Changing religious demographics characterize American universities as well. The Massachusetts Institute of Technology, for example, has twenty-eight student religious organizations on its campus—from the Chinese Bible Fellowship to the Zoroastrian Association—and Wellesley College (with only 2,300 students) has more than twenty-one religions represented on campus. Robert M. Randolph, senior associate dean at MIT, says, "One of the buzz words in universities is diversity. Most people tend to think of that in terms of gender and ethnic diversity. But the greatest diversity we have is religious life."[3] No longer is it only Christian campus ministry groups that target the university in an effort to spread the faith; Islamic study centers and Zen centers strategically located next to universities, working closely with the universities' interfaith centers, are now commonplace.

Perhaps the most visible indicator of the changing religious landscape is the proliferation of non-Christian places of worship or meditation, in both major cities and smaller towns. Over 1,100 mosques and Islamic centers are scattered across the United States.[4] Ornate Hindu temples provide a striking contrast to towering skyscrapers and suburban sprawl, not only in Chicago and Los Angeles but also in more unexpected places like Nashville, the capital of country music. In 1987 the first Shinto shrine on the U.S. mainland was dedicated in Stockton, California. Buddhist temples and meditation centers abound, with the most famous being the Hsi Lai Temple in Hacienda Heights, California. Completed in 1988 at a cost of $30 million, the temple gained instant notoriety when then–Vice President Al Gore visited it and both temple officials and the Democratic Party became embroiled in a political fundraising controversy. In the greater Chicago area alone there is an amazing variety of religious centers, including the first Jain temple to be built outside of India, a Zoroastrian temple, and the structurally magnificent Baha'i house of worship in Wilmette.

But is any of this really new? After all, as far back as recorded history takes us there have been different religious beliefs and practices. And as Robert Wilken observes, the history of Christianity is really a story of ongoing encounter with "religious others."

> Christians . . . have long had to face the challenge of other religions. For the first hundred years of Christian history a traditional religious culture (which was not, as once thought, moribund) set the agenda for many Christian intellectuals, and its spokes-

───

[2]Steve Kloehn, "Far from a Minority," *Chicago Tribune*, August 28, 1997, sec. 1, p. 1.
[3]Beth McMurtrie, "Pluralism and Prayer Under One Roof," *Chronicle of Higher Education*, December 3, 1999, p. A26.
[4]John L. Esposito, "Islam: Lifting the Veil," in *Religion and Ethics Newsweekly*, p. 16.

men energetically contested what seemed to be the pretensions of the new religion. Since the seventh century a large part of the Christian world, Christians
residing in the Eastern Mediterranean, for example, in Egypt, Syria, and Iraq, have
lived in the face of the seemingly invincible presence of Islam, and at a later date
Christians in the great Orthodox capital of Constantinople, as well as those in
Greece, Bulgaria, and the neighboring regions, had to adjust to life under the rule
of Ottoman Turks. Even in the Middle Ages, once thought to be a period of Christian spiritual as well as political hegemony, Western Christian thinkers were challenged by the continued vitality of Jewish communities in their midst and by the
boldness of Islamic philosophy. What is different today, I suspect, is not that Christianity has to confront other religions, but that we now call this situation "religious pluralism." For behind the term "religious pluralism" lurks not so much a
question as an answer, the view that particular traditions cannot be the source of
ultimate truth.[5]

So religious diversity itself is not new, nor are Christian encounters with
other religious traditions. And yet, as Wilken remarks, there is *something* different about the current encounter with other religions that gives the term
"religious pluralism" its distinctively modern sense. There is something
unique about religious diversity in modern societies, as well as the impact of
our awareness of this diversity, that encourages different ways of thinking
about the religions, thereby posing significant challenges to traditional orthodoxies.

The encounter with modern, globalized societies transforms to some extent traditional, established religions. The International Society for Krishna Consciousness is not simply ancient Hinduism in a modern Western setting; it is a
modernized, even Westernized, form of Hinduism. Nor is the user-friendly *zazen*
(sitting meditation) of the Los Angeles Zen Center exactly what one experiences in
the more austere practices of a traditional Zen monastery in Japan. The chic
Tibetan Buddhism of glittering Hollywood parties is a far cry from the sights,
smells and practices one encounters in Lhasa. The selective appropriation of exotic
Eastern symbols and traditions by segments of Western culture often results in
eclectic, syncretistic hybrids that, strictly speaking, are neither Eastern or Western.
The doctrines of karma and rebirth look attractive from the comfort of hot tubs in
Bel Air—who wouldn't want to be reborn into another life of affluence and glam-
our! They appear quite different to those in Southeast Asia for whom life is literally
a painful daily struggle for survival. The fascination with Tibetan Buddhism and the
Dalai Lama in the 1990s was largely driven by a kind of fantasy, a mythical construction of what some celebrities and academics wanted to believe about the pristine spirituality of Tibet—an image used skillfully for Tibetan causes by the Dalai

[5]Robert Wilken, *Remembering the Christian Past* (Grand Rapids, Mich.: Eerdmans, 1995), p. 26.

Lama.[6] Mythical constructions of "the other," along with the collision of traditional religions with the eclecticism and consumerism of modern, globalized cultures, can produce rather unusual combinations of religious symbols. Richard Shweder tells of an especially jarring juxtapositions of symbols:

> A few years ago, for example, I heard a story from Clifford Geertz about a visitor to Japan who wandered into a department store in Tokyo, at a time when the Japanese had begun to take a great interest in the symbolism of the Christmas season. And what symbol of the Christmas season did the visitor discover prominently on display in the Tokyo department store? Santa Claus nailed to a cross![7]

It would be difficult indeed to find two more diametrically opposed symbols than Santa Claus and the cross, and yet some apparently saw nothing incongruous about combining the two in a celebration of Christmas.

But the changing religious landscape of the West is about much more than just the religious diversity of our cities, the proliferation of mosques and temples, or even the bizarre mix of religious symbols (Zen-Catholicism, Christo-paganism, Santa Claus on a cross). Much more significantly, the changes affect how people think about religion in general and the relations among particular religions. This is part of what Wilken means when he says that what is different today is our speaking of the new situation as "religious pluralism," a distinctive consciousness about religious others. But the term "religious pluralism" itself is, of course, ambiguous and can be used in either a descriptive or a normative sense. Descriptively, it refers to the undeniable fact of religious diversity—people do indeed embrace different religious perspectives. This is obvious and not especially controversial.

However, the sense in which we are using it here goes beyond mere recognition of the fact of diversity to embrace a particular view, a normative judgment, about the relations among the major religions—that is, an egalitarian and democratized perspective holding that there is a rough parity among religions concerning truth and soteriological (salvational) effectiveness. In this sense religious pluralism is a distinctive way of thinking *about* religious diversity that affirms such diversity as something inherently good, to be embraced enthusiastically. It is this latter ideological sense that poses special challenges to Christian faith and forms the subject of this book. But as we shall see in the following chapters, the ideological sense of pluralism grows out of, and is sustained in part by awareness of, the fact of religious diversity.

---

[6]For a brilliant analysis of ways in which popular images of the spirituality of Tibet have been constructed and used in the West, see Orville Schell, *Virtual Tibet: Searching for Shangri-La from the Himalayas to Hollywood* (New York: Metropolitan, 2000).

[7]Richard Shweder, "Santa Claus on the Cross," in *The Truth About the Truth: De-confusing and Reconstructing the Postmodern World,* ed. Walter Truett Anderson (New York: G. P. Putnam's Sons, 1995), p. 73.

The Christian faith is based upon the conviction that God has revealed truth about himself and humankind—truth centered in the person and work of Jesus Christ that needs to be both believed and acted upon if sinful human beings are to be restored to a proper relationship with their Creator. The Christian gospel thus has elements of both universality and particularity at its core: universality in that all humankind (including sincere adherents of other religions) are sinners and in need of redemption by God's grace, and in that God desires the salvation of all irrespective of ethnicity, culture or religion; and particularity in that God's salvation comes to us through a particular person, Jesus Christ, the utterly unique incarnation of God who took upon himself the sins of the world.

This understanding of the gospel, however, is regarded by many as not only intellectually untenable but also morally unacceptable in our diverse world. Wilfred Cantwell Smith speaks for many when he states, "It is morally not possible actually to go out into the world and say to devout, intelligent, fellow human beings: 'We are saved and you are damned;' or, 'We believe that we know God, and we are right; you believe that you know God, and you are totally wrong.'"[8] The fact that no informed Christian would express it in quite this way does not detract from Smith's central point, which is that for many people there is something morally repugnant about followers of one religion maintaining that they are correct in their beliefs and that sincere adherents of other religions are mistaken in what *they* believe.

It is not only non-Christians who embrace Smith's critique of traditional Christianity. During the past century, there has been an unprecedented increase in the numbers of those who identify themselves as Christians and who reject the idea that God's truth and salvation are available in Jesus Christ in a manner not found in other religions. During the past fifty years, a growing number of Christians, laity and clergy alike, have embraced the notion that while the Christian faith is "true" and legitimate *for them,* other religions can be equally "true" and legitimate options for others in different circumstances. For example, the following statements, from in-depth interviews with lay Christians conducted by sociologist Christian Smith and his colleagues in their study of American Christianity, are instructive:

- In my mind there is only one God, no matter what you call him. Muslims pray to the same God I do. They call him Allah or whatever, but it's the same entity for all world religions, those that believe in a supreme being. They're talking generally about the same one.

- I am not a believer in missionaries. If we want to go to Africa and provide medical help

---

[8]Wilfred Cantwell Smith, *The Faith of Other Men* (New York: Harper Torchbooks, 1972), pp. 130-31.

and teach people how to farm, great. But if we go to Japan and try to convert Shin-toists, no way. If they came here and tried that on me, I'd get mad, and I think they have every right to feel the same. Christianity is great. If I'm anything I'm a Christian. But I think that others have a right to believe for themselves, and if they go to hell, they just took the wrong turn.

• To say that other religions are wrong is self-centered and egocentric. I am not even comfortable with saying all religions point to the same God. Whatever trips your trig-ger is fine with me, if that's your belief system. We are mortal. Who is to say who is right and wrong? If it helps you get through your life and helps bring meaning to your life, then fine.[9]

These are not radical relativists or atheists but self-confessed Christians who do not regard their comments as incompatible with Christian commitments. In this they are representative of many, both inside and outside the church, for whom the Christian faith is one among many legitimate paths to God. This reflects a perspective that is widespread in popular culture, firmly entrenched among the entertainment and media elite and forms an unofficial orthodoxy in much of academia.

This view grows out of what we might call the pluralistic ethos, a set of assump-tions and values that celebrates diversity of religious experience and expression as something good and healthy, is deeply suspicious of attempts to privilege one tradi-tion or teaching as normative for all, and while skeptical of claims that any particu-lar religious tradition has special access to truth about God, nevertheless freely acknowledges that different people can find religious truth *for them*. At its heart is the conviction that sincere and morally respectable people simply cannot be mis-taken about basic religious beliefs, especially when such beliefs and practices have beneficial effects for the participants. The pluralistic ethos manifests itself in vary-ing ways and degrees of sophistication, from a rather crude, undeveloped intuition that God will accept sincere and good people of whatever faith (and that therefore all religions are equally legitimate options) to sophisticated philosophical models such as that of theologian and philosopher John Hick.

The challenges posed by religious pluralism cannot be dismissed as merely the latest in theological fads that, like so many movements before it, will be replaced by even more bizarre discussions. The issues raised by pluralism are here to stay, and they strike at the heart of Christian faith, touching every major area of theology, including theological method, revelation, the doctrine of God and, most obviously, Christology and soteriology. David Tracy is not far off when he claims, "We are fast approaching the day when it will not be possible to attempt a Christian systematic

[9]Christian Smith et al., *American Evangelicalism: Embattled and Thriving* (Chicago: University of Chicago Press, 1998), pp. 53, 60-61.

theology except in serious conversation with the other great ways."[10] Although mission theorists and practitioners have long been aware of other religions, the issues of pluralism have recently provoked an acute sense of crisis within missiology, raising troubling questions about the nature and even legitimacy of Christian mission. Issues of pluralism are also forcing fresh and complex discussions in the philosophy of religion as questions in religious epistemology and metaphysics are being addressed within the contexts of intercultural and interreligious considerations. All of this has profound implications for theology, missiology and Christian apologetics within culturally and religiously diverse societies.

The late Lesslie Newbigin taught us to ask what a genuinely missiological encounter with Western culture would look like.[11] Missionaries going to other cultures have learned to read the historical, social, cultural and philosophical patterns shaping the worldview of those among whom they minister. Increasingly, those ministering in the West are applying the same tools to the study of Western cultures, and a key element of this missiological engagement with contemporary culture is making sense of the growing attraction of religious pluralism and responding appropriately to it.

Effective response to the multiple challenges of religious pluralism depends upon a proper understanding of the nature of the issues themselves and the factors underlying the attractiveness of pluralism. Thus this book is divided into two parts, with part one exploring the historical, social and cultural contexts within which religious pluralism has emerged and become so influential. A response to some of the issues raised by religious pluralism comprises the chapters of part two.

A proper understanding of, and response to, the challenges of religious pluralism must recognize both the continuity between current issues and those the church has always faced and also the distinctive sense in which today's questions are unique. In other words, the issues of pluralism cannot be understood adequately apart from appreciation of the broader historical, social and intellectual transformations of the past several centuries. The ideology of pluralism did not suddenly appear out of nowhere. Rather, the cumulative influences of the disestablishment of Christianity in Western societies, the increased marginalization of traditional religion in modern life, a deepening skepticism about the claims of orthodox Christianity, and the existential awareness of cultural and religious diversity engendered by globalization work together to erode confidence in the truth of Christian faith in favor of more pluralistic alternatives. Part one argues that the

---

[10]David Tracy, *Dialogue with the Other: The Inter-Religious Dialogue* (Grand Rapids, Mich.: Eerdmans, 1991), p. xi.

[11]See Lesslie Newbigin, *Foolishness to the Greeks: The Gospel and Western Culture* (Grand Rapids, Mich.: Eerdmans, 1986); and Lesslie Newbigin, "Can the West Be Converted?" *International Bulletin of Missionary Research* 11, no. 1 (1987): 2–7.

pluralistic ethos, and the more fully developed models of religious pluralism that grow out of it, are especially influential because of the combined impact of two deeply rooted trends in the modern world: first, widespread loss of confidence in the claims of traditional Christianity, brought about in part by the effects of modernization and the enduring legacy of religious skepticism; and second, the heightened awareness of cultural and religious diversity worldwide induced by the Western "discovery" of the New World and globalization.

It is not uncommon to find explanations of the recent ascendancy of religious pluralism in terms of the transition from "modernity" to "postmodernity," with the popularity of pluralism being taken as clear evidence of this shift. On this model, modernity is identified with the "Enlightenment mentality," which in turn is said to be characterized by optimism concerning human progress through science and technology, belief in universal truth and normative values, the capacity of reason to discover truth and know it with certainty, the push for homogeneity and uniformity, and grand "metanarratives" that explain the vagaries of history. Postmodernity, by contrast, involves loss of optimism and confidence in human progress, incredulity toward metanarratives, skepticism, suspicion of claims to truth, exuberant celebration of diversity, relativism, pragmatism and pluralism.

While not entirely without merit, this model is problematic on several grounds and, in particular, does not help us to understand the historical and cultural dynamics driving religious pluralism. In exploring the context of contemporary religious pluralism, then, part one argues against the idea that there is a sharp dichotomy between modernity and postmodernity and that we have abandoned the former for the latter. Part one proposes an alternative way of understanding cultural history in which the past several centuries are seen as contributing toward an identifiable "culture of modernity" that, rather than being a radical break with earlier times, is actually the intensification and spread of social, cultural and intellectual patterns that have been in place at least since the seventeenth century. Contemporary religious pluralism, part one argues, should be understood in terms of both continuities and discontinuities with the past, with some of the elements of pluralism so evident today having their roots in the sixteenth and seventeenth centuries. In other words, religious pluralism as a way of thinking about religious others is not a rejection of modernity but rather grows out of the ongoing processes of modernization and globalization, along with the intellectual legacy of skepticism about traditional Christianity.

The most influential apologist for religious pluralism in the West is John Hick, and in some ways this book is a sustained response to his views. Hick's journey from being a conservative theologian and defender of Christian orthodoxy to a radical pluralist (the subject of chapter five) exemplifies many of the themes set out in chapters one through four. Consideration of Hick's journey and views thus forms a bridge to part two, in which a response is given to many of the issues raised by religious pluralism.

At the heart of the issues prompted by pluralism are basic philosophical questions about the nature of religious truth and the basis upon which we are to make judgments about rival claims to truth. Thus chapters six through eight examine some of the relevant philosophical issues involved in the debate. John Hick's version of religious pluralism is the most philosophically sophisticated and influential model to date, and it is considered in some detail in chapter seven. In spite of its considerable appeal, I argue that it is weakened by numerous problems. Chapter nine explores the implications of religious pluralism for Christian apologetics. I argue that effectively meeting the challenges of pluralism requires going beyond merely "negative" apologetics and that the church must engage in appropriate forms of "positive" apologetics. Developing a comprehensive theology of religions is an enormous task that goes well beyond the scope of this book. But chapter ten addresses some of the basic issues involved in doing so and proposes an evangelical theological framework for understanding the phenomena of religion.

A brief word about methodology is in order.[12] The discussion in part one draws heavily upon history, the social sciences and philosophy in developing an explanation for the rise of religious pluralism in the late twentieth century. Given the prominence of these disciplines in the discussion, one might assume that religious convictions—belief and unbelief—are merely products of historical, sociocultural conditions, thereby falling victim to a kind of determinism. This, of course, is unacceptable.

We cannot here provide a comprehensive discussion of the many factors involved in expressions of belief or unbelief, but several brief comments might be helpful in locating methodologically the chapters that follow. First, we must recognize that even the terms *belief* and *unbelief* have an element of ambiguity, so that boundaries between them are not always clear-cut. While it is true that, from God's perspective, there is a clear distinction between those who are regenerate (or "saved") and those who are not, and while it is also true that appropriate belief is essential to salvation, on yet another level we can speak in terms of *degrees* of belief or unbelief. This applies both to the content of belief—what it is one believes—and the level of confidence with which one holds that belief. In the latter sense, people hold religious convictions with varying degrees of certitude, so that in some cases belief is joined by doubt and uncertainty.

From the perspective of Christian faith, other religious systems can be regarded

---

[12]In the following paragraphs I have been greatly helped by the insights of my colleague Dr. Bob Priest.

as forms of unbelief in so far as they explicitly reject what Christian faith affirms or they embrace teachings incompatible with Christian faith. Some religions will thus manifest greater unbelief than others, for their divergence from orthodox Christian teachings is greater than others. In this respect Theravada Buddhism, which denies the existence of a Creator God, is further removed from orthodox Christianity than orthodox Judaism or Islam. Although, from a Christian perspective, both Islam and Theravada Buddhism manifest unbelief, the nature of this unbelief is different in each case. Allowing for these ambiguities, then, we can from within the Christian perspective speak of other religious traditions as manifestations of unbelief, although (as I will argue in chapter ten) religions are complex phenomena involving multiple dimensions and cannot be understood merely as unbelief.

Furthermore, there is a delicate relationship between theological and nontheological factors in one's basic worldview and commitments, and excessive emphasis upon either dimension at the expense of the other results in distortion. Human agency is a complex phenomenon that can be understood on several levels. On one level, the ideology of religious pluralism, as a form of unbelief, must be understood fundamentally in theological terms. Pluralism is not something forced upon us by reality but rather, as a form of unbelief, emerges from and serves humankind's sinful tendencies. No Christian should be satisfied with explanations for religious commitments that fail to acknowledge the place of sin in unbelief or the supernatural work of God the Holy Spirit in saving faith. Rejection of the gospel of Jesus Christ is due ultimately to sin and rebellion against what we know to be true and right (Rom 1:18-32). We must also remember that the message of the cross—the very heart of the gospel—is foolishness to unbelievers (1 Cor 1:18-25). The cross is a symbol of human inadequacy, of our inability to save ourselves, and calls for self-denial and even death. In Dietrich Bonhoeffer's poignant words, "When Christ calls a man, he bids him come and die."[13] An invitation to death—death to self, death to sin, possibly even the physical death of martyrdom—is never popular in any culture. Thus there will always be a clash between the demands of following Christ and what the apostle Paul called the "wisdom of the world" (1 Cor 1:21), so that the tension between the gospel and prevailing assumptions can be eliminated only by compromising the gospel. And this we must never do.

We must also acknowledge that, apart from the special work of grace by the Holy Spirit upon our hearts, we cannot understand properly or respond appropriately to the gospel (Jn 3:3, 5-8; 2 Cor 4:4; Eph 2:8-10). Yet even as we affirm that salvation is a gift of God's sovereign grace from start to finish, we must also recognize that Scripture calls unbelievers to repent, believe and accept the gospel of

[13]Dietrich Bonhoeffer, *The Cost of Discipleship* (New York: Macmillan, 1963), p. 99.

Jesus Christ. God's sovereignty in salvation does not mean that the unregenerate are to be entirely passive; we are called, by God's grace, to believe and act upon the gospel.

Having acknowledged the place of sin in unbelief and the necessity of God's grace for salvation, however, it is crucial to recognize that belief and unbelief do not occur in a social or cultural vacuum. Human beings are rooted in particular times and places, so that each person's self-understanding and general worldview are shaped to some extent by society and culture. Although they do not determine our ways of thinking and acting, social and cultural influences do affect us in powerful ways, influencing our understanding of God and the cosmos. While it is true that fundamentally unbelief is rooted in sin—pursuing one's own autonomy and self-gratification rather than embracing God's truth and righteousness—sin manifests itself on various levels in different ways. Although the basic impulse of sin is universal, it expresses itself differently in various cultures. Or as Peter Berger put it in a perceptive reflection upon Paul's words in 1 Corinthians 1, while the gospel is always in tension with the prevailing assumptions of a given society, "the 'wisdom of the world' today always has a sociological address."[14] Thus the "wisdom of the world," while in some ways constant across time and place, looks different in first-century Corinth, seventeenth-century China, nineteenth-century Egypt or twenty-first-century America. The wisdom of the world for many Western societies today has been influenced deeply by the processes of modernization, secularization and globalization and by the intellectual legacies of the past several centuries that reinforce religious skepticism. As these patterns become institutionalized and embedded in culture, they provide powerful obstacles to the acceptance of the gospel.

In other words, however we arrange the various theological and nontheological factors involved in belief or unbelief, we must not lose sight of three basic truths: (1) that the faith that brings salvation is itself a gift of God's grace, given at God's initiative, (2) that sinful human beings are invited, indeed commanded, to repent and accept the gospel, and (3) that both God's invitation and our response are mediated through the social and cultural contexts in which we find ourselves. While the cross itself is always an offense to sinful humanity, there are also contingent historical, social and cultural factors that can inhibit acceptance of the gospel. The values and assumptions associated with religious pluralism are an especially influential set of such factors, and responsible witness in contexts influenced by pluralism must first understand the dynamics behind the rise of pluralism and then respond appropriately to the challenges it presents to Christian faith.

You may be interested to know that I have had the privilege of living much of

---

[14]Peter Berger, *A Far Glory: The Quest for Faith in an Age of Credulity* (New York: Anchor, 1992), p. 12.

my life in Japan, where the Christian community is a tiny minority (less than 1 percent of the total population) in a culture steeped in Buddhist, Shinto, Confucian and assorted folk religious traditions. Returning to the United States in 1993, I encountered religious pluralism in a different context as Christianity, once the dominant religious force in America, now struggles with its diminishing role in a society that increasingly rejects it in favor of fresh alternatives. Interestingly, issues of religious pluralism take somewhat different forms on each side of the Pacific. Many American Christians, for example, long for a much more visible presence for Christian faith in the institutions of the public square (such as prayer in the public schools) whereas most Japanese Christians are deeply suspicious of any hint of the dominant religious tradition (in this case, Shinto) extending its influence in the public sector. Issues of religion and state can appear quite different from the perspective of a minority, as opposed to a majority, religious tradition. At any rate, my experiences in both Japan and the United States have, I think, helped me to appreciate something of the complexity of the issues as well as the distinctive challenges for Christians in each culture.

I have benefited greatly from interaction with colleagues as well as students at Trinity Evangelical Divinity School who have sharpened my thinking through their perceptive comments and questions. Earlier versions of some of these chapters were presented as lectures at Calvin Theological Seminary, the Global Missions Training Center (Seoul), Tokyo Christian University, Canadian Theological Seminary and Wheaton College. I am grateful to these institutions for their gracious hospitality. Drs. D. A. Carson, Doug Geivett, Ben Mitchell, Terry Muck, John Netland, Robert Priest, Doug Sweeney, Tite Tiénou and Paul Hiebert read and commented on portions of the manuscript. I deeply appreciate their thoughtful comments and suggestions. Gary Deddo, of InterVarsity Press, also provided invaluable assistance through his perceptive comments and questions. To each one, thank you. Finally, I would be remiss if I did not also acknowledge my debt to Professor John Hick, under whom I studied at Claremont. For it was Professor Hick who first prompted me to consider seriously the implications of religious pluralism for theology and philosophy, and my views have been formed in large measure by way of response to his version of pluralism. It will be clear in what follows that I do not accept his views on pluralism, but this in no way detracts from my appreciation of him, both as a friend and as a scholar.

PART 1
RELIGIOUS PLURALISM IN CONTEXT

1
SHIFTING PERSPECTIVES ON OTHER RELIGIONS

For the first time since the Constantine victory in A.D. 312 and its consequences, the Christian Church is heading towards a real and spiritual encounter with the great non-Christian religions. Not only because the so-called younger churches, the fruits of the work of modern missions, live in the midst of them, but also because the fast growing interdependence of the whole world forces the existence and vitality of these religions upon us, and makes them a challenge to the Church to manifest in new terms its spiritual and intellectual integrity and value.

HENDRIK KRAEMER, Religion and the Christian Faith

T he half century since Kraemer penned those words has demonstrated the prescience of his observation. Few issues have been as prominent or controversial in recent Christian theological or missiological discourse as the question of the relation of Christianity to non-Christian religious traditions. Since the 1980s there has been an enormous increase, both in volume and in sophistication of discussion, in the theological literature on religious pluralism. In part this is due to the growing exposure in the West to other religions. Our awareness of "religious others" has never been more acute than it is today, forcing the church to deal with new and troubling questions that pose formidable challenges to traditional Christian beliefs and practices.[1] Canon Max Warren, for twenty-one years general secretary of the Church Missionary Society and a major missiological fig-

---

[1]Awareness of diversity presents challenges for other faiths as well as for Christianity. The Muslim scholar Adnan Aslan states, "As a person who was brought up and educated in a traditional Muslim society and who feels strongly about the truth of Islam, I have always considered the question of salvation as one of the vital existential questions in my own life. When I came to England to carry out postgraduate study in Religious Studies, and consequently met several people from very different traditions, the question which came immediately to my mind was whether or not they would be saved. If they are excluded from salvation simply because they were not born to the society to which I was born, then how could I justify the soteriological claims of my religion?" (Adnan Aslan, *Religious Pluralism in Christian and Islamic Philosophy: The Thought of John Hick and Seyyed Hossein Nasr* [Richmond, England: Curzon, 1998], p. ix).

ure in Britain in the mid-twentieth century, correctly perceived the seriousness of the issues when in an address in 1958 he claimed that the impact of agnostic science upon Christianity will turn out to have been mere "child's play" when compared to the challenge presented by non-Christian religions.[2] Writing almost forty years later, Gerald Anderson, one of the most astute observers of missions today, observed, "No issue in missiology is more important, more difficult, more controversial, or more divisive for the days ahead than the theology of religions. . . . This is *the* theological issue for mission in the 1990s and into the twenty-first century."[3]

Although the reasons for the recent prominence of religious pluralism as an issue for the church are varied and complex, it seems clear that more open perspectives on other religions are directly related both to increased exposure to religious diversity and to the cumulative effect of the social and intellectual forces of modernity that tend to undermine confidence in traditional beliefs. The increasingly pervasive exposure in the West to cultural and religious diversity, combined with the erosion of confidence in orthodox Christianity engendered by profound social and intellectual transformations, help to explain the current attraction of pluralistic views on Christianity and other religions. Chapters two through four will explore some of these factors underlying recent shifts in perspectives on other religions, but in this chapter we will first consider the nature of these changes over the past several centuries.

The Traditional Position

Christians have traditionally maintained that God has revealed himself in a unique manner in the Scriptures and preeminently in the incarnation in Jesus of Nazareth, and that sinful humankind can be reconciled to God only through the sinless person and atoning work of Jesus Christ, the one Lord and Savior for all people in all cultures. Allowing for certain distinctives of time and theological tradition, it is safe to say that this has been a central tenet of Christian orthodoxy throughout the past twenty centuries. Accordingly, in the early modern era other religions were regarded by Western Christians largely in negative terms as idolatrous "domains of darkness," and adherents of other religions were thought of as "the heathen" who were "spiritually lost" and in desperate need of the saving gospel of Jesus Christ.

The dominance of this perspective is certainly understandable, for its roots (if not the rather unflattering language in which it has sometimes been expressed) are

---

[2]As quoted in Wilfred Cantwell Smith, "The Christian in a Religiously Plural World," in *Religious Diversity: Essays by Wilfred Cantwell Smith,* ed. Willard G. Oxtoby (New York: Harper & Row, 1976), p. 7.

[3]Gerald H. Anderson, "Theology of Religions and Missiology: A Time of Testing," in *The Good News of the Kingdom: Mission Theology for the Third Millennium,* ed. Charles Van Engen, Dean S. Gilliland and Paul Pierson (Maryknoll, N.Y.: Orbis, 1993), p. 201.

firmly embedded in the New Testament and the practice of the early church. The first Christians were uncompromising monotheists who believed that the one eternal God had decisively revealed himself through the long-awaited Messiah, Jesus of Nazareth. Salvation was available to all—Jews and Gentiles alike—because of God's work on our behalf through Jesus Christ. Moreover, apostolic preaching insisted that salvation was possible only through Jesus Christ. Not surprisingly, then, alternative religious practices and beliefs were largely rejected as idolatrous, and the early church held a consistently critical posture toward the religious practices and beliefs of Hellenistic paganism.[4]

It is tempting to assume that the perplexing problems of religious pluralism we face today are unprecedented, but nothing could be further from the truth.[5] The world of the New Testament was characterized by social, intellectual and religious ferment. Traditional Jewish religious values and beliefs were being challenged by powerful competing forces within the Hellenistic-Roman world. Even within Palestine itself, Jews were confronted with alien beliefs and practices. The many Jews in the Diaspora, scattered throughout the Mediterranean world, were forced to come to grips with the relation between their traditional Jewish religious and cultural heritage and the invigorating intellectual and religious currents from Greece and Rome. Not only did they face the formidable challenge presented by Greek philosophy and literature but also they had to contend with the many popular religious movements of the day—the cults of Asclepius and Artemis-Diana, the "mystery religions" of Osiris and Isis, Mithras, Adonis and Eleusis, the ubiquitous cult of the Roman emperor and the many popularized versions of Stoicism, Cynicism and Epicureanism.[6]

John Ferguson observes that the attitudes of many in the Roman Empire in the first century were marked by tolerance of alien religious beliefs and practices, accommodation and syncretism.[7] The idea that there are multiple ways in which to

---

[4]See, for example, Richard Hess, "Yahweh and His Asherah? Religious Pluralism in the Old Testament World"; John E. Goldingay and Christopher J. H. Wright, " 'Yahweh Our God Yahweh One': The Oneness of God in the Old Testament"; and Thorsten Moritz, " 'Summing Up All Things': Religious Pluralism and Universalism in Ephesians"—all in *One God, One Lord: Christianity in a World of Religious Pluralism,* ed. Andrew D. Clarke and Bruce W. Winter, 2nd ed. (Grand Rapids, Mich.: Baker, 1992). For a comprehensive examination of the biblical data relevant to religious pluralism, see D. A. Carson, *The Gagging of God: Christianity Confronts Pluralism* (Grand Rapids, Mich.: Zondervan, 1996), chapters 5-7.

[5]See Robert Wilken, "Religious Pluralism and Early Christian Thought," in *Remembering the Christian Past* (Grand Rapids, Mich.: Eerdmans, 1995), chapter 2.

[6]See David W. J. Gill, "Behind the Classical Facade: Local Religions in the Roman Empire," and Bruce Winter, "In Public and in Private: Early Christians and Religious Pluralism"—both in *One God, One Lord.* See also James S. Jeffers, *The Greco-Roman World of the New Testament Era* (Downers Grove, Ill.: InterVarsity Press, 1999), chapter 5.

[7]John Ferguson, *Religions of the Roman Empire* (Ithaca, N.Y.: Cornell University Press, 1970), chapter 12.

relate to the divine, with each culture having its own distinctive traditions for doing so, was widespread.[8] The outstanding exceptions to this general pattern were the Jews and the early Christians, for the strict monotheism of Jews and Christians allowed no room for accommodation with the polytheistic traditions of Hellenism and Roman religion. Initially little more than a small minority movement within the Empire, the early Christians faced hostility on all sides. They were attacked by Jews as heretics, persecuted by Rome as a seditious movement, resisted by the masses for their rejection of the popular cults and mystery religions, and ridiculed by the philosophers for their seemingly crude views.[9] It was within this environment that Christians uncompromisingly proclaimed Jesus Christ as the only Lord and Savior for all peoples.

Although there were always those who accepted more accommodating views, it can hardly be denied that the traditional perspective—which regarded Christianity as the only true religion and Jesus Christ as the only Savior—remained dominant within both Roman Catholic and Protestant churches until the nineteenth century. This view prompted the emerging missionary movements of the Catholic and Protestant communities.

Throughout the Middle Ages it was the firm conviction of Catholics that those outside the church were eternally damned—a stance that has been associated with the formula *extra ecclesiam nulla salus* (outside the church no salvation).[10] Introduced by Cyprian in the third century and formalized at the Fourth Lateran Council in 1215, the doctrine was given its most explicit and rigid expression by the Council of Florence in 1442:

> [The Council] firmly believes, professes and proclaims that those not living within the Catholic Church, not only pagans but also Jews and heretics and schismatics, cannot participate in eternal life, but will depart "into everlasting fire which was prepared for the devil and his angels", unless before the end of life the same have

---

[8]Consider the statement of the late-fourth-century Roman prefect Symmachus: "Everyone has his own customs, his own religious practices; the divine mind has assigned to different cities different religions to be their guardians. . . . It is reasonable that whatever everyone worships is really to be considered one and the same. We gaze up at the same stars, the sky covers us all, the same universe encompasses us. What does it matter what practical system we adopt in our search for truth? Not by one avenue only can we arrive at so tremendous a secret" (*Relatio* 8-10, as quoted in Thomas Wiedemann, "Polytheism, Monotheism, and Religious Coexistence: Paganism and Christianity in the Roman Empire," in *Religious Pluralism and Unbelief: Studies Critical and Comparative,* ed. Ian Hamnett [London: Routledge, 1990], pp. 64-65).

[9]See E. C. Dewick, *The Christian Attitude Toward Other Religions* (Cambridge: Cambridge University Press, 1953), pp. 101-2.

[10]For discussion of the phrase *extra ecclesiam nulla salus* in the Roman Catholic context, and for the varying meanings attached to the formula, see Jacques Dupuis, *Toward a Christian Theology of Religious Pluralism* (Maryknoll, N.Y.: Orbis, 1997), pp. 86-101.

been added to the flock. . . . [N]o one, whatever almsgiving he has practiced, even if he has shed blood for the name of Christ, can be saved, unless he has remained in the bosom and unity of the Catholic Church.[11]

Jacques Dupuis reminds us, however, that the primary target of the formula was Jews, heretics and others who were held to be culpable because, having been exposed to the church's teaching, they had willfully rejected it.[12]

Protestants maintained that those apart from the gospel of Jesus Christ were forever lost, and it was this assumption that drove early missionaries to bring the gospel of Christ to the remote peoples of China, Africa, Latin America and the islands of the Pacific. Hudson Taylor, the great missionary to China, vividly expressed this perspective in his challenge to the Student Volunteer Movement in Detroit in 1894: "There is a great Niagara of souls passing into the dark in China. Every day, every week, every month they are passing away! A million a month in China they are dying without God."[13] One simply cannot understand the remarkable Protestant missionary effort of the nineteenth century, including the work of missionary pioneers such as William Carey, Adoniram Judson, David Livingstone and Hudson Taylor, without appreciating the premise underlying their efforts: salvation is to be found only in the person and work of Jesus Christ, and those who die without the saving gospel of Christ face an eternity apart from God.

Early Modern Missions and Religious Others
One might have the impression from current discussions of pluralism that it was Western theologians in the mid-twentieth century who first discovered the problem of Christianity and other religions. In reality, of course, questions about other religions have been prominent among missionaries since the early nineteenth century, with many of the perspectives adopted by theologians today having been anticipated in earlier missiological discussions.

Although he was not the first Protestant missionary, the modern missionary movement is often regarded as beginning with William Carey in India. At a time when many were convinced that Jesus' Great Commission in Matthew 28:19 to "make disciples of all nations" had already been fulfilled by the apostles and thus was no longer applicable, Carey challenged the theological establishment in 1792 by arguing that Christ's command had not been fulfilled and that it was still bind-

---

[11]*Enchiridion Symbolorum,* trans. Roy J. Defarrai, in *The Sources of Catholic Dogma,* ed. Henry Denziger (St. Louis: Herder, 1957), p. 230.

[12]See Dupuis, *Toward a Christian Theology of Religious Pluralism,* pp. 96-99.

[13]As quoted in Grant Wacker, "Second Thoughts on the Great Commission: Liberal Protestants and Foreign Mission, 1890-1940," in *Earthen Vessels: American Evangelicals and Foreign Missions, 1880-1980,* ed. Joel A. Carpenter and Wilbert R. Shenk (Grand Rapids, Mich.: Eerdmans, 1990), p. 285.

ing upon the church.[14] Within several decades numerous missions societies were formed and large numbers of European missionaries spread throughout Asia and Africa, carrying the gospel to those still apart from Christ. The sentiments associated with early missionary endeavors are captured in the comments of missions advocate George Burder at the 1795 inaugural meeting of the Missionary Society (later to become the London Missionary Society):

> I stand up as the advocate of thousands, of millions of souls, perishing for lack of knowledge. I stand up to plead the cause of Christ, too, too long neglected by us all— to plead the cause of the poor benighted heathen—to lay before you their miserable state—to convey to your ears and hearts the cry of their wretchedness—O that it may penetrate your souls—"Come over—Come over, and help us".[15]

As the West increasingly became aware of the large numbers of those who had never heard the gospel of Jesus Christ, there was an outpouring of concern for the salvation of the "heathen," with thousands committing their lives to the foreign mission field. Trying to discern the motives of others is always a perilous enterprise, and undoubtedly missionaries in the nineteenth century—just as Christians today—were prompted by a variety of motives, some more admirable than others. Nevertheless, David Bosch is surely correct in his assessment that "a primary motive of most missionaries was a genuine feeling of concern for others; they knew that the love of God had been shed abroad in their hearts and they were willing to sacrifice themselves for the sake of him who had died for them."[16] Remarkable men such as A. T. Pierson, John R. Mott, Robert Wilder, A. B. Simpson, C. I. Scofield, Robert Speer, T. J. Bach and D. L. Moody inspired generations of missions leaders and practitioners.

In spite of differences on more minor matters, there was a general consensus within Protestant missions on basic theological and strategic issues until the eruption

---

[14]William Carey, *An Enquiry into the Obligations of Christians, to Use Means for the Conversion of the Heathens* (1792). Excerpts from Carey's *Enquiry* are reprinted in *Classical Texts in Mission and World Christianity*, ed. Norman E. Thomas (Maryknoll, N.Y.: Orbis, 1995), pp. 56-57.

[15]As quoted in David Pailin, *Attitudes to Other Religions: Comparative Religion in Seventeenth- and Eighteenth-Century Britain* (Manchester, U.K.: Manchester University Press, 1984), p. 140. Also typical of the times was Burder's mixing of theological motivations for missions with a concern for "civilizing" the heathen. In the same sermon Burder remarked, "Those who are acquainted with the state of the world, need not be informed, that the heathen tribes, are in general, shockingly uncivilized. I have a view more particularly to the inhabitants of the South Sea Islands. Some of their customs are far too delicate to be rehearsed in a Christian audience. On the coast of Terra del Fuego, they are elevated but a small degree above the very brutes. Ought we not to pity fellow-men so degraded in the scale of society; and knowing the vast advantages of a civilized state, endeavor to civilize, may I not say, to *humanize* them?" (Quoted in Pailin, *Attitudes to Other Religions*, pp. 281-82. Emphasis in the original).

[16]David Bosch, *Transforming Mission: Paradigm Shifts in Theology of Mission* (Maryknoll, N.Y.: Orbis, 1991), p. 287.

of the fundamentalist-modernist controversies of the 1920s and 1930s. James Patterson notes that, prior to the controversies, most Protestant missionaries would have accepted the statement in 1920 from the Board of Foreign Missions of the Presbyterian Church in the USA that "the supreme and controlling aim of foreign missions is to make Jesus Christ known to all men as their Divine Savior and Lord and to persuade them to become His disciples."[17] The deity of Jesus Christ as the unique incarnation of God was largely unquestioned. Furthermore, most Protestant missionaries adopted largely negative views of non-Christian religious beliefs and practices, although many acknowledged elements of truth and goodness reflected in them. Salvation was said to be found only in Jesus Christ and, whatever their social or cultural merits, other religions were considered to be fundamentally contrary to God's revelation in Christ. While not neglecting the social dimensions of mission,[18] Protestant missionaries tended to focus upon proclamation of salvation to individuals and to look upon non-Western cultures as obstacles in their way. Non-Christian religions were seen as the cultural matrices within with such individuals were enslaved. D. L. Moody spoke for many when he said, "I look upon this world as a wrecked vessel. God has given me a lifeboat and said to me, 'Moody, save all you can.' "[19] The following statement made in 1896 by Judson Smith, a member of the American Board of Commissioners for Foreign Missions, can be taken as representative of the mainstream of nineteenth-century Protestant missionaries' attitudes toward non-Christian religions:

> Missionaries do not aim to Americanize or Europeanize the people of the Orient, or to bring them under the political control of the great powers of the West or to impose our type of civilization upon them. . . . They have a deeper aim and address a more vital need; they seek to Christianize these peoples, to penetrate their hearts and lives with the truth and spirit of the Gospel, to enthrone Jesus Christ in their souls. . . . There is no faith which Christianity is not worthy to replace, which it is not destined to replace. It is not to share the world *with* Islam, or *with* Buddhism, or *with* any other religious system. It is the one true religion for man as man in the Orient and in the Occident, in the first century and in the twentieth century and as long as time shall last.[20]

---

[17]As quoted in James Alan Patterson, "The Loss of a Protestant Missionary Consensus: Foreign Missions and the Fundamentalist-Modernist Conflict," in *Earthen Vessels,* p. 74.

[18]James Patterson states, "What is remarkable in light of later fundamentalist attacks on the evils of the 'social gospel' is that mission promoters before World War I generally saw no dichotomy between evangelism and social involvement." Patterson, "Loss of a Protestant Missionary Consensus," p. 76.

[19]As quoted in Bosch, *Transforming Mission,* p. 318.

[20]Judson Smith, "Foreign Missions in the Light of Fact," *North American Review* (January 1896): 25; as quoted in Robert E. Speer, *The Finality of Jesus Christ* (New York: Revell, 1933), pp. 161-62. Speer's volume, comprising special lectures at Princeton Theological Seminary and Southern Baptist Theological Seminary in 1932 and 1933, is an eloquent and impressive defense of the traditional perspective that, unfortunately, has been almost totally ignored by more recent debates.

Missions and Colonialism

In thinking about modern missions and religious others we must consider briefly the question of missions and colonialism. The story of Protestant missions and colonialism is a complicated one that often falls victim to the particular agendas of those telling the story. In addressing the issues we must allow for the ambiguities of earlier times, remembering that today we have the benefit of lessons learned over the past several centuries.[21] Nevertheless, some things are clear.

Through the pioneering and sacrificial work of thousands of selfless individuals, the gospel was carried literally worldwide and the church was planted among peoples on all continents, so that by the early twentieth century Christianity, uniquely among the world's religions, was a global religion. And yet the modern missionary movement has had an ambivalent relationship with eighteenth- and nineteenth-century Western imperialism, leaving a legacy that, among other things, has helped make the agenda of religious pluralism attractive today. For many in the West are drawn to pluralism in part out of a deep sense of postcolonialist guilt—and surely there is much in its treatment of non-Western peoples for which the West ought to feel profoundly guilty.[22] But it is often felt today that one way to atone for the past sins of colonialism is to embrace uncritically non-Western cultures and religions, refusing to make negative judgments about their beliefs and practices, and this sentiment naturally finds religious pluralism attractive.

Missions has had an ambiguous relationship with Western colonialism. In many cases there was a connection, whether intentional or not, between Western political, economic and military agendas and missionary endeavors. Given its close link to European and American cultures, at times reinforced through the complicity of missionaries with colonialist institutions, Christianity inevitably came to be identified as a Western religion, thereby assuming both the benefits and the liabilities of Western cultures and the entangling legacy of colonialism. Nineteenth-century missionaries were products of their times, just as we too are shaped by our own environments today, and they exemplified some of the prejudices of their peers. Thus in many minds the "three C's"—Christianity, commerce and civilization—came to exemplify the "blessings" that the West was to "share" with the rest of the

---

[21]Helpful discussions of the subject can be found in Bosch, *Transforming Mission*, pp. 226-30, 302-13; William R. Hutchison, *Errand to the World: American Protestant Thought and Foreign Missions* (Chicago: University of Chicago Press, 1987), especially chapter 7; Stephen Neill, *Colonialism and Christian Missions* (New York: McGraw-Hill, 1966); and Brian Stanley, *The Bible and the Flag: Protestant Missions and British Imperialism in the Nineteenth and Twentieth Centuries* (Leicester, England: Inter-Varsity Press, 1990).

[22]In reflecting upon the mistakes of previous generations we do well to remember the wry observation of the late Lesslie Newbigin: "It is much more pleasant and relaxing to confess the sins of one's ancestors than to be made aware of one's own." Lesslie Newbigin, *A Word in Season: Perspectives on Christian World Missions* (Grand Rapids, Mich.: Eerdmans, 1994), p. 122.

world. Stephen Neill observes:

> Missionaries in the nineteenth century had to some extent yielded to the colonial complex. Only Western man was man in the full sense of the word; he was wise and good, and members of other races, in so far as they became westernized, might share in this wisdom and goodness. But Western man was the leader, and would remain so for a very long time, perhaps for ever.[23]

However, as David Bosch reminds us, "it is simply inadequate to contend that mission was nothing other than the spiritual side of imperialism and always the faithful servant of the latter."[24] Individual missionaries and mission agencies had at best an ambivalent relationship with colonialist institutions and policies. Missionaries certainly did benefit from the protection provided by colonialist powers, but it is also true that colonialist institutions such as the East India Company were often hostile toward missionaries, whom they regarded as subversives who through their ministry among the natives would undermine the colonizers' economic and political interests.[25] Bosch quotes a French governor of Madagascar as saying of missionaries, "What we want is to prepare the indigenous population for manual labor; you turn them into *people.*"[26] Moreover, Vinoth Ramachandra observes that even in India, where the link between colonialism and missions was especially evident, Christian missions cannot be dismissed as merely religious imperialism.

> Christian missions in India are routinely dismissed in contemporary Indian scholarship as simply an adjunct to colonialism. But, in fact, they were the soil from which both modern Hindu reform movements and Indian nationalism sprang. Most of the Indian intellectual and political leadership of the late nineteenth and early twentieth century emerged from Christian schools and colleges. Gandhi may have claimed to have been nurtured in the spiritual atmosphere of the *Bhagavad Gita,* but it was not from this text that he derived his philosophy of *ahimsa* (non-violence) and *satyagraha* ("truth-force"). The deepest influences on Gandhi came from the "renouncer" traditions of Jainism and the New Testament, particularly the Sermon on the Mount as mediated through the works of Tolstoy. Christians in India have long been in the forefront of movements for the emancipation of women, with missionary societies from

---

[23]Stephen Neill, *A History of Christian Missions,* rev. ed. (Hammondsworth, U.K.: Penguin, 1986), p. 220.

[24]Bosch, *Transforming Mission,* p. 310.

[25]Neill, *Colonialism and Christian Missions,* pp. 83-93.

[26]Bosch, *Transforming Mission,* p. 311. Emphasis in original. Bosch explains, "The missionaries did this in many ways. They became friends of the local people, they visited them in their homes. They proclaimed to them that God loved them so much that he sent his only Son for their salvation. They convinced them that, in spite of the way they were being treated by other whites, they had infinite worth in the eyes of the Almighty. They demonstrated this by going out of their way to heal their sick and by offering education to both their boys and their girls. They studied the local languages and in this way proved that they respected the speakers of those languages. In summary, they empowered people who had been weakened and marginalized by the imposition of an alien system."

Britain and the United States often giving the lead where the colonial government was hesitant to tread for fear of upsetting local sensibilities.[27]

Nevertheless, the relation between colonialism and missions was often ambiguous. Indeed, in the eyes of many, Christianity and Western culture were indistinguishable. What missionaries understood to be the confrontation between truth and error, the kingdom of God and the powers of Satan, was often perceived by others as little more than the clash between Western imperialism and indigenous ways of living. The tragic legacy of this era continues to haunt current debates over religious pluralism.

The Fulfillment Theme Emerges

Ironically, even while the modern missionary movement was enjoying unprecedented success and the gospel of Jesus Christ was spreading to all parts of the globe, dramatic changes were occurring in Europe that were to alter forever the Christian community's understanding of itself and its mission in the world. The crucial assumption that God had revealed himself uniquely in the Bible, and thus that the Bible was absolutely trustworthy in all it says, was being eroded by higher critical views of Scripture and the conclusions of Darwinian science. The distinctiveness of Jesus Christ was being challenged by the developing discipline of the history of religions. Common prejudices about non-Europeans as savages were being undermined through extensive contact with the impressive cultures of China, Japan, India and Latin America.

From roughly 1840 onward, Protestant missions became increasingly embroiled in controversy over the theology of religions, culminating in the bitter controversies of the 1920s and 1930s.[28] The disputes were due to various factors, including greater openness to soteriological universalism and rejection of traditional teachings on hell,[29] increased sensitivity on the part of missionaries to indigenous cultures and contextualization of the gospel, and the reflection of missionaries upon their own experiences with deeply pious Muslims, Hindus and Buddhists. In Europe and North America certain theologians provided theological foundations for more open perspectives on other religions. The Anglican theologian F. D. Mau-

---

[27]Vinoth Ramachandra, *Faiths in Conflict? Christian Integrity in a Multicultural World* (Leicester, England: Inter-Varsity Press, 1999), pp. 78-79.

[28]The definitive study of discussions of other religions during this period is Kenneth Cracknell, *Justice, Courtesy, and Love: Theologians and Missionaries Encountering World Religions, 1846-1914* (London: Epworth, 1995). See also Patterson, "Loss of a Protestant Missionary Consensus."

[29]See David J. Powys, "The Nineteenth- and Twentieth-Century Debates About Hell and Universalism," in *Universalism and the Doctrine of Hell*, ed. Nigel M. de S. Cameron (Grand Rapids, Mich.: Baker, 1992), pp. 93-138; and Geoffrey Rowell, *Hell and the Victorians: A Study of the Nineteenth-Century Theological Controversies Concerning Eternal Punishment and the Future Life* (Oxford: Clarendon, 1974).

rice, for example, best known for *The Kingdom of Christ* (1842), in which he emphasized the "actual presence" of the kingdom of Christ in the world as a present reality, published his 1845–1846 Boyle Lectures as *The Religions of the World and Their Relations to Christianity*.[30] Maurice adopted a remarkably positive view of non-Christian religions, admitting God's presence and revelation within them. Thus Islam, Hinduism and Buddhism should not be rejected outright but should be affirmed as serving God's purposes, and missionaries in their encounters with other religions should build upon the "precious fragments of truth" contained within them. Nevertheless, for Maurice there was no question that Christ represented God's supreme and definitive self-revelation, for what was imperfectly anticipated in other religions is made complete in Christianity. Other theologians, such as B. F. Westcott, A. M. Fairbairn, Alexander V. G. Allen and Charles Cuthbert Hall, also influenced theologians and missionaries in adopting more positive views on other religions.[31]

More positive perspectives on other religions were evident at the turn of the century in missionaries Thomas Ebenezer Slater and Robert Allen Hume in India, Timothy Richard in China, Arthur Lloyd in Japan and many others.[32] Greater openness to other faiths was prompted both by the conviction that firm commitment to Christ did not necessitate total rejection of other religions as nothing but "domains of darkness" and a deepening appreciation of the richness of Asian cultures. Embarrassment and dissatisfaction with the close link between Christianity and colonialism, combined with a growing appreciation for the cultural achievements of India, China and Japan, reinforced a more open theological framework. This newer kind of missionary called for more respectful and appreciative attitudes toward religious others, acknowledging what they saw as undeniable truth and beauty in other faiths as incomplete anticipations of what had been definitively revealed in Christ. This more positive perspective eventually came to be called the "fulfillment theme view" of other religions, for it held that what was imperfectly present in other religions was most fully revealed in Christianity.

Although he was not the first to articulate the view, the fulfillment theme has come to be identified primarily with John Nicol Farquhar (1861–1929). Born in Aberdeen and educated at Oxford, Farquhar arrived in India in 1891 as a missionary

---

[30]Frederick Denison Maurice, *The Religions of the World and Their Relations to Christianity* (London: J. W. Parker, 1847). On Maurice's theology of religions, see Cracknell, *Justice, Courtesy, and Love*, chapter 2. Cracknell calls Maurice "the great prophetic thinker of the nineteenth century; the first to plead for justice, courtesy and love when Christians contemplated the meaning of other religions" (p. 35).

[31]The contributions of each theologian to the theology of religions are discussed by Cracknell in *Justice, Courtesy, and Love*, chapter 2.

[32]For discussion of these missionaries, see Cracknell, *Justice, Courtesy, and Love*, chapter 3.

with the London Missionary Society, and after a period of teaching at the Society's college in Calcutta, he was involved in evangelism, writing and lecturing under the auspices of the Indian YMCA, until ill health forced him to leave India in 1923. The last six years of his life Farquhar served as professor of comparative religion at the University of Manchester.

Among Farquhar's many writings, none has been as influential as *The Crown of Hinduism*,[33] a creative work in which "all the main features of Hinduism—as a religion and as a social system—were confronted with the Christian message."[34] Farquhar felt strongly the need for Christian missionaries to develop a positive appreciation for Indian culture and religion, and to present Christianity not as something that radically displaces Hindu traditions but that fulfills or brings to completion that which is already anticipated within them.[35] Farquhar was concerned to develop a theological framework in which Hinduism might be positively appreciated. The dominant theoretical model for understanding religions at the time was in terms of evolutionary development from more "primitive" religions to the "higher" monotheistic religions, culminating (naturally) in Christianity.[36] Farquhar largely adopted this view and regarded Hinduism as not so much false as incomplete, a "less developed" religion that can be appreciated on its own terms but that is to be supplanted by Christianity.

But Farquhar did not for a moment regard Hinduism and Christianity as equally legitimate options. He held that it is in Christ that God has revealed himself in a definitive manner, and it is only in Christ that humankind, regardless of religion or culture, can truly find fulfillment. An evangelist himself, Farquhar claimed, "Our task is to preach the Gospel of Christ and to woo souls to Him; and to that great

---

[33]J. N. Farquhar, *The Crown of Hinduism* (1913; reprint, New Delhi: Oriental Books Reprint Corporation, 1971).

[34]Eric J. Sharpe, *Not to Destroy but to Fulfill: The Contribution of J. N. Farquhar to Protestant Missionary Thought in India Before 1914* (Uppsala, Sweden: Gleerup, 1965), p. 330.

[35]Farquhar states, "All our study of Hinduism and everything we write and say on the subject should be sympathetic. I believe incalculable harm has been done to the Christian cause in India in times past through unsympathetic denunciation of Hinduism. Even if the severe condemnations passed on certain aspects of the religion be quite justifiable, it is bad policy to introduce these things into our addresses and our tracts; for the invariable result is that our audience is alienated. . . . Our aim is to convince the mind and conscience of those who hear us, and we shall do that far more effectively if we eschew the traditional habit of denunciation, and try to lead Hindus to the truth by other paths" (J. N. Farquhar, "Missionary Study of Hinduism" [paper presented to the Calcutta Missionary Conference, May 1905], quoted in Eric J. Sharpe, "J. N. Farquhar," in *Mission Legacies: Biographical Studies of Leaders of the Modern Missionary Movement,* ed. Gerald H. Anderson et al. [Maryknoll, N.Y.: Orbis, 1994], p. 293).

[36]Western views of other cultures and religions at this time were much influenced by the evolutionary anthropology of Edward Burnett Tylor. See J. Samuel Preus, *Explaining Religion: Criticism and Theory from Bodin to Freud* (New Haven, Conn.: Yale University Press, 1987), chapter 7.

end every element in our work should be made strictly subordinate and subservi-ent."[37] Although recognizing truths and noble aspirations in Hinduism, he empha-sized that there is also much in Hindu practice that fails to live up to these ideals and thus degenerates into idolatry. Furthermore, in speaking of fulfillment Farqu-har did not mean that Hindu beliefs and practices should be simply accepted by Christian missionaries just as they are. Basic elements of the Hindu worldview, such as assumptions about endless rebirths and *karma,* are false and thus should be rejected. As Eric Sharpe notes, for Farquhar "fulfillment" really meant "replace-ment," so that Christianity should build upon—but ultimately replace—Hindu-ism.[38] Christianity fulfills Hinduism in the sense that it provides the complete answers both to the questions emerging within Hinduism itself and to those that Hinduism fails to raise, and also in the sense that only in Jesus Christ will India find the resources to address the many problems it faces as it struggles to find its place in the modern world. Thus Farquhar concluded *The Crown of Hinduism* with these words:

> We have already seen how Christ provides the fulfillment of each of the highest aspira-
> tions and aims of Hinduism. A little reflection on the material contained in this chap-
> ter will show that every line of light which is visible in the grossest part of the religion
> reappears in Him set in healthy institutions and spiritual worship. Every true motive
> which in Hinduism has found expression in unclean, debasing, or unhealthy practices
> finds in Him fullest exercise in work for the downtrodden, the ignorant, the sick, and
> the sinful. In Him is focused every ray of light that shines in Hinduism. He is the
> Crown of the faith of India.[39]

Farquhar's views were controversial and he was criticized both by theological conservatives for being too accommodating of Hinduism and by liberals for still insisting upon the finality of Jesus Christ and Christianity. But the fulfillment motif, in varying forms, was to become a dominant theme in twentieth-century theologies of religions.[40]

Theological conservatives were not silent about the growing acceptance of what they perceived to be a naively optimistic view of non-Christian religions. In 1885, for example, Samuel Henry Kellogg, a missionary to India and profes-sor of missions and world religions at Presbyterian Western Theological Semi-nary in Allegheny, Pennsylvania, published *The Light of Asia and the Light of the World,* a passionate rebuttal of Sir Edwin Arnold's 1879 bestseller *The*

---

[37]Farquhar, "Missionary Study of Hinduism," pp. 298-99.
[38]See Sharpe, *Not to Destroy but to Fulfill,* pp. 336-39.
[39]Farquhar, *Crown of Hinduism,* pp. 457-58.
[40]For discussion of the fulfillment motif in reference to Roman Catholic theologians, see Dupuis,
Toward a Christian Theology of Religious Pluralism, pp. 132-43.

Light of Asia, a highly favorable poem about the life of the Buddha.[41] Deeply troubled by the large numbers who were being captivated by the poem's depiction of Buddhism, Kellogg argued that Arnold greatly exaggerated the positive aspects of the Asian religion as well as the extent to which Buddhism and Christianity were in agreement. Kellogg, by contrast, emphasized the "immeasurable disparity between the best that heathenism can offer and the teachings of the Gospel of Christ."[42]

In 1899 Kellogg wrote *A Handbook of Comparative Religion,* a remarkable work that "influenced many missionaries in the last years of the Great Century to take a hard line against other religions."[43] Kellogg's work can be taken as representative of the more traditional Protestant perspective on other religions and, although he wrote fourteen years before Farquhar's *The Crown of Hinduism* appeared, his views provide a powerful counterargument to the already emerging fulfillment theory. The immediate concern that Kellogg addressed was the "widely spread impression that the difference between the various religions of the world has formerly been greatly exaggerated; and that, in particular, the teaching hitherto current in the Church as to the exclusive position held by Christianity as the one and only divinely revealed system of saving truth, is as erroneous as uncharitable."[44] Kellogg goes on to describe the more pluralistic view gaining currency in the late nineteenth century:

> It seems to be imagined by many, that just as we ought to have charity toward our fellow-Christians in various sections of the Church of Christ, who hold on many points religious beliefs different from those which we have been educated to receive, inasmuch as in all that is essential to true religion and acceptance with God, we are truly at one; even so ought we to regard those who are not even Christians in name, but followers of one or other of the great world-religions [sic]. It is strangely fancied that howsoever these may differ from us in many things, yet in all things which are essential to man's eternal well-being, they also are practically at one with Christians; so that, if they but carefully live up to the precepts and observances prescribed in their several religions, it is thought that it is only charitable to suppose that their prospects for the life to come may be, on the whole, as good as our own.[45]

Despite all this, Kellogg was not one to dismiss everything in non-Christian religions as simply demonic and idolatrous. After surveying key teachings of Islam, Hinduism, Buddhism, Confucianism and Shinto, Kellogg readily admitted that

---

[41]Samuel Henry Kellogg, *The Light of Asia and the Light of the World* (London: Macmillan, 1885).
[42]Ibid., pp. xii-xiii.
[43]Cracknell, *Justice, Courtesy, and Love,* p. 14.
[44]Samuel Henry Kellogg, *A Handbook of Comparative Religion* (1899; reprint, Philadelphia: Westminster Press, 1927), p. v.
[45]Ibid., pp. v-vi.

there were some fundamental agreements across religions.[46] Furthermore, after rehearsing the biblical teaching on general revelation, he claimed that "the same Scriptures teach no less clearly that the working of God's Holy Spirit is by no means confined to those who have the revealed Word, but that the eternal Word 'lighteth every man.' " Thus, he says, "let it then be granted, once and for all, that in all the great religions of mankind may be discovered more or less important fragments of Divine truth; and even such truths as are distinctive of Christianity."[47]

However, Kellogg insisted that none of this in any way detracts from the Christian affirmations of the Bible as God's authoritative revelation and of Jesus Christ as uniquely deity, the one Lord and Savior for all peoples, nor from the Christian rejection of other religions as basically false. After reviewing fundamental disagreements between Christianity and other religions, Kellogg concludes,

> [B]eing assured that as an organized and self-consistent system of related truths, Christianity is to be held a true religion, it is not through any lack of charity, but under the constraint of an imperious logical necessity, that we affirm that Islam, Hindooism, Buddhism, Confucianism, in a word, all religions whatsoever other than that of Christ, must be regarded as false.[48]

The question of the destiny of the unevangelized was also widely discussed at the time, and thus Kellogg addressed the issue of "whether men can be saved by other religions than that of Christ." But he made a crucial distinction between two questions: (1) Can one be saved apart from actually hearing the gospel of Jesus Christ? (2) Can one be saved by carefully and sincerely following the dictates of the religion in which one finds oneself? Acknowledging that there is disagreement among Christians on the first question, Kellogg simply notes that "it is perfectly certain that whenever and wherever a man truly repents of all his sin and turns unto God, he will be saved." However, he correctly emphasizes that this is a distinct issue from the question of "whether a man can be saved from sin here and hereafter *by means of a diligent observance of the prescriptions of some other religion than that of Jesus Christ.*"[49] Since the basic assumptions of the major religions not only differ from those of Christianity but in many respects are contradictory among themselves, Kellogg concludes that it makes little sense to speak of a Hindu or Buddhist being "saved," as Christianity understands this term, through faithfully following the prescriptions of Hinduism or Buddhism. The missiological implica-

---

[46]Ibid., pp. 166-67. He noted that there were "important moral and spiritual truths" in other religions and emphasized that "it is of great importance that all Christians, and missionaries especially, recognize and heartily acknowledge such truths as they may find more or less clearly admitted in the religions of those among whom they labor."
[47]Ibid., pp. 168, 170.
[48]Ibid., p. 173.
[49]Ibid., pp. 174-75. Emphasis in the original.

tions of this position are clear, and Kellogg concludes his book with a stirring call to missions: "If the differences between the various religions of the world and the religion of Jesus Christ are such as have been herein set forth, and if the teaching of Christianity be accepted as undoubted truth, then Christian missions to the followers of other religions become a duty so clear that it should be self-evident."[50]

The Debate Intensifies: Continuity or Discontinuity?

Questions about Christian faith and other religions became increasingly controversial in missiological circles during the first four decades of the twentieth century. The first three world missionary conferences, at Edinburgh (1910), Jerusalem (1928) and Tambaram, India (1938), each gave special attention to the issues. The World Missionary Conference held in Edinburgh in 1910 was in many ways a milestone for modern missions and the global church. The immediate concern was the perceived need for careful reflection upon the task of world evangelization, the expectations of which were reflected in the slogan associated with the Student Volunteer Movement in the late nineteenth century: "the evangelization of the world in this generation." There was a basic consensus on the nature of and basis for mission; the questions to be addressed were largely strategic ones about the context in which missions were to take place. The 1910 Edinburgh conference "came at a time of high enthusiasm in the missionary endeavor, and the missionary obligation was considered a self-evident axiom to be obeyed, not to be questioned. . . . The Great Commission of Christ was the only basis needed for missions."[51] And yet the conference organizers were well aware of the formidable challenges facing missions, including rising currents of nationalism and social unrest worldwide and the increasingly pressing question of other religions.[52]

Eight issues were given special attention at the conference, including the question of other religions, which was the focus of Commission IV, "The Missionary Message in Relation to Non-Christian Religions." As part of the preparation for the conference, missionaries all over the world were sent an extensive questionnaire on their perceptions of other religions. Nearly two hundred replies were received, often with extensive comments, providing a wealth of information on missionaries' understandings of Christian mission and its relation to other religious traditions.[53]

---

[50]Ibid., pp. 178-79.

[51]Gerald H. Anderson, "American Protestants in Pursuit of Missions: 1886-1986," *International Bulletin of Missionary Research* 12 (July 1988): 104.

[52]See John R. Mott, *The Decisive Hour of Christian Missions* (London: Church Missionary Society, 1910); and W. H. T. Gairdner, *Echoes from Edinburgh: An Account and Interpretation of the World Missionary Conference* (New York: Revell, 1910), chapter 1.

[53]The responses are summarized in Cracknell, *Justice, Courtesy, and Love*, pp. 191-253. See also Gairdner, *Echoes from Edinburgh*, chapter 10.

Although the missionaries overwhelmingly regarded Christianity as the one true religion and emphasized the need for sharing the gospel with adherents of other faiths, they also consistently called for a change in attitude and demeanor, showing genuine respect and sympathy for other religions rather than ridicule and confrontation. Furthermore, even in 1910 Farquhar's views on fulfillment were well known, and many respondents expressed their own perspectives in terms of a basic continuity between the Christian gospel and other traditions. Kenneth Cracknell observes, "Most of the missionaries responded to the Commissioners in terms of *fulfillment,* and indeed Edinburgh 1910 was the moment of apotheosis of this idea."[54] Although the need for evangelization was not questioned, the manner in which it was to be conducted was being rethought to such an extent that Cracknell refers to the work of the "Missionary Message in Relation to Non-Christian Religions" as "one of the great turning points in the Christian theology of religions."[55]

The world of the 1928 Jerusalem Conference of the International Missionary Council was very different from that of the 1910 Edinburgh conference. The intervening years had witnessed the horrible carnage and devastation of World War I, the Russian Revolution of 1917 and the rise of Communism, emerging movements of nationalism and fascism, an increasingly aggressive secularism and the growing polarization within Protestant Christianity brought about by the fundamentalist-modernist battles. Whereas at Edinburgh there was largely a consensus on the message of the gospel, with changes being called for in the manner in which the gospel was to be shared among those of other faiths, at Jerusalem there was less confidence in the nature of the message itself. The focus at Jerusalem was "The Christian Life and Message in Relation to Non-Christian Systems of Thought and Life," with the two major challenges to missions perceived as secularism and syncretism.[56] But the differences between those who thought of missions in traditional terms, emphasizing the need for evangelism and conversion, and those who openly questioned the traditional position were increasingly evident, prompting concern over theological drift. "Great anxiety was being expressed that in the handling of the issue of the Christian message and its relation to other faiths, there was a discernible shift into syncretism and that the missionary movement was in danger of moving towards the 'social gospel' position, then widely adopted in North America."[57]

Timothy Yates observes that the decade following the Jerusalem conference,

[54]Cracknell, *Justice, Courtesy, and Love,* p. 221. Emphasis in the original.
[55]Ibid., p. xi.
[56]Anderson, "American Protestants," p. 106.
[57]Timothy Yates, *Christian Mission in the Twentieth Century* (Cambridge: Cambridge University Press, 1994), p. 65.

leading up to the 1938 Tambaram Conference of the International Missionary Council, "were years when missiology focussed particularly upon the relationship of Christian faith to other religious traditions."[58] The focal point for the debates was the infamous Laymen's Foreign Missions Inquiry of 1932–1933, a massive research project into Protestant foreign missions funded by John D. Rockefeller Jr. that included visits to mission stations in India, Burma, Japan and China by a fifteen-member commission. The commission compiled a seven-volume final report, with a one-volume version published as *Re-thinking Missions: A Laymen's Inquiry After One Hundred Years,* edited by William Ernest Hocking, professor of philosophy at Harvard University and a Congregationalist layman.[59] Hocking was an early apologist for a new "world faith" that would meet the unprecedented needs of the modern globalized world. He was relentless in promoting a global human religious consciousness that, while transcending particular creeds and institutional religions, would maintain an openness to all faiths and strive for the moral and social transformation of society.[60]

Re-thinking Missions proved to be enormously controversial, for although recognizing the continued importance of missions in some form, it called for a radical reinterpretation of the nature and basis of Christian missions. The report claimed that changing theological convictions about salvation and hell,[61] the challenges of secularism and nationalism, and the emerging "world culture" all demanded that traditional understandings of missions be modified. The real enemies now were not other religions but agnosticism and atheism. Thus Christian missions should not focus upon evangelism with the intention that followers of other religions convert to Christianity; rather, "ministry to the secular needs of men in the spirit of Christ

---

[58]Ibid., p. 94.

[59]See William E. Hocking, ed., *Re-thinking Missions: A Laymen's Inquiry After One Hundred Years* (New York: Harper & Brothers, 1932); Hutchison, *Errand to the World,* pp. 158-75; and Yates, *Christian Mission in the Twentieth Century,* pp. 70-93.

[60]See William E. Hocking, *Living Religions and a World Faith* (New York: Macmillan, 1940); and William E. Hocking, *The Coming World Civilization* (New York: Harper, 1956). Lamin Sanneh observes, "Hocking was the gadfly that perturbed the conscience of his generation. . . . In the main, he put into words the general feeling in many of the mainline Protestant churches, which were reeling from the Great Depression and from the effects of the 1914-18 War. Hocking was the theological equivalent of the League of Nations, and his ambition was similarly to minimize national and religious differences in the interests of global interdependence and solidarity. It would be fair to say that with him Protestant liberalism wrote its verdict on missions" (Lamin Sanneh, "Theology of Mission," in *The Modern Theologians,* ed. David F. Ford, 2nd ed. [Oxford: Blackwell, 1997], p. 567).

[61]Hocking, *Re-thinking Missions,* p. 19. The report stated that in the current theological climate "there is little disposition to believe that sincere and aspiring seekers after God in other religions are to be damned: it has become less concerned in any land to save men from eternal punishment than from the danger of losing the supreme good."

is evangelism."[62] The purpose of missions is not to conquer or displace other religions. Instead Christianity must "make a positive effort, first of all to know and understand the religions around it, then to recognize and associate itself with whatever kindred elements there are in them."[63] The new missionary should "regard himself as a co-worker with the forces which are making for righteousness within every religious system."[64] The missionary "will look forward, not to the destruction of these [non-Christian] religions, but to their continued co-existence with Christianity, each stimulating the other in growth toward the ultimate goal, unity in the completest religious truth."[65] The report was welcomed enthusiastically in liberal circles[66] but was subjected to scathing critiques by the mainstream of the missions movement. Robert E. Speer, Kenneth Scott Latourette and John Mackay all wrote penetrating critiques of the report, rejecting its relativizing tendencies and the questionable theological assumptions upon which it rested. Mackay dismissed it as representing a perspective that was already dated—"the sunset glow of nineteenth century romanticism."[67]

The continuing controversies stimulated by *Re-thinking Missions* provide the context for the third missionary conference of the International Missionary Council, in Tambaram, India, in 1938. One of the central questions addressed at Tambaram was whether God's revelation, as expressed in Christ, is continuous or discontinuous with the beliefs and practices of other religions. To what extent can we discern God's presence and revelatory activity within the non-Christian religions? Not only had the fulfillment theme gained wide acceptance among many missionaries but also more radical voices, such as those expressed in *Re-thinking Missions,* were openly rejecting the need for evangelism and conversion.

The outstanding figure at Tambaram was the Dutch scholar Hendrik Kraemer (1888–1965), a former missionary to Java who had recently been appointed professor of the history of religions at the University of Leiden. Kraemer was asked to prepare a special volume for the conference in which he would "state the fundamental position of the Christian church as a witness-bearing body in the modern world," relating this specifically to "the attitude to be taken by Christians towards other

---

[62]Hocking, *Re-thinking Missions,* p. 68. Emphasis in original.
[63]Ibid., p. 33.
[64]Ibid., p. 40.
[65]Ibid., p. 44.
[66]Pearl Buck, the daughter of missionaries to China, Nobel laureate in literature and sharp critic of traditional missions, commented that *Re-thinking Missions* was "the only book I have ever read which seemed to me literally true in its every observation and right in its every conclusion." As quoted in Yates, *Christian Mission,* p. 90.
[67]As quoted in Anderson, "American Protestants," p. 107.

faiths."[68] The result was *The Christian Message in a Non-Christian World*, widely recognized as a classic statement of the uniqueness and necessity of the Christian gospel, a 450-page work written in a mere seven weeks. In the preface Kraemer noted that "missionary . . . manifestations can only legitimately be called Christian and missionary when they issue directly from the apostolic urgency of gladly witnessing to God and his saving and redeeming Power through Christ."[69] Although he was sensitive to cultural issues and was willing to affirm what is of positive value in other traditions, Kraemer held that Christianity is uniquely "the religion of revelation," and he emphasized a radical discontinuity between what he called the "biblical realism" regarding God's revelation and salvation in Christ and non-Christian religious traditions.[70]

Although Kraemer had a complex and nuanced understanding of other religions,[71] at Tambaram he was highly critical of the increasingly popular fulfillment motif, which emphasized continuity between God's saving action in Jesus Christ and what we find in other religions. Against this, Kraemer emphasized the fundamental discontinuity between God's action in Christ and all human religious expression. Libertus Hoedemaker rightly reminds us that within Kraemer's thought there is room for the notions of continuity and fulfillment, when these are kept within the framework of God's gracious self-disclosure in Christ.[72] Nevertheless, Kraemer's position provoked vigorous debate at Tambaram, with critics such as C. F. Andrews, A. G. Hogg, William Paton, T. C. Chao and others advocating much more positive views on God's presence and work within other religions. The issues debated at Tambaram were not resolved, but the coming of

---

[68]Hendrik Kraemer, *The Christian Message in a Non-Christian World* (New York: Harper & Brothers, 1938), p. v.

[69]Ibid., pp. vi-vii.

[70]Ibid., chapters 3-4. See also Yates, *Christian Mission*, pp. 105-24; and Libertus A. Hoedemaker, "Hendrik Kraemer," in *Mission Legacies*, pp. 508-15.

[71]His more nuanced views are found in later works such as *Religion and the Christian Faith* (London: Lutterworth, 1956) and *World Cultures and World Religions* (London: Lutterworth, 1960).

[72]Hoedemaker states, "Kraemer stressed that one could simply not start on the basis of faith or religion without at least taking into account the unique character of God's revelation in Christ. For Kraemer, the basic choice is: Does one reason about the pilgrimage of the human soul, or about the act of God? On the basis of a clear choice for the latter alternative, it remains quite possible to speak about fulfillment and continuity. But in that case the basic direction of reasoning is not from human religious reality toward Christ but from biblical realism toward human reality. There is always a formal continuity between religious systems and values; there is real and true continuity only insofar as it makes room for the most fundamental discontinuity between God and humankind, which is part and parcel of his revelation in Christ. As long as one does not lose sight of the unique nature and content of this revelation, the concepts of uniqueness and universality, or even of discontinuity and continuity, need not be mutually exclusive" (Hoedemaker, "Hendrik Kraemer," *Mission Legacies*, p. 513).

World War II suspended debate for over a decade.

Vatican II and Other Religions

As noted earlier, with only minor variations, the formula "outside the church there is no salvation" characterized Roman Catholic views of other religions until well into the twentieth century. As exposure to other traditions increased, however, significant efforts were made to soften the tension between God's desire for the salvation of all humankind and the notion of the necessity of the church for salvation.[73] Although one can find clear indicators of more open perspectives among some leading Roman Catholic theologians earlier, it was not until Vatican II (1962–1965) that fundamental changes occurred within Roman Catholicism itself. One of the most influential figures at Vatican II was Karl Rahner, who had developed the theory of the "anonymous Christian."[74] Rahner proposed that, under certain conditions, a sincere Hindu or Buddhist could be regarded as an "anonymous" or "implicit" Christian, and thus be saved, even though this person had not had any contact with the preaching of the gospel or the visible church. This possibility was explicitly acknowledged at Vatican II.

Post-Vatican II Roman Catholicism has adopted a remarkably open perspective on other religions, although it clearly still regards Christianity as the one true religion.[75] Several prominent themes emerge from the documents of Vatican II. First, there is an important sense in which Jesus Christ is held to be normative for all

---

[73]Paul F. Knitter notes that theologians came up with various "ingenious concepts" so as to include within the Catholic church devout and morally exemplary adherents of other faiths, even when they were not explicitly tied to the church in any way. "Saved" non-Christians were said to belong to the "soul" of the church; they were "attached," "linked," "related" to the church; or they were members "imperfectly," "tendentially" or "potentially." Paul F. Knitter, "Roman Catholic Approaches to Other Religions: Developments and Tensions," *International Bulletin of Missionary Research* 8 (April 1984): 50. For a full discussion of various views by Catholic thinkers prior to Vatican II on ways in which those apart from the gospel might nevertheless be saved, see Dupuis, *Toward a Christian Theology of Religious Pluralism,* chapter 4.

[74]See Karl Rahner, "Christianity and Non-Christian Religions," in *Theological Investigations* (Baltimore: Helicon, 1966), 5:115-34; "Anonymous Christian," in *Theological Investigations* (Baltimore: Helicon, 1969), 6:390-98; and "Anonymous Christianity and the Missionary Task of the Church," in *Theological Investigations* (New York: Seabury, 1974), 12:161-78. For a good discussion and defense of Rahner's position, see Gavin D'Costa, *Theology and Religious Pluralism: The Challenge of Other Religions* (Oxford: Blackwell, 1986), chapters 4-5.

[75]There are conflicting views on the implications of Vatican II for Roman Catholic perspectives on other religions. See Knitter, "Roman Catholic Approaches to Other Religions"; Paul F. Knitter, *Jesus and the Other Names: Christian Mission and Global Responsibility* (Maryknoll, N.Y.: Orbis, 1996), chapters 6-7; Thomas F. Stransky, "The Church and Other Religions," *International Bulletin of Missionary Research* 9 (October 1985); Mikka Ruokanen, "Catholic Teaching on Non-Christian Religions at the Second Vatican Council," *International Bulletin of Missionary Research* 14 (April 1990); and Dupuis, *Toward a Christian Theology of Religious Pluralism,* chapters 5-6.

persons, for in the words of *Nostra Aetate,* the "Declaration on the Relation of the Church to Non-Christian Religions," it is "in [Christ], in whom God reconciled all things to himself (2 Cor. 5:18-19), [that] men find the fulness of their religious life."[76] Furthermore, there is still a sense in which the church is held to be necessary for salvation, for as *Lumen Gentium,* the "Dogmatic Constitution on the Church," puts it, "Basing itself upon scripture and tradition, [this holy Council] teaches that the Church, a pilgrim now on earth, is necessary for salvation: the one Christ is mediator and the way of salvation; he is present to us in his body which is the Church."[77]

Given the supremacy and normativity of Christ, and given the necessity (in some sense) of the church for salvation, it follows that the church cannot escape its solemn responsibility to proclaim to all peoples the gracious gospel of Jesus Christ, something the council strongly affirmed in *Ad Gentes,* the "Decree on the Church's Missionary Activity": "Hence the Church has an obligation to proclaim the faith and salvation which comes from Christ. . . . Everyone, therefore, ought to be converted to Christ, who is known through the preaching of the Church, and ought, by baptism, to become incorporated into him, and into the Church which is his body."[78]

And yet Vatican II also clearly opened the door to a much more positive way of looking at other religions. For example, *Lumen Gentium* 16 affirms that "those who have not yet received the Gospel are related to the Church in various ways."[79] And an oft-quoted passage from the same document acknowledges the possibility of salvation apart from actually hearing and responding to the gospel of Jesus Christ.

> Those who, through no fault of their own, do not know the Gospel of Christ or his Church, but who nevertheless seek God with a sincere heart, and, moved by grace, try in their actions to do his will as they know it through the dictates of their conscience—those too may achieve eternal salvation. Nor shall divine providence deny the assistance necessary for salvation to those who, without any fault of theirs, have not yet arrived at an explicit knowledge of God, and who, not without grace, strive to lead a good life. Whatever good or truth is found amongst them is considered by the Church to be a preparation for the Gospel and given by him who enlightens all men that they may at length have life.[80]

Moreover, *Nostra Aetate* makes it plain that non-Christian religions are not to be condemned when it states, "The Catholic Church rejects nothing of what is true

---

[76]*Nostra Aetate,* in A. P. Flannery, ed., *Documents of Vatican II* (Grand Rapids, Mich.: Eerdmans, 1975), p. 739.
[77]Flannery, *Documents of Vatican II,* pp. 365-66.
[78]Ibid., pp. 817, 821.
[79]Ibid., p. 367.
[80]Ibid., pp. 367-68.

and holy in these religions."[81] The document encourages dialogue with adherents of other faiths: "The Church urges her sons to enter with prudence and charity into discussions and collaboration with members of other religions."[82]

Paul Knitter claims that the majority of Catholic theologians interpret the documents of Vatican II as affirming that the non-Christian religions can provide ways of salvation.[83] Jacques Dupuis similarly states:

> The possibility of salvation outside the Church had been recognized by the Church long before Vatican II. . . . If Vatican II innovates in any way on this account, the newness must be seen in the optimistic way in which the council looks at the world at large. . . . What in previous Church documents was affirmed—firmly but cautiously— as a *possibility* based upon God's infinite mercy and in any event to be left to his counsel is being taught by the council with unprecedented assurance: in ways known to him, God can lead those who, through no fault of their own, are ignorant of the Gospel to that faith without which it is impossible to please him (Heb. 11:6).[84]

Post–Vatican II Catholic theology of religions has thus struggled to reconcile the fresh recognition of the possibility of salvation for adherents of other religions with the traditional emphasis upon the normativity of Jesus Christ and the necessity of the church for salvation. In this connection Dupuis points out that Pope John Paul II has had significant influence upon Roman Catholic theology of religions, combining the twin themes of the necessity of evangelism with a recognition of the presence and work of the Holy Spirit outside the church. "It may be said that the singular contribution of Pope John Paul II to a 'theology of religions' consists in the emphasis with which he affirms the operative presence of the Spirit of God in the religious life of non-Christians and the religious traditions to which they belong."[85]

---

[81]Ibid., p. 739.

[82]Ibid.

[83]Knitter, "Roman Catholic Approaches to Other Religions," p. 50. See also Dupuis, *Toward a Christian Theology of Religious Pluralism,* pp. 161-70.

[84]Dupuis, *Toward a Christian Theology of Religious Pluralism,* p. 161. Consider also the following statement made in 1979 by Pietro Rossano, then Secretary of the Vatican Secretariat for Non-Christians: "As for the salvific function of these religions, namely, whether they are or are not paths to salvation, there is no doubt that 'grace and truth' are given through Jesus Christ and by His Spirit (cf John 1:17). Everything would lead one to conclude, however, that gifts of "grace and truth" do reach or may reach the hearts of men and women through the visible, experiential signs of the various religions. The Second Vatican Council is explicit on this point. . . . In this perspective we can conclude by saying that Christ is seen as the origin, center, and destiny of the various religions, as He who brought them to birth, takes them up, purifies them, and fulfills them in order to take them to their eschatological goal, so that 'God may be all in all' (1 Cor. 15:28)" (Pietro Rossano, "Christ's Lordship and Religious Pluralism," in *Mission Trends No. 5: Faith Meets Faith,* ed. Gerald H. Anderson and Thomas F. Stransky [Grand Rapids, Mich.: Eerdmans, 1981], pp. 27-28, 34).

[85]Dupuis, *Toward a Christian Theology of Religious Pluralism,* p. 173.

Christian Faith and Other Religions: Three Paradigms

As we shall see throughout this book, it is the fact that religious pluralism involves a complex cluster of interrelated issues, drawing upon diverse disciplines such as cultural anthropology, comparative religion, history, philosophy and theology, that makes it so difficult to give a simple statement about "other religions." For there is not merely *one* question about religious others; there are multiple, interrelated issues, and what one says about other religions on a given matter depends in part upon the particular question being addressed. This also makes it difficult to categorize the bewildering variety of perspectives on non-Christian religions that have been put forward, for not all discussions deal with the same questions.

Nevertheless, it has become customary in the recent literature to distinguish three broad paradigms for understanding the relation of Christian faith to other religions—exclusivism, inclusivism and pluralism. It is not clear who first introduced these terms, but in *God Has Many Names* (1980) John Hick distinguished these three basic approaches to other religions, although he did not use these terms to designate them.[86] The terms do, however, appear in Alan Race's *Christians and Religious Pluralism* (1983),[87] and they have been widely used since then.

It seems that the term *exclusivism* was introduced into the discussion not by adherents of the traditional perspective but rather by those who rejected this view and wished to cast it in a negative light. It is a pejorative term with unflattering connotations: exclusivists are typically branded as dogmatic, narrow-minded, intolerant, ignorant, arrogant and so on, and those rejecting exclusivism for more accommodating perspectives are regarded as exemplifying the virtues believed deficient in exclusivists.

Evangelicals were largely silent in the formative stages of the debate over religious pluralism, and although they have made significant contributions more recently, they entered the discussion after the agenda and terms of discourse had been largely set by critics of the traditional position. Thus by default evangelicals allowed others to define the category of exclusivism—and to do so in unacceptable terms. Given the many problems associated with the term *exclusivism*, Dennis Okholm and Timothy Phillips have suggested abandoning it in favor of a less offensive label such as *particularism*.[88] I will follow their suggestion and use *particular-*

---

[86]John Hick, *God Has Many Names* (Philadelphia: Westminster Press, 1980), chapter 2.

[87]Alan Race, *Christians and Religious Pluralism* (London: SCM Press, 1983).

[88]Dennis L. Okholm and Timothy R. Phillips, eds., introduction to *Four Views on Salvation in a Pluralistic World* (Grand Rapids, Mich.: Zondervan, 1996), p. 16. For a helpful discussion of the problems of classification, see also Charles Van Engen, *Mission on the Way: Issues in Mission Theology* (Grand Rapids, Mich.: Baker, 1996), pp. 171-81. Van Engen suggests a fourth paradigm, which he calls the "evangelist paradigm," but rather than see this as yet a distinct paradigm, I think it helpful to regard his proposal as a nuanced modification of the particularist model.

ism to refer to what I take to be the broadly traditional position of orthodox Christianity.

Although in *Dissonant Voices* I used the threefold categorization of exclusivism, inclusivism and pluralism,[89] I am increasingly unhappy with this taxonomy as it tends to obscure subtle, but significant, differences among positions and thinkers. Nevertheless, in very broad terms we can distinguish three basic paradigms for understanding the relation of Christianity to other religions. But we should not think of these as three clear-cut categories so much as three points on a broader continuum of perspectives, with both continuities and discontinuities on various issues across the paradigms, depending upon the particular question under consideration. Within each paradigm there is considerable diversity on subsidiary issues, and we must recognize that, as the discussions become increasingly sophisticated and nuanced, it is often quite difficult to locate particular thinkers in terms of the three categories.

The difficulties in identifying particular thinkers with the three categories becomes especially apparent when we consider a group of remarkable twentieth-century missionary theologians who, while quite sympathetic to non-Christian religious traditions, nevertheless ably defended the supremacy of Jesus Christ and the imperative for Christian witness. The writings of Max Warren (1904–1977), Stephen Neill (1900–1984), Kenneth Cragg (b. 1913) and Lesslie Newbigin (1909–1998) do not seem to fall neatly into either the particularist or inclusivist paradigms. Warren advocated Christian witness to Jesus Christ as the one Lord, but he was also very sensitive to the work of the Holy Spirit among adherents of other faiths. Neill, a man of amazing gifts who made significant contributions in New Testament studies and theology as well as history, missiology and comparative religion, has always been difficult to categorize. Deeply involved with the ecumenical movement, Neill was also solidly orthodox in his theology. Firmly commited to the need for evangelism and mission among adherents of other faiths, he also embraced interreligious dialogue as essential to mission. While uncompromising in his insistence upon Jesus Christ as the one Lord and Savior for all peoples, Neill treated other religions with respect, sympathy and appreciation. Similarly Cragg, through a lifetime of study of Islam and extensive experience with Muslims, has combined an uncompromising commitment to the Lordship of Jesus Christ with a highly sympathetic understanding of Islam. Newbigin, one of the founding fathers of the World Council of Churches and a long-time missionary to India, later became a sharp critic of the Council's drift away from theological orthodoxy toward relativism and pluralism. In a steady stream of lectures and writings Newbigin was

---

[89]See Harold Netland, *Dissonant Voices: Religious Pluralism and the Question of Truth* (Grand Rapids, Mich.: Eerdmans, 1991), chapter 1.

uncompromising in his insistence upon Jesus Christ, the incarnate Son of God, as the one Lord and Savior for all humankind, and upon the continuing need for the church to share the gospel with those of other religions, even as he was careful not to limit the activity of the Holy Spirit among religious others.[90] Nevertheless, with proper qualification the three categories can be useful tools for helping us sort out various perspectives on other religions.

Particularism. In broad terms we can say that the traditional perspective of Christianity up until the mid-twentieth century, both Roman Catholic and Protestant, was particularism.[91] This perspective can be described theologically in terms of the following three principles: (1) The Bible is God's distinctive written revelation; it is true and fully authoritative; and thus, where the claims of Scripture are incompatible with those of other faiths, the latter are to be rejected. (2) Jesus Christ is the unique incarnation of God, fully God and fully man, and only through the person and work of Jesus is there the possibility of salvation. (3) God's saving grace is not mediated through the teachings, practices or institutions of other religions.

We should note several things about this position. First, particularism is defined in terms of theological, not social or cultural, exclusivity. Contrary to popular assumptions, there is no reason to suppose that particularists cannot be culturally sensitive or appropriately tolerant and accepting of followers of other religious traditions. Furthermore, particularism as defined here leaves open subsidiary issues over which evangelical Christians often disagree. These include, but are not limited to, the following questions: Is there any truth or value in non-Christian religions, or are they to be dismissed as nothing more than satanic deception and idolatry? Are there points of commonality between Christian faith and other religions? To what extent can we see reflections of general revelation or common grace in other religions? Must one explicitly hear the gospel and respond in faith to the name of Jesus Christ in order to be saved, or is it in principle possible for some to be saved apart from explicitly responding to Jesus Christ?[92] Particularism does not entail

---

[90]See Max Warren, *The Christian Mission* (London: SCM Press, 1951); Max Warren, *I Believe in the Great Commission* (Grand Rapids, Mich.: Eerdmans, 1976); Stephen Neill, *Christian Faith and Other Faiths: The Christian Dialogue with Other Religions* (London: Oxford University Press, 1961); Stephen Neill, *The Supremacy of Jesus* (London: Hodder & Stoughton, 1984); Kenneth Cragg, *Sandals at the Mosque: Christian Presence amid Islam* (New York: Oxford University Press, 1959); Kenneth Cragg, *The Call of the Minaret,* 2nd ed. (Maryknoll, N.Y.: Orbis, 1985); Lesslie Newbigin, *The Open Secret: Sketches for a Missionary Theology* (Grand Rapids, Mich.: Eerdmans, 1978); and Lesslie Newbigin, *The Gospel in a Pluralist Society* (Grand Rapids, Mich.: Eerdmans, 1989).

[91]Obviously Roman Catholics and Protestants would have quite different understandings of some of the relevant doctrines, but I think that with proper qualification both traditions would fit under the general category of particularism.

[92]Some of these issues are addressed in chapter ten.

that all the beliefs of non-Christian religions are false. It does not imply that there is nothing of value in other religions, nor that Christians cannot learn anything from other religions. These are issues on which particularists often disagree, although even the most open particularists have at best a mixed view of other religions. Thus even when due allowance is made for elements of truth, value and beauty in other religions, particularists hold that by and large non-Christian religions provide a false or inaccurate picture of reality and that salvation is not attained through the beliefs and practices of other religious traditions. Central to particularism is the conviction that God has revealed himself definitively through the Scriptures and the incarnation, that Jesus Christ is the one Savior for all people in all cultures and that all people are to acknowledge and worship Jesus as Lord.

In June 1992, under the auspices of the Theological Commission of the World Evangelical Fellowship, eighty-five theologians from twenty-eight countries met in Manila to discuss the theme "The Unique Christ in Our Pluralistic World." The international gathering produced the Manila Declaration, a significant document that expresses nicely the heart of particularism:

> Against . . . pluralism, we affirm that God has acted decisively, supremely, and norma-
> tively in the historical Jesus of Nazareth. In his person and work, Jesus is unique such
> that no one comes to the Father except through him. All salvation in the biblical sense
> of eternal life, life in the kingdom, reconciliation with God and forgiveness of sins
> comes solely from the person and work of Jesus Christ. . . . In our modern pluralistic
> world, many Christians ask: "Is it not possible that there might be salvation in other
> religions?" The question is misleading because it implies that religions have the power
> to save us. This is not true. Only God saves. All people have sinned, all people deserve
> condemnation, all salvation stems solely from the person and atoning work of Jesus
> Christ, and this salvation can be appropriated solely through trust in God's mercy.
>
> The question, therefore, should be rephrased as: "Can those who have never heard of
> Jesus Christ be saved?" Old Testament saints, who did not know the name of Jesus, nev-
> ertheless found salvation. Is it possible that others also might find salvation through
> the blood of Jesus Christ although they do not consciously know the name of Jesus? We
> did not achieve a consensus on how to answer this question. More study is needed.
>
> We did agree that salvation is to be found nowhere else than in Jesus Christ. The
> truth to be found in other religious teachings is not sufficient, in and of itself, to pro-
> vide salvation. We further agreed that universalism (that all people without exception
> will be saved) is not biblical. Lastly, we agreed that our discussion of this issue must not
> in any way undercut the passion to proclaim, without wavering, faltering or tiring, the
> good news of salvation through trust in Jesus Christ.[93]

The Manila Declaration rightly distinguishes particularism from what Clark

---

[93]"The WEF Manila Declaration," in *The Unique Christ in Our Pluralist World,* ed. Bruce J. Nicholls (Grand Rapids, Mich.: Baker, 1994), pp. 14-15.

Pinnock has recently called "restrictivism"[94]—the view that only those who actually hear the gospel of Jesus Christ and respond explicitly in faith to Christ in this life can be saved. Whereas restrictivism is a view about a specific soteriological issue (the necessary conditions for salvation as this relates to the unevangelized), particularism is a perspective about a broader set of issues having to do with Christianity and other religions. Thus while all restrictivists are particularists, not all particularists are restrictivists. The question of the fate of those who never hear the gospel has always been controversial and troubling to sensitive Christians, and various answers have been proposed by those falling within the particularist paradigm.[95] As Okholm and Phillips remind us, some of the most prominent evangelical theologians and missiologists over the years have taken somewhat agnostic positions on the issue.[96] For example, Presbyterian A. T. Pierson—editor of the *Missionary Review of the World* and, according to Dana Robert, "the foremost spokesperson for foreign missions in the late nineteenth century"[97]—was a relent-

---

[94]Clark H. Pinnock, *A Wideness in God's Mercy: The Finality of Jesus Christ in a World of Religions* (Grand Rapids, Mich.: Zondervan, 1992), pp. 12-15. The distinction between exclusivism and restrictivism is also made by John Sanders in the introduction to *What About Those Who Have Never Heard? Three Views on the Destiny of the Unevangelized*, ed. John Sanders (Downers Grove, Ill.: InterVarsity Press, 1995), pp. 12-13; and by Okholm and Phillips, introduction to *Four Views on Salvation in a Pluralistic World*, pp. 16-17.

[95]For a survey of some of the answers proposed, see John Sanders, *No Other Name: An Investigation into the Destiny of the Unevangelized* (Grand Rapids, Mich.: Eerdmans, 1992); Sanders, *What About Those Who Have Never Heard?*; and William V. Crockett and James Sigountos, eds., *Through No Fault of Their Own? The Fate of Those Who Have Never Heard* (Grand Rapids, Mich.: Baker, 1991). Contemporary restrictivists include Ramesh Richard, *The Population of Heaven: A Biblical Response to the Inclusivist Position on Who Will Be Saved* (Chicago: Moody Press, 1994); John Piper, *Let the Nations Be Glad!* (Grand Rapids, Mich.: Baker, 1993); Ronald Nash, *Is Jesus the Only Savior?* (Grand Rapids, Mich.: Zondervan, 1994); and R. Douglas Geivett and W. Gary Phillips, "A Particularist View: An Evidentialist Approach," in *Four Views on Salvation in a Pluralistic World*, pp. 211-45. Evangelical particularists who are not restrictivists and thus are somewhat open on the question of the unevangelized include John Stott, *The Authentic Jesus* (London: Marshall Morgan & Scott, 1985), p. 83; J. I. Packer, "Evangelicals and the Way of Salvation," *Evangelical Affirmations*, ed. Kenneth S. Kantzer and Carl F. H. Henry (Grand Rapids, Mich.: Zondervan, 1990), pp. 121-23; J. I. Packer, *God's Words: Studies of Key Bible Themes* (Downers Grove, Ill.: InterVarsity Press, 1981), p. 210; Klaas Runia, "The Gospel and Religious Pluralism," *Evangelical Review of Theology* 14 (October 1990): 362-63; and Alister McGrath, "A Particularist View: A Post-Enlightenment Approach," in *Four Views on Salvation in a Pluralistic World*; Millard J. Erickson, "Hope for Those Who Haven't Heard? Yes, But . . . ," *Evangelical Missions Quarterly* 11 (April 1975): 122-26; Millard J. Erickson, *How Shall They Be Saved? The Destiny of Those Who Do Not Hear of Jesus* (Grand Rapids, Mich.: Baker, 1996); Christopher J. H. Wright, *What's So Unique About Jesus?* (Eastbourne, England: Monarch, 1990), pp. 36-39; and Daniel B. Clendenin, *Many Gods, Many Lords* (Grand Rapids, Mich.: Baker, 1995).

[96]Okholm and Phillips, introduction to *Four Views on Salvation in a Pluralistic World*, pp. 19-22.

[97]Dana Lee Robert, "Arthur Tappan Pierson and Forward Movements of Late-Nineteenth-Century Evangelism" (Ph.D. diss., Yale University, 1984), p. 165; as quoted in Anderson, "American Protestants," p. 98.

less advocate for world evangelization, yet he did not cut off all hope for those who did not hear the gospel. "If there be anywhere a soul feeling after God, following the light of nature and of conscience, in hope and faith that the Great Unknown will somehow give more light, and lead to life and blessedness, we may safely leave such to His fatherly care."[98]

Although something like the particularist paradigm was dominant within Christianity up until the late nineteenth century, by the turn of the century there were significant changes under way, especially among Protestants, that were to intensify in the twentieth century. We have already noted the profound changes within Roman Catholicism ushered in by Vatican II. By the 1960s and 1970s, much more open and positive views on other religions were common among mainline Protestant theologians as well. Paul Tillich was one of the first major Protestant theologians to give sustained attention to the theology of religions, but it was not long before virtually every major theologian felt compelled to address the subject.[99] The idea that God is present in, and at work through, both the secular realm and non-Christian religious traditions gained widespread acceptance. The more open posture toward those of other faiths was increasingly reflected in the policies and activities of the World Council of Churches (WCC). Questions about the place of dialogue with other religions became increasingly urgent and controversial, and by 1971 a new WCC subunit, Dialogue with Men of Living Faiths and Ideologies, under the Program Unit on Faith and Witness, was formed. Although always controversial, and in spite of a lack of consensus on basic theological issues, interreligious dialogue has been a major part of the WCC's understanding of the mission of the church since 1970.

Inclusivism. These more recent shifts away from particularism toward more open perspectives on other religions have been labeled "inclusivism." Inclusivism is a very broad category that can be defined in terms of the following (admittedly rather ambiguous) principles: (1) There is a sense in which Jesus Christ is

---

[98]Arthur T. Pierson, *The Crisis of Mission: Or, The Voice out of the Cloud* (New York: Carter & Brothers,1886), p. 297. For similar views, see James S. Dennis, *Foreign Missions After a Century* (London: Oliphant, Anderson & Ferrier, 1894), pp. 202-3; and Robert Hall Glover, *The Progress of World-Wide Missions* (New York: Dorna, 1924), p. 25.

[99]See Paul Tillich, *Systematic Theology* (Chicago: University of Chicago Press, 1951-1963), 1:137-44, 218-30; 3: 98-106; Paul Tillich, *Christianity and the Encounter of the World Religions* (New York: Columbia University Press, 1963); and Paul Tillich, *The Future of Religions,* ed. Jerald C. Brauer (New York: Harper & Row, 1966). Gerald H. Anderson, "Christian Mission and Religious Pluralism: A Selected Bibliography of 175 Books in English, 1970-1990," *International Bulletin of Missionary Research* 14, no. 4 (1990): 172-76; and Gerald H. Anderson, "Christian Mission and Religious Pluralism: A Selected Bibliography of Sixty-Seven Books in English, 1991-1998," *International Bulletin of Missionary Research* 22, no. 4 (1998): 159-61.

unique, normative or superior to other religious figures, and in some sense it is through Christ that salvation is made available. (2) God's grace and salvation, which are somehow based upon Jesus Christ, are also available and efficacious through other religions. (3) Thus other religions are generally to be regarded positively as part of God's purposes for humankind. The statements are deliberately ambiguous to allow for considerable diversity among inclusivists on a range of issues.[100] Some inclusivists hold fast to traditional doctrines such as the Trinity and two-nature Christology, thus accepting Jesus Christ as fully God and fully man; others reject orthodox Christology but still regard Jesus as being somehow distinctive as the one through whom God has been preeminently present and active on behalf of humankind. Some inclusivists accept traditional language about sin, atonement and salvation; others do not. Nevertheless, the core of inclusivism is the desire to maintain in some sense the uniqueness of Jesus Christ while also admitting that God's grace and salvation (however these are understood) are present and effective in and through other religions as well.

Pluralism. By the late 1970s and 1980s, a noticeable shift in the discussion took place as more radical perspectives were advanced and a growing number of leading Western theologians called for rejection of an assumption shared by both particularists and inclusivists: that there is something significantly superior to, or normative about, Jesus Christ and Christianity. The 1987 publication of *The Myth of Christian Uniqueness* was something of a watershed event, intended by the contributors to the volume to serve as a "crossing of a theological Rubicon" or a public embrace of a genuinely pluralistic view of religions. Editor Paul Knitter stated, "Through this collection of essays we hope to show that such a pluralist turn is taking shape, that it is being proposed by a variety of reputable Christian thinkers, and

---

[100]Some representative inclusivistic works include Dupuis, *Toward a Christian Theology of Religious Pluralism;* Gavin D'Costa, ed., *Christian Uniqueness Reconsidered: The Myth of a Pluralistic Theology of Religions* (Maryknoll, N.Y.: Orbis, 1990); D'Costa, *Theology and Religious Pluralism;* Richard Henry Drummond, *Toward a New Age in Christian Theology* (Maryknoll, N.Y.: Orbis, 1985); Pinnock, *Wideness in God's Mercy;* Clark H. Pinnock, "An Inclusivist View," in *Four Views on Salvation in a Pluralistic World,* pp. 93-23, 141-48; Wolfhart Pannenberg, "The Religions from the Perspective of Christian Theology and the Self-Interpretation of Christianity in Relation to the Non-Christian Religions," *Modern Theology* 9, no. 3 (1993): 285-97; Hans Küng, "The World Religions in God's Plan of Salvation," in *Christian Revelation and World Religions,* ed. J. Neuner (London: Burns & Oates, 1967), pp. 25-66; and Hans Küng, "What Is True Religion? Toward an Ecumenical Criteriology," in *Toward a Universal Theology of Religion,* ed. L. Swidler (Maryknoll, N.Y.: Orbis, 1987), pp. 231-50. Mark Heim also identifies himself as an inclusivist, but by advocating a genuine plurality of soteriological ends which are both sought and actually realized in the diverse religions he moves well beyond most inclusivists. Heim's creative proposal illustrates the difficulties of placing certain thinkers within the traditional categories. See S. Mark Heim, *Salvations: Truth and Difference in Religion* (Maryknoll, N.Y.: Orbis, 1995) and S. Mark Heim, *The Depth of the Riches: A Trinitarian Theology of Religious Ends* (Grand Rapids, Mich.: Eerdmans, 2001).

that therefore it represents a viable, though still inchoate and controversial, option for Christian believers."[101] Contributors to the volume included some of the most influential figures in contemporary theology, such as Gordon Kaufman, John Hick, Langdon Gilkey, Wilfred Cantwell Smith, Raimundo Panikkar, Rosemary Radford Ruether and Tom Driver.

The term *pluralism* itself, as already pointed out in the introduction to this book, is ambiguous. It can refer simply to the undeniable fact of religious diversity, for people do indeed embrace different religious perspectives. This is obvious and not particularly controversial. But the sense in which we are using it here goes beyond mere recognition of the fact of diversity to refer to a particular view about the relations among the major religions, namely an egalitarian and democratized perspective that maintains a rough parity among religions concerning religious truth. Pluralism, then, holds that salvation (or enlightenment or liberation) should be acknowledged as present and effective in its own way in each religion. No single religion can claim to be somehow normative and superior to all others, for all religions are in their own way complex historically and culturally conditioned human responses to the one divine reality. Thus, although Christians can hold that Jesus is unique and normative *for them,* they cannot claim that Jesus is unique or normative in an objective or universal sense. Jesus may be the savior for Christians, but he is not the one Savior for all peoples.[102]

Since the late 1970s, religious pluralism has come to be associated primarily with the theologian and philosopher of religion John Hick, whose 1986 Gifford Lectures were published as *An Interpretation of Religion.*[103] This work is without question the most sophisticated and rigorous model for a genuinely pluralistic understanding of the religions, and it has been enormously influential in religious studies and philosophy of religion. At the heart of Hick's pluralist model is the idea that "the great world faiths embody different perceptions and conceptions of, and correspondingly different responses to, the Real [the religious ultimate] from within the major variant ways of being human; and that within each of them the

---

[101]Paul F. Knitter, preface to *The Myth of Christian Uniqueness,* ed. John H. Hick and Paul F. Knitter (Maryknoll, N.Y.: Orbis, 1987), p. viii.

[102]Some contemporary pluralists include Gordon Kaufman, "Religious Diversity, Historical Consciousness, and Christian Theology," in *Myth of Christian Uniqueness,* pp. 3-15; Langdon Gilkey, "Plurality and Its Theological Implications," in *Myth of Christian Uniqueness,* pp. 37-50; Paul F. Knitter, *No Other Name? A Critical Survey of Christian Attitudes Toward the World Religions* (Maryknoll, N.Y.: Orbis, 1985); Paul F. Knitter, *One Earth, Many Religions: Multifaith Dialogue and Global Responsibility* (Maryknoll, N.Y.: Orbis, 1995); Knitter, *Jesus and the Other Names;* Wilfred Cantwell Smith, *Towards a World Theology* (London: Macmillan, 1981); Keith Ward, *A Vision to Pursue* (London: SCM Press, 1991); Keith Ward, *Religion and Revelation* (New York: Oxford University Press, 1994); and N. Ross Reat and Edmund Perry, *A World Theology: The Central Spiritual Reality of Humankind* (New York: Cambridge University Press, 1991).

[103]John Hick, *An Interpretation of Religion* (New Haven, Conn.: Yale University Press, 1989).

transformation of human existence from self-centredness to Reality-centredness is taking place. These traditions are accordingly to be regarded as alternative soteriological 'spaces' within which, or 'ways' along which, men and women find salvation/liberation/ultimate fulfillment."[104]

In other words, all religions (or at least the "major" ones) are in their own ways complex historically and culturally conditioned human responses to the one ultimate Reality. We will explore Hick's theory of religious pluralism in greater detail in chapters five and seven.

The trend toward more pluralistic ways of understanding the relation between Christianity and other religions is not confined to the West. The issues of pluralism have long been of special interest to Christian thinkers in Asia, and pluralistic models have been advanced by leading Asian thinkers such as Stanley Samartha, Aloysius Pieris, Seiichi Yagi and Raimundo Panikkar.[105] Pluralistic views on the religions are deeply entrenched in certain academic circles, especially in religious studies. But it is not merely the latest academic fad; pluralistic themes are common among ordinary people who have never heard of John Hick or the academic debates on other religions. Although pluralism finds increasingly sophisticated expression among scholars, it is also a perspective that is widely accepted in a rudimentary form throughout popular culture, and its influence is increasingly felt within the church as well. It is thus essential that the church understand and respond appropriately to the cultural changes driving pluralism.

---

[104]Ibid., p. 240.

[105]Stanley Samartha, "The Cross and the Rainbow," in *Myth of Christian Uniqueness;* Stanley Samartha, *One Christ—Many Religions: Toward a Revised Christology* (Maryknoll, N.Y.: Orbis, 1991); Aloysius Pieris, *An Asian Theology of Liberation* (Maryknoll, N.Y.: Orbis, 1988); Aloysius Pieris, *Love Meets Wisdom: A Christian Experience of Buddhism* (Maryknoll, N.Y.: Orbis, 1988); Aloysius Pieris, *Basic Issues in Asian Buddhism and Christianity* (Maryknoll, N.Y.: Orbis, 1996); Seiichi Yagi, " 'I' in the Words of Jesus," in *Myth of Christian Uniqueness,* pp. 117-34; Raimundo Panikkar, *The Unknown Christ of Hinduism: Towards an Ecumenical Christophany,* rev. ed. (London: Dartman, Longman & Todd, 1981); Raimundo Panikkar, "The Jordan, the Tiber, and the Ganges," in *Myth of Christian Uniqueness,* pp. 89-116; Raimundo Panikkar, *The Silence of God: The Answer of the Buddha* (Maryknoll, N.Y.: Orbis, 1989); and Raimundo Panikkar, *The Cosmotheandric Experience: Emerging Religious Consciousness* (Maryknoll, N.Y.: Orbis, 1993).

2

CONTOURS
OF THE PRESENT

The Culture of Modernity

A massive intellectual revolution is taking place that is perhaps as great as that which marked off the modern world from the Middle Ages.

DIOGENES ALLEN, Christian Belief in a Postmodern World

Postmodernity . . . is the age of over-exposure to otherness—because, in traveling, you put yourself into a different reality; because, as a result of immigration, a different reality comes to you; because, with no physical movement at all, only the relentless and ever-increasing flow of information, cultures interpenetrate.

WALTER TRUETT ANDERSON, The Truth About the Truth

We have not moved beyond modernity but are living precisely through a phase of its radicalisation.

ANTHONY GIDDENS, The Consequences of Modernity

We saw in chapter one that dramatic changes have taken place within the past century with respect to how Christians view other religions. Particularism, the traditional perspective, has come under increasing attack, with more inclusivist and pluralist views gaining in prominence. In the broader culture outside the church, pluralism has of course been popular for some time.

Religious pluralism presents some daunting challenges to orthodox Christianity. But before we can consider responses, we must first understand the factors underlying this shift toward pluralism. In this and the next two chapters we will be developing a framework for understanding recent cultural changes and the growing plausibility of religious pluralism in the West. We will first examine a model that has been quite influential among Christian thinkers since the 1980s: the modernity/postmodernity model. This way of understanding cultural history maintains that the West has now moved beyond modernity to postmodernity. The attraction of religious pluralism is then seen as a function of this cultural shift toward postmodernity. Although this model has been very influential among evangelicals, I will argue that the distinction is problematic on several counts and that it is not particularly helpful in explaining the cultural dynamics behind religious pluralism today. Although there clearly is a sense in which the early twenty-first century is significantly different from previous eras, along with these profound changes there are deeply rooted continuities with earlier times that must not be overlooked.

John Hick is the most influential defender of religious pluralism in the West today, and his views will be carefully examined in chapters five and seven. But it is interesting to see how others have perceived Hick's theory of pluralism. Some have criticized it for being too modernist (and thus out of step with contemporary postmodern realities), while others have attacked it for capitulating to the relativism of postmodernity.[1] The fact that Hick's pluralism is interpreted as exemplifying the vices of both modernity and postmodernity might, of course, simply mean that his theory is exceptionally problematic. But while Hick's proposal does face significant difficulties, as we shall see in chapter seven, this ambivalence suggests more about the problems in distinguishing modernity from postmodernity than it does about Hick's own views.

Developing comprehensive models for explaining large domains of human activity across temporal, cultural and geographical expanses is no easy task, and attempts to do so with respect to the past four hundred years of Western history face the danger of reductionism. While we can discern certain dominant patterns and themes at particular times, we must be careful not to give undue emphasis to some patterns at the expense of others or to impose a misleading homogeneity upon what are actually very heterogeneous movements. Models serve investigational purposes by accounting for particular phenomena, and their value is directly proportional to their ability to explain the relevant data. Our concern here is not to develop a comprehensive paradigm that systematically accounts for all of the past five centuries of Western cultural history but rather to suggest some of the salient themes that help to make sense of the plausibility of religious pluralism today.

In particular, I suggest that it is the widespread loss of confidence in traditional

---

[1]On Hick's theory as a vestige of modernism, see John V. Apczynski, "John Hick's Theocentrism: Revolutionary or Implicitly Exclusivist?" *Modern Theology* 8, no. 1 (1992); Alister McGrath, *A Passion for Truth: The Intellectual Coherence of Evangelicalism* (Downers Grove, Ill.: InterVarsity Press, 1996), chapter 5; Kieran Flanagan, "Theological Pluralism: A Sociological Critique," in *Religious Pluralism and Unbelief: Studies Critical and Comparative*, ed. Ian Hamnett (London: Routledge, 1990), pp. 81-113; and Gavin D'Costa, *The Meeting of Religions and the Trinity* (Maryknoll, N.Y.: Orbis, 2000), chapter 1. For Hick as a postmodernist, see Robert Cook, "Postmodernism, Pluralism and John Hick," *Themelios* 19, no. 1 (1993): 10-12.

religious (which in the West means Christian) perspectives, combined with the increasing awareness of cultural and religious diversity, that has shaped the epistemological and cultural context of religious pluralism. While the modernity/postmodernity model perhaps has merit in other contexts, I do not think it helps us understand the dynamics behind the cultural shifts toward religious pluralism. After looking briefly at the modernity/postmodernity model, I will note some problems with it and will argue that a more satisfactory framework for understanding recent cultural change is what I will call the "culture of modernity," a model that draws upon intellectual history as well as the themes of modernization and globalization from the social sciences.

From Modernity to Postmodernity?

There is little question that our world has been undergoing rapid and profound transitions that are changing how we think of ourselves and others, but what is less clear is the nature and long-term significance of these transformations. In the 1980s and 1990s it became virtually axiomatic, at least in some academic quarters, that the West was undergoing a massive cultural shift from modernity to postmodernity. But as the term itself indicates, postmodernity is parasitic upon modernity, and therefore much depends upon how we understand modernity. But this is precisely the problem, for in spite of the voluminous literature on the subject, there is little consensus over even basic definitions. Barry Smart observed over a decade ago that "one of the remarkable features of contributions to debates on this issue is the extent to which key terms and ideas have evaded clarification, and this applies not only in respect of the family of terms associated with 'modern' but in addition, if not to an even greater extent, in relation to 'postmodern' and its conceptual constellation."[2]

In her helpful study *The Post-Modern and the Post-Industrial: A Critical Analysis,* Margaret Rose examines the bewildering variety of ways in which *modern, postmodern* and their cognates have been used during the twentieth century.[3] For example, one of the earliest uses of *postmodern* was by Arnold Toynbee in *A Study of History* (1939) to refer to the period from 1914 onward, inaugurated by World War I.[4] For Toynbee, modernity has a close affinity with Western societies and culture, and thus the postmodern age is characterized by, among other things, the emerging prominence of the non-Western nations and the growing significance of non-Christian religions.

---

[2]Barry Smart, "Modernity, Postmodernity, and the Present," in *Theories of Modernity and Postmodernity,* ed. Bryan Turner (London: Sage, 1990), p. 16.
[3]Margaret Rose, *The Post-Modern and the Post-Industrial: A Critical Analysis* (Cambridge: Cambridge University Press, 1991).
[4]Ibid., p. 9.

Postmodern also came to be used as a way of describing the social and economic changes brought about by the rapid growth of new technologies, especially tele-communications, prompting a shift from an industrial to a postindustrial society. Daniel Bell, for example, drew attention to the social implications of postindustrial societies that have moved from a goods-producing economy to a service economy, with ever-increasing levels of technological specialization. "Broadly speaking, if industrial society is based on machine technology, post-industrial society is shaped by an intellectual technology. And if capital and labor are the major structural features of industrial society, information and knowledge are those of post-industrial society."[5] The post–World War II world has become increasingly dominated by the institutions and processes associated with advertising and consumerism; bewildering innovations in electronics, computer technology and telecommunications; proliferation of the mass media; the phenomenal growth of information technologies and services, and the influence of the entertainment industries. The writings of Marshall McLuhan on the growing impact of electronic communication systems, producing a kind of "global village," articulated the perception of globalized, technology-dependent societies of the late twentieth century rapidly moving into a postmodern era.[6] McLuhan's metaphor has been updated to "global city" or, in the words of the Commission on Global Governance of the United Nations (1995), "our global neighborhood," to capture the urbanized, posttraditional nature of global interconnectedness.[7]

But *postmodernity* is also often used in a much broader sense to refer to a kind of cultural critique of the West that emerged in the 1960s and 1970s. According to John McGowan, this critique was "resolutely antifoundationalist—eschewing all appeals to ontological or epistemological or ethical absolutes—while also proclaiming itself resolutely radical in its commitment to the transformation of the existing Western social order."[8] By the 1960s, there were significant changes at work, especially in the Anglo-American and French philosophical traditions, questioning earlier assumptions and paradigms. About the same time, a new generation of writers, artists and architects began to react against modernism in the arts. The 1960s were a time of cultural upheaval, social unrest and radical questioning of the political and social status quo. The year 1968, in particular, was one rocked by

---

[5]Daniel Bell, foreword to *The Coming of Post-Industrial Society* (New York: Basic, 1976); as quoted in *From Modernism to Postmodernism: An Anthology,* ed. Lawrence Cahoone (Oxford: Blackwell, 1996), p. 427.
[6]Edmund Carpenter and Marshall McLuhan, eds., *Explorations in Communications* (Boston: Beacon, 1960); Marshall McLuhan, *Understanding Media* (London: Routledge, 1964); Marshall McLuhan and Q. Fiore, *The Medium Is the Message: An Inventory of Effects* (London: Lane, 1967).
[7]John Tomlinson, *Globalization and Culture* (Chicago: University of Chicago Press, 1999), p. 181.
[8]John McGowan, *Postmodernism and Its Critics* (Ithaca, N.Y.: Cornell University Press, 1991), p. ix.

explosive demonstrations against the establishment by university students in Chicago, London, Paris, Mexico City, Tokyo and many other cities. Since the 1970s, the term *postmodern* has been used of a variety of literary, philosophical, social and political trends linked by their critique of established "modern" values, assumptions and institutions. Postmodernity in this sense refers to a broad range of late-twentieth-century intellectual and cultural movements in the fine arts, architecture, communications media, politics, the social sciences, literary theory and hermeneutics, and philosophy that perhaps are connected more by what they reject than by what they affirm.

Historical postmodernism. Lawrence Cahoone suggests that the term *postmodernism* is used to refer to at least three distinct perspectives—historical postmodernism, methodological postmodernism and positive postmodernism.[9] Historical postmodernism claims that the social, political or cultural transformations of the recent past are sufficiently significant that we are now in a distinctively different era than that of modernism. This is a historical judgment based upon perceived changes distinguishing contemporary social and cultural patterns from the previous period. The historical era of modernism is said to have passed, and although it is not entirely clear what will replace it, *postmodernism* refers to this new emerging historical context. One can, of course, agree with this historical observation without necessarily making value judgments, positive or negative, about the changes themselves. The views of Toynbee and Bell noted above include assumptions about just this kind of historical transition.

The value of a historical judgment about the transition from modernity to postmodernity will depend in part upon our ability to identify clearly points that demarcate the latter from the former. But what exactly are the historical boundaries of the modern era? In his insightful work *Cosmopolis: The Hidden Agenda of Modernity,* Stephen Toulmin catalogs a surprising variety of dates and events that have been suggested for the origin of modernity: 1436 and Gutenberg's adoption of movable type, 1520 and Luther's rebellion against church authority, 1648 and the end of the Thirty Years War, 1776 and the American Revolution, 1789 and the French Revolution, 1895 and the publication of Freud's *Intrepretation of Dreams,* and so on.[10] Different dates clearly serve different purposes when it comes to setting the historical parameters of modernity.

If there is uncertainty about the beginning of modernity, there is even greater ambiguity concerning its termination. Some see the end of modernity already in the French Revolution of 1789; for others, the end comes with the 1781 publication

---

[9]See Cahoone, introduction to *From Modernism to Postmodernism,* p. 17.
[10]Stephen Toulmin, *Cosmopolis: The Hidden Agenda of Modernity* (Chicago: University of Chicago Press, 1990), p. 5.

of Kant's *Critique of Pure Reason* or the 1883 publication of Nietzsche's *Thus Spake Zarathustra;* and still others mark the 1989 destruction of the Berlin Wall as the end of modernity. And if there is such difficulty identifying the historical parameters of modernity, then we should expect the notion of postmodernity to be equally imprecise (Is Kant modern or postmodern? What about nineteenth-century Romanticism? What about Nietzsche?). Of course, disagreement concerning the temporal boundaries of modernity and postmodernity does not in itself entail that the distinction is without value, but it should make us cautious about sweeping pronouncements concerning this transition.

Methodological postmodernism. In Cahoone's taxonomy, methodological post-modernism goes beyond historical postmodernism in that it involves a preference for postmodernity over modernity. Methodological postmodernism includes a variety of views that, despite their many differences, are united in their rejection of the idea that we can have secure foundations to knowledge or arrive at truths about reality that are universal and unchanging. Included here, also, is a deep suspicion about the possibility of knowledge of the "real" or "objective" world (often expressed in the language of ontological nonrealism);[11] rejection of the idea of determinate or enduring "essences" (such as the "self"); suspicion of the notion of fixed meanings in texts or language; a preference for the local, specific and transitory over against the universal and unchanging; celebration of diversity in all of its forms; and the convergence of all of the above in strongly "perspectivist" and relativistic epistemologies. Methodological postmodernism denies the transcendence or objectivity of norms such as truth, goodness, beauty, justice and rationality.[12] It embraces skeptical and relativistic epistemologies that are prompted in large measure by heightened awareness of disagreement and diversity, or in some cases it abandons epistemology entirely.[13]

---

[11]Ontology is the study of being. Realism and nonrealism adopt opposing views on the ontological status of a wide range of things, including physical objects, moral values and norms, numbers and the principles of mathematics, logical principles, entities postulated in the physical sciences and so on. To be a realist with respect to a particular domain is to maintain that the objects within that domain have reality independent of individual or collective states of consciousness; they have mind-independent reality. Nonrealists deny this and maintain that the objects of our experience are not ontologically independent of our experiences. One can, of course, be a realist with respect to one domain (physical objects) and a nonrealist with respect to others (moral principles), and there are many versions of both realism and nonrealism. See Michael Devitt, *Realism and Truth,* 2nd ed. (Oxford: Blackwell, 1991), chapter 1.

[12]By "transcendence or objectivity," I mean that the norms have extramental reality or validity and cannot be reduced to individual or collective states of human consciousness. The norms exist and have validity whether anyone is aware of them or not, or whether they are accepted or rejected by particular groups of people.

[13]For a helpful introductory discussion of some of the epistemological themes associated with postmodernity, see Stanley Grenz, *A Primer on Postmodernity* (Grand Rapids, Mich.: Eerdmans, 1996); and J. Andrew Kirk and Kevin J. Vanhoozer, eds., *To Stake a Claim: Mission and the Western Crisis of Knowledge* (Maryknoll, N.Y.: Orbis, 1999), chapters 1-3.

As an intellectual movement, or rather as a collection of interrelated movements, postmodernity is especially identified with Michel Foucault (1926–1984), Jacques Derrida (b. 1930), Jean-François Lyotard (b. 1924) and Richard Rorty (b. 1931). Foucault, French philosopher and social critic, is remembered for his unique approach to intellectual history, the "archaeology of knowledge."[14] His concern was not with uncovering the past as it actually was or arriving at some indisputable, universal truths about the past. Indeed his method was intended to show that such presumed objectivity of historical knowledge was impossible. Foucault especially attacked a cluster of assumptions concerning knowledge that were identified with the Enlightenment: the assumption that there is an objective body of knowledge "out there" waiting to be discovered; the assumption that the proper use of reason will produce universally valid, neutral and value-free knowledge; and the assumption that the pursuit of such knowledge is necessarily good and benefits all humankind rather than just certain classes of people. He launched a subtle but penetrating critique of this view of knowledge through his "archaeological" investigations of the social and historical circumstances within which ideas are advanced and accepted. Adopting from Nietzsche the notion of "genealogy" in unmasking claims to knowledge—that is, the attempt to undermine all claims to universal truth by uncovering the circumstances in which such claims are made and the particular agendas at work in such assertions—Foucault contended that all truth or knowledge claims are implicitly or explicitly assertions of power over others. What is accepted as knowledge is actually the result of a "will to knowledge" that establishes its own "truth" and is "a system of ordered procedures for the production, regulation, distribution, circulation and operation of statements."[15]

Jacques Derrida's reputation as a philosopher is well established in Europe, although in the United States he is known more for his influence upon literary the-

---

[14]See Michel Foucault, *The Archeology of Knowledge and the Discourse on Language,* trans. A. M. Sheridan Smith (New York: Pantheon, 1972).

[15]As quoted in Grenz, *Primer on Postmodernism,* p. 133. Foucault states, "The important thing here, I believe, is that truth isn't outside power, or lacking in power: contrary to a myth whose history and functions would repay further study, truth isn't the reward of free spirits, the child of protracted solitude, nor the privilege of those who have succeeded in liberating themselves. Truth is a thing of this world: it is produced only by virtue of multiple forms of constraint. And it induces regular effects of power. Each society has its regime of truth, its general politics of truth: that is, the types of discourse which it accepts and makes function as true; the mechanisms and instances which enable one to distinguish true and false statements, the means by which each is sanctioned; the techniques and procedures accorded value in the acquisition of truth; the status of those who are charged with saying what counts as true" (Michel Foucault, "Truth and Power," in *The Foucault Reader,* ed. Paul Rabinow [New York: Pantheon, 1984], pp. 72-73).

ory than philosophy.[16] Derrida's writings are notoriously difficult to interpret, but throughout his many works one may find two interrelated themes: a concern with language and meaning, and a sustained attack upon what he sees as the confusions of traditional Western philosophy. Indeed his critique of Western philosophy for its "logocentrism" stems from his nonrealist understanding of language and meaning. Derrida rejects the assumption that our concepts, words or language refer to fixed or objective realities and meanings "out there." He emphasizes elements of ambiguity, indeterminacy, metaphor and multiple meanings in an effort to show that "meaning" is not something fixed and determinate, which we are able to uncover by carefully studying written texts through proper hermeneutical methods, but rather is open-ended and indeterminate, consisting of the set of linguistic and textual relationships themselves and not something beyond that to which they point. This obviously has enormous implications for literary theory and hermeneutics, implications that find expression in the popular movement known as "deconstruction." Deconstruction defies clear definition, but Stanley Grenz has helpfully characterized it as a movement that "involves the use of certain philosophical or philological assumptions to launch an assault on logocentrism, understood as the assumption that something lies beyond our system of linguistic signs to which a written work can refer to substantiate its claim to be an authentic statement."[17]

Less prolific a writer than Derrida is Jean-François Lyotard, a French philosopher known especially for his work *The Postmodern Condition: A Report on Knowledge.* In an oft-quoted statement Lyotard defines postmodernity as "incredulity toward metanarratives," with a metanarrative understood as a grand schema, comprehensive system or explanatory framework intended to make sense of our world.[18] Religions such as Christianity and Islam include religious metanarratives; secular metanarrratives can be found in Marxism or Hegelianism. For Lyotard,

---

[16]Derrida is a prolific writer. Among his more influential works are *Of Grammatology,* trans. Gayatri Chakravorty Spivak (Baltimore: Johns Hopkins University Press, 1975); *Margins of Philosophy,* trans. Alan Bass (Chicago: University of Chicago Press, 1980); *Speech and Phenomena and Other Essays on Husserl's Theory of Signs,* trans. David Allinson (Evanston, Ill.: Northwestern University Press, 1973); *Writing and Difference,* trans. Alan Bass (Chicago: University of Chicago Press, 1978). Helpful discussions of Derrida's thought can be found in Christopher Norris, *Derrida* (Cambridge, Mass.: Harvard University Press, 1987); and Grenz, *Primer on Postmodernism,* pp. 138-50.

[17]Grenz, *Primer on Postmodernism,* p. 148. For Derrida's influence on deconstruction, see Christopher Norris, *Deconstruction: Theory and Practice,* rev. ed. (London: Routledge, 1991). For helpful critiques of deconstruction, see John Ellis, *Against Deconstruction* (Princeton, N.J.: Princeton University Press, 1989); D. A. Carson, *The Gagging of God: Christianity Confronts Pluralism* (Grand Rapids, Mich.: Zondervan, 1996), especially pp. 107-16; and Kevin J. Vanhoozer, *Is There a Meaning in This Text? The Bible, the Reader, and the Morality of Literary Knowledge* (Grand Rapids, Mich.: Zondervan, 1998).

[18]Jean-François Lyotard, *The Postmodern Condition: A Report on Knowledge,* trans. Geoff Bennington and Brian Massumi (Minneapolis: University of Minnesota Press, 1984), p. xxiv.

modernity was characterized by an implicit metanarrative arising from the Enlightenment that emphasized the power of reason and universal truth, our capacity to know reality objectively, and continual progress in perfecting human society. According to Lyotard, such metanarratives have lost their ability to persuade and legitimize contemporary institutions and assumptions, thereby thrusting us into a postmodern stage with its multiplicity of heterogeneous and incommensurable perspectives and agendas.

Undoubtedly the most influential postmodern philosophical figure in the United States today is Richard Rorty. Although coming from a very different tradition, Rorty shares Derrida's rejection of the modern concern with secure foundations for knowledge. Initially a fairly traditional analytic philosopher, Rorty in 1979 published *Philosophy and the Mirror of Nature*, a work that argued against what he saw as a mistaken assumption underlying modern philosophy—the idea that the mind is a "mirror of nature" and that with proper epistemological constraints our knowledge can accurately represent or picture reality.[19] Rorty rejects the suggestion that it is possible for us to make objective or nonarbitrary judgments about conflicting beliefs from a transcendent or objective standpoint. His critique of epistemology includes rejection of a representational or correspondence understanding of truth as well as foundationalism in knowledge. He understands both truth and knowledge in pragmatic terms as socially constructed conventions for "what works." The carefree relativism of postmodernism is captured well in a quip often attributed to Rorty: "Truth is whatever your peers will let you get away with." Although these are not his exact words, they do illustrate the conventionalism and pragmatism implicit not only in Rorty but also in many other postmodern thinkers as well.[20]

In more recent writings Rorty has softened the relativistic themes somewhat,

---

[19]Richard Rorty, *Philosophy and the Mirror of Nature* (Princeton, N.J.: Princeton University Press, 1979). See also Rorty's *The Consequences of Pragmatism* (Minneapolis: University of Minnesota Press, 1982) and *Objectivity, Relativism, and Truth* (Cambridge: Cambridge University Press, 1991).

[20]What Rorty does say is the following: "Can we treat the study of 'the nature of human knowledge' just as the study of certain ways in which human beings interact, or does it require an ontological foundation (involving some specifically philosophical way of describing human beings)? Shall we take 'S knows that p' (or 'S knows noninferentially that p' or 'S believes incorrigibly that p,' or 'S's knowledge that p is certain') as a remark about the relation between subject and object, between nature and its mirror?" Rorty rejects the idea that knowledge is a matter of our thoughts mirroring reality and thus he adopts the first alternative, which "leads to a pragmatic view of truth and a therapeutic approach to ontology." Rorty observes that this pragmatic approach goes against attempts "to make truth something more than what Dewey called 'warranted assertability': more than what our peers, *ceteris paribus*, let us get away with saying" (Rorty, *Philosophy and the Mirror of Nature*, pp. 175-76). See also the exchange between Rorty and Charles Taylor in Richard Rorty, "Taylor on Truth," and Charles Taylor, "Charles Taylor Replies," in *Philosophy in an Age of Pluralism: The Philosophy of Charles Taylor in Question*, ed. James Tully (Cambridge: Cambridge University Press, 1994), pp. 20-33, 219-22.

admitting, "Truth is, to be sure, an absolute notion, in the following sense: 'true for me but not for you' and 'true in my culture but not in yours' are weird, pointless locutions." But he continues to reject the "appearance-reality distinction," claiming that "there are many ways to talk about what is going on, and that none of them gets closer to the way things are in themselves than any other." Although truth itself might be an absolute notion, "we have no criterion of truth other than justification," and justification "will always be relative to audiences." Thus, even if "true" is an absolute term, "its conditions of application will always be relative."[21]

Positive postmodernism. Although methodological postmodernism is largely negative in that it is defined in terms of its rejection of modernity's epistemological assumptions and agendas, positive postmodernism goes beyond this to attempt a positive reinterpretation of basic issues. It takes the critique of modernity seriously, but rather than dismissing fundamental questions about humankind, society, art, politics, the self or God entirely, it reformulates them on the basis of postmodernist values and assumptions.[22] Such postmodernist writings characteristically stress the limited and perspectival nature of all inquiry and the futility of trying to arrive at certainty in knowledge, but they do so while trying to avoid the incoherencies of thoroughgoing relativism. Among evangelical thinkers, Nancey Murphy and Stanley Grenz are examples of positive or constructive postmodernists.[23]

The threefold classification by Cahoone is helpful, and it reminds us that postmodernity is not a clearly defined uniform movement but rather includes a variety of quite disparate thinkers and agendas united more by what they reject—the "Enlightenment worldview" or, more accurately, what they take to be the Enlightenment worldview—than by what they accept. Although Foucault, Derrida, Lyotard and Rorty are all highly creative thinkers in their own right, the common

---

[21]Richard Rorty, *Truth and Progress: Philosophical Papers* (Cambridge: Cambridge University Press, 1998), 3:1-2.

[22]See David Ray Griffin, William A. Beardslee and Joe Holland, *Varieties of Postmodern Theology* (Albany: State University of New York Press, 1989); David Ray Griffin, "Introduction: Constructive Postmodern Philosophy," in *Founders of Constructive Postmodern Philosophy,* ed. David Ray Griffin (Albany: State University of New York Press, 1993), pp. 1-42; and David Ray Griffin, *God and Religion in the Postmodern World: Essays in Postmodern Theology* (Albany: State University of New York Press, 1989).

[23]See Nancey Murphy, "Philosophical Resources for Postmodern Evangelical Theology," *Christian Scholars Review* 26, no. 2 (1996), pp. 184-205; Nancey Murphy, *Beyond Liberalism and Fundamentalism: How Modern and Postmodern Philosophy Set the Theological Agenda* (Valley Forge, Penn.: Trinity Press International, 1996); Nancey Murphy, *Anglo-American Postmodernity: Philosophical Perspectives on Science, Religion, and Ethics* (Boulder, Colo.: Westview, 1997); Stanley Grenz, *Revisioning Evangelical Theology: A Fresh Agenda for the Twenty-First Century* (Downers Grove, Ill.: InterVarsity Press, 1993); and Stanley Grenz, *Theology for the Community of God* (Nashville: Broadman & Holman, 1994).

perception that their thought represents a radical departure from previous philosophical traditions is somewhat misleading. For all, in varying degrees, share an epistemological skepticism and critique of metaphysics that has dominated Western philosophy since the time of Immanuel Kant. Furthermore, while it would be grossly inaccurate to dismiss them as nothing more than a rehash of classical skepticism, there are some striking similarities between certain postmodernist thinkers and the nineteenth-century philosopher Friedrich Nietzsche as well as some fascinating parallels with the Sophists of fifth-century B.C. Athens.[24]

Modernity and the Enlightenment

Postmodernity is generally understood in terms of its contrast with modernity, and modernity in turn is identified with the Enlightenment—or the "Enlightenment project," to use Jürgen Habermas's influential phrase.[25] In this model "modernity" and "Enlightenment project" are virtually synonyms of each other, with "postmodernity" being defined in terms of the rejection of this Enlightenment mentality. Moreover, this model claims that, since Western culture has largely rejected the assumptions and ideals of the Enlightenment, we are now in postmodernity.

But what do advocates of this model mean when they refer to the Enlightenment mentality? Habermas, himself a sympathetic critic of the Enlightenment project who has devoted his life's work to reformulating and defending what he sees as valuable in the Enlightenment, has expressed the dynamics of modernity in this way:

> The project of modernity, formulated in the eighteenth century by the Enlightenment *philosophes,* consists of a relentless development of the objectivating sciences, the universalistic bases of morality and law, and autonomous art in accordance with their internal logic but at the same time a release of the cognitive potentials thus accumulated from their esoteric high forms and their utilisation in praxis; that is, in the rational organisation of living conditions and social relations. Proponents of the Enlightenment . . . still held the extravagant expectation that the arts and sciences would further not only the control of the forces of nature but also the understanding of self and the world, moral progress, justice in social institutions, and even human happiness.[26]

---

[24]A number of scholars have also pointed out basic similarities between these postmodernist thinkers and some non-Western thinkers and movements. See David L. Hall, "Modern China and the Postmodern West," in *Culture and Modernity: East-West Philosophic Perspectives,* ed. Eliot Deutsch (Honolulu: University of Hawaii Press, 1991), pp. 50-70.

[25]Jürgen Habermas, *The Philosophical Discourse of Modernity,* trans. Frederick Lawrence (Cambridge, Mass.: MIT Press, 1987).

[26]Jürgen Habermas, "Modernity: An Unfinished Project," in *The Post-Modern Reader,* ed. Charles Jencks (New York: St. Martin's, 1992), pp. 162-63; as quoted in Grenz, *Primer on Postmodernism* (Grand Rapids, Mich.: Eerdmans, 1996), p. 3.

Similarly David Harvey, in his influential work *The Condition of Postmodernity*, also sees a close relationship between modernity and the Enlightenment and emphasizes the place of knowledge, truth and progress in Enlightenment thought.

> The Enlightenment project . . . took it as axiomatic that there was only one possible answer to any question. From this it followed that the world could be controlled and rationally ordered if we could only picture and represent it rightly. But this presumed that there existed a single correct mode of representation which, if we could uncover it (and this is what scientific and mathematical endeavors were all about), would provide the means to Enlightenment ends.[27]

Harvey notes that the Enlightenment "embraced the idea of progress, and actively sought that break with history and tradition which modernity espouses. It was, above all, a secular movement that sought the demystification and desacralization of knowledge and social organization in order to liberate human beings from their chains."[28]

The term *Enlightenment* generally is used to refer to a particular intellectual movement—or rather, several distinct but related movements—that began in England in the seventeenth century, developed in France and Scotland during the eighteenth century and then spread throughout Europe and North America.[29] The English (1688) and French (1789) revolutions provide convenient historical markers for this movement, although certain characteristic Enlightenment assumptions can be found earlier and its influence certainly has extended far beyond the end of the eighteenth century. Sometimes the terms "the Enlightenment" and "the Age of Reason" are used synonymously, although strictly speaking the latter title refers to the heavy rationalism of seventeenth-century thinkers such as Descartes, Leibniz and Spinoza whereas "the Enlightenment" denotes distinctive cultural and intellectual movements of the eighteenth century. Although Enlightenment thinkers certainly did emphasize reason, in general they had much more modest expectations on what reason could deliver than did the earlier rationalists.[30]

The Enlightenment movement was generated by the cultured elite and in

---

[27]David Harvey, *The Condition of Postmodernity: An Enquiry into the Origins of Cultural Change* (Cambridge, Mass.: Blackwell, 1990), p. 27.

[28]Ibid., pp. 12-13.

[29]Some helpful works on the Enlightenment include Ernst Cassirer, *The Philosophy of the Enlightenment* (Princeton, N.J.: Princeton University Press, 1951); Peter Gay, *The Rise of Modern Paganism*, vol. 1 of *The Enlightenment: An Interpretation,* and *The Science of Freedom,* vol. 2 of *The Enlightenment: An Interpretation* (New York: W. W. Norton, 1966); Norman Hampson, *The Enlightenment: An Evaluation of Its Assumptions, Attitudes, and Values* (Hammondsworth, England: Penguin, 1968); and Paul Hazard, *European Thought in the Eighteenth Century: From Montesquieu to Lessing* (New Haven, Conn.: Yale University Press, 1954).

[30]See Franklin L. Baumer, *Modern European Thought: Continuity and Change in Ideas, 1600-1950* (New York: Macmillan, 1977), pp. 142-43.

France centered around the *philosophes,* a diverse group of scientists, writers, statesmen and other intellectuals who were bound together by their common support of the developing natural sciences, their attack upon what they regarded as irrational and superstitious traditions (especially the authoritarianism of the established church), and their commitment to more liberal and tolerant political and social institutions. The Enlightenment was not an entirely uniform movement, with the French Enlightenment considerably more radical and antireligious than the Scottish or German movements. Nevertheless, there were common themes linking the various thinkers and movements, with the commonalities appearing more in *how* people thought than in *what* they believed. Lester Crocker observes that the Enlightenment "way of thinking set in place in Western culture a new dominant mode that was to persist into the future: the free play of critical and constructive reason, employing available knowledge, in the humanistic search for a better society, better behaviour, greater happiness on earth, a better understanding of what men are capable of, and what can and should be done with them."[31] The Enlightenment was a movement that, for all of its disparate personalities, beliefs and agendas, was held together by certain common assumptions about reason, science, progress, and how the proper use of our increasing knowledge might improve human life.

As a particular historical movement, the Enlightenment was over by the beginning of the nineteenth century, although its legacy is still with us. But for many today the Enlightenment represents more than just a particular historical period; it has become a kind of conceptual symbol for certain values and assumptions, an ideology or worldview that transcends particular historical periods, and it is in this sense that the Enlightenment mentality is said to have been dominant in the West from the late eighteenth century until well into the twentieth century. Thus modernity is said to be a worldview characterized by an emphasis upon the capacity of reason to uncover universal truths; the rejection of superstition and religious authoritarianism; an understanding of science as producing ever more accurate pictures of the universe and the human person; an expectation that science, technology and education working together will eradicate problems and progressively improve human life; and a general toleration for various creeds and ways of life, so long as they do not conflict with what reason sanctions.

And it is this worldview that is said to have been rejected and replaced by postmodernity. Thus Lawrence Cahoone notes that "postmodernism is the latest move in the critique of the Enlightenment," and David Harvey defines postmodernity as the condition in which the world finds itself after the collapse of the Enlighten-

---

[31]Lester G. Crocker, introduction to *The Blackwell Companion to the Enlightenment,* ed. John W. Yolton (Cambridge, Mass.: Blackwell, 1991), p. 1.

ment project.[32] On this understanding, then, postmodernity involves the rejection of the assumption that reason leads us to ever-expanding knowledge of reality and that dramatic developments in science and technology result in ever-greater progress for humankind.

Many theologians, including many evangelicals, have been strongly influenced by this understanding of the relation between modernity and the Enlightenment. But perhaps no one has done more to focus the attention of evangelicals on the impact of the Enlightenment upon modern Western culture than the late missiologist and theologian Lesslie Newbigin.[33] Newbigin is well known for placing the issues of gospel and culture on the agenda for the Western church by forcefully raising the question "Can the West be converted?"[34] Although he never developed a systematic model for understanding modernity or postmodernity, Newbigin regarded contemporary Western societies as having been powerfully shaped by Enlightenment assumptions. According to Newbigin, one of the most pernicious influences of the Enlightenment is the modern demand for absolute certainty in all areas of knowledge, including religion, an unattainable ideal that he traces back to the dominant influence of René Descartes upon modern thought.[35]

There is, of course, much to be said for this identification of modernity with the Enlightenment, for clearly Enlightenment assumptions have shaped modern Western cultures in significant ways. However, simply to identify modernity with the Enlightenment, and in particular to understand subsequent Western culture as defined by René Descartes's agenda and assumptions, is both historically misleading and inadequate to account for the cultural and intellectual patterns driving religious pluralism today. James C. Livingston notes:

> All too often, "Modernity" has been identified with the Enlightenment—or, more candidly, with a caricature of the Enlightenment—resulting from selective attention to those thinkers and writings that represent the most egregious excesses of eighteenth century rationalism, abstraction, materialism, or belief in an inevitable historical progress. The Enlightenment was, of course, a far more complex and variegated phenomenon. . . . But, more to my point, "Modernity" has not been shaped exclusively by

[32]Cahoone, introduction to *From Modernism to Postmodernism,* p. 2; Harvey, *Condition of Postmodernity,* p. 27.

[33]See Lesslie Newbigin, *Foolishness to the Greeks: The Gospel and Western Culture* (Grand Rapids, Mich.: Eerdmans, 1986); *The Gospel in a Pluralist Society* (Grand Rapids, Mich.: Eerdmans, 1989); *Truth to Tell: The Gospel as Public Truth* (Grand Rapids, Mich.: Eerdmans, 1991); "Truth and Authority in Modernity," in *Faith and Modernity,* ed. Philip Sampson, Vinay Samuel and Chris Sugden (Oxford: Regnum/Lynx, 1994), pp. 60-88.

[34]See Lesslie Newbigin, "Can the West Be Converted?" *International Bulletin of Missionary Research* 11 (1987): 2-7.

[35]See, for example, *Truth to Tell,* pp. 25-30; *Gospel in a Pluralist Society,* chapters 3-5; and "Truth and Authority in Modernity," pp. 61-70.

the Enlightenment. The Modern Age also is deeply infused with the spirit, feelings, and values of various Romanticisms, with the ideas and sensibilities we find in Wordsworth and Coleridge, in Hamann and Hegel, in Lamennais and Newman, in Kierkegaard and Nietzsche, or in the divided psyche of Chateaubriand. . . . [We can see] in manifestations of contemporary post-Modernism—its critique of metaphysics and the claim to possess incorrigible foundations of knowledge and belief, its attention to how rationality and knowledge are embedded in distinctive languages and cultures, and its critique of liberal individualism—that all these have their roots in the fertile soil of both the Enlightenment and Romanticism, which, respectively, have shaped our complex and pluralistic modern world.[36]

The problem with the casual identification of modernity with the Enlightenment, then, is twofold: First, this model is misleading and reductionistic in its treatment both of the historical Enlightenment and the two centuries that followed. Second, the particular patterns and dynamics usually associated with post-modernity—skepticism about metanarratives, distrust of rationality, relativism, fascination with diversity and difference—actually have deep roots in the early modern period and can best be accounted for not as a recent rejection of Enlightenment rationalism but rather as the culmination of the social transformations brought about by modernization and the intellectual currents of the past four centuries. We will consider briefly the views of Enlightenment thinkers on reason before going on to suggest an alternative way of understanding cultural transformation.

The Enlightenment and Reason

The Enlightenment is frequently portrayed, especially by Christian theologians, as a movement intoxicated by an excessive confidence in the powers of human reason to solve all problems. That reason was central to Enlightenment thinkers is beyond dispute, although it was often regarded with considerably more ambivalence than is generally recognized. The Enlightenment manifested a qualified confidence in reason as our only guide to truth—an assumption more apparent in some thinkers than others, but one that was never far from the constraining undercurrents of skepticism.

Enlightenment thinkers certainly did recognize the capacity of reason to arrive at some universally valid and normative truths. Properly disciplined and unencumbered by inhibiting factors, reason was regarded as capable of discovering significant truths about the universe and human affairs. However, certain external factors—notably the religious authoritarianism associated with the church and

---

[36]James C. Livingston, *The Enlightenment and the Nineteenth Century,* vol. 1 of *Modern Christian Thought,* 2nd ed. (Upper Saddle River, N.J.: Prentice-Hall, 1997), p. 3.

traditional religion—were believed to have corrupted the natural operation of reason. As Crane Brinton puts it, "Church, state, social and economic class, superstition, ignorance, prejudice, poverty, and vice all seemed to work together to impede the proper functioning of Reason."[37]

Enlightenment, then, was held to be the liberation of the rational capacity of humankind from the shackles of medieval Christendom that inhibited its free expression.[38] Thus Immanuel Kant, the last and arguably the greatest of the Enlightenment thinkers, in a seminal essay states:

> Enlightenment is man's emergence from his self-imposed nonage. Nonage is the inability to use one's own understanding without another's guidance. This nonage is self-imposed if its cause lies not in lack of understanding but in indecision and lack of courage to use one's own mind without another's guidance. Dare to know! *(Sapere aude!)* "Have the courage to use your own understanding" is therefore the motto of the Enlightenment.[39]

In the same essay Kant links the enlightened use of reason to the themes of freedom and autonomy: "This enlightenment requires nothing but *freedom*—and the most innocent of all that may be called 'freedom': freedom to make public use of one's reason in all matters."[40]

The eighteenth-century emphasis upon reason, however, must be distinguished from the seventeenth-century rationalism of Descartes, Leibniz and Spinoza. The earlier rationalists' desire to construct a comprehensive metaphysical system

---

[37]Crane Brinton, "The Enlightenment," in *The Encyclopedia of Philosophy*, ed. Paul Edwards (New York: Macmillan, 1967), 2:520.

[38]Franklin Baumer describes one of the more bizarre episodes of the Enlightenment: "On the morning of November 10, 1793 (or the twentieth Brumaire of the Year II, according to the Revolutionary calendar), there took place in the Cathedral of Notre Dame of Paris an extraordinary religious event. This was the Festival of Liberty and Reason, proclaimed three days before by the mayor of the city. As spectators, officials of the Commune and Department of Paris together with a great concourse of plain citizens, entered the cathedral, they saw, some doubtless with astonishment, the insignia of Christianity covered up and their place taken by the symbols of a strange new religion. Rising up in the nave was an improvised mountain, at the top of which perched a small Greek temple dedicated 'To Philosophy' and adorned on both sides by the busts of philosophers, probably Voltaire, Rousseau, Franklin, and Montesquieu. Halfway down the side of the mountain a torch of Truth burned before an altar of Reason. Then ensued a bizarre ceremony which culminated in the emergence from the temple of a beautiful woman, an actress of the Paris Opera, dressed in red, white, and blue garments, who personified Liberty. The spectators proceeded to render homage to Liberty by stretching out their arms and singing a hymn, the words of which were written by Marie Joseph Chénier: 'Come, holy Liberty, inhabit this temple, Become the goddess of the French people.' Soon thereafter the Constitutional Convention decreed that Notre Dame should be known as the temple of Reason" (Franklin L. Baumer, *Religion and the Rise of Scepticism* [New York: Harcourt Brace, 1960], pp. 35-36).

[39]Immanuel Kant, "What Is Enlightenment?" trans. Peter Gay, in *The Enlightenment: A Comprehensive Anthology*, ed. Peter Gay (New York: Simon & Schuster, 1973), p. 384.

[40]Ibid., p. 385.

through rigorous deduction from indubitable premises, yielding absolute certainty in all areas of inquiry, was largely abandoned by later eighteenth-century thinkers.[41] With the Enlightenment there is a clear shift away from earlier rationalism toward empiricism, or the focus upon human experience, especially sense experience, as the source of knowledge. If we are to pick a seventeenth-century thinker who anticipates Enlightenment perspectives, it would not be René Descartes but rather John Locke, for it was Locke's empiricist epistemology, along with the new experimental scientific methodology of Isaac Newton, and of Francis Bacon before him, that shaped eighteenth-century views on reason. And Newton's method, especially as outlined in his *Opticks,* was not that of strict deduction but instead was based upon analysis of the data of experience. The revolutionary developments in mathematical science, astronomy, physics and biology during the sixteenth and seventeenth centuries—exemplified in the work of Bacon, Kepler, Galileo, Harvey, Boyle and, of course, Newton—naturally raised expectations about what the rigorous application of reason and careful experimentation might accomplish.[42]

Not surprisingly, then, the Enlightenment carried with it a powerful sense of optimism about human progress. "As science seemed to establish itself on an impregnable basis of experimentally verified fact, doubt and confusion eventually gave way to self-confidence, the belief that the unknown was merely the undiscovered, and the general assumption—unprecedented in the Christian era—that man was to a great extent the master of his own destiny."[43] With the liberation of reason from religious authoritarianism and superstition, the growing influence of modern science, and the remarkable developments of early technology, it was natural to suppose that human society could progress indefinitely. Significantly, at the heart of this optimistic vision was rejection of the traditional Christian understanding of original sin in favor of views of human nature that emphasized a natural capacity for virtue and moral perfectibility, given the proper conditions

---

[41]See Cassirer, *Philosophy of the Enlightenment,* pp. 6-7; Hazard, *European Thought in the Eighteenth Century,* part 1, chapter 3.

[42]Norman Hampson describes the enormous impact of Newton's empirical method upon the intellectual climate of Europe: "We may concentrate on [Newton's] law of gravity. The beautiful simplicity of a single law which appeared to explain the operation of every kind of earthly and celestial movement was a triumphant example of the possibilities of the new learning. Human reasoning, operating by means of careful observation and checking its conclusions by further observation or experiment, could for the first time in the history of man reveal the mechanism of the natural world in which he had lived for so long like a fearful and wondering child. Nature, instead of being a mere collection of phenomena, a hotch-potch of occult influences or the canvas on which an inscrutable Providence painted its mysterious symbols, was a system of intelligible forces. God was a mathematician whose calculations, although infinite in their subtle complexity, were accessible to man's intelligence" (Hampson, *Enlightenment,* pp. 37-38).

[43]Ibid., p. 35.

and education.[44] For example, Condorcet's ecstatic vision, as expressed in his *Sketch of the Progress of the Human Mind* (1795), of a world governed by enlightened reason, enjoying ever-new dimensions of progress and human flourishing, may be extreme even by Enlightenment standards, but it captured well the giddy optimism of the times. Ignorance was on the retreat. Common sense and enlightened reason would eventually eliminate political discord between nations. Developments in medicine would progressively eradicate common diseases, lengthening human life indefinitely. Enlightened education and liberation from authoritarianism would ensure a just and equitable society, free of tyranny, superstition and dogmatism. In short, Condorcet confidently claimed, "We may conclude . . . that the perfectability of man is indefinite."[45]

But we must also remember that some of the leading figures of the Enlightenment were actually quite modest, even skeptical, in their views on reason. As we shall see in chapter four, the specter of skepticism haunted the early modern period, so that the heavy rationalism of the seventeenth century must be understood in part as a calculated response to the widespread skepticism (doubt about human ability to know truth) and fideism (reliance on faith alone, not reason) of the time. Furthermore, skeptical themes were prominent in some of the leading Enlightenment thinkers, most notably David Hume, who can hardly be accused of having excessive confidence in reason. And of course, the great irony is that in spite of Immanuel Kant's conviction that his critical philosophy had established the foundations of knowledge, his contemporaries recognized correctly that in fact his "Copernican revolution" merely made the problems of skepticism more intractable. Thus Sylvana Tomaselli notes that "it would be a mistake to think of reason as the rallying cry of Enlightenment thinkers except in so far as it was opposed to faith, and the Age of Reason as opposed to the Age of Superstition."[46] Similarly Peter Gay has argued persuasively that the *philosophes'* views should not be understood as unqualified confidence in reason alone so much as a revolt against seventeenth-century rationalism accompanied by a strong commitment to ongoing criticism.

> The *philosophes'* glorification of criticism and their qualified repudiation of metaphysics make it obvious that the Enlightenment was not an Age of Reason but a Revolt Against Rationalism. This revolt took two closely related forms: it rejected the assertion that reason is the sole, or even dominant, spring of action; and it denied that all

[44]See Cassirer, *Philosophy of the Enlightenment*, p. 159.
[45]Antoine-Nicolas de Condorcet, "Sketch of the Progress of the Human Mind," in Gay, *Enlightenment: A Comprehensive Anthology*, p. 808. Ironically, Condorcet's utopian essay was written in 1793 after the brutality of the French Revolution, while he was in hiding, and was published only after his death.
[46]Sylvana Tomaselli, "Reason," in *Blackwell Companion to the Enlightenment*, p. 446.

mysteries in the world can be penetrated by inquiry. The claim for the omnicompetence of criticism was in no way a claim for the omnipotence of reason. It was a political demand for the right to question everything, rather than the assertion that all could be known or mastered by rationality.[47]

What united Enlightenment thinkers, in spite of their many differences, was their common commitment to the virtues of criticism in all areas of life, but preeminently in religion.[48] As Diderot put it, "All things must be examined, debated, investigated without exception and without regard for anyone's feelings."[49] Thus Gay contends that the eighteenth century should be understood as the "Age of Criticism" rather than the "Age of Reason."[50]

Nevertheless, the role of reason was central to the unremitting attack upon orthodox Christianity as irrational, and it is this as much as anything else that reinforces the popular image today of the Enlightenment as a movement obsessed with reason. Even more skeptical thinkers, such as David Hume, were quite confident about reason's capacity to debunk the superstitions of traditional Christianity. Enlightenment thinkers were not necessarily against all religion; indeed, explicit atheism was rare outside of France.[51] But there was a sustained effort to cleanse religion of anything perceived to be contrary to reason, thereby restoring a pure, rational and natural religion common to all humankind.[52] The "scandal of particularity," which emphasized the utterly unique manner in which God has revealed himself through the Old and New Testaments, as well as the distinctiveness of Jesus

---

[47]Gay, *Rise of Modern Paganism*, p. 141.

[48]Peter Gay, introduction to *Enlightenment: A Comprehensive Anthology*, p. 17. Paul Hazard highlights the effective use made of non-Western (Persian, Chinese, African, Native American) symbols and "voices," both real and imagined, in the critique of European civilization. This motif, of course, culminated in the biting satire of Jonathan Swift's *Gulliver's Travels*. See Hazard, *European Thought in the Eighteenth Century*, part 1, chapter 1.

[49]Denis Diderot, "Encyclopedia," in Gay, *Enlightenment: A Comprehensive Anthology*, p. 289.

[50]Gay, introduction to *Enlightenment: A Comprehensive Anthology*, p. 19. The skepticism inherent in the thought of Enlightenment figures such as David Hume and Immanuel Kant will be considered in chapter three.

[51]See Michael Hunter and David Wooton, eds., *Atheism from the Reformation to the Enlightenment* (Oxford: Clarendon, 1992).

[52]Eighteenth-century thinkers were not particularly original in their attacks upon religious beliefs. Enlightenment figures deliberately went back to the earlier Greek and Roman writers and their critiques of popular religion, borrowing heavily from thinkers such as Lucretius (d. 54 B.C.), the Roman poet and philosopher, and Cicero (d. 43 B.C.), the Roman orator and poet. Lucretius's *De rerum natura*, with its polemical attack upon religious superstition and ignorance, was enormously influential in the eighteenth century. Almost two thousand years before the Enlightenment Lucretius argued that reason and "science" alone provide adequate understanding of the cosmos and that religion is nothing more than ignorant superstition. The ignorant masses "create" gods in their own images, and although religion serves certain pragmatic functions, it cannot be accepted as true. Voltaire, Diderot and Hume were all strongly influenced by Lucretius. See Gay, *Rise of Modern Paganism*, pp. 72-203.

Christ as God incarnate, the only Savior for all peoples, was bitterly attacked by Enlightenment thinkers as irrational.[53] The concept of divine special revelation was deemed unnecessary since the essence of "true religion" was said to be accessible to the disciplined and unprejudiced reason alone. Thus John Toland wrote *Christianity Not Mysterious: Or a Treatise Shewing That There Is Nothing in the Gospel Contrary to Reason, Nor Above It: And That No Christian Doctrine Can Be Properly Called a Mystery* (1696). The title alone eliminates any mystery concerning Toland's agenda. In sum, although they rejected orthodox Christianity with its commitment to a God who intervenes supernaturally in human affairs through miracles, reveals himself uniquely through the Bible and became incarnate in Jesus Christ, many Enlightenment thinkers were sympathetic to a kind of "natural religion" purged of all superstition and accessible to the dispassionate reflection of enlightened reason.[54]

The Problem of Reductionism
Reductionism occurs when an explanatory model fails to take into account properly the heterogeneity of the phenomena to be explained, or when it gives undue emphasis to certain items while ignoring others. Reductionistic explanations account for diverse data by reducing the complexity to a few simple principles or categories, in the process distorting the nature of what is to be explained. The popular understanding of modernity as the Enlightenment mentality, and of postmodernity as the rejection of this worldview, tends to be reductionistic unless it is carefully qualified.

For example, identifying modernity with the Enlightenment tends to minimize other intellectual and social movements of the time, thereby granting it more influence than it deserves. Not everyone in the eighteenth century was enamored with Enlightenment thought, for as Crane Brinton reminds us, "The generation that matured about 1800 felt for the Enlightened a contempt as deep as any on record."[55] Owen Chadwick points out that much of nineteenth-century England rejected Enlightenment assumptions, for the Enlightenment "stood for much that the nineteenth century despised."[56] Romanticism, the late-eighteenth- and early-

---

[53]See Gerald Cragg, *Reason and Authority in the Eighteenth Century* (Cambridge: Cambridge University Press, 1964); Hazard, *European Thought in the Eighteenth Century*, pp. 44-129; and Gerald R. McDermott, *Jonathan Edwards Confronts the Gods: Christian Theology, Enlightenment Religion, and Non-Christian Faiths* (New York: Oxford University Press, 2000), chapter 1.

[54]See Peter Harrison, *"Religion" and the Religions in the English Enlightenment* (Cambridge: Cambridge University Press, 1990).

[55]Brinton, "Enlightenment," p. 524.

[56]Owen Chadwick, *The Secularization of the European Mind in the Nineteenth Century* (Cambridge: Cambridge University Press, 1975), p. 144.

CONTOURS OF THE PRESENT

nineteenth-century movement affecting the fine arts, literature and philosophy, is often portrayed as a countermovement to the Enlightenment, or in John Stuart Mill's phrase, a reaction "against the narrowness of the eighteenth century."[57] And certainly it included rejection of some of the Enlightenment's central tenets. But Romanticism also shared some traits with the Enlightenment, making it difficult to categorize particular thinkers. Were thinkers such as Goethe, Lessing and Schiller part of the Enlightenment or Romanticism, or both? What of Rousseau? This is not to suggest that no distinction between the Enlightenment and Romanticism can be made—clearly they were different movements—but simply to caution against reductionistic treatments that are insensitive to the complexities within cultural movements.

We must also remember that the eighteenth century included significant movements of religious revival, so that reactionary movements against orthodox Christianity and dramatic growth and revitalization of the church took place simultaneously. Pietism emerged in the seventeenth century and became a formidable force within Protestantism, with Count Nicholas Ludwig von Zinzendorf and the Moravian community helping to launch the modern missionary movement. The Age of Enlightenment was also the time of John Wesley and the rise of Methodism in England, resulting in widespread spiritual and social renewal, as exemplified in William Wilberforce's attack upon slavery. George Whitefield was electrifying thousands with his dramatic preaching. A series of sweeping religious revivals—the Great Awakening in the American colonies between roughly 1726 and 1760, the Evangelical Revival in England from roughly 1787 to 1825, and the Second Great Awakening at the end of the eighteenth century—transformed the lives of thousands. And of course, the nineteenth and twentieth centuries produced an enormous variety of thinkers and movements—some hostile to Christian faith and others catalysts for renewal within the church—that do not neatly fit within the Enlightenment framework. In other words, the eighteenth-century Enlightenment was just one intellectual movement of the past three hundred years, and while it did exert considerable influence upon later developments, it was not the sole, nor perhaps even the dominant, force shaping late-twentieth-century Western cultures.

The problem of reductionism can also be seen in an overemphasis upon intellectuals and ideas in shaping cultural patterns. Those who identify modernity with the Enlightenment tend to adopt a "history of ideas" approach to cultural change, focusing upon particular ideas and then interpreting modernity and postmodernity in terms of their respective stances toward these beliefs. They give special attention to pivotal thinkers, and they understand broader social and cultural trends as the

---

[57]As quoted in Baumer, *Modern European Thought,* p. 270.

product of these thinkers' ideas. There is much to commend this approach, for clearly ideas often have significant consequences, and leading thinkers have had enormous effects upon society and popular culture. One need only mention the names of David Hume, Immanuel Kant, Ludwig Feuerbach, Sigmund Freud, Friedrich Nietzsche, Charles Darwin, Bertrand Russell, Ludwig Wittgenstein, Aldous Huxley or Carl Sagan to be reminded that the ideas of prominent individuals can have a profound impact upon others. To take just one of the more obvious and tragic examples of modern times, the ideas of Karl Marx, adapted and implemented by ruthless despots such as Josef Stalin, Mao Zedong, Pol Pot and a host of lesser tyrants, have had disastrous consequences for millions of people.

However, a history-of-ideas approach *by itself* is inadequate for understanding contemporary cultural changes. Intellectual history alone will not explain the dynamics of popular culture, where the influence of intellectuals is marginal at best. Thus, in discussing the secularization in Europe, Owen Chadwick observes, "That is why the problem of secularization is not the same as the problem of enlightenment. Enlightenment was of the few. Secularization is of the many."[58] Applying this to the question how best to understand modernity, then, debating the respective merits of modernity or postmodernity by analyzing the assumptions of representative thinkers (Foucault and Derrida versus Descartes and Locke), while instructive in its own way, is of limited value in helping us to grasp the dynamics of widespread cultural change among ordinary persons, most of whom have little awareness of such academic discussions. To be sure, we dare not ignore the impact of intellectuals upon culture. We must recognize, for example, the impact of radical deconstructionists upon many through their influence in the universities and the media. And in chapter four we will consider the effect of various intellectual movements upon religious skepticism. But the point here is that ideas and thinkers do

---

[58]Chadwick, *Secularization of the European Mind,* p. 9. Chadwick, who himself combines intellectual history with social history in his study of the secularization of the common people, puts the issues succinctly: "Social history or intellectual history? Orthodox Christianity was proved untrue because miracles became improbable, and Genesis was proved to be myth by science, and philosophical axioms were transformed by intellectual processes derived from the Enlightenment, and the intellectual revolution passed from universities to newspaper, and newspaper to drawing-room, and drawing-room to housekeeper's parlour, and newspaper to working-men's clubs—are *ideas* what moved the souls of men? Or did the working-man, thrust by economic development into a new and more impersonal class-structure, develop a consciousness of his class, and distrust or hatred of the middle-class, and find the churches middle-class institutions, and start to beat them with whatever sticks lay to hand, and found the weapons of atheist pamphleteers and potted handbooks of evolutionary science? Did men's minds move because educated men told them their axioms about God needed changing, or did they move because they felt a need to be 'free' from their fellow-men and that seemed to mean being 'free' from God? Was the process [of secularization] the result of new knowledge, or the result of a new development of society? . . . Men do not fathom intellectual history if they ask about nothing but the intellect" (ibid., pp. 12-13).

not emerge and gain plausibility in a sociocultural vacuum. Thus, in trying to understand the widespread acceptance today of religious pluralism, not only among the academic elite but also among the less educated, we need to consider factors other than merely ideas that affect belief and behavior on a popular level. A proper understanding of cultural change, then, will draw upon both intellectual history and broader social developments in an integrated manner, recognizing that each dimension affects and reinforces the other. In other words, we should look to both the intellectual legacies of the past, and how they are being expanded or challenged today, as well as the social and cultural transformations of the past few centuries that shape the present context.

Modernity and Modernization

It is helpful to supplement more philosophical understandings of modernity with insights from the social sciences on modernization. Although it is difficult to locate precisely the beginning of modernization, there clearly is a sense in which modern societies can be distinguished from premodern societies, and what lies at the heart of this distinction is the process of modernization. But what exactly is modernization? Peter Berger has defined modernization as "the institutional concomitants of technologically induced economic growth." Modernization thus "consists in the growth and diffusion of a set of institutions rooted in the transformation of the economy by means of technology."[59] The ongoing processes of modernization, then, are rooted in social institutions and structures associated with dramatic developments in technology and the economic transformations stimulated by such innovations, with the ramifications of these changes extending into virtually all areas of social life.

At the heart of modernization are the economic and social transformations growing out of the Industrial Revolution in Europe. Beginning especially in the late seventeenth century was a remarkable series of developments in industry and early technology resulting in significant changes in methods of producing goods other than crops. Increasingly sophisticated machines, such as the steam engine in 1769, were developed, enabling more efficient production and transportation of goods. The Industrial Revolution originally centered in Great Britain and was focused upon the textile manufacturing industry, but it gradually spread throughout Europe and North America, and eventually its effects were felt worldwide. Technological development affected not only manufacturing industries but also transportation and communication. Industrialization set in motion developments that continue today, as technological innovations continue to increase the effi-

---

[59]Peter Berger, Brigitte Berger and Hansfried Kellner, *The Homeless Mind: Modernization and Consciousness* (New York: Vintage, 1973), p. 9.

ciency with which a tremendous variety of goods and services are made available to more and more people worldwide. Technological changes profoundly altered social life as well, as the steam locomotive made possible a general mobility of people. Long-distance travel became faster and easier, thereby encouraging mobility and loosening the ties with local places.

The twentieth century saw these developments accelerate at a dizzying rate, as technological advances revolutionized transportation (airplane travel, the automobile, high-speed rail service, space travel), communication (telephone, satellite, e-mail, the World Wide Web), living conditions (central heating and air conditioning, automatic dishwashers), health care and life expectancy (penicillin, artificial hearts), entertainment (movies, compact discs, theme parks), education (research universities, community colleges, distance education) and the virtual worlds created by computer technology and digitization. While there certainly are differences between the industrialization of the West in the nineteenth century, with its predominance of goods produced through factories and heavy industries, and the kind of service-sector goods and information-based technologies that dominate today's economic landscape, this should not obscure the fact that what we have today is still part of the ongoing process of technological development stemming from modernization.[60]

While we must avoid simplistic stereotypes, it is probably safe to say that premodern societies were characterized by populations scattered throughout relatively isolated and self-contained rural communities, dependence upon agriculture, and a rather narrow range of life options available to members. Furthermore, in premodern societies almost all aspects of human life were shaped by "deeply rooted traditional modes of thought and behavior that are almost without exception, religious or sacred in character."[61] Modern societies, by contrast, are characterized by a population concentration in centralized urban areas; an intensified division of labor, along with a high degree of institutional specialization and segmentation; and economic and production spheres that are based upon an increasingly sophisticated technology. Considerable sociocultural pluralism or diversity characterize modern societies, and the worldview of the modern person tends to be rational and secular, open to innovation and not bound by traditional sanctions.

One of the most significant consequences of modernization has been urbanization. The massive shift from rural communities to urban centers constitutes one of the great social transitions of modern times. In Great Britain, the early pioneer in industrialization, the year 1801 saw about one-fifth of the population living in

---

[60]See Rose, *Post-Modern and the Post-Industrial*, pp. 28-29.
[61]James Davison Hunter, "What Is Modernity? Historical Roots and Contemporary Features," in *Faith and Modernity*, p. 15.

towns and cities of ten thousand or more inhabitants. By 1851 that figure had risen to two-fifths, and if smaller towns of from five thousand to ten thousand are included, more than half of the population was urbanized. By 1901 three-quarters of the population lived in cities of ten thousand or more (half the population in cities of twenty thousand or more). "In the span of a century a largely rural society had become a largely urban one."[62] By 1900 most of Europe had joined in the processes of industrialization and urbanization, so that by 1985, 70 percent of Europe (excepting the Soviet Union) was urbanized.

Urbanization is today a global phenomenon, with many of the most rapidly growing urban centers in the non-Western world. In 1950 six of the ten largest metropolitan areas were in Europe or North America, with New York the only city with more than 10 million residents. By 1995 only two of the top ten cities (New York and Los Angeles) were from Europe or North America. Leading the list was Tokyo/Yokohama, with just under 27 million residents. Other top cities included Mexico City, São Paulo, Bombay, Shanghai, Beijing, Calcutta and Seoul.[63] The United Nations reports that at the turn of the millennium, for the first time in history, urban dwellers outnumbered those in more traditional rural areas, with the urban population growing three times faster than that of rural communities.[64] The sweeping social changes brought about by urbanization that took place over almost two centuries in the West are compressed into merely a few decades in Asia, Latin America and Africa.

Modernization does not simply affect how we live, by producing more conveniences and more efficient ways of doing things; it also influences how we understand ourselves and the world around us. Max Weber, one of the earliest social theorists to consider carefully the impact of modernization upon society, regarded the increasing rationalization of all areas of life that accompanied the emergence of free-market capitalism and the various institutions associated with it a major effect of modernization.[65] Other effects include the increased bureaucratization of social life, the rise of the modern nation-state, the increasing application of scientific methodology and assumptions to all areas of social life, and the social fragmentation resulting from separation of family from business enterprises and the emer-

---

[62]Krishan Kumar, "Modernization and Industrialization," in *The New Encyclopaedia Britannica*, (Chicago: Encyclopaedia Britannica, 1998), 24:284.

[63]From the United Nations Population Fund, as cited in Colin McMahan, "Hope and Poverty Gravitate to Cities for World's Poor," *Chicago Tribune*, June 2, 1996, sec. 1, p. 10.

[64]United Nations, *World Population Prospects: The 1996 Revision* (New York: United Nations, 1998), pp. 2, 29; as cited in Roger Greenway and Timothy M. Monsma, *Cities: Missions' New Frontier*, 2nd ed. (Grand Rapids, Mich.: Baker, 2000), p. 13.

[65]See Max Weber, *The Protestant Ethic and the Spirit of Capitalism* (London: Allen & Unwin, 1930); Max Weber, *The Sociology of Religion* (London: Methuen, 1966); and Max Weber, *Economy and Society: An Outline of Interpretive Sociology* (New York: Badminister, 1968).

gence of autonomous urban business institutions. Weber's concern was with rationalization as a way of thinking and acting under the influence of modernization such that both public and personal life become increasingly dominated by "the purposive orientation of one's actions with respect to the actions of others and with respect to the means employed in achieving freely chosen ends."[66] Or as Bryan Turner puts it, for Weber "modernity is the outcome in cultural, social, and political terms of the broad process of rationalization by which the world is controlled and regulated by an ethic of world mastery. . . . The modernized project is the imposition of rationality (in terms of means-ends schemes) to the total environment."[67]

Thus modern people tend to develop what Peter Berger calls a distinctive "cognitive style," or way of thinking and behaving, shaped by modern institutions and practices.[68] For example, those working in vocations connected with technological production—whether traditional heavy industries or more recent telecommunications and information technologies—are affected in their basic approach to life by the nature of their work and its environment. The values of efficiency, productivity and the maximization of results (bigger is better, more for less) come to characterize one's general orientation to life. Predictability, control and concern for proper procedure become important values, not only in the workplace but in other spheres of life as well. One's life becomes governed by a "functional rationality" that exerts increasing rational control and by a problem-solving approach to all aspects of life, including social relations.

Globalization

The astonishing technological developments of the twentieth century, especially in transportation and communication, heightened our sense of the world as "one place," smaller and more intimately interrelated than before. We are aware of the unprecedented degree to which patterns of contemporary life are interconnected worldwide in complex ways that transcend geographical, national and cultural boundaries. In order to grasp the dynamics behind the current fascination with religious pluralism, it is crucial to understand the nature and impact of globalization.

One way to think about globalization is in terms of the increasing homogeneity or

---

[66]Craig M. Gay, "An Ironic Cage: The Rationalization of Modern Economic Life," in *Faith and Modernity*, p. 253. For Weber's views on rationality, see Stephen Kalberg, "Max Weber's Types of Rationality: Cornerstone for the Analysis of Rationalization Processes in History," *American Journal of Sociology* 85, no. 5 (1980): 1145-79.

[67]Bryan Turner, *Orientalism, Postmodernism, and Globalism* (London: Routledge, 1994), p. 79.

[68]See Berger et al., *Homeless Mind,* chapters 1-2. For a penetrating analysis of the influences of the cognitive style of modernity upon Christians, see Craig Gay, *The Way of the (Modern) World: Or, Why It's Tempting to Live As If God Doesn't Exist* (Grand Rapids, Mich.: Eerdmans, 1998).

commonality in certain areas that we find throughout the world, commonalities that cross ethnic, religious and political boundaries. This is sometimes called the homogenization thesis, since it emphasizes ways in which previously disparate groups are becoming similar. Those who frequently travel worldwide, for example, and who spend most of their time overseas in airport terminals, five-star hotels and expensive entertainment spots, are often struck by the "obvious Westernization" of the world. After all, one has ready access to CNN and e-mail, McDonald's and Starbucks, and is never far away from someone fluent in English. Globalization is thus very much a matter of transplanting the comforts and efficiencies of home worldwide. Yet if one were to wander away from the airport or Hilton and explore the ordinary lives of people in Bangkok, Mexico City or Bombay, it would quickly become apparent that such impressions are misleading.

Globalization is more subtle than the homogenization thesis suggests, and it can best be understood in terms of the notions of complex interrelatedness or interconnectedness on multiple levels across traditional boundaries. Thus John Tomlinson speaks of globalization as "complex connectivity," by which he means "the rapidly developing and ever-densening network of interconnections and interdependencies that characterize modern social life."[69] And Anthony Giddens defines globalization as "the intensification of worldwide social relations which link distant localities in such a way that local happenings are shaped by events occurring many miles away and vice versa."[70] What initially appear to be merely local events—selection of a new pope, the May 1989 Tiananmen massacre, collapse of the Hong Kong stock market—have powerful repercussions around the globe, and in turn the "local" events themselves are partly shaped by developments and expectations worldwide.

But it is not merely the fact of growing interrelatedness that is significant; it is our heightened *awareness* of this interconnectivity, and the effects of this consciousness upon us, that make globalization so important for understanding cultural change today. This aspect is captured nicely in Malcolm Waters's definition of globalization as "a social process in which the constraints of geography on social and cultural arrangements recede and *in which people become increasingly aware that they are receding.*"[71]

Globalization is directly linked to modernization, for, as many social theorists recognize, modernity is inherently globalizing.[72] Waters notes that globalization is

---

[69]Tomlinson, *Globalization and Culture*, p. 2.

[70]Anthony Giddens, *The Consequences of Modernity* (Stanford, Calif.: Stanford University Press, 1990), p. 64.

[71]Malcolm Waters, *Globalization* (New York: Routledge, 1995), p. 3. My emphasis.

[72]Two of the chief theorists on globalization disagree over the relation of globalization to modernization. Roland Robertson views the patterns of globalization as predating modernization and the rise of capitalism, although the latter greatly accelerate the process, whereas Anthony Giddens sees globalization as a direct consequence of modernization. See Robertson, *Globalization: Social Theory and Global Culture* (Newbury Park, Calif.: Sage, 1992), and Giddens, *Consequences of Modernity.*

"the direct consequence of the expansion of European culture across the planet via settlement, colonization and cultural mimesis."[73] The pattern of globalization as we know it emerged in the fifteenth and sixteenth centuries, and in the following centuries it became increasingly rooted in the economic developments associated with modern capitalism and the political alignments of the Western powers. The interrelatedness of globalization is evident in the political dimension, especially in the post-Cold War era. For with the rise of the modern era, the earlier world empires were gradually replaced by the nation-state as a distinctive social and political unit.[74] The Cold War realigned the world in terms of bipolar relationships—the "First" and "Second" Worlds representing the democratic/capitalist and communist/socialist nations, respectively, with the "Third" World resisting such political commitments. However, the revolutionary changes of 1989 and the collapse of the former Soviet Union have ushered in a new stage characterized politically not by bipolar but multipolar relationships.[75]

Closely related to the political dimension is economic interdependence. Roland Robertson notes that "economic interdependence and interpenetration at the global level constitute the most commonly and explicitly specified ingredient and dynamic of globalization."[76] Examples of economic and political interdependence abound. Robert Schreiter observes that with the collapse of socialist systems in 1989 there has been a resurgence of market capitalism worldwide and an intensification of a global economic system characterized by "its ignoring of national boundaries, its ability to move capital quickly, and its engagement in short-term projects that maximize the profit margin."[77] The extent to which economic rela-

---

[73]Waters, *Globalization,* p. 3.

[74]Immanuel Wallerstein has given much attention to the political and economic aspects of globalization in developing his model of globalization as producing an identifiable "world-system." See Wallerstein, *The Capitalist World Economy* (Cambridge: Cambridge University Press, 1979); *The Politics of the World Economy: The States, the Movements and the Civilizations* (Cambridge: Cambridge University Press, 1984); and "World-Systems Analysis," in *Social Theory Today,* ed. Anthony Giddens and J. Turner (Stanford, Calif.: Stanford University Press, 1987).

[75]Related to, and yet transcending, explicitly political concerns are the growing numbers of intergovernmental organizations (United Nations, World Bank, International Monetary Fund and so on) and international nongovernmental organizations (Greenpeace, Association of Commonwealth Universities, World Council of Churches, World Moslem Congress, International Olympic Committee and so on). Waters states that by 1992 there were over three thousand intergovernmental organizations and over fifteen thousand international nongovernmental organizations. Waters, *Globalization,* pp. 111-13.

[76]Roland Robertson, "Globalization, Modernization, and Postmodernization: The Ambiguous Position of Religion," in *Religion and Global Order,* ed. Roland Robertson and William Garrett (New York: Paragon, 1991), p. 282.

[77]Robert Schreiter, *The New Catholicity: Theology Between the Global and the Local* (Maryknoll, N.Y.: Orbis, 1997), p 7.

tions have become globalized was vividly illustrated in the financial crises of 1997–1998, which immediately linked events in Bangkok to Seoul, Tokyo, New York, London, Mexico City, Rio de Janeiro and Moscow, threatening financial markets worldwide.

The political and economic interrelatedness among nations is both sustained by and reflected in the astonishing developments in communication technologies, so that messages and visual images can now be communicated almost instantaneously worldwide. Thomas Friedman remarks that "globalization has its own defining technologies: computerization, miniaturization, digitization, satellite communications, fiber optics and the Internet."[78] Whereas the symbol of the Cold War was the Berlin Wall, separating people in both literal and metaphorical senses, the symbol of globalization is the World Wide Web, which links people across traditional barriers, thereby extending the influences of modernization to the remotest parts of the earth. And it is here that we begin to discern patterns in globalization that directly affect cultures.

Globalization and Culture

Many have called attention to what seems to be an emerging global popular culture resulting from increased contact among peoples worldwide. The jet engine significantly cut travel times, and thus what used to be the prerogatives of only the wealthy or adventuresome now are routine for many, as ordinary businessmen and tourists circle the globe. The twentieth century also saw massive demographic changes worldwide, as large numbers of people migrated, for economic or political reasons, from traditional homelands to new places of residence. But even more significant is the increased contact between disparate groups through the telecommunications and entertainment media, so that one need not leave home in Beijing or Billings in order to participate in the emerging global popular culture. Malcolm Waters argues that popular culture has shown a greater tendency toward globalization than either the political or the economic sector.[79] We are aware of increased cultural commonalities across national and ethnic boundaries, so that Gillette's chairman Alfred M. Zein is not far off when he observes that "kids on the streets in Tokyo have more in common with kids on the streets of London than they do with their parents."[80] What they have in common includes tastes in food, music, clothing and entertainment as well as educational processes preparing them for a technologically sophisticated world.

---

[78]Thomas Friedman, *The Lexus and the Olive Tree: Understanding Globalization* (New York: Farrar, Straus & Giroux, 1999), p. 8.

[79]Waters, *Globalization,* p. 125.

[80]As quoted in Benjamin Barber, *Jihad vs. McWorld: How Globalization and Tribalism Are Reshaping the World* (New York: Ballantine, 1996), p. 105.

Such commonalities produce what Benjamin Barber has termed the culture of "McWorld," or the increasingly global culture shaped by "onrushing economic, technological, and ecological forces that demand integration and uniformity and that mesmerize peoples everywhere with fast music, fast computers, and fast food—MTV, Macintosh, and McDonald's—pressing nations into one homogenous global theme park, one McWorld tied together by communications, information, entertainment, and commerce."[81] While undoubtedly a bit hyperbolic, Barber's characterization is a good expression of the homogenization thesis, which sees globalization as "synchronization to the demands of a standardized consumer culture, making everywhere seem more or less the same."[82] On this understanding, globalization is producing a cultural nightmare in which the rich distinctives of local cultures are being replaced by the bland uniformities of Western consumerist societies.

It is important to recognize the extent to which disparate peoples and places are being linked by common symbols, values and behavior, although, as we shall see, the homogenization thesis needs careful qualification. For good or ill, the globe is being connected through a common means of communication, the English language. Over two-thirds of the world's scientists write in English, three-fourths of the world's mail is written in English and 80 percent of all the information in the world's electronic retrieval systems is stored in English.[83] Or we might consider the increasing commonalities in eating habits signified by the global spread of McDonald's, the epitome of the fast food industry, which serves 20 million customers around the world every day.[84] What is passed on in the proliferation of fast food outlets worldwide is not simply a new taste for hamburgers and French fries but, much more subtly, a set of values emphasizing efficiency in production, predictability, gratification of desires and so on. McDonald's is not only a way of eating; it is a way of life.

What Benjamin Barber calls the "infotainment telesector"—the "wedding of telecommunications technologies with information and entertainment software"—is especially significant in cultivating a global popular culture.[85] It would be difficult indeed to exaggerate the impact worldwide of MTV, CNN and the pop-

---

[81]Ibid., p. 4.

[82]Tomlinson, *Globalization and Culture,* p. 6.

[83]D. Crystal, *The Cambridge Encyclopaedia of Language* (Cambridge: Cambridge University Press, 1987), p. 358; as cited in Tomlinson, *Globalization and Culture,* p. 78.

[84]Barber, *Jihad vs. McWorld,* p. 23. The case of McDonald's raises the question of who "owns" the symbols of globalized culture. A number of years ago, while I was living in Japan, a young boy asked me in all seriousness whether we had McDonald's in the United States! Symbolically, McDonald's was thoroughly Japanese as far as this boy was concerned.

[85]Barber, *Jihad vs. McWorld,* p. 60.

ular music industry. The movies of Hollywood and cable television carry the idealized visions of modern Western affluent lifestyles into the squalid theaters and impoverished homes of Asia, Africa and Latin America, raising unrealistic expectations of what might be and whetting appetites for more. "McWorld" is preeminently about consumerism. As Waters puts it, "Under a consumer culture, consumption becomes the main form of self-expression and the chief source of identity. It implies that both material and non-material items, including kinship, affection, art, and the intellect become commodified, that is their value is assessed by the context of their exchange, rather than the context of their production or use."[86] As we shall see in chapter four, consumerism has powerfully affected how people think about religion and spirituality, encouraging eclecticism and pluralism.

It is important to see that globalization is not merely the Westernization of the world or, more specifically, the imposition of Western consumer culture upon the rest of the world. The simple identification of globalization with Westernization is misleading in that it confuses the question of the origin of modernization and globalization with their current status and effects.[87] It is of course true that modernization and the mechanisms of free-market capitalism began in Europe and that, in this sense, modernity clearly is linked to Western culture. It is also indisputable that Western economic, political, social and cultural institutions were "exported" to the non-Western world through colonialism. But it is crucial to see that, although modernization had its origins in the West, the institutions and processes associated with it are today genuinely global and that the influences from it move in all directions simultaneously. As Giddens observes,

> The first phase of globalization was plainly governed, primarily, by the expansion of the West, and the institutions which originated in the West. No other civilization made anything like as pervasive an impact on the world, or shaped it so much in its own image. . . . Although still dominated by Western power, globalization today can no longer be spoken of only as a matter of one-way imperialism. . . . Increasingly there is no obvious "direction" to globalization at all and its ramifications are more or less ever present. The current phase of globalization, then, should not be confused with the preceding one, whose structures it acts increasingly to subvert.[88]

Furthermore, as Benjamin Barber reminds us, even as globalization promotes increased interconnectedness and commonalities across ethnic, religious, cultural

---

[86]Waters, *Globalization*, p. 140.

[87]See Tomlinson, *Globalization and Culture*, pp. 63-70, 91-92; Giddens, *Consequences of Modernity*, p. 52; and Robertson, *Globalization*, p. 27.

[88]Anthony Giddens, "Living in a Post-Traditional Society," in *Reflexive Modernization*, ed. U. Beck, A. Giddens and S. Lash (Cambridge: Polity, 1994), p. 96; as quoted in Tomlinson, *Globalization and Culture*, p. 92.

and national boundaries, powerful countermodernizing reactions emphasize local distinctives opposed to the global.[89] Even as we find greater uniformity worldwide on one level, tenacious reactionary movements championing local distinctives gain popular support on another level. Such movements can take the form of religious fundamentalisms, nationalistic movements or the revival of ethnic identities, and they occur in the West as well as in non-Western societies. Thus, in speaking of increased commonalities worldwide induced by globalization, we must also be sensitive to the strong undercurrents of resistance that reinforce perceived local distinctives.

Similarly, globalization cannot be construed as the elimination of local cultural distinctives, for indigenous patterns do not disappear with the advent of modernization. Hong Kong is not Nairobi, and neither is identical with Miami or London. The influences of globalization interact with indigenous social and cultural patterns, and in many cases what results is not the disappearance of the latter but rather a fresh expression in which the new coexists with the old. The local will always remain and have a kind of priority over the global, not least because, as Tomlinson notes, we are physically embodied creatures and thus are inextricably rooted in particular localities. "Local life occupies the majority of space and time."[90]

But globalization means that, for all of the differences between peoples on the local level, there is increased interrelatedness symbolically connecting groups of people previously separated by geography, ethnicity, politics and religion. As Waters puts it, "A globalized culture admits a continuous flow of ideas, information, commitment, values and tastes mediated through mobile individuals, symbolic tokens, and electronic simulations."[91] What is especially significant for our purposes is the manner in which globalization transforms local cultural distinctives: "The paradigmatic experience of global modernity for most people . . . is that of staying in one place but experiencing the 'displacement' that global modernity *brings to them.*"[92]

Awareness of the impact of globalization upon local settings is prompting rethinking of some of the standard assumptions about culture.[93] In particular, models that view culture as an entity tied to a particular group of people living in a clearly defined time and place are challenged by the blurring of boundaries that accompanies globalization. We often think of cultures as clearly defined, static systems, each of which is entirely distinctive and different from the rest. Thus we speak of the culture of Athens in the fifth century B.C. or of the fifteenth-century

---

[89]See Barber, *Jihad vs. McWorld,* pp. 155-216, where Barber provides many examples from France, Germany, Spain, Switzerland, Canada and the United States as well as the non-Western world.

[90]Tomlinson, *Globalization and Culture,* p. 9.

[91]Waters, *Globalization,* p. 126.

[92]Tomlinson, *Globalization and Culture,* p. 9. Emphasis in original.

[93]See Tomlinson, *Globalization and Culture,* pp. 27-28.

Incas in the Andes or of the eighteenth-century Japanese under the Tokugawa *bakufu*—each of these as isolated and self-contained entities. But looking at cultures in this way is misleading in that it emphasizes the differences that mark each as unique while ignoring commonalities across geographic, ethnic, linguistic and religious boundaries. It is in part this way of thinking about cultures that makes cultural relativism so enormously attractive.

But we must remember that, historically, cultures have not been self-enclosed, bounded systems untouched by other peoples and ways. Nor have cultures been static, frozen in a kind of "pure" pristine state. Cultures have always been, in varying degrees, fluid and unbounded, as groups of people have interacted with each other over time, resulting in cultural change as elements from other contexts are absorbed. While this has always been true of societies and cultures to some extent, it is undeniable that today cultures, languages and religious traditions have much more extensive contact with each other, resulting in greater "shared space" than at earlier times.

Not surprisingly, then, there is an extensive academic discussion today over the concept of culture itself, with critics claiming that the very concept of "a culture" is flawed by a fixation upon "boundedness, homogeneity, coherence, stability, and structure whereas social reality is characterized by variability, inconsistencies, conflict, change, and individual agency."[94] While it would be rash to throw out the concept of culture because of past abuses, we should recognize the fluid, unbounded and imprecise nature of culture. At the heart of the notion of culture is the idea of identifiable commonalities relating to life patterns that link together particular people. Cultural anthropologist Clifford Geertz defines culture as "an historically transmitted pattern of meanings embodied in symbols, a system of inherited conceptions expressed in symbolic forms by means of which men communicate, perpetuate, and develop their knowledge about and attitudes toward life."[95] Culture, then, involves meanings conveyed through symbolic forms, by which people "make sense" of life experiences, finding their place and purpose within the cosmos. Cultural symbols include not only words and concepts but also rituals, institutions, modes of artistic expression, social mores and so on.

Now the notion of culture is inherently ambiguous, so that we can speak, for example, of both a single American culture as well as various distinctive American subcultures (the culture of second-generation Korean-Americans in Los Angeles, African-American culture, the academic culture of Ivy League schools, the culture

---

[94]Christoph Brumann, "Why a Successful Concept Should Not be Discarded," *Current Anthropology* 40, supplement (February 1999): S1. See the responses to Brumann's essay in the same issue for a good introduction to the debate.

[95]Clifford Geertz, *The Interpretation of Cultures* (New York: Random House, 1973), p. 89.

of the Teamsters union members and so on). It is important to see that this ambiguity is not due to an unnecessarily imprecise definition but rather to the fluidity of the reality that the definition is trying to capture.

If we adopt a more fluid, unbounded understanding of culture and apply it to globalization, it makes sense to speak of a global culture even while recognizing distinctive local cultures that retain their own identities throughout globalization. The dynamics between the global and the local can be understood in terms of the reflexive impact of encounters with other social and cultural contexts upon local patterns. As Peter Beyer notes:

> Globalization . . . is more than the spread of one historically existing culture at the expense of all others. It is also the creation of a new global culture with its attendant social structures, one which increasingly becomes the broader social context of all particular cultures in the world, including those of the West. The spread of the global social reality is therefore quite as much at the "expense" of the latter as it is of non-Western cultures. Globalization theories cannot describe contemporary global society as simply the extension of a particular society and its culture (that is, as one part becoming the whole) because these also change dramatically in the process.[96]

Anthony Giddens, in particular, has emphasized the *reflexivity* of modernity and globalization as well as the destabilizing effects of such reflexivity upon traditional structures and patterns. Modernity and globalization present individuals and societies with constantly new information, images and possibilities that implicitly call into question traditional patterns. "Modernity's reflexivity refers to the susceptibility of most aspects of social activity, and material relations with nature, to chronic revision in the light of new information or knowledge."[97] It is not necessarily that the flow of new information forces us to give up what we have traditionally accepted; we might continue to maintain the same beliefs or practices, but we do so with the awareness that they must be situated in relation to the world "out there," with its alternative possibilities. This reflexivity can undermine traditional certainties, raising doubt and a more tentative approach to knowledge, affecting even popular confidence in science.

> The reflexivity of modernity actually undermines the certainty of knowledge, even in the core domains of natural science. Science depends, not on inductive accumulation of proofs, but on the methodological principle of doubt. No matter how cherished, and apparently well established, a given scientific tenet might be, it is open to revision—or might have to be discarded altogether—in light of new ideas or findings. The integral

---

[96]Peter Beyer, *Religion and Globalization* (Thousand Oaks, Calif.: Sage Publications, 1994), p. 9.
[97]Anthony Giddens, *Modernity and Self-Identity: Self and Society in the Late Modern Age* (Stanford, Calif.: Stanford University Press, 1991), p. 20. See also Giddens, *Consequences of Modernity*, pp. 36-45.

relation between modernity and radical doubt is an issue which, once exposed to view, is not only disturbing to philosophers but is *existentially troubling* for ordinary individuals.[98]

Giddens's point about reflexivity undermining confidence in the natural sciences is an important one and applies to other areas as well, so that ongoing exposure to other cultures and religions through globalization often erodes confidence in traditional religious commitments.

The Culture of Modernity

We have sketched in rather general terms two ways in which we might understand recent cultural changes: a model that identifies modernity with the Enlightenment and holds that the Enlightenment project has now largely been abandoned in favor of postmodernity; and a perspective that sees modernity in terms of the ongoing processes of modernization and globalization. Both models have strengths and weaknesses, but the two approaches are not mutually exclusive and an adequate understanding of both past history and present cultural dynamics requires integrating insights from intellectual history with sociological understandings of modernization and globalization.

We might include insights from both approaches in a "culture of modernity" as a framework for understanding cultural history. To speak of a culture of modernity in the singular runs the risk of exaggerating homogeneity at the expense of local cultural distinctives. After all, there is enormous variety among societies in the West, to say nothing of modern non-Western societies. And yet clearly there are significant commonalities as well, not merely between, say, British and German cultures in the 1850s and those in Europe today but also between American and Japanese cultures today. We might speak of cultures of modernity in the plural, thereby recognizing the significant cultural commonalities *and* differences, so that the culture of modernity as seen in Mexico City will not be thought of as identical to that in London or Tokyo. And yet even speaking of cultures of modernity in the plural suggests that there is *something* that each of these has in common, and what they have in common might just as easily be referred to by the rubric "culture of modernity." There is no entirely satisfactory way to speak of these matters, but I will use "culture of modernity" to refer to the increasingly common cultural symbols, values and institutions that modernized societies share, recognizing that each of these cultures will be significantly different from the others.

Accordingly, we might define the culture of modernity as the product of two sets of factors: first, as the increasingly globalized culture that is rooted in the processes

---

[98]Giddens, *Modernity and Self-Identity*, p. 21. Emphasis in original. The relativizing effects of globalization is also a theme in Robertson, *Globalization*.

of modernization associated with the economic, industrial and social transformations originating in sixteenth-century Europe and progressively moving worldwide; and second, as the intellectual heritage of the West during the past three hundred years. The latter includes not only the influences of the eighteenth-century Enlightenment but also the many other intellectual movements of the past several centuries. The intellectual legacy of the West is legitimized and transmitted, increasingly worldwide, through the influences of the modern university and the educated elite. In speaking of the culture of modernity, or perhaps a metaculture of modernity, then, we are referring to the increasingly globalized pattern of symbolic meanings, which transcend geographic, ethnic, political and religious boundaries, by means of which geographically disparate peoples understand themselves and the world.

Several significant consequences follow from this model. The first is that modernity cannot be defined in terms of a particular historical era, although clearly the period from the sixteenth through the twentieth centuries in Europe and North America is especially significant. Furthermore, modernity should not be considered simply a Western phenomenon, although it has been most evident in the West because the processes of modernization are most entrenched there.

Another consequence is that, although modernity exhibits certain constants worldwide, there is also considerable variability in the particular forms that it might take throughout the world. The structures and institutions of modernization might be fairly constant, but the particular impact of this upon a given society will vary, depending both upon the nature of the indigenous culture and its stage in the process of modernization. In other words, while we should expect to see certain commonalities in different societies as they undergo modernization, we should also be sensitive to differences. The culture of modernity is not something a particular society either has or does not have in completed form; rather, we should think in terms of a continuum of modernization, with different societies existing at various stages on the continuum.

Finally, we should note that in this model the common distinction between modernity and postmodernity becomes imprecise and not particularly helpful. If modernity is equated simply with the Enlightenment worldview, then it makes sense to think of those who reject the assumptions and values of the Enlightenment as postmodern. But it is difficult to think in terms of postmodernity if modernity is defined in terms of the ongoing processes of modernization and their many ramifications. For to do so suggests that one might somehow get beyond the social structures and dynamics of modernization, so that their impact is no longer felt. But this is increasingly impossible in the contemporary world. Thus "postmodernity" is not so much an alternative to modernity as it is a recent stage in the ongoing process of coming to terms with modernization. Anthony Giddens argues persuasively that at the heart of what is often called "postmodernity" is a deep sense of disorientation brought about by the rapid and widespread changes of recent decades, producing in many the sense of "being caught up in a universe of events we do not fully understand, and which seems in large part outside our control."[99] Yet far from this signaling our transition to a period of genuine postmodernity, Giddens holds, "we are moving into one in which the consequences of modernity are becoming more radicalised and universalised than before."[100]

In chapter four we will consider how the culture of modernity affects religious beliefs and behavior, noting in particular some implications from this for the current issues of religious pluralism. But first we must pursue one aspect of globalization by considering briefly the growing exposure in the West, during the modern era, to other religious traditions, for this too has helped to shape the context for current debates over religious pluralism.

---

[99]Giddens, *Consequences of Modernity*, pp. 2-3.
[100]Ibid., p. 3. See also Giddens, *Modernity and Self-Identity*, chapter 1.

3

DISCOVERING
RELIGIOUS OTHERS

The question of the "truth" of what we think probably only arises when we become aware of "others" who think and act differently.

RICHARD E. WENTZ, *The Culture of Religious Pluralism*

There is little question that a significant factor in the current attraction of religious pluralism in the West is increased exposure to non-Western cultures and non-Christian religions. But many assume that such awareness of religious others is a relatively recent phenomenon, distinctive of the post–World War II era. While widespread exposure to other cultures and religions is a late-twentieth-century development, it is important to see that the West has had significant encounters with East Asian religions for over five centuries and that along with this there has been a growing dissatisfaction among many people with traditional Christian perspectives, expressing itself in greater openness to other religions. In other words, the late-twentieth-century fascination with pluralism is not a radical departure from the past so much as it is a marked intensification of patterns already present in the West for a long time.

In this chapter we will look at the West's ongoing fascination with the East since the sixteenth century, noting how awareness of religious others often undermined traditional perspectives. This, of course, is not the whole story. Along with the trend toward greater openness to other religions, there was the very different response expressed in the massive Protestant missionary movement, in which the gospel of Jesus Christ was taken to adherents of other religions around the globe. The proper response to increased awareness of religious diversity among conservative Protestants was exertion of ever-greater efforts toward world evangelization and conversion of "the heathen." And yet, as we saw in chapter one, even within the modern missionary movement the issues of other religions could not be ignored, as missiological debates altered in significant ways both the understanding and the practice of modern missions.

New Worlds and New Peoples

At the beginning of the fifteenth century, European Christendom knew almost nothing about the many cultures beyond its borders. But this changed dramatically as a series of voyages of exploration by Christopher Columbus (1492), Vasco da Gama (1497–1499), Pedro Cabral (1500), Ferdinand Magellan (1519–1522) and others introduced to Europe the many peoples of the Americas, Africa and Asia. The year 1492 marked a watershed in how Europeans, including Christians, viewed the world and, in turn, understood themselves.[1] The sheer numbers and enormous diversity among the peoples of the New World forced a rethinking of common assumptions about the world and Europe's place in it. Paul Hiebert articulates some of the questions prompted by these early encounters:

> Were these creatures of the new worlds humans? Did they have souls that needed to be saved? Could they be enslaved or killed? These raised profound questions not only of geography, but also of sociology, economics, politics, and theology. . . . In 1537 Pope Paul III proclaimed in *Sublimis Deus,* "the Indians are true men." If so, how should Christians relate to them? The answer was that they were pagans and heathens. They were not Christian heretics, nor Muslim infidels who rejected Christian truth. They were people who never had the opportunity to hear the gospel.[2]

But this raised further issues. It had previously been accepted that most of the world had been exposed to the teachings of the church, and thus those who chose to remain outside the church—heretics, Jews, Muslims—were culpable for their unbelief. It was now clear, however, that large numbers of people had not actually rejected the church, since they had not yet even heard of it. In his massive study of the Roman Catholic Church's views on other religions, Jacques Dupuis regards 1492 as the pivotal point in the history of Christian relations with religious others. For from that point on, the powerful social and intellectual currents pushing for more accommodating and pluralistic views were unleashed. "[Columbus's 'discovery' of the New World] called on theologians to reconsider the entire case of the requisites for salvation. No longer would it be possible to hold, without qualification, that faith in Jesus Christ and belonging to the Church were absolutely required for salvation."[3]

---

[1]For a fascinating account of the clash of civilizations in 1492—a clash not only of the New World and the Old but of Christendom and Islam, of Christians and Jews, of Europe and the rest of the world—see Bernard Lewis, *Cultures in Conflict: Christians, Muslims, and Jews in the Age of Discovery* (New York: Oxford University Press, 1995).

[2]Paul Hiebert, "Critical Issues in the Social Sciences and Their Implications for Mission Studies," *Missiology* 24, no. 1 (1996): 67. See also Bernard McGrane, *Beyond Anthropology: Society and the Other* (New York: Columbia University Press, 1989), chapter 1.

[3]Jacques Dupuis, *Toward a Christian Theology of Religious Pluralism* (Maryknoll, N.Y.: Orbis, 1997), pp. 110-11.

From the seventeenth century through the early twentieth century, the West became increasingly involved with the cultures of Asia, not only through voyages of exploration and missionary endeavors but also through the entangling ties of colonialism. This is a fascinating period during which very different cultures collided, challenging and transforming accepted traditions on both sides. Yet it is also a deeply tragic chapter of human history, when peoples in the Americas, Africa and Asia were colonized and exploited for Western gain. While it is true that during this time Asian cultures were changed significantly by Western influences, we must not forget that the West itself was also transformed in subtle but profound ways by its encounter with the East. As Hendrik Kraemer put it, "It is not only in the East that there has been, and still is, an 'Invasion' with its ensuing reactions and responses, full of disturbance and renewed vigour. There is also an Eastern Invasion in the West, more hidden and less spectacular than the Western Invasion, but truly significant."[4] Similarly, J. J. Clarke comments:

> This encounter of ideas between East and West over a considerable historical period is surprising enough in itself. What is all the more paradoxical is that it occurred in the period of the rapid extension of Western military and economic power over the nations of South and East Asia, a period in which Western global superiority was being exerted and celebrated in so many fields of cultural endeavor. . . . [I]t remains a matter of astonishment that generations of intellectuals and scholars, followed by an ever-growing sample of the educated public, have sought insight and inspiration in far-off lands in the East, and have endeavoured to incorporate the Orient into their own thinking.[5]

European encounters with non-Christian religions in the seventeenth and eighteenth centuries stimulated a surprising number of theological writings on the subject. Most were concerned to demonstrate the errors of "paganism" and the superiority of Christianity, but some were remarkably perceptive in their struggles with fresh questions.[6] The Dutch jurist and Arminian theologian Hugo Grotius (1583–1645), for example, wrote *On the Truth of the Christian Religion* (1627), intended as a missionary training manual in evidences for the truth of Christianity for those working among Muslims and other non-Christians. Even the Puritan divine Richard Baxter (1615–1691) addressed the question of other religions in his *The Reasons of the Christian Religion* (1667). Although unambiguously holding that God's definitive self-revelation is in the Christian Scriptures and thus that Christianity is the only true religion, and in spite of his strong concern for evangelism, as expressed in his *A Call to the*

---

[4]Hendrik Kraemer, *World Cultures and World Religions: The Coming Dialogue* (Philadelphia: Westminster Press, 1960), p. 228.
[5]J. J. Clarke, *Oriental Enlightenment: The Encounter Between Asian and Western Thought* (London: Routledge, 1997), p. 6.
[6]See David A. Pailin, *Attitudes to Other Religions: Comparative Religion in Seventeenth- and Eighteenth-Century Britain* (Manchester, U.K.: Manchester University Press, 1984), chapter 1.

Unconverted (1657), Baxter was remarkably moderate in his appraisal of other religions, including Islam, recognizing goodness and truth in them.[7]

In an important study Gerald McDermott shows that Jonathan Edwards (1703–1758), American Calvinist theologian and philosopher, was well aware of other religions and thought deeply about the theological implications of recent European "discoveries" of the many peoples who had never heard the gospel of Jesus Christ. At the time of his death Edwards had compiled extensive notes on other religions (over sixty entries in his notebooks), and McDermott argues persuasively that Edwards was preparing a powerful theological response to the deists' use of other religions in their attacks upon Christian orthodoxy.[8] Since Edwards never published a theology of religions, his views must be reconstructed from unpublished manuscripts and notes. According to McDermott, Edwards "viewed non-Christian religions not as nether-worlds of unmixed darkness but as traditions once visited by and still retaining traces of the light of revelation." However, although he was apparently groping for ways to fit non-Christian religions within the scope of providential revelatory history, Edwards did not waver in his commitment to the "scandal of particularity"—God's unique special revelation in the Scriptures and the incarnation in Jesus Christ—which so upset the deists. "Edwards found a way to acknowledge genuine religious truth outside the Judeo-Christian world while at the same time holding fast to a particular and historical revelation."[9]

The Problem of Conflicting Religions

The voyages of exploration in the sixteenth century, and the resulting "discoveries"

---

[7]On Islam, Baxter stated, "In the Religion of the Mahumetans I finde much good, viz. A Confession of only one God, and most of the Natural parts of Religion; a vehement opposition to all Idolatry; A testimony to the Veracity of Moses, and of Christ; that Christ is the Word of God, and a great Prophet, and the Writings of the Apostles true: All this therefore where Christianity is approved, must be embraced." Baxter goes on to say that "there is no doubt but God hath made use of Mahumet as a great Scourge to the Idolaters of the World; as well as to Christians who had abused their sacred priviledges and blessings." Nevertheless, he rejected the Islamic claims about Muhammad being the "chief of prophets" and the Qur'an as the Word of God. See "Of the several Religions which are in the world," excerpt from Richard Baxter, *The Reasons of the Christian Religion* (1667), as reprinted in Pailin, *Attitudes to Other Religions*, pp. 156-57.

[8]Gerald R. McDermott, *Jonathan Edwards Confronts the Gods: Christian Theology, Enlightenment Religion, and Non-Christian Faiths* (New York: Oxford University Press, 2000), p. 5.

[9]Ibid., pp. 12-13. In his notes Edwards is fascinated by the *prisca theologia*, the tradition developed by early Christian apologists holding that "vestiges of true religion" were to be found among the Greeks and other non-Christian traditions, due to creation and an original revelation that was then passed on by the Jews. Drawing upon this and his careful compilation of notes about other religions, Edwards responded to the deists by arguing that all people had received revelation and that knowledge of true religion among the heathen was from revelation and not the light of natural reason. See McDermott, *Jonathan Edwards Confronts the Gods*, especially chapters 4-7.

of the Americas, Asia and Africa, occurred at a time of intellectual and religious unrest within Europe. The social, political and religious transformations associated with the Protestant Reformation, prompted by Martin Luther's protest in 1517 against the sale of indulgences, were especially significant. Although the heart of the Reformation was a strong theological response to the corruption and degeneracy of late medieval Catholicism, its legacy was to affect much more than just theology and the church, for in its wake came a period of open conflict and competition among different religious communities, each claiming to represent the one true Christian faith. Whereas earlier the religious beliefs and practices of most Europeans were largely controlled by the church, the church itself was now divided. For the first time there was a real option in religious allegiances, and indeed among the Reformers themselves one might choose to follow the Lutherans, the Zwinglians, the Calvinists or the Anabaptists. From that point on, choice was to become increasingly significant in the religious landscape of the West.

Throughout the sixteenth century, strictly theological issues increasingly became entangled with political and social agendas, with local rulers often using competing religious movements for their own ends. The Peace of Augsburg (1555) in Germany formalized the relationship between ruler and religion so that the religious choice of the ruler became that of the subjects as well. "He who rules a territory determines its religion" became the watchword. Much of the sixteenth and seventeenth centuries on the Continent and in England were characterized by intrigue, violent conflict and bloody wars, not only between Catholics and Protestants but among various Protestant groups as well, culminating in the brutal devastation of the Thirty Years War (1618–1648).[10]

The Reformation challenge to the authority of Rome, combined with the Renaissance revival of interest in classical skepticism[11] and the social and political turmoil in Europe, produced a crisis in religious epistemology: How are we to decide among the many rival claims to religious authority and truth? The senseless devastation and slaughter of the Thirty Years War, fought in part over religious issues, produced a weary impatience with religious disputes and highlighted the need for a rational and peaceful means of settling such differences.[12] It is within

---

[10]We must avoid the simplistic view that regards the "Wars of Religion" as motivated merely by religious or theological differences. Although theological disputes were clearly involved, the wars were also prompted by a variety of other social and political factors, including "the aggrandizement of the emerging State over the decaying remnants of the medieval ecclesial order" (William T. Cavanaugh, " 'A Fire Strong Enough to Consume the House': The Wars of Religion and the Rise of the State," *Modern Theology* 11, no. 4 [1995]: 398).

[11]See chapter four.

[12]See Richard Popkin, *The History of Scepticism from Erasmus to Spinoza* (Berkeley and Los Angeles: University of California Press, 1979), chapter 1.

this context that we must understand the thought of Jean Bodin and Lord Herbert of Cherbury, two remarkable thinkers who anticipate many of the themes of the late twentieth century in their attempt to come to grips with religious diversity and conflict.

Although Jean Bodin (1530–1596), a distinguished lawyer and diplomat, lived prior to the Thirty Years War, he was deeply troubled by the religious conflict in Europe. He was also well aware of the discoveries of new religious traditions outside of Christendom. In his *Colloquium of the Seven About Secrets of the Sublime,*[13] seven men—a Catholic, a Calvinist, a Lutheran, a Muslim, a Jew and two persons not identified with any confessional tradition—engage in a vigorous dialogue over religious differences and truth. When a Christian participant asks, "Who can doubt that the Christian religion is the true religion or rather the only one?" the answer from another (surely representing Bodin) bluntly states the problem: "Almost the whole world."[14]

Bodin was troubled by the clearly contradictory claims advanced by the various religious communities and yet he did not believe that any one religion could establish itself definitively as true and the others as false. To the contrary, he held that the endless conflict among them and the variety of their beliefs "belied their claims to exclusive possession of true religion and divine approval."[15] What was needed, he felt, was to go beyond the mutually contradictory claims of the individual religions to uncover the origin of religion in general, and then on that basis to make rational judgments about particular beliefs and practices.

Interestingly, the three Christian participants in the dialogue express the views that Bodin himself finds especially problematic in religion: exclusivity, intolerance and dogmatism in insisting upon the truth of one's own position; a willingness to use coercion against one's rivals; and beliefs that are regarded as contrary to reason (original sin, incarnation).[16] Bodin held that God had created human beings with a capacity for religious expression, a kind of original or natural religion that human beings have somehow distorted, resulting in the many varied religions observable today. Thus the religious impulse itself is from God; the varied religious expressions are due to human creativity and distortion. Senamus, who apparently represents Bodin in the dialogue, champions an enlightened tolerance and pragmatism

---

[13]Jean Bodin, *Colloquium of the Seven About Secrets of the Sublime,* trans. Marion Kuntz (Princeton, N.J.: Princeton University Press, 1975). Although written in 1593, the work was not published until 1857. Nevertheless, it was circulated widely during Bodin's lifetime and became something of an underground classic among the freethinkers.

[14]As quoted in J. Samuel Preus, *Explaining Religion: Criticism and Theory from Bodin to Freud* (New Haven, Conn.: Yale University Press, 1987), p. 3.

[15]Ibid., p. 4.

[16]Ibid., p. 8.

that allows for various religions to flourish since we have no way of determining which, if any among them, is uniquely true. In general, religion is good for society (Bodin had no time for atheism) so long as superstition and dogmatism are eliminated. Senamus claims to worship at all the shrines "of all the religions, wherever they are, so as not to be considered an atheist by wicked example and also that others may hold in awe the divine."[17]

Like Bodin before him, Lord Herbert of Cherbury (1583–1648) was troubled by the religious conflicts plaguing Europe. A diplomat, soldier of fortune and English ambassador to Paris from 1619 to 1624, Herbert had firsthand experience in war, including conflicts between Protestants and Catholics as well as between Arminians and Calvinists. J. Samuel Preus observes, "It is no wonder, then, that he perceived the great problem of his time, in the sphere of religion, to be the question of how to resolve contradiction and conflict and to establish peace, both in minds and in society. Integrally related to that problem was the one that preoccupied the philosophy of the time: the question of criteria for truth."[18] Herbert, as Bodin before him, held that the root cause of religious conflict was the conviction by each competing tradition that it alone held the truths leading to salvation.[19] Herbert believed that some universal criterion for religious truth was necessary, since "the wretched terror-stricken mass have no refuge, unless some immovable foundations of truth resting on *universal consent* are established, to which they can turn amid the doubts of theology and philosophy."[20]

Lord Herbert published in 1624 *De veritate*, or *On Truth As It Is Distinguished from Revelation, Probability, Possibility and Falsehood,* an ambitious work on epistemology that also proposed some "common notions" that could be used as criteria for recognizing authentic religion and for judging among rival claims and practices.[21] He assumed that the foundation upon which such judgments could be made must be a standard rooted in universal consent, upon which all religions fundamentally agree. "We have to search for what is by universal consent acknowledged in religion. . . . [For] universal consent [is] the final test of truth."[22] Herbert assumed that, given God's creation and universal providence, we ought to expect to

---

[17]As quoted in Preus, *Explaining Religion*, p. 19.

[18]Ibid., p. 24.

[19]Ibid., p. 25.

[20]Herbert of Cherbury, as quoted in James C. Livingston, *The Enlightenment and the Nineteenth Century*, vol. 1 of *Modern Christian Thought*, 2nd ed. (Upper Saddle River, N.J.: Prentice-Hall, 1997), p. 15. Emphasis in the original.

[21]See the selection from *De veritate* reprinted in "Common Notions Concerning Religion," in *Christianity and Plurality: Classical and Contemporary Readings,* ed. Richard J. Plantinga (Oxford: Blackwell, 1999), pp. 171-81.

[22]*De veritate,* as quoted in Roger Johnson, "Natural Religion, Common Notions, and the Study of Religions: Lord Herbert of Cherbury (1583-1648)," *Religion* 24 (July 1994): 216.

find basic commonalities shared by all religions at all times in all places.

Herbert claimed that five common notions in religion can be established by universal consent. These are the following: (1) that there is a supreme God, (2) that this sovereign deity ought to be worshiped, (3) that the connection between virtue and piety is the most important part of religious practice, (4) that wickedness and vice must be expiated by repentance, and (5) that there is reward or punishment in the afterlife. According to Lord Herbert,

> It follows from these considerations that the Dogmas which recognize a sovereign Deity enjoin us to worship Him, command us to lead a holy life, lead us to repent of our sins, and warn us of future recompense or punishment, proceed from God and are inscribed within us in the form of Common Notions. But those dogmas which postulate a plurality of Gods, which do not forbid crimes and sins, which rail against penitence, and which express doubts about the eternal state of the soul cannot be considered either Common Notions or truths. Accordingly, every religion, if we consider it comprehensively, is not good; nor can we admit that salvation is open to men in every religion. For how could anyone who believes more than is necessary, but who does less than he ought, be saved? But I am convinced that in every religion, and indeed in every individual conscience, either through Grace or Nature, sufficient means are granted to men to win God's goodwill; while all additional and peculiar features which are found at any period must be referred to their inventors.[23]

Herbert clearly did not believe that all beliefs and practices found in the religions were acceptable; those that deviated from the "common notions" were not. But he did hold that, despite surface differences in beliefs and practices, among all religions there is a rudimentary awareness and acceptance of these five beliefs.[24]

In spite of the fact that Herbert carefully studied the available data on non-Christian religions, both those of the ancient world and those of the New World, one might well question the "universal consent" claimed for these "common notions." Some forms of Hinduism, Jainism and Buddhism would reject the obvious theism underlying Herbert's notions, and thus these notions seem to be informed more by his Christian assumptions than by careful phenomenology, or the study of actual human behavior.[25] But Herbert's methodology and conclusions are significant for several reasons. First, although Herbert himself did not abandon

---

[23]Herbert of Cherbury, "Common Notions Concerning Religion," p. 178.

[24]There has been much discussion over just what Herbert meant by the "common notions" and how they operate among diverse peoples. Preus observes that "a sensible interpretation is that rather than innate *ideas,* there is an innate religious *sense* that accounts for religion's very existence, in addition to which there are reliable critical faculties for identifying the true and discriminating it from the false, when it is experienced. Religion is universal because of *something* innate; its fundamental ideas emerge as experience is interpreted through innate but not predetermined faculties" (J. Samuel Preus, *Explaining Religion,* p. 28).

[25]See Johnson, "Natural Religion," p. 217.

Christian theism, his approach resulted in a leveling of the religious playing field. No longer could Christianity be granted the privileged status of the one true religion, with the implication that all others are false; all religions, including Christianity, are to be seen as a mixture of good and evil, truth and falsehood, depending upon the degree to which they adhere to the "common notions." Not only did this divest Christianity of its exclusive claim to truth but also it elevated non-Christian religions, including those of the Incas and Aztecs in the New World. Second, although it would be anachronistic to attribute to Herbert the later ideas of deism and natural religion, his discussion of the "common notions" was very influential among the deists a generation after him. Finally, Herbert was arguably the first in the English-speaking world "to ground religious truth not in the claims of a divine revelation mediated by tradition, but in those universal truths imprinted upon the mind or heart by God or Nature."[26] This is a theme that, in varying forms, was to be prominent among later pluralistic thinkers.

The Enlightened Rational Religion of Confucius

As the West progressively deepened its encounters with Asian cultures and religions, it passed through various stages in which first one, then another, exotic religion of the East became the object of fascination. Intellectuals looked first to the "rational natural religion" of Confucius, then to the dark mysticism of Vedanta Hinduism and finally to the agnostic empiricism of Buddhism for inspiration. What is striking is that each stage of these encounters was prompted in part by disillusionment with Western traditions and was often linked to an explicit rejection of classical Christianity. Dissatisfaction with aspects of Western culture led to a search for correctives in the wisdom of the East, so that gleanings from Eastern religions were frequently used as a means of undermining traditional Christian institutions, values and assumptions.[27]

European awareness of China in the eighteenth century was due primarily to the travels and reports of the Jesuit missionaries to China.[28] Some of the classical Confucian texts, translated into Latin and published in Paris in 1687, were widely read in Europe. Confucius and the early Chinese literati were portrayed by the Jesuits as rational theists who had arrived at belief in God through natural theology and who had

---

[26]Ibid., p. 214. For Lord Herbert's impact upon later deists, as well as discussion of the deists' views of Asian religions, see Wilhelm Halbfass, *India and Europe: An Essay in Understanding* (Albany: State University of New York Press, 1988), chapter 4; and McDermott, *Jonathan Edwards Confronts the Gods*, chapter 1.

[27]See, for example, Clarke, *Oriental Enlightenment*, pp. 55, 60, 69. In the following discussion I am especially indebted to Clarke's fine treatment of the subject (pp. 39-53).

[28]On the impact in Europe of the Jesuit missions, see P. J. Marshall and Glyndwr Williams, *The Great Map of Mankind: British Perceptions of the World in the Age of Enlightenment* (London: J. M. Dent, 1982), chapters 3-4. On the Jesuits in China, see Andrew C. Ross, *A Vision Betrayed: The Jesuits in Japan and China, 1542-1742* (Maryknoll, N.Y.: Orbis, 1994).

adopted a moral system compatible with Christian theism. The picture of Confucius as an enlightened, rational, moral theist who rejected religious superstition was enthusiastically embraced by many Western intellectuals as a positive corrective to Christianity. Michel de Montaigne used reports about China to support his relativism and call for greater religious tolerance. Pierre Bayle appealed to China's great antiquity in an effort to undermine traditional interpretations of biblical chronology, and he contrasted what he saw as China's religious tolerance with the dogmatism and authoritarianism of the church. The German philosopher Leibniz, who was in regular correspondence with Jesuit missionaries, had an ongoing fascination with China and wrote two substantial works on China, including a treatise on Chinese philosophy.[29] Voltaire, a bitter critic of traditional Christianity, portrayed Chinese moral and political philosophy as inherently superior to the authoritarianism and dogmatism of Christian principles and institutions. Similarly British deists depicted the Chinese as Eastern representatives of a natural, moral religion that is discernible by enlightened reason, devoid of any superstition.[30] Matthew Tindal, for example, emphasized that Confucian moral teachings (which he claimed were fully equal to Christian principles) were based solely upon rational reflection and not revelation. Tindal welcomed Leibniz's earlier suggestion that China should send missionaries to Europe, stating, "I am so far from thinking the maxims of Confucius and Jesus Christ differ, that I think the plain and simple maxims of the former will help illustrate the more obscure ones of the latter."[31]

However, the tide soon turned and fascination with China decreased toward the end of the eighteenth century, so that thinkers such as Jean-Jacques Rousseau and Condorcet criticized Chinese society as decadent, irrational and unnatural. Contrasting the "decadence" of Chinese civilization with the "noble savage" living in the state of nature, Rousseau declared that "there is no sin to which [the Chinese] are not prone, no crime which is not common among them."[32]

---

[29]On Leibniz and Confucianism, see David E. Mungello, *Leibniz and Confucianism: The Search for Accord* (Honolulu: University of Hawaii Press, 1977). Leibniz had a deep interest in ecumenism and sought not merely harmony between Roman Catholics and Protestants in Europe but also a genuinely global ecumenism in which "the revealed religion of the West would be an equal trade for the natural theology and ethics of China." Ibid., p. 9.

[30]Exposure to other religions was a significant factor in the seventeenth- and eighteenth-century debates over "natural religion." See Pailin, *Attitudes to Other Religions,* chapter 3; as well as David A. Pailin, "The Confused and Confusing Story of Natural Religion," *Religion* 24 (July 1994): 199-212.

[31]As quoted in Clarke, *Oriental Enlightenment,* p. 51.

[32]As quoted in ibid., p. 53. There were also a few Asian visitors to Europe at this time, sometimes with tragic consequences. For a fascinating account of a Chinese convert to Catholicism who accompanied a French missionary back to France in 1722, see Jonathan D. Spence, *The Question of Hu* (New York: Alfred A. Knopf, 1988). The Japanese novelist Shusaku Endo provides a haunting historical novel, based upon an actual incident, about a group of Japanese who accompany a Catholic missionary in 1613 first to Mexico and then to Madrid and Rome (Shusaku Endo, *The Samurai,* trans. Van C. Gessel [New York: Harper & Row, 1982]).

The Lure of India and Vedanta

India had been part of the consciousness of Europe since at least the seventeenth century, but the increasing domination of the Indian subcontinent by Britain in the following century stimulated a deeper interest in its culture and religion. Thinkers associated with Romanticism led the way in looking to India as a fresh source of spiritual and moral vision. Again, the turn East was prompted in part by a desire to correct perceived inadequacies of the West.

> As in the Enlightenment period, the primary intellectual impetus for the new oriental-ism lay not so much in disinterested scholarship as in the growing sense of disillusion-ment with prevailing European modes of thought and belief, on the one side Judeo-Christianity whose spiritual traditions were proving unsatisfactory, and on the other the materialism and anti-religious stance of the Enlightenment which appeared to abolish the possibility of the spirit altogether.[33]

The Bhagavad-Gita, first translated into English in 1785, was widely read. Writers such as Shelley, Byron and Coleridge all showed awareness of Indian religious and philosophical themes. But it was primarily in Germany that the Romantic interest in Indian thought was strongest. In spite of the rich diversity of Indian thought, Europeans tended to identify Indian religion primarily with the idealism of Advaita (Nondualist) Vedanta philosophy.[34] The deepest wisdom of India was held to be in the sacred writings known as the Upanishads, with their monistic tendencies identifying the *atman,* or soul, with Brahman, the one ultimate reality. Parallels between Vedanta Hinduism and German idealist philosophy, which viewed the defining reality as *Geist* (spirit), were observed. It was the monistic themes of the Upanishads—the belief that ultimately all reality is one unified whole and that this reality is fundamentally spiritual in nature, with the material world being in some respect illusory—that captured the German idealists. Just as the earlier Enlightenment thinkers had seen in the natural religion of Confucianism a corrective to the alleged superstition of Christianity, so now the spiritual idealism of Vedanta Hinduism offered Romanticists an ideal with which to critique the rationalism and materialism characterizing European culture.

Both Johann Gottfried Herder, a German Lutheran pastor and philosopher, and Goethe, the poet and dramatist, understood the basic outlines of Hindu thought. The idealism of F. W. J. Schelling was influenced by Eastern ideas, and in his lectures of 1802 Schelling claimed that the sacred texts of the Indians were superior to the Bible.[35] Friedrich von Schlegel studied Sanskrit and seems to have embraced

---

[33]Clarke, *Oriental Enlightenment,* p. 55.
[34]See Richard King, *Orientalism and Religion: Postcolonial Theory, India and the "Mystic East"* (New York: Routledge, 1999), chapter 6.
[35]Ibid., p. 63.

the view that underlying all the religious traditions is a kind of "universal revelation" or "single truth" that is expressed variously in different languages and cultures.[36] But few nineteenth-century thinkers were as deeply immersed in the thought of India as the German philosopher Arthur Schopenhauer. Although largely ignored by twentieth-century philosophers, Schopenhauer was one of the most widely read and influential thinkers of his day. An idealist influenced by neo-Kantian thought, he studied the Upanishads and later became one of the first Europeans to take Buddhism seriously. Schopenhauer was a sharp critic of Christianity and suggested that anything of value in Christianity actually has its source in Asia: "Christianity taught only what the whole of Asia knew already long before and even better."[37]

Across the Atlantic as well there was growing awareness of Asian religions. As a result of trade and exploration, the massive worldwide missionary effort and increased immigration, the United States entered a period of engagement with Asian religions in the 1840s.[38] The American Transcendentalists, like the European Romanticists, were fascinated by the religious thought of the East.[39] Ralph Waldo Emerson was especially taken with the Vedanta philosophy of Hinduism and the Bhagavad-Gita. Emerson's friend and colleague Henry David Thoreau enthused over the wisdom of the East: "I bathe my intellect in the stupendous and cosmological philosophy of the *Bhagavat Geeta* . . . in comparison with which our modern world in its literature seems puny and trivial."[40] Like their European Romanticist counterparts, the Transcendentalists not only noted what they saw as parallels between Hinduism and their version of Unitarian moral theism but also used their image of Hinduism to undermine the exclusivism of Christianity and promote what Arthur Versluis calls the "Transcendentalist vision"—the idea that "the best of the past and of all the world's religions and literatures will flower in a new American literary religion."[41] This eclectic vision was promoted by James F. Clarke's popular *Ten Great Religions* (1871), one of the first works in English to set out the views of major non-Christian religions.[42]

---

[36]Ibid., p. 65.

[37]As quoted in Clarke, *Oriental Enlightenment,* p. 69. On Schopenhauer's somewhat confused understanding of Hinduism and Buddhism, see Halbfass, *India and Europe,* chapter 7.

[38]Thomas A. Tweed, general introduction to *Asian Religions in America: A Documentary History,* ed. Thomas A. Tweed and Stephen Prothero (New York: Oxford University Press, 1999), p. 2.

[39]See Arthur Versluis, *American Transcendentalism and Asian Religions* (New York: Oxford University Press, 1993).

[40]As quoted in Clarke, *Oriental Enlightenment,* p. 86.

[41]Versluis, *American Transcendentalism and Asian Religions,* p. 10.

[42]Excerpts from Clarke's *Ten Great Religions* can be found in *Asian Religions in America,* pp. 114-18.

The Dharma Comes West

The impact of Buddhism upon Europe and America was even more pervasive than had been that of Confucianism or Hinduism earlier. Whereas the latter religions had been enthusiastically embraced by a relatively small, although very influential, group of thinkers, by the late nineteenth century the popular attraction of Buddhism was so great that some prominent Christians began to speak of it publicly as a threat to Christianity. The appeal of Buddhism can be seen in the remarkable reception that greeted publication in 1879 of Sir Edwin Arnold's epic poem on the life of the Buddha, *The Light of Asia*.[43] Carl Jackson observes:

> It has been estimated that *[The Light of Asia]* went through sixty English and eighty American editions and that between five hundred thousand and one million copies were sold in Great Britain and the United States. Enthusiastically reviewed and widely quoted, hotly attacked and passionately defended, perhaps no work on Buddhism has ever approached its popular success. Certainly, no event in the late nineteenth century did more to rivet attention on Buddhism.[44]

This is an extraordinary response for any work of poetry, let alone one dealing with the life of a religious leader. But the time was ripe for an elegant and sympathetic account of the Buddha as a sincere seeker after religious truth. Shunning the more controversial aspects of Buddhist teaching, Arnold concentrated "on the Buddhist elements that most closely paralleled the traditions of Christianity, creating the impression of a fundamental similarity between Christian and Buddhist experiences."[45]

The attraction of Buddhism at this time must be understood within the context of the crisis of faith that Christianity was undergoing in the late nineteenth century. The authority of Christianity was being challenged by positivism, Darwinism and the higher criticism of Scripture, and so "the newly disseminated Buddhist teachings had a great appeal to many seeking a religious alternative to the Christian tradition, and became a veritable battle-ground between Christianity on the one hand and the forces of atheism and secularisation on the other."[46] In England Thomas Huxley, who gave us the word *agnosticism,* stated in his Romanes Lectures of 1893 that the agnostic character of Buddhism made it especially appealing to his

---

[43]Edwin Arnold, *The Light of Asia, or the Great Renunciation* (New York: A. L. Burt, 1879).

[44]Carl T. Jackson, *The Oriental Religions and American Thought: Nineteenth-Century Explorations* (Westport, Conn.: Greenwood, 1981), p. 143.

[45]Ibid., p. 144. Among the more bizarre responses to Arnold's work was one by Felix Oswald, a medical doctor, who argued that Jesus in fact had been a Buddhist! Ibid., p. 148. *The Light of Asia* also had a profound impact upon the spiritual development of Mahatma Gandhi. See Mohandas Karamchad Gandhi, "Extracts from *The Story of My Experiments with Truth,*" in *Christianity Through Non-Christian Eyes,* ed. Paul J. Griffiths (Maryknoll, N.Y.: Orbis, 1990), p. 219.

[46]Clarke, *Oriental Enlightenment,* p. 81.

contemporaries.[47] The following year Paul Carus published *The Gospel of Buddha,* a highly sympathetic and influential portrayal of Buddhism as a rational faith. And in 1897 the Japanese Zen Buddhist D. T. Suzuki moved to La Salle, Illinois, to work with Paul Carus at Open Court Publishing, thus beginning a long and distinguished career as an apologist and popularizer of Buddhism in the West.[48]

History is full of the ironies of unintended consequences, one of which is the fact that it was in part the very success of nineteenth-century missions that introduced non-Christian religions to Western audiences. Western missionaries encompassed the globe, spreading the gospel of Jesus Christ throughout Asia, the islands of the Pacific, Latin America and much of Africa, sending back to constituencies at home haunting images of millions of "heathen" and "pagans" oppressed by spiritual darkness.[49] Especially significant are the unintended consequences of the missionaries' study of other religions and the translation of their sacred texts into European languages.[50] For example, William Carey, early missionary to India, felt that missionaries needed to understand the religious context of those to whom they ministered, and thus, in addition to his translations of the Bible into Bengali, Sanskrit and Marathi, he also translated Hindu sacred texts, including much of the massive Ramayana, into English.[51] Classical texts of Confucianism and Taoism were translated into English by James Legge, who, after a distinguished missionary career in Hong Kong, accepted a professorship in Chinese studies at Oxford University.[52] Works prepared by missionaries for the training of missionaries, such as the Reverend Spence Hardy's *A Manual of Buddhism* (1853), also had the effect of propagating in the West the very religions they were seeking to conquer.[53] Improvements in printing and publication meant that by the 1850s there were many works explaining Buddhism with wide circulation among the increasingly better educated laity. T. W. Rhys Davids, together with his wife, founded the Pali

---

[47]Ibid., p. 72.

[48]On D. T. Suzuki in the West, see Larry A. Fader, "D. T. Suzuki's Contribution to the West," and Masao Abe, "The Influence of D. T. Suzuki in the West," both in *A Zen Life: D. T. Suzuki Remembered,* ed. Masao Abe (New York: Weatherhill, 1986), pp. 95-117; and Robert H. Sharf, "The Zen of Japanese Nationalism," in *Curators of the Buddha: The Study of Buddhism Under Colonialism,* ed. Donald S. Lopez Jr. (Chicago: University of Chicago Press, 1995), pp. 107-60.

[49]For samples of missionary correspondence in which non-Christian religions are depicted, see "Robert Morrison's Letter from China (1809)," "Adoniram and Ann Judson, a Mission in Burma (1832)" and "Dr. Judson's Opinion on Some of the Tenets of Buddhism"—all in Tweed and Prothero, *Asian Religions in America,* pp. 35-42.

[50]See Eric Sharpe, *Comparative Religion: A History,* 2nd ed. (La Salle, Ill.: Open Court, 1986), pp. 145-46.

[51]Stephen Neill, *A History of Christian Missions,* rev. 2nd ed. (Hammondsworth, England: Penguin, 1986), pp. 224-25.

[52]See Lauren F. Pfister, "The Legacy of James Legge," *International Bulletin of Missionary Research* 22, no. 2 (1998): 77-82.

[53]Clarke, *Oriental Enlightenment,* p. 74.

Text Society, which was devoted to the translation and publication of the Pali Buddhist scriptures.[54] But undoubtedly the one most responsible for the translation, publication and study of the scriptures of Asian religions was Friedrich Max Müller, one of the pioneers of comparative religion and a professor at Oxford University. Müller edited *Sacred Books of the East,* a monumental project of translating the sacred scriptures of the major Asian religions into English.[55]

Perennialism: The East in the West

By the mid-twentieth century, Eastern influences were readily apparent throughout Europe and North America. Then by the 1990s, the symbols of Hindu, Buddhist and Taoist spirituality were so prevalent that it was increasingly difficult to distinguish "the East" from "the West." The cumulative effects of two devastating world wars, culminating in the terrors of the atomic bomb and the Cold War; the economic catastrophe of the Great Depression; violent anticolonialist movements of nationalism throughout Africa, Asia and Latin America; disillusionment with the rampant consumerism and materialism of Western societies; the perception of institutional Christianity as an irrelevant vestige of a bygone era; and a deepening disenchantment with science and technology produced an ethos increasingly skeptical about traditional Western assumptions and institutions. J. J. Clarke eloquently summarizes the factors that have worked to make Eastern religious alternatives to Christianity attractive, thereby increasing the plausibility of a general religious pluralism as well.

> The theme of moral and cultural decline is indeed one of the dominant themes of the East-West encounter throughout the whole modern period. . . . [The whole of the modern world has been] characterized by cultural, social, and intellectual transformations which produced a deep sense of uncertainty and anxiety, expressed in such terms as "anomie", "alienation", and "the homeless mind", a major consequence of which has been the calling into question of traditional beliefs and values, and the relativising of all world views. These factors have acquired both wider and more acute significance in the twentieth century where the plurality of belief systems, and hence the risks and conflicts associated with choice, has emerged as an issue of fundamental importance in cultural and intellectual debates. We have been obliged in this century to confront not only a disturbing—yet at the same time stimulating and inspiring—transformation and pluralisation of cultures and institutions, but also an unprecedented fragmentation and dissolution of traditional ways of thinking about the world, of values, and of matters of ultimate concern. Above all, the century has experienced a collapse of spiritual authority and a crisis of religious faith which, while representing the mat-

---

[54]By the time of his death, the Society had published ninety-four volumes (twenty-six thousand pages) of the Buddhist scriptures. Clarke, *Oriental Enlightenment,* p. 75.
[55]On the influence of Max Müller, see Sharpe, *Comparative Religion,* pp. 35-46.

uration of factors that have been germinating in the West since the Enlightenment period, has had unprecedented cultural consequences in recent times.[56]

Disillusionment with established Western social and cultural patterns emerged in the 1950s with the Beat existentialists and burst into full expression with the more radical movements of the 1960s. Significantly, the countercultural movements of both decades drew heavily upon Eastern religious symbols and spiritual practices as alternatives to the perceived decadence of the West.[57] Swami Paramahamsa Yogananda, who established the Hindu Self-Realization Fellowship in 1935, published the *Autobiography of a Yogi* (1946), a countercultural classic of the 1960s and 1970s. Buddhist themes and symbolism were prominent in Beat poet Jack Kerouac's "Dharma Bums" (1958) and Gary Snyder's "Smokey the Bear Sutra" (1969).[58] Whereas the earlier interest in Asian religions centered primarily upon the study of translations of sacred texts from Hinduism and Buddhism, by the 1960s large numbers of Westerners were traveling to India and Japan to study with the Eastern masters, thereby acquiring enlightenment directly. An influential group of Western thinkers, having made the obligatory pilgrimage to the East, became effective apologists for Eastern traditions. Richard Alpert, who taught psychology at Stanford, Berkeley and Harvard, journeyed to a temple in the Himalayas in 1967 to study under Neem Karoli Baba. Alpert returned to America the following year as Ram Dass, a guru in his own right, and wrote *Be Here Now* (1971) and *The Only Dance There Is* (1974). The attraction of Eastern mysticism was enhanced with the 1968 visit by the Beatles to India and their public identification with the Maharishi Mahesh Yogi of Transcendental Meditation (TM) fame. Alan Watts, a prolific writer and popularizer of Zen for the West, described his own spiritual orientation as "between Mahayana Buddhism and Taoism, with a certain leaning towards Vedanta and Catholicism, or rather the Orthodox Church of Eastern Europe."[59] This happy eclecticism, freely mixing elements from various traditions, characterized much of the Western appropriation of Eastern religions.

A group of Asian intellectuals emerged who were well acquainted with Western intellectual traditions and who devoted themselves to interpreting and advancing Eastern religious perspectives among the cultural elite in the West. Mention has

---

[56]Clarke, *Oriental Enlightenment,* pp. 109, 96.

[57]See Robert S. Ellwood, *The Sixties Spiritual Awakening: American Religion Moving from Modern to Postmodern* (New Brunswick, N.J.: Rutgers University Press, 1994); Robert S. Ellwood, *Alternative Altars: Unconventional and Eastern Spirituality in America* (Chicago: University of Chicago Press, 1979); and Harvey Cox, *Turning East: The Promise and Peril of the New Orientalism* (New York: Simon & Schuster, 1977).

[58]See Tweed and Prothero, *Asian Religions in America,* pp. 196-200, 342-45.

[59]As quoted in "Alan Watts: 'Beginning a Counterculture' " (1972), in *Asian Religions in America,* p. 229.

already been made of D. T. Suzuki and his enormous influence; others included Swami Vivekananda, founder of the Ramakrishna Mission and the Vedanta Society; the Indian poet and Nobel laureate Rabindranath Tagore; the Indian philosopher Sri Aurobindo; the Hindu philosopher and first Spalding Professor of Eastern Religions and Ethics at Oxford, Sarvepalli Radhakrishnan; and more recently, the Japanese Zen Buddhist Masao Abe; and Tenzin Gyatso, the current Dalai Lama of Tibetan Buddhism.[60] Less distinguished, but equally influential in their own ways, were the ubiquitous self-proclaimed holy men and gurus—such as Maharishi Mahesh Yogi and TM, A. C. Bhaktivedanta Swami Prabhupada and the International Society for Krishna Consciousness, and Bhagwan Shree Rajneesh and Rajneeshpuram—who attracted large followings and considerable media coverage.

By the 1980s and 1990s, what had been countercultural and somewhat avant-garde became mainstream and chic in the form of the New Age movement. The New Age movement is an eclectic and rather amorphous movement that combines elements of ancient paganism, the occult, Eastern religions and some Judeo-Christian themes with pop psychology and an obsession with what Paul Heelas has termed "self-spirituality."[61] Although not a religion as such, and certainly not an organized conspiracy as some have thought, New Age themes and practices, many of which draw explicitly upon Hindu, Buddhist and Taoist teachings, have been legitimized through their acceptance by leading media and entertainment personalities as well as, to some extent, educational institutions. By the 1990s, Buddhism, especially Tibetan Buddhism, was chic within the entertainment industry, as celebrities such as Richard Gere, Tina Turner, Adam Yauch of the Beastie Boys, Herbie Hancock and Steven Seagal publicly embraced it.[62] Two major films on the Dalai Lama and Tibetan Buddhism, *Seven Years in Tibet* and *Kundun,* premiered in 1997.[63]

While many in the West were content to dabble in various Eastern traditions without carefully considering the doctrinal issues involved, others gave serious thought to the philosophical questions raised by alternative religions. Beginning in the late nineteenth century, a significant group of thinkers put forward what has come to be called "perennial philosophy," namely the view that at root all religions

---

[60]See Jane Naomi Iwamura, "The Oriental Monk in American Popular Culture," in *Religion and Popular Culture in America,* ed. Bruce David Forbes and Jeffrey H. Mahan (Berkeley: University of California Press, 2000), pp. 25-43.

[61]See Paul Heelas, *The New Age Movement: The Celebration of the Self and the Sacralization of Modernity* (Oxford: Blackwell, 1996).

[62]See David Van Biema, "Buddhism in America," *Time,* October 13, 1997, pp. 72-84.

[63]On the symbolic meanings of Tibet and the Dalai Lama for the West, see Orville Schell, *Virtual Tibet: Searching for Shangri-La from the Himalayas to Hollywood* (New York: Metropolitan Books, 2000).

teach the same esoteric truth. Perennialism found expression in the Theosophical Society, founded in 1875 by Madame Blavatsky and Colonel H. S. Olcott. In 1878 Blavatsky and Olcott traveled to India and Ceylon, where they publicly adopted Buddhism. The central message of Theosophy (the term means "divine wisdom") is that "all phenomena arise out of an eternal, unitary principle which is spiritual in essence and which is manifested most conspicuously in individual enlightened souls."[64] Blavatsky claimed, "Truth remains one, and there is not a religion, whether Christian or heathen, that is not firmly built upon the rock of ages—God and immortal spirit."[65] Blavatsky's writings increasingly incorporated Hindu and Buddhist themes and looked to the East for true wisdom.

An influential expression of perennialism is found in Aldous Huxley's *The Perennial Philosophy* (1945). Huxley read widely in world religions, and after settling in the United States in 1937, he became closely associated with the Vedanta Center in California, where, with Christopher Isherwood and Gerald Heard, he edited the magazine *Vedanta and the West.*[66] Huxley was convinced that the key to the problems of the modern West lay in the spirituality of India, especially in the Vedanta philosophy of Hinduism as popularized by Vivekananda. Huxley described the *philosophia perennis* as "the metaphysic that recognizes a divine Reality substantial to the world of things and lives and minds; the psychology that finds in the soul something similar to, or even identical with, divine Reality; the ethic that places man's final end in the knowledge of the immanent and transcendent Ground of all being."[67] Huxley claimed that "rudiments of the Perennial Philosophy may be found among the traditionary lore of primitive peoples in every region of the world, and in its fully developed forms it has a place in every one of the higher religions."[68]

Paul Heelas has pointed out that perennialism is also characteristic of much New Age thought. Although New Agers reject much of institutional, traditional religion (they are into "spirituality" not "religion"), they unashamedly draw upon ancient religious traditions, whether Hindu, Buddhist or shamanic. Something at the heart of the religious practices of indigenous peoples of ancient Egypt, Peru, North America and India is said to be common to all the great world religions, and this common wisdom can be accessed by spiritually sensitive people today.

> Having little or no faith in the external realm of traditional belief, New Agers can
> ignore apparently significant differences between religious traditions, dismissing
> them as due to historical contingencies and ego-operations. But they do have faith in

---

[64]Clarke, *Oriental Enlightenment*, p. 89.
[65]Helena Blavatsky, *Isis Unveiled* (Wheaton, Ill.: Theosophical Publishing House, 1972), 1:467, as quoted in Heelas, *New Age Movement*, p. 27.
[66]Clarke, *Oriental Enlightenment*, p. 134.
[67]Aldous Huxley, *The Perennial Philosophy* (London: Grafton, 1985), p. 10.
[68]Ibid.

that wisdom which is experienced as lying at the heart of the religious domain as a whole. From the detraditionalized stance of the New Age what matters is the "arcane", the "esoteric", the "hidden wisdom", the "inner or secret tradition", the "ageless wisdom." . . . The perennialized viewpoint involves going beyond traditions as normally conceived, going beyond differences to find—by way of experience—the inner, esoteric core. This means that New Agers can "draw" on traditions whilst bypassing their explicit authoritative doctrines, dogmas, and moral codes. Instead, in detraditionalized fashion, they can discern—by way of their own experience, their gnosis or experiential knowledge—those spiritual truths which lie at the heart of, say, Vedanta or shamanism.[69]

Although perennialism, as distinct from a more general religious pluralism, has never been dominant within the academy, some recent academic advocates of the perennial philosophy include Frithjof Schuon, Huston Smith and the Muslim philosopher Seyyed Hossein Nasr.[70] Perennial philosophy is not the same thing as the more sophisticated model of religious pluralism advanced by John Hick, which will be examined in chapter seven, although there are some similarities between the two perspectives. In both there is the attempt to go beyond the apparent differences and incompatibilities among the religions to affirm that the major religious traditions are all more or less acceptable ways to respond to the one divine reality.[71]

A Tale of Two Parliaments

One way to appreciate the changes in perspectives on other religions is to look at two remarkable events in the United States occurring a century apart, each of which has become a significant symbol for how American society views religious diversity. By the late nineteenth century Westerners were already beginning to be more open to non-Christian religions, but it was only in the late twentieth century that what were previously minority perspectives became widely accepted and dominant views, not only among non-Christians but also within Roman Catholicism and Protestantism. This shift in perspectives can be illustrated by contrasting the 1893 World Parliament of Religions with the 1993 Parliament of the World's Religions.

---

[69]Heelas, *New Age Movement,* pp. 27-28.
[70]Frithjof Schuon, *The Transcendent Unity of Religions,* trans. Peter Townsend, rev. ed. (New York: Harper & Row, 1975); Huston Smith, *Forgotten Truth* (New York: Harper & Row, 1976); Huston Smith, *Beyond the Post-Modern Mind* (New York: Crossroad, 1982); Huston Smith, "Is There a Perennial Philosophy?" *Journal of the American Academy of Religion* 55, no. 3 (1987): 553-66; Seyyed Hossein Nasr, *Knowledge and the Sacred* (Albany: State University of New York Press, 1981); Seyyed Hossein Nasr, "In Quest of the Eternal Sophia," in *Philosophers Critiques D'eux Memes—Philosophische Selhstbetrachtungen,* ed. Andre Mercier and Suilar Maja (Bern, Switzerland: Peter Lang, 1980), 6:109-31.
[71]For a fascinating comparison of the pluralism of John Hick with the perennialism of Seyyed Hossein Nasr, see Adnan Aslan, *Religious Pluralism in Christian and Islamic Philosophy: The Thought of John Hick and Seyyed Hossein Nasr* (Richmond, England: Curzon, 1998).

The World's Parliament of Religions was held September 11-27, 1893, in Chicago, in conjunction with the World's Columbian Exposition, a technological extravaganza celebrating the four hundredth anniversary of Columbus's arrival in the Western hemisphere.[72] This was a time of enormous Western self-confidence, due both to the remarkable technological achievements in the West and the spread of Western political, economic and cultural influence worldwide through colonialism. The 1893 Columbian Exposition was the last of a series of nineteenth-century exhibitions celebrating Western achievements, and the World's Parliament of Religions naturally shared the spirit of optimism and confidence in the ongoing progress of civilization—by which, of course, was meant Western, "Christian" civilization.

Forty-one different religious groups—including Christian, Jewish, Hindu, Buddhist, Shinto, Confucian, Jain, Zoroastrian and Muslim traditions—were represented at the 1893 Parliament. Although foreign delegates came from non-Western nations such as India, Japan, Turkey, Lebanon, China, Ceylon and Siam, the non-Christian representation was uneven at best and failed not only to represent religious diversity globally but even to portray the growing diversity within North America. Only one Jain and one Muslim participated.[73] Native American traditions were represented by an academic anthropologist. Western Protestant missionaries presented papers on Eastern religious traditions.

A variety of expectations and agendas were at work during the conference. Many saw the parliament as a chance to promote a more open-minded, respectful approach toward other traditions, and thus they emphasized religious unity in pursuit of a more harmonious world in the twentieth century. Others, such as John Henry Barrows, pastor of Chicago's prestigious First Presbyterian Church and chairman of the parliament, as well as many active missionaries from overseas, viewed the event "as an unparalleled opportunity to present the Christian cause persuasively to the admiration and consent of all who could reach an unbiased opinion."[74] Barrows regarded the parliament as an unprecedented opportunity for Christian witness. And then there were the many critics of the parliament who refused to participate on the grounds that doing so would grant unwarranted legit-

---

[72]In the following comparison of the two parliaments I am indebted to the fine analysis of Alan Neely, "The Parliaments of the World's Religions: 1893 and 1993," *International Bulletin of Missionary Research* 18 (April 1994): 60-64.

[73]The Muslim, Mohammed Alexander Russell Webb, was actually an American, a former Presbyterian and ambassador to the Philippines who had dabbled in both Buddhism and Theosophy prior to his conversion to Islam. See Alan Neely, "The Parliaments of the World's Religions: 1893 and 1993," p. 61; and Jackson, *Oriental Religions and American Thought*, p. 251.

[74]James A. Kirk, "The 1893 World's Parliament of Religions," *Studies in Interreligious Dialogue* 3 (1993): 121-22.

imacy to non-Christian religions. Evangelist D. L. Moody held an evangelistic rally across the street from the parliament, "praying for the souls of the delegates every day that the meetings were in session."[75] Conservative Protestants were concerned that the conference would have a negative effect upon commitment to missions in foreign lands. A. T. Pierson, a leading missions advocate, for example, observed— correctly, as it turned out—that the parliament would give the broad impression that Christianity *"may not be the only Divine religion."*[76]

Nevertheless, in spite of the generally positive tone toward other religions reflected in the proceedings, the first parliament was an unabashedly Christian event. It was planned and directed primarily by Christians, the overwhelming majority of the official delegates were Christians and two-thirds of the papers presented were by Christians. At least a dozen Christian missionaries were featured in the program. Christian hymns were sung, the Lord's Prayer was repeated in each day's worship, and the final session ended with the triumphal singing of Handel's "Hallelujah Chorus." Some of the Christian participants were quite direct in their insistence on the exclusive truth of Christianity. For example, Professor William Wilkinson of the University of Chicago, in his paper "The Attitude of Christianity to Other Religions," explicitly rejected the fulfillment theme: "Of any ethnic religion, therefore, can it be said that it is a true religion, only not perfect? Christianity says, No." Rejecting non-Christian religions as false religions, Wilkinson stated, "The attitude, therefore, of Christianity towards religions other than itself is an attitude of universal, absolute, eternal, unappeasable hostility; while toward all men everywhere, the adherents of false religions by no means excepted, its attitude is an attitude of grace, mercy, and peace, for whosoever will."[77]

But Wilkinson's perspective was clearly a minority view, with most participants accepting more irenic perspectives on other religions. Nevertheless, as Alan Neely observes:

> The first parliament was predominantly a Christian extravaganza based on an underlying assumption held by many of the leaders, including John Henry Barrows, that Christianity would eventually triumph over all other religions. The sessions provided an ideal setting for presenting Christianity as morally, spiritually, and materially superior to all other religious traditions, and they served to vindicate the Christian belief in the rightness of their burgeoning missionary enterprise. Barrows would later declare that anyone present during the 1893 meeting or who read the record of the proceed-

---

[75]Ibid.

[76]As quoted in Martin Marty, *The Irony of It All, 1893-1919,* vol. 1 of *Modern American Religion* (Chicago: University of Chicago Press, 1986), p. 22. Emphasis in the original.

[77]William C. Wilkinson, "The Attitude of Christianity to Other Religions," in *The Dawn of Religious Pluralism: Voices from the World's Parliament of Religions, 1893,* ed. Richard Hughes Seager (La Salle, Ill.: Open Court, 1993), pp. 321-22.

ings could not help but be aware that the first parliament "was a great Christian demonstration with a non-Christian section which added color and picturesque effect."[78]

This was the heyday of Protestant theological liberalism, and the unifying theme—at least in the minds of the organizers—was the "fatherhood of God" and the "universal brotherhood of man."[79] In his official welcome to participants, Charles Bonney, the driving force behind the parliament, stated that the mission of the conference was "to unite all Religion against all irreligion; to make the golden rule the basis of this union; and to present to the world the substantial unity of many religions in the good deeds of the religious life."[80] The motto of the parliament was "Have we not all one Father? Hath not God created us?" (Mal 2:10). That the planners of the parliament had a theistic, if not explicitly Christian, framework and agenda in mind is evident from the ground rules for the conference, one of which stated that an objective of the conference was "to indicate the impregnable foundations of Theism, and the reasons for man's faith in Immortality, and thus unite and strengthen the forces adverse to a materialistic philosophy of the universe."[81] The fact that not all religions are theistic or share common understandings of the person and the afterlife was not perceived to be a problem, although the Buddhist, Jain and Confucian delegates in their presentations pointed out the inadequacy of defining religion in theistic terms.

We saw in chapter one that by the 1890s there was a vigorous discussion among missionaries and theologians on the question of other religions. And yet even the most theologically liberal still tended to think in terms of the fulfillment motif, according to which other religions were at best preparation for, and anticipations of, what is most completely revealed in Jesus Christ and Christianity. This broadly inclusivist perspective characterized Barrows's approach to other religions. Joseph Kitagawa remarks that,

> To Barrows, the plurality of religions was a genuine mystery, but he was certain that the deity whom Jews and Christians worship had something to do with all these religions of the world. He asked, "Why should Christians not be glad to learn what God has wrought through Buddha and Zoroaster—through the sages of China, and the prophets of India and the prophet of Islam?"[82]

---

[78]Neely, "Parliaments of the World's Religions," p. 62.

[79]See William R. Hutchison, *Errand to the World: American Protestant Thought and Foreign Missions* (Chicago: University of Chicago Press, 1987), pp. 105-6.

[80]Charles Carroll Bonney, "Words of Welcome," in *Dawn of Religious Pluralism*, p. 21. Bonney, a commited Swedenborgian, was using a monotheistic understanding of religion, which he defined as "the love and worship of God and the love and service of man." Ibid., p. 17.

[81]Kirk, "1893 World's Parliament of Religions," p. 127.

[82]Joseph M. Kitagawa, "The 1893 World's Parliament of Religions and its Legacy," in *The History of Religions: Understanding Human Experience* (Atlanta: Scholars, 1987), p. 363.

Yet in his final comments to conference participants, Chairman Barrows spoke freely and clearly about his commitment to Jesus Christ: "I desire that the last word which I speak to the Parliament shall be in the name of Him to whom I owe life and truth and hope and all things, who reconciles all contradictions, pacifies all antagonisms, and who from the throne of His heavenly kingdom directs the serene and unwearied omnipotence of redeeming love—Jesus Christ, the savior of the world."[83] The official report of the parliament concluded that the conference "did emphasize and illustrate the great Evangelical claim that the historic Christ is divine, the sufficient and only saviour of mankind."[84] Thus what is striking about the 1893 parliament is the strong liberal Protestant Christian presence, which, while willing to acknowledge many beauties and truths in other religions, nevertheless staunchly retained the clear superiority of Christianity.

The Asian participants, however, saw things rather differently. The three most significant Asian religious figures at the Parliament—the Hindu Swami Vivekananda from India, the Buddhist Dharmapala from Ceylon and the Japanese Buddhist Shaku Soen—all viewed the conference as presenting them with an unprecedented "platform from which to address the whole world."[85] Vivekananda, who had an electrifying effect upon the conference and was hailed by the *New York Times* as "undoubtedly the greatest figure in the Parliament of Religions,"[86] emerged as the symbol of reasoned tolerance.

> Do I wish that the Christian would become Hindu? God forbid. Do I wish that the Hindu or Buddhist would become Christian? God forbid. . . . The Christian is not to become a Hindu or a Buddhist, nor a Buddhist to become a Christian. But each must assimilate the others and yet preserve its individuality and grow to its own law of growth.[87]

The Japanese Buddhist delegation returned to Japan convinced that the parlia-

---

[83]As quoted in Kirk, "1893 World's Parliament of Religions," p. 131. Reflecting later upon the benefits of the parliament, Barrows emphasized the opportunity for Christians to share their faith in an unprecedented manner to leaders from other faiths, and stimulation of the study of comparative religions, which, he was convinced, would reveal the superiority of Christianity. See John Henry Barrows, "Results of the Parliament of Religions" (1894) in *A Museum of Faiths: Histories and Legacies of the 1893 World's Parliament of Religions,* ed. Eric J. Ziolkowski (Atlanta: Scholars, 1993), pp. 131-47.

[84]From John Henry Barrows, *The World's Parliament of Religions,* (Chicago: Parliament, 1893), 2:1569.

[85]Kitagawa, "1893 World's Parliament of Religions and Its Legacy," p. 359.

[86]Marcus Baybrooke, *Inter-Faith Organizations, 1893-1979: An Historical Directory* (New York: Edwin Mellen, 1980), pp. 6-7.

[87]Vivekananda, "Impromptu Comments," in *Dawn of Religious Pluralism,* pp. 336-37. Staying on in the West for four years, Vivekananda preached the gospel of neo-Vedanta Hinduism in America and England and started the Ramakrishna Order.

ment had demonstrated that a materialistic and hedonistic America was hungering for Eastern spirituality.

> The Japanese Buddhists did not hesitate to proclaim that the parliament was a unique breakthrough for Buddhist mission. The Buddhist presence was characterized as "an epoch-making, unprecedented happening, unheard-of in history." It was felt that the situation was ripe for "Buddhism in Japan in the Far East to turn the wheel of Dharma in America in the Far West." At the dawn of the twentieth century Buddhism was appearing at the scene of world culture spreading the unfathomable light and compassion of the Buddha. A representative Buddhist journal concluded that the parliament was "the most brilliant fact in the history of Buddhism."[88]

The perceptions of the Japanese Buddhists were not far off, for it is generally acknowledged that one of the enduring effects of the 1893 Parliament was greatly increased exposure in the West to Asian religions, resulting in their legitimation as viable religious alternatives in Western societies.[89]

In 1993 Chicago hosted the second Parliament of the World's Religions—but what a difference a century makes! America in 1993 was far more diverse culturally and religiously than it was in 1893. By the 1990s, there were an estimated 5.5 million Muslims, 4 million Buddhists and 1.3 million Hindus in the United States. Chicago alone had roughly 250,000 Muslims, 155,000 Buddhists, 100,000 Hindus, 2,500 Jains as well as many adherents of other traditions and the ubiquitous New Agers.[90]

Over six thousand participants representing 125 different religious groups gathered in Chicago August 28–September 5, 1993, for an exuberant celebration of religious diversity. Participants included Baha'is, Buddhists, Christians, Confucians, Hindus, Jains, Jews, Muslims, Native American religionists, neo-pagans, Rastafarians, Shintoists, Taoists, Theosophists, Unitarians, venerators of Isis and various earth spirits, Zoroastrians and many others. Whereas the 1893 parliament had been

---

[88]Notto Thelle, *Buddhism and Christianity in Japan: From Conflict to Dialogue, 1854-1899* (Honolulu: University of Hawaii Press, 1987), pp. 221-22. Joseph Kitagawa points out a further unintended consequence of the 1893 Parliament. We have already noted the dominance of the fulfillment theme among Protestants at the parliament. Asian religious reformers such as Vivekananda, Dharmapala and Shaku Soen also adopted the fulfillment motif but turned it on its head. Instead of recognizing Christianity as the fulfillment of Asian religions, they reversed the formula, interpreting other religions, including Christianity, from their own distinctive Hindu or Buddhist perspectives. Christianity "properly understood," then, becomes an anticipation of what is most fully realized in Hinduism or Buddhism. This was to become an increasingly popular form of Hindu and Buddhist apologetics. See Kitagawa, "1893 World's Parliament of Religions and Its Legacy," p. 366.
[89]See Richard Hughes Seager, general introduction to *Dawn of Religious Pluralism*, pp. 9-11.
[90]The figures are from Michael Hirsley, "Common Cause," *Chicago Tribune Magazine*, August 29, 1993, p. 16; and Diana L. Eck, "America's New Religious Landscape," in *Religion and Ethics Newsweekly: Viewers Guide* (New York: Thirteen/WNET, 1998), p. 2.

criticized for its heavy Christian presence and failure to represent adequately the diversity in the world, this was hardly a problem in 1993. The conference included not only plenary sessions and over six hundred seminars on a wide range of issues but also opportunities for expressions of worship from the various traditions, prayers, meditation, dancing and singing.[91] Prayers were offered by Christians, Jews and Muslims; Buddhists led in silent meditation. A priestess of Isis invoked the deities of this world for their assistance in eradicating earth's problems. The Bible was read, the Qur'an was recited and Hindu mantras were chanted. Wiccans held a full moon ritual in Chicago's Grant Park—an event unimaginable at the 1893 parliament.

Gone in 1993 was the heady optimism of 1893. The intervening century had witnessed two world wars as well as countless regional conflicts; the proliferation of nuclear weapons; the waste of natural resources and destruction of the environment; the rise of ethnic tensions, resulting in multiple genocides; and a continuing population explosion straining existing resources. Thus the focus of the 1993 parliament was on the need for various religious traditions to work together to tackle the many daunting problems plaguing the world at the turn of the millennium. Ecological concerns were dominant, and representatives of "earth-based spiritualities, foremost among them neopagans, formed a significant part of the total assembly."[92] Much attention was given to the role of religion in fighting racism, the exploitation of the earth's natural resources, hunger and poverty, injustice and oppression. The parliament issued a declaration, *Toward a Global Ethic,* which called on all religious communities to "strive for a just social and economic order, in which everyone has an equal chance to reach full potential as a human being" and to commit themselves "to a culture of non-violence, respect, justice, and peace."[93]

---

[91]See Hendrik M. Vroom, "Chicago 1993: The Parliament of the World's Religions," *Studies in Interreligious Dialogue* 3 (1993): 115.

[92]Richard Seager, "The Two Parliaments, the 1893 Original and the Centennial of 1993: A Historian's View," in *The Community of Religions: Voices and Images of the Parliament of the World's Religions,* ed. Wayne Teasdale and George Cairns (New York: Continuum, 1996), pp. 29-30.

[93]Parliament of the World's Religions, introduction to *A Global Ethic: The Declaration of the Parliament of the World's Religions,* ed. Hans Küng and Karl-Josef Kuschel (New York: Continuum, 1993), p. 15. Yet not all was peace and harmony at the parliament; speakers were occasionally challenged with raucous debate and rude interruptions. A Kashmiri speaker, for example, accused the Republic of India of occupying Kashmir and suppressing the population, a charge that was promptly met by angry protests from Hindus demanding that the speaker be silenced. The presence of Louis Farrakhan of the Nation of Islam caused four Jewish groups to pull out of the conference. The Greek Orthodox Diocese of Chicago withdrew from the parliament because of the presence of nontheistic religious groups, stating, "It would be inconceivable for Orthodox Christianity to establish a perceived relationship with groups which possess no belief in God or a supreme being" (quoted in John Zipperer, "The Elusive Quest for Religious Harmony," *Christianity Today,* October 4, 1993, p. 43).

One of the greatest differences between the two parliaments is the nature of the Christian participation in each event. Although prominent Christians were present in 1993, no one would characterize the second parliament as a "Christian event" in any sense of the term. Gone was the triumphalism of 1893, which held that through the parliament proceedings adherents of other religions would see the clear superiority of Jesus Christ and Christian faith. Many Christian participants in 1993 would have questioned whether that is even a desirable objective. Alan Neely observes, "[The parliament] was predominantly an other-than-Christian assembly, with the Christians who were present maintaining a modest profile and assiduously avoiding Christian claims of uniqueness or superiority."[94]

Whereas in 1893 it was the Christians who emphasized the uniqueness and superiority of Christian faith, in 1993 it was not the Christians but those of other faiths who were aggressive in pushing their religions. In 1893 Christians presented papers with titles such as "The Truthfulness of Holy Scripture," "Christianity a Religion of Facts," "Christ the Savior of the World" and "The Message of Christianity to Other Religions." But Christian apologetics of this kind had no place in 1993.[95] It was now the Hindus who presented papers on "The Genuine Authentic Religion We Need Today" and "Bhakti Marga and the Unity of Religion"; it was a Muslim who spoke on "Mohammed the Model for Humanity"; and it was a Jain who informed the world of "The Solution of Present-Day World Problems from a Jain Perspective." Reflecting on the parliament, Neely remarked, "[T]hroughout the eight days of the 1993 meeting, I repeatedly wondered why there was hardly a word and not a single paper that set forth in a clear and comprehensive fashion what Christianity is today, who Jesus Christ is, what Christians believe, the Christian basis of religious authority, or the Christian view of the *Missio Dei* or the mission of the church."[96]

Part of the answer to Neely's question lies in the unfortunate fact that conservative Protestants largely boycotted the event out of a desire not to be identified with anything granting legitimacy to other religions. But surely much of the answer also is found in the profound cultural changes transforming America during the twentieth century. Christian participants in the 1893 parliament, in spite of their considerable openness to other religions, took it for granted that Christianity was the one true religion and that Jesus Christ is clearly superior to other religious leaders. But for many Christians in 1993, and certainly for those most prominent at

---

[94]Neely, "Parliaments of the World's Religions," p. 62.

[95]Neely comments, "By and large Christians who read papers or who spoke in 1993 appeared to be consciously avoiding any intimation of theological exclusivism or superiority, and Protestant evangelicals who likely would have made traditional claims for Christianity either did not attend the parliament or chose to be spectators" (ibid., p. 63).

[96]Ibid.

the parliament, it was precisely these issues concerning the superiority of Christianity and Jesus Christ that were most problematic.

Implicit in many of the presentations and activities at the 1993 parliament was the assumption that each religious tradition is in its own way legitimate and right for its adherents, that no one should attempt to persuade followers of other religious paths to change allegiances, and that what is needed today is for each tradition to accept all others as partners in our common search for truth and human well-being. If Swami Vivekananda was the media favorite at the 1893 Parliament, in 1993 that honor surely went to the Dalai Lama, head of the Gelugpa order of Tibetan Buddhism and reincarnation of the *bodhisattva* Avalokitesvara. This implicit assumption was explicit in the Dalai Lama's closing talk on "The Importance of Religious Harmony" before some twenty thousand people crowded into Grant Park on Chicago's lakefront. Echoing the sentiments expressed by Vivekananda a century earlier, the Dalai Lama, who (at least in the West) has become the symbol of tolerance and religious harmony, stated:

> Each religion has its own philosophy and there are similarities as well as differences among the various traditions. What is important is what is suitable for a particular person. We should look at the underlying purpose of religion and not merely at the abstract details of theology or metaphysics. All religions make the betterment of humanity their primary concern. When we view the different religions as essentially instruments to develop a good heart—love and respect for others, a true sense of community—we can appreciate what they have in common. . . . Everyone feels that his or her form of religious practice is the best. I myself feel that Buddhism is best for me. But this does not mean that Buddhism is best for everyone else.[97]

This captures well not only the pluralistic ethos of the 1993 parliament but also that of the broader culture today, which enthusiastically hailed the conference as a new milestone in interreligious relations.

Orientalism

Discussion of the European and American "discovery" of East Asian religions would be incomplete without some reference to the much-debated subject of Orientalism. Although the term "Orientalism" has been used at least since the 1830s to refer to that branch of scholarship that uses Western methods and categories to understand the East, with the 1978 publication of Edward Said's *Orientalism* it assumed a special meaning, signifying "the complicity between Western academic accounts of the nature of 'the Orient' and the hegemonic political agendas of Western impe-

---

[97]His Holiness the Dalai Lama, "The Importance of Religious Harmony," in *Community of Religions*, pp. 17-18. Despite the pluralistic overtones in his comments, the Dalai Lama is not really a religious pluralist (see pp. 216-18).

rialism."[98] Said subjected Western scholars' discourse about non-Western peoples and cultures to a stinging critique, arguing that their depictions of "the Orient" (which for Said referred more to the Middle East and Islam than to East Asian cultures) were inextricably linked to the social and political agendas of European colonialism.[99]

Orientalism is thus about the ways in which the West looks at "the Orient," viewing it from within the framework of Western experiences and interests. This in itself is hardly controversial, for everyone to some extent interprets what is different in terms of what is familiar. But Said's point is more than just that Western attempts to understand the East were impaired by Western ethnocentrism and cultural blinders. Drawing heavily from Michel Foucault's discussions on the relation between knowledge and power, Said argues that, for example, the British and French representations of the peoples of the Middle East were both shaped by and served to reinforce the agendas of colonialism. He contends that "ideas, cultures, and histories cannot seriously be understood or studied without their force, or more precisely their configuration of power, also being studied."[100] Consequently, far from dispassionately and objectively explaining the Orient "as it really is," earlier European scholars misrepresented it, imposing upon Eastern cultures and religions the categories and interpretive interests of Western scholars, then used this mythological image to marginalize and control the cultures of the East. Thus Said speaks of Orientalism as "a way of coming to terms with the Orient that is based upon the Orient's special place in European Western experience"[101]—and the "special place" refers, of course, to the West's colonialist interests in Asia. Orientalism thus grows out of and reinforces the Western desire to control non-Western peoples.

Orientalist discourse made a sharp dichotomy between "the Orient" and "the Occident," with sweeping generalizations on both sides that accentuated differences and reinforced the sense of privilege and superiority of the West at the expense of the East. Bryan Turner observes, "Orientalism is a discourse which represents the exotic, erotic, strange Orient as a comprehensible, intelligible phenomenon within a network of categories, tables and concepts by which the Orient is simultaneously defined and controlled. To know is to subordinate."[102] Thus Western culture was depicted as energetic, rational, scientific, controlled, mature and moral, whereas the Orient was perceived as lascivious, irrational, mystical, unpre-

---

[98]King, *Orientalism and Religion,* p. 83.
[99]Edward Said, *Orientalism* (New York: Vintage, 1978).
[100]Ibid., p. 5.
[101]Ibid., p. 1.
[102]Bryan S. Turner, *Orientalism, Postmodernism, and Globalism* (London: Routledge, 1994), p. 21.

dictable, childish and cruel. Broad generalizations about both "the East" and "the West" abounded, with little sensitivity to the complex heterogeneity of either.

Said's thesis has generated vigorous debate, and while many of his claims have been accepted, scholars have also pointed out that matters are not quite as simple as he sometimes suggests.[103] Without pretending to resolve the issues here, several points should be noted. First, in one sense what Said discusses is a subcategory of the broader question about how we understand "the other." Understanding other cultures has always presented challenges and involves a measure of translation, or taking what is strange and different and re-presenting it in terms that are familiar. In itself this is not particularly controversial, for if we were unable to do this successfully, understanding across boundaries—whether linguistic, cultural, religious or historical—would be impossible. And yet clearly *some* understanding of "the other" in these contexts does occur. So Orientalism should not be understood in such a way that it rules out the possibility of understanding across cultural boundaries.

Furthermore, while fully recognizing, along with Foucault and Said, that knowledge is power and that to have knowledge of a thing is in some sense "to dominate it, to have authority over it," we must avoid reductionism. For it is one thing to say that Orientalist depictions of Eastern peoples and cultures were not always accurate and that they often, whether intentionally or not, were both shaped by and furthered colonialist aims. It is something else again to dismiss Western characterizations of the East as *nothing but* social constructions legitimizing colonialists ends.[104] Some nineteenth-century studies of Asian cultures were remarkably accurate and perceptive, in spite of their association with colonialist agendas. Moreover, the thesis that Orientalist discourse is always associated with colonialist agendas is misleading, as Germany certainly had its share of Orientalist scholars although it had no Eastern empire to control, and Japan was the object of Orientalist discourse without ever having been colonized by the West.[105]

But what is especially important for our purposes is the way in which Said's insights can be applied to scholarly discourse—both Eastern and Western—about

---

[103]For critical responses to Said, see especially Bruce Robbins, "The East Is a Career: Edward Said and the Logics of Professionalism"; and Richard G. Fox, "East of Said"—both in *Edward Said: A Critical Reader*, ed. Michael Sprinker (Oxford: Blackwell, 1992), pp. 48-73, 144-56; David Kopf, "Hermeneutics Versus History," *Journal of Asian Studies* 39, no. 3 (1980): 495-506; and Fred Dallmayr, *Beyond Orientalism: Essays on Cross-Cultural Encounter* (Albany: State University of New York Press, 1996).

[104]"If discourse produces its own objects of enquiry and if there is no alternative to discourse, then there is little point in attempting to replace Oriental discourse with some improved or correct analysis of 'the Orient.'" (Turner, *Orientalism, Postmodernism and Globalism,* p. 101).

[105]See King, *Orientalism and Religion,* p. 85; and Richard H. Minear, "Orientalism and the Study of Japan," *Journal of Asian Studies* 39, no. 3 (1980): 507-17.

Hinduism and Buddhism. Scholars such as Richard King demonstrate how early Western thinkers sometimes promoted misleading stereotypes about Indian religious traditions, caricatures that often served to reinforce a sense of superiority about Western (Christian) religion and philosophy. For example, in the early academic study of religion, not only was the category of religion itself shaped by Western, and often Christian, assumptions—so that disproportionate attention was given to the place of doctrine and sacred scriptures in defining other religions—but there was also a tendency to homogenize the many disparate traditions under a single unifying category such as "Hinduism," thereby giving the illusion of greater homogeneity than was often the case.[106] The category Hinduism itself was a modern one, introduced by Europeans to make sense of the bewildering diversity of Indian religious beliefs and practices. But in categorizing the many diverse traditions as all Hinduism, scholars minimized the differences in favor of a search for the "essence" of Hinduism that all traditions share. To speak of Hinduism as a clearly defined entity, then, is in a sense to fall victim to a caricature that distorts the remarkable diversity of Indian religious life.

Not only did Western scholars ignore the rich diversity of Eastern traditions but also Hinduism and Buddhism were routinely characterized as mystical, irrational and morally deficient in contrast to the rationality and moral superiority of Western (Christian) religion. From the late nineteenth century on, there was an increasing tendency "to emphasize the 'mystical' nature of Hinduism by reference to the 'esoteric' literature known as the Vedanta, the end of the Vedas—namely, the *Upanishads.*"[107] Thus for European scholars the nondualistic monism of Advaita Vedanta and the eighth-century philosopher Shankara came to define the essence of Hinduism, strengthening the perception of the essentially mystical and monistic nature of Eastern thought. The reality, of course, is that Indian religious and philosophical traditions are extremely diverse, with Advaita Vedanta merely one—and not necessarily even the most significant—of many different traditions.[108] And yet this reductionistic understanding of Hinduism persists, so that the "mystical East" continues to be played off against the "rational West." Both stereotypes are misleading, for both "the East" and "the West" are largely constructions that obscure the enormous diversity within Eastern and Western cultures.

Recent scholars have rightly pointed out that engaging in misleading generalizations about "the other" to further one's own agenda is not just a matter of the

---

[106]King, *Orientalism and Religion,* chapters 2-4.

[107]Ibid., p. 119.

[108]See Dallmayr, *Beyond Orientalism,* chapter 6. For a helpful guide to the diversity of Indian philosophical and religious traditions, see Ninian Smart, *Doctrine and Argument in Indian Philosophy* (London: Allen & Unwin, 1964).

West controlling a passive East for its own ends. There is also a kind of "reverse Orientalism" as well, as Asian scholars manipulate the symbols and discourse of Orientalism in order to shape the West's understanding of the East. For example, as noted above, the stereotype of "the East" as mystical, intuitive and irrational was simplistic and served to marginalize Indian religious traditions among those scholars who prized rationality in religion. And yet for others, such as the "romantic Orientalists" of nineteenth-century Romanticism and Transcendentalism as well as more recent New Agers, it is precisely the perceived mysticism and spirituality of the East that commended Asian religions over the stale rationalism of Western traditions. Although still a distortion, romantic Orientalism's understanding of Eastern thought as esoteric mysticism thus became a way of advancing the sense of superiority of Eastern spirituality to (Western) Christianity.

Some leading Asian intellectuals picked up on this, and so Richard King speaks of "ways in which indigenous peoples of the East have used, manipulated and constructed their own positive responses to colonialism using Orientalist conceptions."[109] Thus, for example, part of the legacy of colonialism and the encounter between India and European cultures was the revitalization of Hindu intellectual movements that sought to reassert Indian identity and encourage nationalistic aspirations through a renewed emphasis upon the unique spirituality of Hinduism. A distinguished group of modern Hindu thinkers such as Rammohun Roy, Dayananda Saraswati, Swami Vivekananda, Mohandas K. Gandhi and Sarvepalli Radhakrishnan made skillful use of the symbolism of the spiritual East in developing their apologetic for modern Hinduism as the antidote for the crass materialism and nihilism of Western culture.

The effective use of Orientalist discourse to enhance Western appreciation of Eastern religious traditions is perhaps most evident in some nineteenth- and twentieth-century Japanese interpreters of Buddhism to the West. D. T. Suzuki was a master of this, and his writings are replete with sweeping generalizations contrasting the materialism of the West with the mystical spirituality of the East, by which he of course meant his particular interpretation of Japanese Zen. In an important study of Suzuki, Robert Sharf states:

> While Suzuki's Zen claimed a privileged perspective that transcended cultural difference, it was at the same time contrived as the antithesis of everything Suzuki found deplorable about the West. . . . We read repeatedly that the "West" is materialistic, the "East" spiritual, that the West is aggressive and imperialistic, while the East extols nonviolence and harmony, that the West values rationality, the East intuitive wisdom, that the West is dualistic, the East monistic, and that while the West is individualistic, setting man apart from nature, the East is communalistic, viewing man as one with

---

[109]King, *Orientalism and Religion,* p. 86.

nature. In short, his image of the East in general, and Japan in particular, is little more than a romantic inversion of Japanese negative stereotypes of the West.[110]

This agenda has been continued by the Kyoto School of Japanese Buddhism, associated with Kitaro Nishida, Keiji Nishitani, Hajime Tanabe and Masao Abe, who have carefully crafted a distinctive understanding of Japanese Zen as epitomizing Eastern insights.[111] The attraction of Eastern traditions in the West is due in part to the skillful and effective use of Orientalist symbols in depicting a profound Eastern spirituality as the antidote to Western rationalistic materialism.

---

[110]Robert H. Sharf, "Whose Zen? Zen Nationalism Revisited," in *Rude Awakenings: Zen, the Kyoto School, and the Question of Nationalism,* ed. James W. Heisig and John C. Maraldo (Honolulu: University of Hawaii Press, 1994), pp. 47-48. On Suzuki's unique interpretation of Zen, see David Kalupahana, *A History of Buddhist Philosophy: Continuities and Discontinuities* (Honolulu: University of Hawaii Press, 1992), pp. 228-36.

[111]See King, *Orientalism and Religion,* chapters 4-6; Dallmayr, *Beyond Orientalism,* chapter 3. Also helpful are the essays in Lopez, *Curators of the Buddha;* and Galen Amstutz, *Interpreting Amida: History and Orientalism in the Study of Pure Land Buddhism* (Albany: State University of New York Press, 1997). A vigorous debate has been going on in recent years over the complicity of some leading Japanese scholars associated with the Kyoto School in Japanese nationalism and militarism in the 1930s. See the essays in Heisig and Maraldo, *Rude Awakenings.*

4

RELIGION & SPIRITUALITY
IN THE CULTURE
OF MODERNITY

In the United States the norms of secularism are largely taken for granted. Although blatant defenses of atheism are seldom articulated, there is little in the official wisdom of public institutions that validates the sacred except as personal conviction or as quaint tradition. Such norms do not prevent spirituality from expressing itself. But they do influence how it is expressed.

ROBERT WUTHNOW, *After Heaven*

We do have a problem of belief, and it not only raises the question of why we should believe in God but why we should believe in *this* God. There are others, after all, and today they are made available in an unprecedented way through the religious supermarket of modern pluralism.

PETER BERGER, *A Far Glory*

As the nineteenth century drew to a close, two very different expectations about the future of religions in the modern age could be found among Western thinkers. There were those such as Karl Marx who held that the relentless advancement of modernization, under the impact of education and science, would eventually eliminate the need for religion, and thus religion would simply "wither away."[1] This assumption survives in some forms of the secularization thesis, which will be considered later in this chapter.

Quite different expectations were held by some nineteenth-century missionaries, who fully anticipated the elimination of non-Christian religions through the worldwide advance of the Christian gospel. For example, Lars Dahle, general secretary of the Norwegian Missionary Society, after analyzing the statistics of the growth of the Christian church worldwide during the nineteenth

---

[1]For the views of Marx on religion, see J. Samuel Preus, *Explaining Religion: Criticism and Theory from Bodin to Freud* (New Haven, Conn.: Yale University Press, 1987), chapter 6; and Daniel L. Pals, *Seven Theories of Religion* (New York: Oxford University Press, 1996), chapter 4.

century, confidently predicted in 1900 that by "the year 1990 the entire human race would be won for the Christian faith."[2]

Needless to say, both expectations have gone unrealized. Religion in general has not disappeared. Indeed highly modernized, technologically sophisticated societies continue to manifest remarkable religious vitality. But neither has Christianity replaced non-Christian religions.[3] In spite of the significant growth of the Christian church in the past two hundred years, non-Christian religious traditions continue to flourish. As David Bosch notes, for some people this fact prompts some disconcerting questions: "The Christian faith is still a minority religion, at best holding its own in relation to the overall world population. And if Christianity is no longer successful, is it still unique and true?"[4]

In this chapter we will bring together several themes concerning the impact of the culture of modernity upon religious assumptions and attitudes, observing how they enhance the plausibility of religious pluralism. In particular the ethos of pluralism is supported by the cumulative effects of skepticism about traditional Christianity, sustained exposure to religious diversity, and the emphasis upon pragmatism and personal experience reflected in the privatization of religion that produce what Wade Clark Roof calls the "quest culture."

> In my judgment, the current religious situation in the United States is characterized not so much by a loss of faith as a qualitative shift from unquestioned belief to a more open, questioning mood. . . . A set of social and cultural transformations have created a quest culture, a search for certainty, but also the hope for a more authentic, intrinsically satisfying life.[5]

Roof considers these changes in religious expression to be directly related to the social and cultural transformations brought about by modernization and globalization.

> The emergence of a global world, an influx of new immigrants and cultures, widespread changes in values and beliefs, the immense role of the media and visual imagery in shaping contemporary life, an expanding consumer-oriented culture targeting the self as an arena for marketing, the erosion of many traditional forms of commu-

---

[2]David Bosch, *Transforming Mission: Paradigm Shifts in Theology of Mission* (Maryknoll, N.Y.: Orbis, 1991), p. 6.

[3]A more somber assessment of missions success is reflected in the statement by Canon Max Warren, general secretary of the Church Missionary Society: "We have marched around alien Jerichos the requisite number of times. We have sounded the trumpets. And the walls have not collapsed" (quoted in Wilfred Cantwell Smith, "The Christian in a Religiously Plural World," in *Religious Diversity: Essays by Wilfred Cantwell Smith,* ed. Willard G. Oxtoby [New York: Harper & Row, 1976], p. 7).

[4]Bosch, *Transforming Mission,* p. 6.

[5]Wade Clark Roof, *Spiritual Marketplace: Baby Boomers and the Remaking of American Religion* (Princeton, N.J.: Princeton University Press, 1999), pp. 9-10.

nity—all point to major realignments in religion and culture. . . . Old certainties collapse as new mysteries arise. It seems not just coincidental that the metaphor of a
spiritual quest takes on significance just when many of traditional religion's underpin-
nings of the culture have become more tenuous.[6]

We will return to the theme of spiritual quest later, but first we will examine the
place of skepticism in undermining confidence in orthodox Christianity.

The Crisis of Faith

We have been considering the historical, social and cultural factors affecting religious belief, noting especially the changes that contribute to the plausibility of religious pluralism. A caveat here is in order, to remind us that such social and
cultural factors never determine belief or unbelief. No one is merely the product of
sociocultural influences. Individuals regularly challenge and rise above the cumulative influences of their environments, and cultures themselves are continually
undergoing change. More significantly, we must always remember that at the heart
of unbelief is sin, human rebellion against God and his ways and the pursuit of
human autonomy. In so far as commitment to religious pluralism is an expression
of unbelief in the gospel of Jesus Christ, then—whatever else it involves—it is a
manifestation of the sinful drive for autonomy from God and his truth. Thus religious pluralism is never merely a sociocultural response to diversity; it also
includes a theological response to God's revelation in Christ.

And yet sin operates in many ways on multiple levels, including the social and
cultural patterns influencing how we think and act. While all persons are
accountable before God for how they respond to what they know to be true and
right, one's cultural environment shapes both one's understanding of God's revelation and one's response to it. The plausibility structures of a particular society—the set of institutions, values and assumptions that support the plausibility
of certain beliefs—can either encourage or discourage commitment to Christian
faith. Plausibility structures vary from culture to culture in their impact upon
Christian belief, so that, apart from the grace of God, someone living in seventeenth-century Kyoto (for example) would have greater obstacles to overcome in
believing the gospel than someone living in seventeenth-century London.
Although sin and unbelief are constants among humankind, each culture and age
presents its own special obstacles to Christian faith. A particularly significant
obstacle for many in the West is the ideology of religious pluralism, and thus it is
important to understand the dynamics that make it so attractive. To appreciate
this we must consider religious pluralism within the broader context of the crisis

---

[6]Ibid., p. 8.

of faith that has plagued orthodox Christianity in the West since the early modern period.[7] And this requires some understanding of the social and intellectual currents of the past several centuries that have helped to shape the present.

The participants in a recent international, multiyear study project called "Toward a Missiology of Western Culture" correctly observed that "one of the features characteristic of modern Western culture is epistemological uncertainty, seen in the generally decreasing confidence that any adequate basis for knowing can be found."[8] Writing in 1960, Franklin Baumer called the twentieth century "one of the great sceptical epochs of history."[9] Roof similarly observes that "the legacy of doubt, suspicion, and distrust of institutions and of religious authority permeates the mainstream culture."[10] Whereas this is often taken to indicate a cultural shift away from the certainties of "modernity" to the uncertainties of "postmodernity," it is better to see this as a perennial problem but one that has assumed more sophisticated expression within the last century.

Epistemological uncertainty is evident in the deep skepticism with which many treat the core claims of the Christian gospel. The Christian faith is rooted in certain events concerning the life, teachings, death and resurrection of Jesus of Nazareth two thousand years ago in Palestine. Unlike some other religious traditions with a more tenuous relation to historical events, Christianity stands upon the historicity of the New Testament account of Jesus Christ, or what C. Stephen Evans has called "the incarnational narrative." This is "the account of how the divine Word took on human flesh, was born as a baby, lived a life characterized by miraculous healing and authoritative teaching, died a cruel and voluntary death for the sake of redeeming sinful humans, was raised by God to life, and now abides with God, awaiting the time of his glorious return and ultimate triumph."[11] Furthermore, Christians have traditionally maintained that salvation—that is, forgiveness for sin and reconciliation with God, resulting in a qualitatively new life both now and for eternity—is based upon the divine person and work of Jesus Christ on the cross and requires a response in faith to what God in Christ has done on our behalf. In other words, the events of Jesus' life do matter. As the apostle Paul put it in reference to the resur-

---

[7]A helpful overview of Christian thought in the modern era is James C. Livingston, *The Enlightenment and the Nineteenth Century*, vol. 1 of *Modern Christian Thought*, 2nd ed. (Upper Saddle River, N.J.: Prentice-Hall, 1997); and James C. Livingston, Francis Schüssler Fiorenza et al., *The Twentieth Century*, vol. 2 of *Modern Christian Thought*, 2nd ed. (Upper Saddle River, N.J.: Prentice-Hall, 2000).

[8]Introduction to *To Stake a Claim: Mission and the Western Crisis of Knowledge*, ed. J. Andrew Kirk and Kevin J. Vanhoozer (Maryknoll, N.Y.: Orbis, 1999), p. xiv.

[9]Franklin L. Baumer, *Religion and the Rise of Scepticism* (New York: Harcourt Brace, 1960), p. 3.

[10]Roof, *Spiritual Marketplace*, p. 56.

[11]C. Stephen Evans, *The Historical Christ and the Jesus of Faith: The Incarnational Narrative as History* (Oxford: Clarendon, 1996), p. 5.

rection, "If Christ has not been raised, your faith is futile; you are still in your sins" (1 Cor 15:17). And yet the story about Jesus in the New Testament, which until the twentieth century was widely accepted by Christians as true and authoritative, is regarded by many today—both inside and outside the church—as highly problematical. As Evans observes, "To put it bluntly and simply, we have become unsure whether the events happened, and uncertain about whether we can know that they happened, even if they did."[12]

There are, of course, many factors involved in the loss of confidence in the truth of Scripture's incarnational narrative, including the rise of modern biblical criticism. While in many ways the rigorous and careful study of the New Testament has helped us to understand the world of the first century and the meanings of biblical texts much better, it can hardly be denied that radical biblical criticism has produced pervasive skepticism about the events recorded in Scripture. Due to the skeptical assumptions underlying the methodologies of the more radical scholars, it is taken for granted in many circles that what we have in the New Testament are not the actual words and deeds of Jesus of Nazareth but instead the early church's picture of Jesus' life and teaching, a creative reconstruction concerning which we have no way of knowing whether it reflects accurately the historical Jesus. This approach naturally regards with suspicion any attempt to justify theological positions merely by appealing to what the New Testament record portrays Jesus as saying and doing. On these grounds, no longer can one justify Christian insistence upon the exclusivity of salvation in Christ alone simply by referring to texts such as John 14:6 or Acts 4:12, which speak of Jesus as the only Savior. Skeptical assumptions about the New Testament are not limited to a select group of academics but find wide acceptance in the culture at large, due not only to the influence of radical scholarship in the academic world but also to the widespread coverage of groups such as the Jesus Seminar in the popular media.

But religious skepticism affects more than merely radical biblical criticism. In a sense anyone undergoing a secular university education in the West is immersed in religious skepticism and relativism. As Roof observes, "Educating college populations in the humanities and the social sciences, on critical biblical scholarship, the world religions, semiotics, and hermeneutics further contributed to a more relativistic understanding of religious truth."[13] We should not assume that this is simply a recent "postmodern" reaction to the heavy rationalism of the Enlightenment. On the one hand, it is true that religious skepticism and relativism are more pervasive today than in the 1780s, and part of what drives contemporary skepticism is dissatisfaction with what is perceived in earlier thinkers as a naive confidence in the pow-

[12]Ibid., p. 13
[13]Roof, *Spiritual Marketplace*, p. 55.

ers of reason. One of the ironies of the modern world is that, far from attaining the epistemological certainty in all areas of inquiry that Descartes and others dreamed of, the past several centuries have been marked by a deepening epistemological skepticism, particularly in religious matters.[14]

On the other hand, contemporary skepticism is not a recent development, a sharp break with an excessively rationalistic modernity. As Baumer notes, "Present day religious scepticism . . . would not be what it is, would certainly not be as pervasive as it is, had it not been for the development of a powerful sceptical tradition over four centuries and more."[15] The legacy of skepticism is significant for understanding contemporary religious pluralism, for pluralism thrives within a relativistic ethos that rejects traditional Christianity as untenable but is open to new religious alternatives. Religious skepticism can take one of two forms, either a general skepticism about the existence of God and a supernatural realm or a more restricted skepticism about the claims of a particular religious tradition to exclusive truth and efficacy in salvation. It is primarily the second form that feeds into religious pluralism, but it often grows out of the same basic concerns driving the more general skepticism. Contemporary religious skepticism is also quite selective, so that it rejects traditional orthodoxies as untenable but allows for extraordinary credulity toward new religious practices. We will look briefly at skepticism in the ancient Greek and early modern European contexts, noting in particular the link between skepticism and the awareness of cultural diversity, for both in classical and early modern times the plausibility of skepticism was tied to the appeal to widespread diversity and disagreement—factors that became even more pronounced in the twentieth century.

The Legacy of Ancient Skepticism

A rather sophisticated early expression of skepticism emerged with the Sophists, a

---

[14]One can, of course, be skeptical about religious issues without maintaining skepticism about knowledge in general. Many are quite willing to speak in terms of universal truth in the physical sciences and history, for example, while remaining deeply skeptical about any truth claims in religion. While there are many, especially in the social sciences, cultural studies and literary studies, who embrace varying degrees of skepticism and relativism, there are also many who have considerable confidence in the capacities of reason. Scientism—the view that the hard physical sciences provide the paradigm and criteria for all genuine knowledge—is hardly extinct, as the continued popularity of thinkers such as Carl Sagan, Stephen Jay Gould, Richard Dawkins and Stephen Hawking illustrate. Furthermore, with the recent explosion of new technologies for information and entertainment, it hardly seems that people in general are less enamored of science than they were previously, even if the naive optimism of a previous era has been tempered by the realization of the evils to which science can contribute. It is surely significant that *Time* magazine named Albert Einstein, the icon of modern science, as "Person of the Century." Many of those with the strongest confidence in reason's capacity for knowledge in science are also the most skeptical about the claims of religion.

[15]Baumer, *Religion and the Rise of Scepticism,* pp. 3-4.

group of itinerant teachers of rhetoric who exerted enormous influence in fifth-century B.C. Athens.[16] The chief Sophists were not natives of Athens but came from elsewhere—Protagoras from Abdera in Thrace, Gorgias from southern Sicily, Thrasymachus from Chalcedon—and they challenged the reigning assumptions in Athens by pointing out the rich diversity of beliefs and customs in the Mediterranean world. Through persuasive argumentation they forced Athenians to consider whether their beliefs and customs were based upon truth (according to nature, the way things are) or were merely the products of social convention. There was little question about the Sophists' answer, as reflected in the famous dictum of Protagoras: "Man is the measure of all things, of the things that are that they are, and of the things that are not that they are not."[17] The apparent implication is that each person understands the world individually from his or her (relative) perspective; there are no (or at least we have no access to) general universal truths. The Sophists were particularly skeptical about claims to religious knowledge or universal moral truths. Protagoras stated, "Concerning the gods I am not in a position to know either that (or how) they are, or what they are like in appearance; for there are many things that are preventing knowledge, the obscurity of the matter and the brevity of human life."[18]

So great was the impact of the Sophists that much of Plato's impressive philosophical work can be seen as a refutation of their views. But in spite of Plato's incisive response, skepticism was not eliminated and, in one of history's many ironies, Plato's Academy eventually became the home of Academic Skepticism. Prompted by an earlier Socratic observation—"All I know is that I know nothing"—Academic Skepticism developed arguments that undercut any attempt to establish knowledge based upon sense experience or reason.[19] Academic Skepticism flourished through the first century B.C. and finds expression in Cicero's *Academica* and *De natura deorum*.

An even more radical skepticism, known as Pyrrhonian Skepticism because of its identification with Pyrrho of Elis, advocated withholding judgments of any kind on all issues concerning which there are conflicting opinions.[20] The only surviving

---

[16]On the Sophists, see W. K. C. Guthrie, *A History of Greek Philosophy* (Cambridge: Cambridge University Press, 1969), vol. 3, pt. 1; and G. B. Kerferd, *The Sophistic Movement* (Cambridge: Cambridge University Press, 1981).

[17]Quoted in Guthrie, *History of Greek Philosophy*, p. 183.

[18]Quoted in Kerferd, *Sophistic Movement*, p. 165.

[19]Richard Popkin, *The History of Scepticism from Erasmus to Spinoza* (Berkeley and Los Angeles: University of California Press, 1979), p. xiii. See also Popkin, "Skeptics and Skepticism," in *The Encyclopedia of Religion*, ed. Mircea Eliade, vol. 13 (New York: Macmillan, 1987), pp. 341-43.

[20]Pyrrho was said to have accompanied Alexander the Great on his conquests through northern India and there to have encountered Indian religious ascetics (or "naked sophists" as the Greeks called them). There are tantalizing similarities between aspects of Pyrrhonism and Indian skeptical traditions, although any kind of dependence is impossible to establish. See J. J. Clarke, *Oriental Enlightenment: The Encounter Between Asian and Western Thought* (London: Routledge, 1997), p. 38.

texts of Pyrrhonian Skepticism are those included in Sextus Empiricus's third-century A.D. *Outlines of Pyrrhonism* and *Against the Dogmatists*. Pyrrhonism "was an ability, or mental attitude, for opposing evidence both pro and con on any question about what was non-evident, so that one would suspend judgment on the question. This state of mind then led to a state of *ataraxia,* quietude, or unperturbedness, in which the sceptic was no longer concerned or worried about matters beyond appearances."[21] With respect to religion, Pyrrhonian Skepticism refused even to answer the question "Do the gods exist?" on the grounds that we simply cannot know. And yet such skepticism was not regarded as incompatible with religious practice; following the prevailing religious customs was acceptable so long as one withheld judgment about the question of truth.

The tradition of Greek skepticism, especially Pyrrhonian Skepticism, had a profound effect upon European thought in the sixteenth and seventeenth centuries. The social, intellectual and religious ferment stimulated by the Renaissance and the Reformation, along with the brutal devastation of the Thirty Years War (1618–1648), with its strong religious overtones, left Europe increasingly fragmented and greatly diminished the traditional authority of the institutional Catholic church. But the new uncertainties extended far beyond the institutional church. An unintended consequence of the Reformation challenge to traditional Catholic authority structures was raising in a fresh way the perennial problem of criteria: Given the competing claims to religious authority and truth, how does one justify claims to religious truth? By what criteria does one distinguish between legitimate and illegitimate claims to truth? Significantly, the crisis of religious authority coincided with the rediscovery of ancient Greek and Roman skepticism and with fresh encounters with the strange cultures and religions of the New World.[22]

Sextus Empiricus's *Outlines of Pyrrhonism* was first translated into Latin in 1562, and it would be difficult to exaggerate the impact of Sextus upon subsequent intellectual history. Julia Annas and Jonathan Barnes state, "It was the rediscovery of Sextus and of Greek scepticism which shaped the course of philosophy for the next three hundred years."[23] Sextus persuasively presented all of the classical arguments for skepticism—the unreliability of our senses and the widespread disagree-

---

[21]Popkin, *History of Scepticism,* p. xv.

[22]See Popkin, *History of Scepticism,* chapters 1-2; Baumer, *Religion and the Rise of Scepticism,* pp. 96-111.

[23]Julia Annas and Jonathan Barnes, *The Modes of Scepticism: Ancient Texts and Modern Interpretations* (Cambridge: Cambridge University Press, 1985), p. 5. See also Charles B. Schmitt, "The Rediscovery of Ancient Skepticism in Modern Times," in *The Skeptical Tradition,* ed. Myles Burnyeat (Berkeley and Los Angeles: University of California Press, 1983), pp. 225-51; and Brian P. Copenhaver and Charles B. Schmitt, *Renaissance Philosophy* (New York: Oxford University Press, 1992), chapter 4.

ment among apparently reasonable people about the most basic issues—to undercut any claims to certain knowledge. Of special interest for our purposes is the effective use made of the appeal to differences across cultures to undermine beliefs about universal moral truth.[24]

The influence of Sextus is clearly evident in the 1580 publication of Michel de Montaigne's *In Defense of Raymond Sebond,* a masterful work in which the classical arguments for skepticism are marshaled in the service of faith.[25] Difficult questions of interpretation are involved here, but according to a common view, Montaigne's intention was to demonstrate the presumptuous illusions and pride of those who thought that human reason—apart from God's special revelation—could attain certainty in knowledge, and thus he represents what Terence Penelhum has called "skeptical fideism."[26] Certainty about theological matters is strictly a gift of faith and not the product of rational analysis. Human reasoning is dependent upon the senses, which are notoriously unreliable, and wise thinkers have disagreed on even the most basic issues. How then can we expect reason to produce certainty and knowledge? "All things produced by our reasoning and powers, whether true or false, are subject to doubt and debate. . . . Let us confess ingenuously that we acquire truth through God alone, and by faith, for it is not learned from nature and by our reason."[27]

Montaigne was a contemporary of Jean Bodin, and like his countryman, he was troubled by the problems posed by competing religious claims. But Montaigne did not see how reason could settle the question of which religious authority to recognize, and thus he held that each of us should simply accept that faith into which we are born. Rationally assessing the truth or falsity of various perspectives presupposes that we have access to nonarbitrary criteria for such assessment—something Montaigne denied.[28] Religious commitment is thus reduced to a matter of geography.

---

[24]See Annas and Barnes, *Modes of Scepticism,* pp. 151-71, for examples from Sextus and discussion of his use of this in argument. Other ancient writers influential in the early modern era included the Roman poet Lucretius, whose *On the Nature of Things* was a scathing attack upon popular religion as ignorant superstition, and Cicero, especially as the author of *The Nature of the Gods.* In the eighteenth century both Voltaire and David Hume drew from the writings of Lucretius and Cicero.

[25]See Michel de Montaigne, *In Defense of Raymond Sebond,* trans. Arthur H. Beattie (New York: Frederick Ungar, 1959).

[26]Terence Penelhum, "Skepticism and Fideism," in *Skeptical Tradition,* pp. 287-88. Popkin, *History of Scepticism,* chapter 3, adopts a similar perspective. For a contrasting view, which understands Montaigne to be rejecting Christian belief while still upholding Christianity for social and political purposes, see Alan Levine, "Skepticism, Self, and Toleration in Montaigne's Political Thought," in *Early Modern Skepticism and the Origins of Toleration,* ed. Alan Levine (New York: Lexington, 1999), pp. 51-75.

[27]Montaigne, *In Defense of Raymond Sebond,* pp. 67-68.

[28]See Popkin, *History of Scepticism,* p. 53.

Centuries before, Sextus had advanced a kind of cultural relativism that grew out of his observation of the very different beliefs and practices among peoples of the ancient world. Montaigne also appealed repeatedly to the sixteenth century's growing awareness of diversity of customs in the New World to undermine what he regarded as a misplaced confidence in reason. His most extensive treatment of the subject is in the remarkable essay "Of Cannibals," in which Montaigne claimed that "everyone gives the title of barbarism to everything that is not according to his usage; as, indeed, we have no other criterion of truth and reason than the example and pattern of the opinions and customs of the country wherein we live."[29]

> This sort of learned scepticism is made more persuasive by Montaigne, not only by quoting ancient authors, as previous sceptics had done, but by coupling the impact of the rediscovery of the ancient world with the discovery of the New World. On the other side of the Atlantic Ocean another cultural universe existed, with different standards and ideals. On what basis could we ever judge whether the outlook of the noble savages was better or worse than our own? The message that the merits of all human opinions are relative to the cultures in which they have been produced was put forth by Montaigne, as a new type of sceptical realization, one that was to have far-reaching effects even four centuries later.[30]

The appeal to cultural diversity to support skepticism was also made by Montaigne's friend and intellectual disciple the French priest Father Pierre Charron (1541–1603). Charron's *On Wisdom* (1603) was a systematic presentation of Pyrrhonian Skepticism and cultural relativism, ostensibly as part of a fideistic defense of Catholicism against Calvinism and unbelief. Montaigne and Charron thus illustrate the general trend at this time of appealing to cultural and religious diversity to undermine claims to universal truths. As Tullio Gregory puts it, Charron's skepticism "is a self-conscious response to the discovery of the multiplicity and the diversity of intellectual and moral worlds, to the new civilizations and religions that one could learn about by reading the reports of travellers who had explored the Far East and the New World."[31] Charron stated that reason is "capable of finding an appearance of rationality in anything, witness the fact that whatever is held to be impious, unjust, disgraceful in one place is pious, just, and honourable in another; one cannot name a single law, custom, or belief that is universally either approved or condemned."[32] Gregory observes that defenders of Christian orthodoxy began to

---

[29]Michel de Montaigne, "Of Cannibals," in *Montaigne: Collected Essays,* ed. Blanchard Bates, trans. Charles Cotton and W. Hazlitt (New York: Random House, 1949), pp. 77-78.

[30]Popkin, *History of Scepticism,* p. 53.

[31]Tullio Gregory, "Charron's 'Scandalous Book,' " in *Atheism from the Reformation to the Enlightenment,* ed. Michael Hunter and David Wooten (Oxford: Clarendon, 1992), pp. 89-90.

[32]Pierre Charron, *On Wisdom* 1.16.132, quoted in Gregory, "Charron's 'Scandalous Book,' " p. 92.

regard travel as a cause of libertinism and atheism, so effective was the experience of cultural and religious diversity in undermining traditional religious convictions.[33] Montaigne and Charron, then, illustrate not only the widespread skepticism of the sixteenth century but also the link between the growing awareness of diversity in the world and a resulting skepticism or relativism. As Brian Copenhaver and Charles Schmitt note, it was Montaigne who made relativism a modern problem in a supposedly Christian culture.[34]

No one understood more clearly the skeptical challenges posed by Sextus Empiricus, as mediated through Montaigne and Charron, than the great French mathematician and philosopher René Descartes (1596–1650).[35] Descartes's relentless search for certainty—his obsession with "clear and distinct ideas"—cannot be appreciated apart from the broader context of the deepening epistemological skepticism of seventeenth-century Europe. Against the skeptics, Descartes and other seventeenth-century rationalists held that we have a nonempirical and rational means of attaining truth and that the kind of certainty we have in mathematics can be secured in other domains as well. Philosophy, it was believed, along with the emerging sciences and mathematics, could provide a comprehensive system of knowledge in all fields. The rationalists' assumptions and agenda were enormously optimistic, and it did not take long for their views to come under severe attack.[36]

Modern Religious Skepticism

The legacy of classical skepticism found fresh and sophisticated expression in the work of the eighteenth-century Scottish philosopher David Hume (1711–1776). Hume's *A Treatise of Human Nature* (1739), initially published when he was only

---

[33]Gregory, "Charron's 'Scandalous Book,' " p. 91. On the relativizing effects of travel during the seventeenth century, see Paul Hazard, *The European Mind: 1680-1715* (London: Hollis & Carter, 1953), part 1, chapter 1.

[34]Copenhaver and Schmitt, *Renaissance Philosophy*, p. 346. Similarly Robert Solomon and Kathleen Higgins suggest that Montaigne, not Descartes, be considered the first modern philosopher. Robert C. Solomon and Kathleen M. Higgins, *A Short History of Philosophy* (New York: Oxford University Press, 1996), pp. 178-80.

[35]On the significance of Montaigne for understanding Descartes, see Popkin, *History of Scepticism*, chapter 3; Stephen Toulmin, *Cosmopolis: The Hidden Agenda of Modernity* (Chicago: University of Chicago Press, 1990), pp. 36-44; and E. M. Curley, *Descartes Against the Skeptics* (Cambridge: Harvard University Press, 1978), chapters 1-2.

[36]Richard Popkin notes that during the fifty-year period immediately after Descartes "the basic structure of the 'new' philosophy [Descartes's rationalism] was dissected, analyzed, and destroyed, leaving wounds of such magnitude that philosophy has never really recovered from them. The marvelous optimism with which Descartes launched the modern intellectual world was to be gradually so completely eroded during the second half of the seventeenth century that philosophy could carry on thereafter only by changing its character, and denying its previous role" (Richard Popkin, *The High Road to Pyrrhonism*, ed. Richard A. Watson and James E. Force [Indianapolis: Hackett, 1980], p. 12).

twenty-eight, sets out his empiricist epistemology, which maintains that all of the content of the mind is derived from experience and natural dispositions.[37] Hume distinguished between two faculties for belief formation—"reason" and "imagination." Imagination can be understood both as our ability to reproduce ideas based upon past experiences and as the seat of our propensities to form beliefs. In the latter sense, imagination is essentially "human nature," or our natural tendencies for belief formation. Whereas most philosophers emphasize the role of reason above natural propensities, Hume did precisely the opposite, arguing that reason alone is incapable of establishing even our most commonly accepted beliefs. He challenged, for example, the claim to knowledge about causal relationships between any two entities, stating that, although we naturally assume causality because of "nature and custom," it is impossible to demonstrate through reason any causal relationship.[38] Not only did Hume's attack present difficulties for the emerging disciplines of science but also it undercut popular contemporary moves in Christian apologetics that relied upon causality in arguments for God's existence.

For Hume, then, belief was not based upon rational considerations but rather was a product of our natural dispositions or propensities. Hume openly acknowledged the skeptical implications of this, admitting to being "ready to reject all belief and reasoning" and saying that he could "look upon no opinion even as more probable or likely than another."[39] Most of what we accept in ordinary life—confidence in reason to settle disputes, the reliability of memory, the reality of other minds, the reliability of the senses—are products, not of rational reflection, but rather of our natural dispositions to believe and act in certain ways. "Reason is, and ought to be, the slave of the passions, and can never pretend to any other office than to serve and obey them."[40] This should not, however, alter significantly how we go about our ordinary lives, for what reason is unable to deliver nature itself has produced.

> Most fortunately it happens that since reason is incapable of dispelling these clouds [of doubt], nature herself suffices for that purpose. . . . I dine, I play a game of backgammon, I converse and am merry with my friends; and when after three or four hours' amusement, I would return to these speculations, they appear so cold and strained and

---

[37]For helpful introductions to Hume's epistemology, see David Fate Norton, *David Hume: Common Sense Moralist, Skeptical Metaphysician* (Princeton, N.J.: Princeton University Press, 1982); and Barry Stroud, *Hume* (London: Routledge & Kegan Paul, 1977). The best treatment of the religious implications of Hume's epistemology is Keith Yandell, *Hume's "Inexplicable Mystery": His Views on Religion* (Philadelphia: Temple University Press, 1990).

[38]David Hume, *Enquiry Concerning Human Understanding*, 3rd ed., rev. P. H. Nidditch (Oxford: Clarendon, 1975), pp. 26-27.

[39]See David Hume, *A Treatise of Human Nature*, ed. L. A. Selby-Bigge (Oxford: Clarendon, 1965), pp. 268-69.

[40]Ibid., p. 415.

ridiculous that I cannot find in my heart to enter into them any farther. Here then I find myself absolutely and necessarily determined to live and talk and act like other people in the common affairs of life.[41]

Whereas sixteenth-century thinkers such as Montaigne regarded skepticism as an ally to faith, with Hume skepticism becomes aggressively anti-Christian. Hume returned repeatedly to the subject of religion, which he referred to as "the established superstition." In the notorious essay "Of Miracles" Hume launched a twofold attack upon the heart of contemporary apologetics: he argued, first, that even if a miracle were in principle possible we could never have sufficient evidence for believing that any given phenomenon is indeed a miracle and not simply an anomaly, and second, that in fact the available evidence for Christian miracles is deficient.[42] In sharp contrast to religious pluralists today, who hold that apparently incompatible truth claims from various religions need not mean that at least some of the claims are false, Hume bluntly stated, "In matters of religion, whatever is different is contrary." Applying this dictum to the question of miracles, Hume argued that various religions all appeal to miracles in support of their different claims, and since incompatible claims cannot all be true, the rival claims based upon such alleged miracles have a mutually canceling effect.[43]

The *Dialogues Concerning Natural Religion* (published posthumously in 1779) unleashed a penetrating attack upon natural theology in general and the teleological argument in particular. *The Natural History of Religion* (1757), an early effort in the history-of-religions genre, was Hume's attempt to provide an account of religion in strictly naturalistic (and highly unflattering) terms. While he recognized that religious belief was rooted in human nature—he spoke of a "universal propensity to believe in invisible, intelligent power" as "a general attendant of human nature"—Hume regarded religion as detrimental to both individual and social

---

[41]Ibid., p. 269.

[42]Hume, *Enquiry Concerning Human Understanding,* pp. 109-31. For discussion of Hume's attack on miracles, see Colin Brown, *Miracles and the Critical Mind* (Grand Rapids, Mich.: Eerdmans, 1984), chapter 4; and Keith Yandell, *Hume's "Inexplicable Mystery,"* chapter 15.

[43]Hume states: "[I]n matters of religion, whatever is different is contrary; and . . . it is impossible the religions of ancient Rome, of Turkey, of Siam, and of China should all of them, be established on any solid foundation. Every miracle, therefore, pretended to have been wrought in any of these religions (and all of them abound in miracles), as its direct scope is to establish the particular system to which it is attributed; so has it the same force, though more indirectly, to overthrow every other system. In destroying a rival system, it likewise destroys the credit of those miracles, on which that system was established; so that all the prodigies of different religions are to be regarded as contrary facts, and the evidences of these prodigies, whether weak or strong, as opposite to each other" (David Hume, "Of Miracles," in *David Hume: Writings on Religion,* ed. Antony Flew [La Salle, Ill.: Open Court, 1993], pp. 75-76).

well-being.[44] Sounding a theme that was to become prominent in later critiques of Christianity, Hume contended that monotheism (Christianity) was inherently intolerant whereas polytheism tended to be more tolerant of diverse views. "The intolerance of almost all religions, which have maintained the unity of God, is as remarkable as the contrary principle of polytheists."[45] The final words of Hume's *Natural History of Religion* bear striking resemblance to Cicero's conclusion of his *De natura deorum,* and they express concisely Hume's detached skepticism about religious claims:

> The whole [God's existence] is a riddle, an enigma, an inexplicable mystery. Doubt, uncertainty, suspense of judgment appear the only result of our most accurate scrutiny, concerning this subject. But such is the frailty of human reason, and such the irresistible contagion of opinion, that even this deliberate doubt could scarcely be upheld; did we not enlarge our view, and opposing one species of superstition to another, set them a quarreling; while we ourselves, during their fury and contention, happily make our escape into the calm, though obscure, regions of philosophy.[46]

Peter Gay portrays Hume as the prototypical Enlightenment figure, courageously embracing the implications of modern skepticism.

> [Hume] was willing to live with uncertainty, with no supernatural justifications, no complete explanations, no promise of permanent stability, with guides of mere probable validity; and what is more, he lived in his world without complaining, a cheerful Stoic. Hume, therefore, more decisively than many of his brethren in the Enlightenment, stands at the threshold of modernity and exhibits its risks and its possibilities. Without melodrama but with the sober eloquence one would expect from an accomplished classicist, Hume makes plain that since God is silent, man is his own master: he must live in a disenchanted world, submit everything to criticism, and make his own way.[47]

In this Hume exemplifies not only a powerful current within eighteenth-century intellectual life but also many today who remain deeply skeptical about the claims of religion.

Significantly, the critical philosophy of the German philosopher Immanuel Kant (1724–1804) was stimulated by a desire to respond to the skepticism of Hume.

---

[44]David Hume, "The Natural History of Religion," in *David Hume,* p. 181. On Hume's views of the relations among religion, human nature and morality, see Yandell, *Hume's "Inexplicable Mystery,"* pp. 25-35.

[45]Hume, "Natural History of Religion," pp. 146-47.

[46]Ibid., p. 182. Much earlier Cicero had concluded his *On the Nature of the Gods* with the following reflection: "This more or less is what I have to say about the nature of the gods: it is not my design to disprove [belief in the gods], but to bring you to understand how obscure it is and how difficult to explain" (Cicero, *De natura deorum,* trans. H. Rackham [New York: Putnam, 1933], p. 381).

[47]Peter Gay, *The Rise of Modern Paganism,* vol. 1 of *The Enlightenment: An Interpretation* (New York: W. W. Norton, 1966), p. 419.

Kant stands in a pivotal position in the history of Western thought, for while he clearly was a product of the eighteenth-century Enlightenment and in many ways exemplified its values and agenda, he also marks a transition into a new era in which Enlightenment assumptions about the universality and objectivity of reason were rejected in favor of relativism and perspectivism.

There is considerable irony in the fact that, although Kant's intention was to secure an epistemological foundation, in ethics as well as in other areas, for the sense of universality and necessity associated with the then-dominant Newtonian model of science, the actual effect of his thought was precisely the opposite.[48] Kant's most significant work, the *Critique of Pure Reason* (1781), was an attempt to determine the possibilities and limitations of reason, particularly with respect to the questions of metaphysics. Kant thought that the kind of objectivity and certainty we have in mathematics and the sciences—but which he thought we do *not* have in metaphysics, including theology—can be explained by reversing the traditional relation between the mind and extramental reality. Instead of supposing that the mind is passive and conforms to the nature of external objects, Kant suggested that the objects of knowledge actually conform in a significant way to the nature of the human understanding.

> Hitherto it has been assumed that all of our knowledge must conform to objects. But all attempts to extend our knowledge of objects by establishing something in regard to them a priori, by means of concepts, have, on this assumption, ended in failure. We must make trial whether we may not have more success in the tasks of metaphysics, if we suppose that objects must conform to our knowledge. This would better agree with what is desired, namely, that it should be possible to have knowledge of objects a priori, determining something in regard to them prior to their being given.[49]

His "Copernican revolution" in epistemology involved the thesis that the mind plays a determinative role in our knowledge by organizing and systematizing the sensory input presented to us. It does this by imposing concepts or categories for understanding (which are themselves part of the mind or noetic structure) upon the raw sense data received from outside of us, and in this way the mind deter-

---

[48]Good treatments of Kant's epistemology can be found in A. C. Ewing, *A Short Commentary on Kant's Critique of Pure Reason* (Chicago: University of Chicago Press, 1938); Stephen Korner, *Kant* (Hammondsworth, England: Penguin, 1955); and *The Cambridge Companion to Kant,* ed. P. Guyer (Cambridge: Cambridge University Press, 1992). For the implications of Kant's views for religion, see Allen Wood, *Kant's Moral Religion* (Ithaca, N.Y.: Cornell University Press, 1970); and *Kant's Philosophy of Religion Reconsidered,* ed. Philip J. Rossi and Michael Wreen (Bloomington: Indiana University Press, 1991).

[49]Immanuel Kant, preface to the second edition of *Critique of Pure Reason,* trans. Norman Kemp Smith (New York: St. Martin's, 1929), p. 22.

mines the particular form taken by our experience. Kant's views are highly original, and he developed them in a complex argument that we cannot explore here. But we might summarize his conclusions by noting that Kant thought his model enables us to account for the necessity and universality we find in Newtonian physics (and which he thought characterized ethics as well) since it is the human noetic structure itself, which Kant assumed was the same in all rational persons, that produces such concepts. However, this came at enormous cost, for in Kant's theory, knowledge of metaphysics (God, freedom, the immortality of the soul) is ruled out, since metaphysics deals with matters that are beyond the realm of possible experience. Our knowledge is restricted to the realm of possible empirical experience, or the phenomena (appearances); we have no knowledge of the noumena (the "things in themselves"), or that which is beyond possible experience.

Strictly speaking, then, we can have no knowledge of God, and in fact Kant subjected the traditional theistic arguments to a rigorous critique. Nevertheless, although we have no knowledge about God, we can be entitled on the grounds of "practical reason," or the implications from our experience of moral obligation, to postulate the reality of God.[50] Thus, although he rejected traditional metaphysics, Kant allowed for a kind of "rational faith" on moral grounds, and in *Religion Within the Limits of Reason Alone* (1793) he attempted a complete reinterpretation of orthodox Christianity in terms of moral theology, calling for a "pure, rational religion." Kant held that rational morality, and the natural religion arising from it, must be equally accessible and credible to all people irrespective of time and place. He thus explicitly rejected the "scandal of particularity" of orthodox Christianity, with its claims about special revelation and a particular incarnation, arguing that a religion based upon a particular revelation to a specific people cannot be normative for all people since it lacks the universality and necessity required of genuine religion.[51] What is required for a genuinely rational religion (which for Kant was the only acceptable kind) is universality, or equal access to the essential truths of religion for all people at all times and in all places, and the certainty of truth that comes only from reason and cannot be derived from the contingencies of history.

This "scandal of particularity," although in somewhat different form from that expressed by Kant, remains at the heart of today's dissatisfaction with the traditional Christian position on other religions. Moreover, Kant's universal moral reli-

---

[50]See Immanuel Kant, *Critique of Practical Reason,* trans. Lewis White Beck (New York: Macmillan, 1993), pp. 130-31.

[51]See Immanuel Kant, *Religion Within the Limits of Reason Alone*, trans. Theodore M. Greene and Hoyt H. Hudson (New York: Harper Torchbooks, 1934), pp. 100, 105, 110-11, 175-77. See also Allen Wood, "Kant's Deism," and Denis Savage, "Kant's Rejection of Divine Revelation and His Theory of Radical Evil"—both in *Kant's Philosophy of Religion Reconsidered*, pp. 1-21, 54-76.

gion has some strong similarities to certain forms of contemporary religious pluralism, such as that of John Hick, whose model we will consider in chapter seven.

Perspectivism

The impact of Kant upon subsequent Western thought has been enormous. However, in spite of his desire to steer clear of subjectivism, and in spite of his desire to preserve the objectivity, necessity and universality of our judgments about the world, Kant's philosophy actually had the opposite effect and was used even in his lifetime to support more relativistic and subjectivist views. Kant himself rejected the relativistic interpretations of his thought, contending that the constraints imposed upon our experience through the categories of the understanding, although in some sense "self-thought" *(selbstgedachte)*, nevertheless arise apart from merely our subjective contribution.[52] But both Kant's contemporaries and those who followed him, such as Fichte and Schelling, were often more impressed by the active part played by the understanding in ordering our experience than with Kant's attempts to secure the objectivity and universality of our judgments. Given this emphasis upon the active interpretive role of the mind, it was not a large step to question Kant's assumption that the mind, the noetic structure, functions in the same manner for all rational beings. From there it was again an easy move to conclude that there are many alternative ways of interpreting reality, and indeed to speak of alternative realities themselves.

But of course it is not only the mind that shapes our experiences. Exposure to the many peoples of the world stimulated new disciplines such as cultural anthropology and comparative religions, which emphasized the diversity of belief and practice and the roles of culture and religion in shaping perceptions of reality. A remarkable thinker who gave early expression to many themes that were to become entrenched in modern cultural relativism was Johann Gottfried Herder (1744–1803), who came under Kant's influence while studying at the University of Königsberg. Herder was greatly impressed by what he saw as the role of language in the development of consciousness, so that in a real sense we are creatures of our language and our world is "created" through language.[53] However, as Herder was well aware, this emphasis upon language, combined with the enormous diversity of the world's cultures and

---

[52]On the various interpretations of Kant with respect to the question of subjectivism and relativism, see Terry F. Godlove Jr., *Religion, Interpretation, and Diversity of Belief: The Framework Model from Kant to Durkheim to Davidson* (New York: Cambridge University Press, 1989), chapter 1.

[53]See James C. Livingston, *The Enlightenment and the Nineteenth Century*, vol. 1 of *Modern Christian Thought*, 2nd ed. (Upper Saddle, N.J.: Prentice-Hall, 1997), pp. 74-77; and Patrick Gardiner, "German Philosophy and the Rise of Relativism," *The Monist* 64 (April 1981): 138-54.

languages, has strong relativistic implications. Although a Lutheran minister, Herder recognized the implications of such relativism for religion.

> The import of Herder's cultural pluralism for religion and for Christianity emerge in his *First Dialogue Concerning National Religions* (1802). The conversation between two friends turns to the pathos of one ancestral religion being forced upon a foreign people, with the consequence of the people not only losing their own religion but raising the question of the legitimacy of the universal claims of Christianity. "Would you be annoyed," the one friend asks, "if I hold Christianity to be the religion *of all religions,* of all peoples?" The second friend replies, "What distinguishes peoples?" Both have to agree that it is language and the shaping of a distinct physiognomy of the corporate soul. But, then, does it not follow that the language in which the heart of a people speaks most deeply from its soul and most lovingly of the gods must be the language of its own mother tongue, the language "in which we love, pray, and dream"?[54]

Herder was deeply bothered by what he perceived as the destruction of indigenous cultural and religious patterns through missionary activities. As a pluralist, he called for recognizing the legitimacy and efficacy of each local religion; as a Lutheran, he still held, in some sense, to the distinctive truth of Christianity. Herder called for a change in attitude:

> In this way no foreign language or religion will tyrannize the language and character of another nation. . . . Every nation blossoms like a tree from its own roots. Christianity, that is, *the true conviction about God and human beings,* is nothing but the pure dew of heaven for all nations that, moreover, does not change any tree's character or type of fruit, and does not strip any human beings of their own nature. . . . Every religion would strive, according to and within its own context, to be better, no, the best of its kind without measuring and comparing itself to others. . . . I do not need to tell you that in this way the so-called propagation and expansion of Christianity would win a different character.[55]

It is not at all clear how the dual themes of the legitimacy of local religions and "Christianity [as] the true conviction about God and human beings" were to be harmonized.

The seeds of modern relativism,[56] which were sown by sixteenth-century think-

---

[54]Livingston, *Enlightenment and the Nineteenth Century*, p. 75.

[55]Johann Gottfried Herder, *First Dialogue Concerning National Religions*, as quoted in Livingston, *Enlightenment and the Nineteenth Century*, p. 77. Emphasis in original.

[56]Although today skepticism is often linked with relativism, the two are not identical. Skepticism typically denies, or at least calls into question, our capacity to know truth, but it does not necessarily deny that there is such a thing as truth. Relativism comes in many forms and degrees, but at its heart is the claim that truth (or knowledge or rationality norms) is not unchanging or universally normative for all peoples but rather is relative to particular contexts. Relativism does not deny the possibility of arriving at truth (indeed it assumes this), but it does deny that this "truth" is independent of particular contexts and applies to all people. On the relation between skepticism and relativism, see Paul K. Moser, Dwayne H. Mulder and J. D. Trout, *The Theory of Knowledge: A Thematic Introduction* (New York: Oxford University Press, 1998), pp. 8-14.

ers such as Montaigne, came to full fruition in the nineteenth and twentieth centuries. The new social sciences—sociology, psychology and cultural anthropology in particular—tended to undermine confidence in the truth of orthodox Christianity both by providing alternative, naturalistic explanations for religious phenomena that made no appeal to the supernatural dimension and by emphasizing the significance of "this worldly" contextual factors in conditioning religious belief and behavior. John Passmore observes, "The main tendency of nineteenth century thought was toward the conclusion that both 'things' and facts about things are dependent for their existence and their nature upon the operations of the mind."[57] In the twentieth century the influential works of Ludwig Wittgenstein, Willard V. O. Quine, Thomas Kuhn, Richard Rorty and many others have emphasized the inescapably perspectival nature of human belief and the difficulties of rising above our particular frameworks to attain objectivity in knowledge. The role of social and cultural factors in shaping (determining?) belief is central to the sociology-of-knowledge movement, which gained special prominence in the mid-twentieth century.[58] It has thus become virtually axiomatic in many academic circles that we cannot have access to reality itself but only to our varying, limited perspectives on reality, with no nonarbitrary way of determining which, if any, perspective is in fact true.

Pluralism and Tolerance

One of the striking features of modern, Western democratic societies is the priority they place upon tolerance. Alan Levine states, "Toleration is one of the most attractive and widespread ideals of our day. It is a cornerstone of liberalism, a key protection for both individual citizens and minority groups, and in general is the predominant ethos of all moral civilizations in the modern world."[59] Thus it is easy to forget that throughout history most societies have not been tolerant—at least with respect to diversity of religious belief and practice—as we understand the term today.

In popular consciousness tolerance and pluralism are linked in the perception that particularism (the view that one religion is distinctively true and thus normative for all peoples) is inherently intolerant of other faiths whereas pluralism, which holds that all religions are equally legitimate responses to the religious ultimate, is appropriately tolerant. Condemnation of particularism as immoral is often accompanied by the judgment that the nonmonotheistic religions of Asia have his-

---

[57]John Passmore, *A Hundred Years of Philosophy*, 2nd ed. (Hammondsworth, England: Penguin, 1966), p. 174.

[58]See Peter L. Berger and Thomas Luckmann, *The Social Construction of Reality* (Hammondsworth, England: Penguin, 1973).

[59]Alan Levine, "The Prehistory of Toleration and Varieties of Skepticism," introduction to *Early Modern Skepticism*, p. 1.

torically been much more tolerant of other faiths than has Christianity.[60] This perception, which was widespread among Enlightenment figures, has been skillfully cultivated by modern Asian thinkers such as Vivekananda, Radhakrishnan, and D. T. Suzuki in their apologetic for Eastern spirituality.[61]

Unfortunately, the historical record is considerably messier than this common assumption suggests. While it is certainly true that Christianity has a long and shameful history of mistreating religious others—Jews, Muslims and the indigenous peoples of the New World in particular—it must also be admitted that other religious traditions have their own legacies of religious violence. History is full of examples of brutal wars and fighting between various religious communities. Christians slaughtered Muslims and Jews. Muslims in turn massacred Christians and Jews. Muslims and Hindus fought bitterly in the Indian subcontinent. Baha'is have faced systematic persecution from Muslims. Even Buddhists—widely regarded as paragons of compassion, tolerance and serenity—have had their bloody internal feuds with fellow Buddhists, and more recently some Buddhists have attacked Christians in Sri Lanka. The dramatic rise during the past decades in the persecution of Christians at the hands of militant Hindus in India and of Muslims in Indonesia and Sudan, for example, should give pause to those who assume that Christians have a monopoly on religious intolerance.

Our primary concern here, however, is with the perceived connection between tolerance and pluralism, and I suggest that the link between the two depends upon a shift in the meaning of tolerance as well as some assumptions about the relation among religions. Traditionally, the notion of tolerance has included "the deliberate decision to refrain from prohibiting, hindering, or otherwise coercively interfering with conduct [or beliefs] of which one disapproves, although one has the power to do so."[62] As Jay Newman reminds us, tolerance is "the acceptance in one sense of something one does not accept in another sense."[63] Significantly, the modern call for tolerance emerged initially in response to the brutal wars of the sixteenth and seventeenth centuries, as recognition of the futility of trying to settle religious disputes by force led to a grudging willingness to allow for a measure of diversity of belief and practice. The classic case for religious tolerance—within carefully

---

[60]See, for example, Gustav Mensching, *Tolerance and Truth in Religion*, trans. H. J. Klimkeit (University, Alabama: University of Alabama Press, 1971).

[61]See the fine discussion on tolerance and inclusivism in Indian religious traditions in Wilhelm Halbfass, *India and Europe: An Essay in Understanding* (Albany: State University of New York Press, 1988), pp. 403-18.

[62]John Horton, "Toleration," in *Routledge Encyclopedia of Philosophy*, ed. Edward Craig (London: Routledge, 1998), 9:429-30.

[63]Jay Newman, *Foundations of Religious Tolerance* (Toronto: University of Toronto Press, 1982), p. 5.

defined limits—is found in John Locke's *A Letter Concerning Toleration* (1689) and *Two Treatises on Government* (1690).[64]

More recently, however, the meaning of tolerance has changed so that to be tolerant of another religion is often regarded as a matter of not saying anything negative about that religion's beliefs or practices. Thus, for example, Christians who hold that salvation is available only through Jesus Christ, and that sincere Hindus or Muslims are mistaken in their basic beliefs, are routinely dismissed as intolerant. Similarly attempts to persuade a Buddhist or Hindu to change fundamental religious commitments and to accept Jesus Christ as Lord are considered intolerant since this implies that there is something deficient in Buddhism or Hinduism. This redefinition of tolerance is closely related to the reign of "political correctness" during the 1980s and 1990s, for out of a legitimate desire to take seriously the diversity of our societies there developed the misguided expectation that one should never do or say anything that some other group might find offensive. And it was generally accepted that stating, or even implying, that sincerely held religious convictions are false or inadequate is offensive and thus intolerant.[65] The implication of this new understanding, however, is that any time one disagrees with someone else's sincerely held convictions one is necessarily intolerant.

But something else is also at work in the association of tolerance with pluralism, and that is rejection of the view that Christianity is distinctively true in favor of either a general skepticism or a more pluralistic view of religions. Interestingly, John Locke believed that Christianity was true and his arguments for religious tolerance were based upon the Christian notion of the significance of conscience (genuine belief could not be coerced but must come voluntarily) and the idea that the proper function of government is to maintain civil order, not to save souls. However, other early thinkers such as Michel de Montaigne, Jean Bodin, Baruch Spinoza, Pierre Bayle, Jean-Jacques Rousseau, Voltaire and Denis Diderot argued for religious tolerance in part because of skepticism—since we are unable to determine which, if any, religious tradition is true, prudence demands that we allow for diversity of belief and practice so long as the public welfare is not jeopardized.[66]

The call for a detached and enlightened tolerance, based upon our inability to

---

[64]Locke was unwilling to extend tolerance to Roman Catholics, because they owed their allegiance to a foreign power, or to atheists, since atheism would undermine the moral fabric of society. See John Locke, *A Letter on Toleration*, trans. J. W. Gough (Oxford: Clarendon, 1968), pp. 131-35; and Nathan Tarcov, "John Locke and the Foundations of Toleration," in *Early Modern Skepticism*, pp. 179-93.

[65]See the helpful discussion on this and related issues in S. D. Gaede, *When Tolerance Is No Virtue: Political Correctness, Multiculturalism, and the Future of Truth and Justice* (Downers Grove, Ill.: InterVarsity Press, 1993).

[66]See the collection of essays in *Early Modern Skepticism and the Origins of Toleration*.

determine the truth of rival religious claims, was given eloquent expression by the Enlightenment philosopher and dramatist Gotthold Ephraim Lessing in *Nathan the Wise* (1779). Set in Jerusalem during the Third Crusade in the twelfth century, this dramatic poem involves a dialogue between Nathan, a rich Jewish merchant, and Saladin, the Muslim ruler. When Saladin challenges Nathan by asking which of Judaism, Christianity or Islam is the true religion, Nathan replies by telling the parable of the three rings. A wealthy man in the East had a priceless ring with magical powers, so that whoever wore the ring and trusted in its strength was said to be loved by God and humanity. The ring was passed down from father to son through several generations, until it came to a man with three sons whom the father loved equally. The father promised each of the sons the ring, and rather than choose among them, he had a skillful jeweler make two other rings identical to the original and, upon his death, gave each son a ring. After discovering that there were now three rings, the brothers began to quarrel among themselves as to who had the true ring. In a telling phrase, which surely speaks for Lessing, Nathan says:

[The brothers] investigate, recriminate, and wrangle—all in vain—
Which was the true original genuine ring
Was undemonstrable—
Almost as much as now by us is undemonstrable
The one true faith.[67]

The brothers approach a wise judge to settle the controversy, but the judge responds by saying, "Let each believe his own to be the true and genuine ring" and live in a manner showing "humility, hearty forbearance, true benevolence, and resignation to the will of God."[68] Since we are unable to determine which religion is true, let each one—Jew, Christian and Muslim—continue in his religion but with a tolerant acceptance of the others as brothers.

Tolerance of religious diversity on the basis of skepticism is also at work today. Stan Gaede correctly points out that much of the multiculturalism agenda is driven, not by commitment to truth, but by "a deep moral and ontological relativism."[69] Skepticism about the possibility of determining truth in the midst of competing religious claims, the breakdown of traditional community life that had sustained common visions of the true and the good, rampant consumerism and individualism that feed upon pragmatism—all of this encourages an uncritical tolerance that refuses to make negative judgments about alternative beliefs and practices. "[T]olerance is a value that conforms nicely to the world we live in. Having

---

[67]Gotthold Ephraim Lessing, *Nathan the Wise*, ed. George Alexander Kohut, trans. Patrick Maxwell (New York: Bloch, 1939), p. 249.
[68]Ibid., pp. 252-53.
[69]Gaede, *When Tolerance Is No Virtue*, p. 37.

pretty much decided that truth is not attainable, we have made tolerance of a plurality of truths a virtue. Having no truths worth defending, we have made nondefensiveness a mark of distinction."[70]

Once the forces pushing for greater toleration of dissenting religious perspectives were unleashed, especially with the disestablishment of religion and the freedom of religious expression guaranteed in the American Constitution, modern societies were well on the way to an environment in which virtually all views, religious and irreligious, were to be protected. As Owen Chadwick puts it:

> From the moment that European opinion decided for toleration, it decided for an eventual free market in opinion. . . . Once concede equality to a distinctive group, you could not confine it to that group. You could not confine it to Protestants; nor, later, to Christians; nor, at last, to believers in God. A free market in some opinions became a free market in all opinions. . . . In Christian countries divided in religion, a free market in opinions became a reality; on grounds of conscience, and duty of toleration, and principles of equity, and expediency in a world of disagreement. In the leading countries of western Europe it finally became a reality between 1860 and 1890.[71]

Chadwick reminds us that the push for greater religious tolerance was not unrelated to what historians and sociologists have called the secularization of Western societies.

Secularization

Modern religious skepticism is often linked to the notion of secularization, so that, it is said, as Western societies became modernized they were increasingly secularized, resulting in widespread loss of confidence in Christian teachings and institutions. Yet few subjects are as problematic or controversial as that of secularization. On one level, what the secularization thesis is intended to explain seems clear enough. As James Davison Hunter puts it, the heart of secularization includes the notion that "being religious is not as easy as it used to be,"[72] or perhaps we should say that being religious *in a traditional sense* is not as easy as it used to be. But there is no consensus on the extent to which this is the case or just how it is that modern life renders traditional religion problematic. A thorough discussion of secularization is impossible, but we will highlight briefly the traditional thesis, noting some difficulties with it. We will then suggest some alternative ways of looking at religion in the modern world that help to account for the move toward religious pluralism. We will conclude

---

[70]Ibid., p. 27.

[71]Owen Chadwick, *The Secularization of the European Mind in the Nineteenth Century* (Cambridge: Cambridge University Press, 1975), pp. 21, 27.

[72]James Davison Hunter, *American Evangelicalism: Conservative Religion and the Quandary of Modernity* (New Brunswick, N.J.: Rutgers University Press, 1983), p. 4.

the chapter by pointing out several significant challenges to orthodox Christian faith posed by the culture of modernity's impact upon religious belief.

In the early twentieth century sociologists, drawing upon the work of pioneers in social theory such as Auguste Comte, Emile Durkheim, Max Weber and Karl Marx (arguably the most influential social theorist of the nineteenth century),[73] often assumed that modernization had an almost inevitable secularizing effect upon societies. Bryan Wilson, probably the most influential and respected advocate of the traditional model, defines secularization as "the process in which religious consciousness, activities, and institutions lose social significance. It indicates that religion becomes marginal to the operation of the social system, and that the essential functions for the operation of society become rationalized, passing out of the control of agencies devoted to the supernatural."[74] Wilson contends that secularization "relates essentially to a process of decline in religious activities, beliefs, ways of thinking, and institutions that occurs primarily in association with, or as unconscious or unintended consequences of, other processes of social structural change."[75] Similarly, Steve Bruce suggests that we think of secularization in terms of the following three interrelated changes: the decline of popular involvement with churches; the decline in scope and influence of religious institutions; and the decline in the popularity and influence of religious beliefs.[76] At least two crucial

---

[73]Owen Chadwick claims, "Marxism was the most powerful philosophy of secularization in the nineteenth century." Chadwick, *Secularization of the European Mind*, p. 66. On the early development of the secularization thesis, as well as an overview of contemporary debates over secularization, see Alan Aldridge, *Religion in the Contemporary World: A Sociological Introduction* (Cambridge: Polity, 2000), chapters 4-5. Secularization must be distinguished from secularism. Secularization is said to be an observable historical process affecting the place, significance and nature of religion in societies that undergo modernization. Thus historians and sociologists should be able to determine the extent to which, if at all, the process has taken place in a particular society, and their doing so is (or ought to be) independent of what they might happen to believe about religion. Secularism, on the other hand, is an ideology or way of thinking that not only is thoroughly naturalistic in its assumptions but also often is actively opposed to religious beliefs and institutions. It is possible, then, for a commited Christian to defend the secularization thesis as an accurate description of what has in fact happened in history without thereby endorsing the ideology of secularism. See David Lyon, *The Steeple's Shadow: On the Myths and Realities of Secularization* (Grand Rapids, Mich.: Eerdmans, 1985), pp. 30-32.

[74]Bryan Wilson, "Secularization," in *The Encyclopaedia of Religion*, ed. Mircea Eliade (New York: Macmillan, 1987), 12:160. See also Bryan Wilson, *Religion in Secular Society* (London: C. A. Watts, 1966); and Bryan Wilson, *Religion in Sociological Perspective* (Oxford: Oxford University Press, 1982). For critical discussion of the traditional model, see *Religion and Modernization: Sociologists and Historians Debate the Secularization Thesis*, ed. Steve Bruce (Oxford: Clarendon, 1982); David Martin, *A General Theory of Secularization* (Oxford: Blackwell, 1978); and David Lyon, "Rethinking Secularization: Retrospect and Prospect," *Review of Religious Research* 26 (March 1985): 228-43.

[75]Wilson, "Secularization," p. 159.

[76]Steve Bruce, *Religion in the Modern World: From Cathedrals to Cults* (New York: Oxford University Press, 1996), p. 26.

assumptions are operative here: first, that there is an identifiable prior state in which traditional religion flourished and in reference to which we can speak of its subsequent decline, and second, that the declining fortunes of religion are not merely accidental but are somehow related to the changes induced by modernization.

The prior state against which secularization is generally measured is premodern Europe, which was dominated by the Catholic Church. We must be careful here not to idealize the past by presuming that, for example, thirteenth-century Europe included a perfectly cohesive social order in which everyone not only was deeply committed to but also consistently acted upon clearly religious values and assumptions. Undoubtedly even at the height of Christendom there were varying degrees of confidence in Christian beliefs and considerable variance in consistency of practice with professed belief. However, even allowing for this, certain patterns can be discerned that suggest, at least in some areas, a decline in the significance of religious institutions, practices and beliefs. Whereas in premodern societies religion served as a kind of "sacred canopy," to use Peter Berger's language, giving integration and meaning to the diverse aspects of one's life,[77] there does seem to be in some societies a dissolution of this more or less unified religious worldview, and it is this that is said to constitute secularization.

The secularization thesis is most compelling when we use clearly measurable indicators such as church attendance and apply them to modern Europe. For example, after presenting statistical data on church attendance in several European countries during the nineteenth and twentieth centuries, Steve Bruce concludes, "Different countries show different rates of decline and different sorts of measures show different aspects of the change, but the direction of change in all indices of involvement in institutional religion is the same: downward."[78] Similarly Grace Davie observes that the data from 1981 and 1990 studies of the European Values System Study Group, which examined social and moral values as well as religious beliefs across fifteen European countries, reveal a significant shift away from traditional commitments and participation in institutional religion, especially among younger respondents.[79]

Although the secularization thesis has some plausibility when applied to northern Europe, it simply does not fit the patterns of modern societies elsewhere in the

---

[77]Peter Berger, *The Sacred Canopy: Elements of a Sociological Theory of Religion* (New York: Anchor, 1967).

[78]Bruce, *Religion in the Modern World*, p. 31.

[79]See the summary of data in Grace Davie, "Europe: The Exception That Proves the Rule?" in *The Desecularization of the World: Resurgent Religion and World Politics*, ed. Peter L. Berger (Grand Rapids, Mich.: Eerdmans; Washington: Ethics and Policy Center, 1999), pp. 65-83.

world.[80] The United States, for example, is surely one of the most modernized societies on earth, and yet religion flourishes in America. George Gallup reported in 1996 that one-third of the adult American population claimed to have experienced "a profound spiritual experience . . . which has been life changing."[81] In the same study 96 percent of Americans affirmed "belief in God or in a universal spirit," 84 percent of respondents said they believe Jesus Christ is God or the Son of God, and 43 percent said they attended church or synagogue within the past seven days. Amassing an impressive array of statistics, Roger Finke and Rodney Stark argue that the past fifty years is the most "churched" half century in U.S. history.[82] In a different study, Finke claims:

> The historical evidence on religion in the USA does not support the traditional model of secularization. . . . Instead, the evidence displays the vitality of religious organizations and the continuing commitment of individuals. Rather than declining, church adherence rates have shown a rapid increase in the nineteenth century and remarkable stability throughout the twentieth.[83]

Furthermore, Christian Smith and his colleagues have argued that, contrary to what the secularization thesis would lead us to expect, American evangelicalism is thriving and flourishing, not in spite of the pressures of modernity and pluralism but precisely because of these challenges.

> For decades, sociologists of religion have operated on the belief that cultural pluralism, social differentiation, and religious diversity within a society undermine the plausibility and strength of religion. The inherent logic of this approach—framed by the theoretical literature on modernization and secularization—has tended to produce fairly pessimistic portrayals of the fate of evangelicalism in the modern world. We have seen, however, that modern American evangelicalism is thriving. . . . American evangelicalism, we contend, is strong not because it is shielded against, but because it is—or at least perceives itself to be—embattled with forces that seem to oppose or threaten it. Indeed, evangelicalism, we suggest, thrives on distinction, engagement, tension, conflict, and threat.[84]

---

[80]For an excellent discussion of the inappropriateness of the secularization thesis for Southeast Asia, see T. N. Madan, "Secularism in Its Place," *Journal of Asian Studies* 46, no. 4 (1987): 747-59. On difficulties with the secularization thesis in modern Japan, see Winston Davis, *Japanese Religion and Society: Paradigms of Structure and Change* (New York: State University of New York Press, 1992), chapter 7; Jan Swyngedouw, "Secularization in a Japanese Context," *Japanese Journal of Religious Studies* 3, no. 4 (1976): 283-306; and Munakata Iwao, "The Ambivalent Effects of Modernization on Traditional Folk Religion of Japan," *Japanese Journal of Religious Studies* 3, nos. 2-3 (June-September 1976): 99-126.

[81]George Gallup Jr., *Religion in America: 1996* (Princeton, N.J.: Princeton Religion Research Center, 1996), p. 4.

[82]See Roger Finke and Rodney Stark, *The Churching of America, 1776-1990* (New Brunswick, N.J.: Rutgers University Press, 1992), pp. 15-16.

[83]Roger Finke, "An Unsecular America," in *Religion and Modernization*, pp. 163-64.

[84]Christian Smith et al., *American Evangelicalism: Embattled and Thriving* (Chicago: University of Chicago Press, 1998), p. 89.

Recent discussions have shown just how complex the entire subject is and how difficult it can be to derive any significant generalizations from the data. Much depends upon where one looks and how one measures religious vitality and commitment. Conflicting data from different modern societies have caused many—including Peter Berger, an early defender of the traditional model—to question the usefulness of the traditional secularization thesis. Moreover, Berger has rightly raised the question about how we choose cases that are to be normative: Why suppose that the decline in religious participation and belief in Sweden, for example, rather than the religious vitality of the United States, is normative for understanding modernization and religion?

> I think what I and most other sociologists of religion wrote in the 1960s about secularization was a mistake. Our underlying argument was that secularization and modernity go hand in hand. With more modernization comes more secularization. . . . Most of the world today is certainly not secular. It's very religious. So is the U.S. The one exception to this is Western Europe. One of the most interesting questions in the sociology of religion today is not, How do you explain the fundamentalism in Iran? but, Why is Western Europe different?[85]

Berger correctly observes that "the world today is massively religious, is *anything but* the secularized world that had been predicted (whether joyfully or despondently) by so many analysts of modernity."[86] One of the remarkable developments of the late twentieth century was the resurgence of religious expression throughout the world, manifesting itself in, for example, the many powerful revitalization movements (often lumped together misleadingly under the label *fundamentalism)* in Christianity, Hinduism and Islam; the astonishing number and variety of new religious movements; or the amorphous eclecticism of New Age teachings and practices. At the very least, the relationship between modernity and religion is considerably more complex than the secularization thesis suggests.

But even if we reject the traditional secularization thesis, it is clear that modernization has affected religious institutions and commitments. Institutionally, this can be seen in the social differentiation of modern life. With the increased complexity of modern societies, more specialized institutions have developed to handle specific functions previously carried out by religious insti-

---

[85]Peter Berger, "Epistemological Modesty: An Interview with Peter Berger," *Christian Century,* October 29, 1997, p. 974.
[86]Peter L. Berger, "The Desecularization of the World: A Global Overview," in *Desecularization of the World,* p. 9. Grace Davie reports that fully 70 percent of respondents to the European Values System Study Group claimed to believe in God, with the highest percentages in Ireland (96 percent) and Italy (83 percent) and the lowest in Sweden (15 percent) and France (57 percent). While the percentage of Europeans who do not profess to believe in God is significant, it is still a clear minority. Davie, "Europe," p. 70.

tutions.[87] Functions once performed by the church—marriage, education, health care, conflict resolution, funerals—are assumed by nonreligious institutions, which in turn come to dominate and define the public sector. Differentiation and social pluralization are also exemplified in the modern dichotomy between the public and private worlds.[88] The public sector becomes increasingly dominated by public secular institutions, with religious institutions, symbols and beliefs relegated to the private sphere. The public sector is ruled by an implicit consensus on what is true and what the proper procedures are for discovering truth, and educational institutions are expected to pass on to the young the knowledge our enlightened scientific age has uncovered. Since religion, in contrast to the hard sciences, does not enjoy any consensus concerning truth—witness the widely divergent truth claims made by the various religions and the lack of agreement as to how we might even settle such disputes—public expressions of religious belief are discouraged.[89] Whether we should continue to use the language of secularization to speak of these changes or find an alternative model is something that, fortunately, we do not need to resolve here.

From Religion to Spirituality

The culture of modernity does place significant pressure upon traditional religious belief and practice. It is not so much that modernity causes believers to become atheists but rather that what is believed and the manner in which religious commitments are expressed change. This is most apparent with the more controversial and publicly offensive beliefs, such as belief in hell or the exclusivity of salvation through Jesus Christ. Christian teaching on hell has never been particularly popular, but it was widely accepted in the church up until modern times, and in the medieval world it was an accepted part of the broader worldview of most Europeans. No longer. Belief in hell and damnation is routinely dismissed today as a vestige of a less sophisticated era. Writing a half century ago, the atheist philosopher Bertrand Russell captured the ethos of the times when he quipped, "Hell is neither so certain nor so hot as it used to be."[90]

---

[87]See Roy Wallis and Steve Bruce, "Secularization: The Orthodox Model," in *Religion and Modernization*, pp. 12-13; and Peter Berger, Brigitte Berger and Hansfried Kellner, *The Homeless Mind: Modernization and Consciousness* (New York: Vintage, 1973), chapter 3.

[88]See Berger et al., *Homeless Mind*, p. 80; and Anthony Giddens, *Modernity and Self-Identity: Self and Society in the Late Modern Age* (Stanford, Calif.: Stanford University Press, 1991), p. 150.

[89]See Stephen Carter, *The Culture of Disbelief: How American Law and Politics Trivialize Religious Devotion* (New York: Basic, 1993); and Richard John Neuhaus, *The Naked Public Square: Religion and Democracy in America* (Grand Rapids, Mich.: Eerdmans, 1984).

[90]Bertrand Russell, *Why I Am Not a Christian* (New York: Simon & Schuster, 1957), p. 195. A remarkably high percentage of Americans still affirm belief in some kind of judgment and hell. A 1996 study by Gallup found that 73 percent of American respondents still believe in hell, although

Similarly, the traditional beliefs about the uniqueness of Jesus Christ as the only Lord and Savior for all humankind have been the subject of intense debate in recent years. The pressures today against this kind of exclusivism are enormous. Reflecting upon the results of his study of college and seminary students in the 1980s, James Davison Hunter observed that "the exclusivism and finality of the Christian soteriology is also the single most socially offensive aspect of Christian theology; the single most important source of contention between Christians and non-Christians. . . . In the face of intense religious and cultural pluralism in the past century, the pressures to deny Christianity's exclusive claims to truth have been fantastic."[91]

Along with these changes are what Roof calls the "soft" undercurrents of change in religious expression. For example, he observes that "popular discourses about 'religion' and 'spirituality,' about the 'self' and 'experience,' about 'God' and 'faith' all point to subtle—but crucially important—shifts in the meaning of everyday religious life."[92] Significantly, fewer people are comfortable with the language of "religion," preferring to speak instead of "spirituality." More than merely a semantic switch is at work here, for the two terms signify different ways of thinking about and responding to the issues. *Religion* connotes rigid, authoritarian, oppressive institutions; dogmatism and lack of openness to alternative perspectives; and cold formalism or ritualism. *Spirituality,* by contrast, suggests flexibility and creativity; tolerance and respect for alternative insights from all peoples and cultures; room for doubt and searching; and an emphasis upon personal experience. It is hardly surprising, then, that people readily admit to having deep interest in spirituality while carefully distancing themselves from religion.

This shift is nicely charted for us by Robert Wuthnow in his excellent work *After Heaven: Spirituality in America Since the 1950s.*[93] Wuthnow argues that the last half of the twentieth century has witnessed massive changes in spiritual beliefs and practices. He suggests that "a traditional spirituality of inhabiting sacred places has

---

we are not told what they understand by the term. Also, 80 percent expect to be called before God on judgment day to answer for their sins. However, there does not seem to be much anxiety over this prospect as fully 77 percent rate their chances of going to heaven as excellent or good. Gallup, *Religion in America*, p. 22.

[91]James Davison Hunter, *Evangelicalism: The Coming Generation* (Chicago: University of Chicago Press, 1987), p. 34. A 1994 Gallup Youth Survey found that the majority of teenagers agree very much (29 percent) or somewhat (35 percent) with the statement that "all religions are about equally good." Only 35 percent disagreed with this assertion (cited in Gallup, *Religion in America,* p. 45). Similarly Roof found in his research on American Baby Boomers and religion that just over one-fourth of self-identified evangelicals agreed that "all the religions of the world are equally true and good" (Roof, *Spiritual Marketplace*, p. 84).

[92]Roof, *Spiritual Marketplace*, pp. 3-4.

[93]Robert Wuthnow, *After Heaven: Spirituality in America Since the 1950s* (Berkeley and Los Angeles: University of California Press, 1998).

RELIGION & SPIRITUALITY IN THE CULTURE OF MODERNITY

given way to a new spirituality of seeking—that people have been losing faith in a metaphysic that can make them feel at home in the universe and that they increasingly negotiate among competing glimpses of the sacred, seeking partial knowledge and practical wisdom."[94] The shift in popular discourse from "religion" to "spirituality" is captured nicely in Wuthnow's perception of a transition from a spirituality of "dwelling" or "place" to a spirituality of "seeking" or "journey."[95]

By spirituality of dwelling or place, Wuthnow means an orientation that links spirituality to participation in institutional religion and is marked by sharply drawn symbolic boundaries. Spirituality is indicated by membership in the organization and "being there," so that "if one is faithful in showing up for prayers or singing the right hymns or attending services, then one is part of the community that God blesses."[96] Spirituality of place flourishes in times of social and cultural stability and cohesion and found clearest expression in the United States during the 1950s.[97]

With the cultural upheaval of the 1960s, however, America experienced a sharp move away from a spirituality of place to a spirituality of seeking or journey. "The 1960s began with Christian theologians declaring that God was dead; it ended with millions of Americans finding that God could be approached and made relevant to their lives in more ways than they had ever imagined."[98] Interest in spirituality continued unabated in the next three decades, with the 1980s and 1990s distinguished by the eclecticism of the New Age movement and the popular fascination with angels and miracles. The new spirituality of seeking views the spiritual life as an ongoing journey or quest, with the process as important as the destination. Spirituality here is more ambiguous, with vague and open boundaries and loose connections, if any, with religious institutions. Eclecticism and openness to diversity on many levels is the operative principle. Doubt and uncertainty are embraced, and truth is personalized.

Spirituality of seeking fits nicely in an age marked by uncertainty and cultural upheaval, especially when such uncertainties call into question one's own identity. Grand metaphysical narratives are replaced with more subjective, personal narratives of exploration. "People who are faced with a dizzying array of choices and who experience so much uncertainty and change that they must negotiate their relationships, if not their very identities, are likely to find it easier to imagine that the sacred manifests itself at odd times and in less predictable ways."[99] Wuthnow

---

[94]Ibid., p. 3.
[95]Wuthnow's discussion of the spirituality of seeking or journeying parallels Roof's depiction of the "quest culture."
[96]Wuthnow, *After Heaven*, p. 41.
[97]Ibid., chapter 2.
[98]Ibid., p. 53.
[99]Ibid., p. 7.

rightly links the rise of the spirituality of seeking with the emphasis in the 1960s upon "freedom of choice" and consumerism. "The freedom that living in a secure community of like-minded individuals offered was gradually replaced by a freedom to exercise choice in a marketplace of ideas and lifestyles. Freedom of choice was attractive to those who in fact were confronted with an immense array of alternatives."[100]

One of the implications of this is that religious commitment is no longer automatic. Multiple religious options present the opportunity—or rather the necessity—for choice. As Peter Berger observes:

> Cultural plurality is experienced by the individual, not just as something external—all those people he bumps into—but as an internal reality, a set of options present in his mind. In other words, the different cultures he encounters in his social environment are transformed into alternative scenarios, options, for his own life. The very phrase "religious preference" (another American contribution to the language of modernity!) perfectly catches this fact: The individual's religion is not something irrevocably given, a *datum* that he can change no more than he can change his genetic inheritance; rather, religion becomes choice, a product of the individual's ongoing project of world and self-construction.[101]

The contours of one's worldview can no longer simply be taken for granted as part of one's nature and identity, received from others. Whether one is to be religious at all and, if so, how one expresses religious commitments are increasingly matters of choice.

But the possibility of choice, while providing opportunities, also raises perplexing questions: Given the many different, conflicting religious alternatives, and given the cacophony of voices claiming religious authority, how is one to know which path to follow? On what basis is one to choose among the various options? In contexts marked by diversity and religious skepticism, choice is increasingly based upon pragmatic factors. Religious decisions are made much like those in other domains. As Berger notes, "There comes to be a smooth continuity between consumer choices in different areas of life—a preference for this brand of automobile as against another, for this sexual lifestyle as against another, and finally a decision to settle for a particular 'religious preference.' "[102]

What Wuthnow calls the spirituality of seeking, or what Roof calls the quest culture, is closely related to the late-twentieth-century preoccupation with the self. The uncertainties of modern life remove many of the stabilizing factors that help to

---

[100]Ibid., 83.

[101]Peter Berger, *A Far Glory: The Quest for Faith in an Age of Credulity* (New York: Anchor, 1992), p. 67.

[102]Peter Berger, *The Heretical Imperative: Contemporary Possibilities of Religious Affirmation* (New York: Doubleday, 1979), p. 17.

define the self, so it is not surprising to see a heightened focus upon the language of self and therapy in the late modern period.[103] Roof remarks, "The real story of American religious life in this half-century is the *rise of a new sovereign self* that defines and sets limits on the very meaning of the divine."[104] The loss of transcendence and the accompanying focus upon self and this-worldly ends can be seen clearly in what Paul Heelas calls the "Self-spirituality" of the New Age movement.[105] Similarly Steve Bruce notes that, although the New Age movement often presents itself as countercultural or postmodern, it in fact exemplifies the individualism and consumerism of modernity:

> [T]here is one sense in which the New Age is a perfect product of its time: an exemplification of modernity rather than a rejection of it. It is the acme of consumerism. It is individualism raised to a new plane. The eclecticism of the New Age is not just a matter of being tolerant of behavioural differences or of supposing that we all have an equal right to act as we wish provided it does not harm others. It is going further than that to suppose not only that we can all discern truth, but that what we all variously discern is true. The individual consumer is not only the final arbiter of what he or she wants to believe and practise but also the final arbiter of truth and falsity. It is individualism taken to the level of epistemology, so that in place of the sectarian arguments over which revelation best embodied the one truth, there is complete relativism.[106]

These shifts in religious expression and commitment have obvious implications for religious pluralism. The notion that one religion is true, and that others that are incompatible with it are false, makes little sense in a free market of religions. Truth (if indeed one even continues to think in terms of truth) is understood in pragmatic terms that focus upon personal experience and benefits. One does not expect a particular religion to provide objectively true answers to basic questions about human origins and destiny, answers that apply to all people in all cultures at all times. What counts is whether the spiritual practices meet the needs (desires?) of the practitioner. Each person must discover for himself or herself what is right and best, recognizing that the journey to such discovery might take strange turns and draw upon a variety of traditions.

---

[103]Many writers have called attention to this feature of modern life. See, for example, Craig Gay, *The Way of the (Modern) World: Or, Why It's Tempting to Live As If God Doesn't Exist* (Grand Rapids, Mich.: Eerdmans, 1998); Christopher Lasch, *The Culture of Narcissism: American Life in an Age of Diminishing Expectations* (New York: Warner, 1979); David F. Wells, *No Place for Truth: Or, Whatever Happened to Evangelical Theology?* (Grand Rapids, Mich.: Eerdmans, 1993); and David F. Wells, *God in the Wasteland: The Reality of Truth in a World of Fading Dreams* (Grand Rapids, Mich.: Eerdmans, 1994).

[104]Roof, *Spiritual Marketplace*, p. 130. Emphasis in the original.

[105]Paul Heelas, *The New Age Movement: The Celebration of Self and the Sacralization of Modernity* (Oxford: Blackwell, 1996), p. 2.

[106]Bruce, *Religion in the Modern World*, pp. 221-22.

Modernity's Challenges to Christian Faith

There can be little doubt that modernization has had many positive effects. The remarkable spread of the gospel throughout the nineteenth and twentieth centuries, so that Christianity today is well established around the world, would have been impossible apart from technological advances in transportation, medicine and communication. Furthermore, although modernization has had the effect of undermining aspects of traditional Christianity in the West, the destabilizing forces of modernity have also worked to the advantage of Christian faith in some non-Western societies by weakening traditional religious and social constraints, thus enabling Christianity to become a genuine alternative.

But whatever its benefits, the challenges that the culture of modernity poses for Christian faith are formidable. The values and assumptions associated with the culture of modernity, along with some of the institutions of modern societies, tend to reinforce perspectives that conflict sharply with orthodox Christian belief and practice. We will note in particular three challenges to which the church must give careful attention in coming decades. The first is simply the perennial issue of religious skepticism. The idea that we can know religious truth, that fundamental questions about God's existence, nature and relation to humankind can be answered with any degree of intellectual satisfaction, strikes many today as naive. Religious skepticism is especially pronounced in the academy. Although the academic study of religion is popular and respectable, to suggest that we actually take seriously the truth claims implicit in religious beliefs and behavior is to invite incredulity.

But not all skeptics about traditional Christian faith dismiss religion altogether, for religious skepticism can be remarkably selective in its application. While many remain skeptical about the claims to exclusive truth on the part of any given religion, there is often a striking credulity toward religion in general. Thus, although the particular claims of a specific religion might be rejected, there is a sense that the religions (plural) are not entirely delusory but are somehow all in touch with spiritual realities. And this leads to the challenge of religious pluralism, which strikes at the central Christian affirmation of the distinctiveness and exclusivity of Jesus Christ as the one Lord and Savior for all peoples. The notion that one particular religious figure and one religious perspective can be universally valid and normative for all people in all cultures is widely dismissed today as morally and intellectually untenable in our pluralistic world.

But there is yet a third challenge to Christian faith. Not long ago it was generally accepted in the West, even among non-Christians, that Christianity and Jesus Christ were in some sense privileged and superior to other religious traditions. No longer. Since the eighteenth century, there have been those who have deliberately looked to the East for alternatives to Christianity and Western cultural traditions. What was earlier a small but persistent stream of thinkers looking East has today grown into a powerful current that includes not only increasing numbers of academics but also influential leaders in popular culture.

It is not only Westerners who are attracted to the wisdom of the East; Eastern thinkers are also rediscovering in their ancient heritage what they find lacking in the West. Hindus such Sarvepalli Radhakrishnan, and Buddhists such as Gunapala Dharmasiri and Masao Abe, have carefully studied Western thought and Christian theology and have rejected both in favor of traditional Eastern perspectives. They represent a growing movement, including Eastern and Western intellectuals, that is looking to Eastern religious and philosophical traditions for answers not found in Western paradigms. Although their impact upon society at large is still modest, their influence upon popular culture can be expected to increase in coming decades, given globalization and the increasing influence of Eastern views in academic sectors. Therefore, here is a fresh challenge to Christian faith: Even if in principle it is granted that one religious tradition might be superior to the rest, why should we assume that Christianity is in this privileged position? After all, why Jesus and not the Buddha? The effectiveness of Christian witness in our pluralistic world depends in part upon the church's response to these issues.

5

JOHN HICK'S
JOURNEY TO PLURALISM

If we define salvation as being forgiven and accepted by God because of the atoning death of Jesus, then it is a tautology that Christianity alone knows and teaches the saving truth that we must take Jesus as our lord and saviour, plead his atoning death, and enter into the church as the community of the redeemed, in which the fruits of the Spirit abound.

JOHN HICK, *A Christian Theology of Religions*

Christianity's implicit or explicit claim to a unique superiority, as the central focus of God's saving activity on earth, has come to seem increasingly implausible within the new global consciousness of our time.

JOHN HICK, *The Metaphor of God Incarnate*

No one has done more to champion the cause of religious pluralism within the Western academic world than John Hick. One of the most influential philosophers of religion and theologians of the twentieth century, Hick has, since the late 1970s, been an indefatigable apologist for pluralism. We will conclude part one and our consideration of the historical and cultural factors leading to religious pluralism by looking at the career of John Hick, especially the transition in his thought from Christian orthodoxy to radical pluralism.

John Hick is a prolific writer who has made significant contributions to philosophy, religious studies and theology. Whereas many academics devote their entire careers to working within fairly narrow confines, establishing their reputations by writing on one or two major issues, Hick's writings cover an amazing variety of subjects. Hick has contributed to discussions in religious epistemology, theodicy, Christology and religious pluralism to the extent that—whether one agrees with him or not—serious work in any of these areas cannot ignore his views, and indeed more often than not the nature of the debates themselves have been influenced by his pen. One way to study developments in philosophy of religion and theology in the West during the past half century is to review Hick's writings, beginning with his first publication in 1952,[1] as well as the many responses they stimulate. For in Hick's writings we see reflected the major issues and turning points in philosophical theology over the past five decades.

There is considerable irony in the fact that, although he is well known today as a radical pluralist, earlier in his career Hick distinguished himself as an articulate apologist for Christian orthodoxy at a time when philosophy was aggressively hostile to religion. We will examine Hick's model of religious pluralism in some detail in chapter seven, but it might be instructive here to consider briefly his journey to pluralism, since some of the factors instrumental in Hick's theological changes are also at work on a more popular level among many today.

Any division of a life as rich and productive as Hick's into distinct stages will be somewhat arbitrary, but his interests and changes in perspective over time lend themselves to a threefold distinction among early, middle and later stages. The early stage was marked by theological convictions that were broadly orthodox and philosophical interests in religious epistemology that were developed by way of response to the sharp critiques of religious belief so influential in the 1950s and 1960s. The second stage was characterized by a greater degree of theological questioning and significant movement away from orthodoxy on several issues. The third stage finds Hick making a clear break with orthodoxy and fully embracing religious pluralism. In reviewing these transitions we will highlight Hick's views in religious epistemology and Christology, for it is his conclusions in these areas that shape his later model on religious pluralism.

Beginnings: The Epistemological Framework

John Hick was born in Scarborough, Yorkshire, England, in 1922. Although as a child he was not particularly involved in the institutional church, Hick, when reflecting later upon his early years, writes that he has always had "a rather strong sense of the reality of God as the personal and loving lord of the universe, and of life as having a meaning within God's purpose."[2] At the age of eighteen, while a law student at Uni-

---

[1]John Hick, "The Will to Believe: William James's Theory of Faith," *London Quarterly & Holborn Review,* October 1952, pp. 290-95.

[2]John Hick, *God Has Many Names* (Philadelphia: Westminster Press, 1980), p. 14. Hick has provided autobiographical reflections on his theological and intellectual career in several writings, including "A Spiritual Journey," in *God Has Many Names,* pp. 13-28; "Three Controversies," in *Problems of Religious Pluralism* (New York: St. Martin's, 1985), pp. 1-15; "A Personal Note," in *Disputed Questions in Theology and the Philosophy of Religion* (New Haven, Conn.: Yale University Press, 1993), pp. 139-45; and "A Pluralist View," in *Four Views on Salvation in a Pluralistic World,* ed. Dennis L. Okholm and Timothy R. Phillips (Grand Rapids, Mich.: Zondervan, 1995), pp. 29-39. Helpful overviews of Hick's theological career can be found in Paul Badham, "The Philosophical Theology of John Hick," in *A John Hick Reader,* ed. Paul Badham (Philadelphia: Trinity Press International, 1990), pp. 1-14; and Paul R. Eddy, "John Hick's Theological Pilgrimage," in *Proceedings of the Wheaton Theology Conference: The Challenge of Religious Pluralism, An Evangelical Analysis and Response* (Wheaton, Ill.: Wheaton Theology Conference, Wheaton College, 1992), pp. 26-38.

versity College, Hull, Hick "underwent a spiritual conversion in which the whole world of Christian belief and experience came vividly to life, and I became a Christian of a strongly evangelical and indeed fundamentalist kind."[3] Hick states that at this time, "I accepted as a whole and without question the entire evangelical package of theology—the verbal inspiration of the Bible; Creation and Fall; Jesus as God the Son incarnate, born of a virgin, conscious of his divine nature, and performing miracles of divine power; redemption by his blood from sin and guilt; Jesus' bodily resurrection, ascension, and future return in glory; heaven and hell."[4]

He then transferred to the University of Edinburgh, where he graduated with first class honors in philosophy in 1948. While at Edinburgh, Hick was active in the Bible studies and prayer meetings of the Evangelical Union. However, his studies were interrupted by service in World War II (as a pacifist, he served in the ambulance unit in Egypt and Greece), and upon his return to Edinburgh after the war, Hick found that he was no longer comfortable with the more conservative nature of the Evangelical Union. He began asking questions about the Bible and Christian belief, but rather than finding the answers he sought, he felt that the questions themselves were unwelcome. Thus, he says, "I drifted apart from the conservative evangelical student movement, though continuing for many years to be what I would now describe as theologically conservative."[5]

Hick went on for graduate studies, completing the D.Phil. in religious epistemology at Oxford in 1950, then pursuing theological studies at Cambridge. For three years he served as pastor of the Belford Presbyterian Church (now United Reformed Church), Northumberland. He then moved to the United States for his first teaching position, in philosophy of religion at Cornell University. In 1959 Hick moved to Princeton Theological Seminary as the Stuart Professor of Christian Philosophy, where he remained until 1964. Shortly after his move to Princeton, Hick was embroiled in theological controversy as he attempted to transfer his ministerial credentials from the Presbytery of Berwick in England to the Presbytery of New Brunswick, in the United States, of the United Presbyterian Church. Hick's questioning of traditional Presbyterian beliefs such as the predestination of many to eternal hell, the verbal inspiration of the Bible and the virgin birth of Jesus resulted in his credentials not being accepted within the New Brunswick presbytery.[6] Theological controversy, in one form or another, was to follow Hick throughout his academic life.

Hick's approach to the epistemology of religion has remained fundamentally

---

[3]Hick, *God Has Many Names*, p. 14.
[4]Hick, "Pluralist View," p. 30.
[5]Ibid., p. 32.
[6]See Hick, "Three Controversies," pp. 1-4.

consistent throughout his long career. He set out the basic framework in his first book, published in 1957 as *Faith and Knowledge,* and has not significantly modified it since.[7] The immediate context of the book was the challenge to Christian faith posed by the legacy of logical positivism, an influential movement associated with the Vienna Circle, a group of philosophers, physicists and mathematicians who met regularly in Vienna in the 1920s.[8] Logical positivism was inspired by radical empiricism and verificationism, and it dominated the Anglo-American philosophical world throughout the 1930s and 1940s. Positivism was best known for its notorious "verifiability criterion of meaning," which was intended to discriminate between "cognitively meaningful" (genuinely informative) statements and those that, although appearing to be informative about the nature of reality, were literally "meaningless." Only statements that satisfied this criterion could be considered cognitively meaningful and thus either true or false. Although it proved impossible to formulate an acceptable version of the verifiability criterion of meaning—and this failure resulted in the demise of the movement by the 1960s—the central idea was that genuinely meaningful or informative statements must, at least in principle, be capable of being verified or falsified by some specifiable experiences. The clear implication from this requirement was that most of metaphysics and ethics (including theology) was cognitively meaningless or uninformative about reality. Religious utterances, whatever else they might be doing, were not making statements about reality that were true or false.[9]

It is difficult for us from our vantage point today to appreciate the magnitude of the challenge that logical positivism posed to Christian thinkers in the 1940s and 1950s. Christian theism was fighting for its very life in the academy. Positivism presented a distinctive challenge, for whereas earlier critics had argued against the truth of Christian belief, the positivists claimed that utterances about God, sin and the afterlife were not even the kind of statements that *could* be true or false. Unless

---

[7]John Hick, *Faith and Knowledge* (Ithaca, N.Y.: Cornell University Press, 1957). A second, revised edition followed in 1966, also published by Cornell University Press.

[8]For helpful introductions to logical positivism, see A. J. Ayer, ed., *Logical Positivism* (Glencoe, Ill.: Free Press, 1959); and Oswald Hanfling, *Logical Positivism* (New York: Columbia University Press, 1981). For its impact upon theology, see Malcolm L. Diamond and Thomas V. Litzenburg Jr., eds., *The Logic of God: Theology and Verification* (Indianapolis: Bobbs-Merrill, 1975); and R. S. Heimbeck, *Theology and Meaning: A Critique of Metatheological Skepticism* (Stanford, Calif.: Stanford University Press, 1969).

[9]The logical positivists were consciously following David Hume, who in a famous passage made much the same point 150 years earlier. "If we take in our hand any volume of school metaphysics, for instance, let us ask 'Does it contain any abstract reasoning concerning quantity or number?' No. 'Does it contain any experimental reasoning concerning matters of fact and existence?' No. Commit it then to the flames; for it can contain nothing but sophistry and illusion" (David Hume, *Enquiries Concerning Human Understanding and Concerning the Principles of Morals*, ed. L. A. Selby-Bigge, 3rd ed. [Oxford: Clarendon, 1975], p. 165).

theists could show that such statements met the verifiability criterion, "God talk" was to be dismissed as uninformative about reality (though perhaps psychologically comforting or ethically motivating). Theologians panicked and scrambled about madly, trying to appease their critics and salvage their calling. Some philosophers and theologians accepted the positivists' conclusions and reinterpreted religious statements in "noncognitivist" terms, so that religious statements (including doctrinal formulations) were regarded as not making claims that were either true or false but rather were serving other, noncognitive functions.[10]

It was within this intellectual context that John Hick began his career, responding to the positivists in defense of orthodox Christian theism. Although we cannot explore Hick's religious epistemology in depth here, we should mention several themes from *Faith and Knowledge* that have continued to shape his later views on religious pluralism.[11] The originality of Hick's approach lay in his rejection of classical natural theology, and its preoccupation with the traditional theistic proofs, in favor of a more modest attempt to show the rationality of Christian belief. The common expectation at the time was that the best way to defend Christian theism was to demonstrate (preferably through a sound deductive argument) God's existence and then to establish other truths about Jesus Christ and the Bible on that basis. But Hick rejected this approach, acknowledging at the beginning of *Faith and Knowledge* that the traditional arguments for God's existence are either clearly unsound or at best inconclusive.[12] Hick did not attempt to demonstrate the *truth* of

---

[10]See, for example, Antony Flew, R. M. Hare and Basil Mitchell, "Theology and Falsification," R. B. Braithwaite, "An Empiricist's View of the Nature of Religious Belief," and D. Z. Phillips, "Religious Beliefs and Language Games"—all in *The Philosophy of Religion*, ed. Basil Mitchell (Oxford: Oxford University Press, 1971).

[11]Hick first established his reputation by developing the notion of "eschatological verification" in response to the positivists' challenge. Hick insisted that Christian statements were indeed assertions about the nature of reality that were either true or false and thus were "factually informative." He introduced eschatological verification in *Faith and Knowledge* in 1957, but it was his 1960 article "Theology and Verification" (*Theology Today* 17 [April 1960]: 12-31) that placed Hick at the center of the debate. Hick argued that the positivists' challenge could be met on their own terms since Christian theism contains within it the possibility of the experiential confirmation of basic Christian beliefs. For example, the statement "God exists" is factually informative since there are conceivable states of affairs (perhaps not in this life but in a life to come) that would remove all grounds for rationally doubting the truth of the statement. And thus the statement is in principle confirmable and should be accepted as "factually informative." Hick's proposal has often been misunderstood as his answer to the question of how we know whether Christian theism is true. But eschatological verification was never intended to settle that question. It was specifically directed to the positivists' demand for an experientially verifiable state of affairs that could show that religious statements do indeed make "factually informative" claims about reality that are true or false. See John Hick, "Eschatological Verification Reconsidered," *Religious Studies* 13 (June 1977): 189-202.

[12]Hick, *Faith and Knowledge*, pp. 4-5. See also his "Rational Theistic Belief Without Proofs," in *Arguments for the Existence of God* (New York: Herder & Herder, 1971), chapter 7.

Christian theism but rather argued that it could be entirely *reasonable* or *rational* for a Christian in certain circumstances to believe in God. Moreover, Hick argued that this more modest form of justification for Christian belief rests not upon theistic arguments but rather upon certain kinds of experience, what the Christian takes to be experiences of the presence and activity of God.

> We become conscious of the existence of other objects in the universe, whether things or persons, either by experiencing them for ourselves or by inferring their existence from evidences within our experience. The awareness of God reported by the ordinary religious believer is of the former kind. He professes, not to have inferred that there is a God, but that God as a living being has entered into his own experience. He claims to enjoy something which he describes as an experience of God.[13]

As we shall see in chapter eight, it is not unusual for philosophers today to make the same move in trying to establish the acceptability of religious belief by appealing to religious experience. But this was a novel approach for an analytic philosopher in 1957.

In defending the rationality of Christian belief Hick introduced several ideas that were later to be integral to his model of religious pluralism. These are the notions of "experiencing-as," or the inherently interpretive nature of all experience; the religious ambiguity of the world; and "cognitive freedom" and faith as the interpretive element within religious experience. Each of these Hick introduced in *Faith and Knowledge,* and each continued to shape Hick's epistemology over the next three decades, remaining central to the epistemological framework of his later religious pluralism.

Hick distinguished three dimensions of existence implicit in our experiences: the natural or physical, the human and ethical, and the divine or religious realms. Each dimension is distinctive, with its own order of significance, and cannot be reduced to the others. The natural dimension is the most basic, followed by the human and then the religious dimensions. Hick argued that on each level there is an irreducible element of interpretation involved in our experience. "In the case of each of these realms, the natural, the human, and the divine, a basic act of interpretation is required which discloses to us the existence of the sphere in question, thus providing the ground for our multifarious detailed interpretations within that sphere."[14]

Furthermore, Hick argued that the degree of epistemological ambiguity, and hence the need for interpretation, increases with each level, so that interpretation is involved least in our experiences of the physical world, more in our experiences

---

[13]Hick, *Faith and Knowledge*, p. 95.
[14]Ibid., pp. 107-8.

of relationships with others, and most in the religious dimension with experience of God. Ludwig Wittgenstein's *Philosophical Investigations,* published in 1953, had called attention to the ambiguity of puzzle pictures, in which (for example) a drawing could be interpreted either as a rabbit or as a duck. In seeing the picture, we see it as a duck or we see it as a rabbit.[15] Hick picked up on Wittgenstein's notion of "seeing-as" and extended it to include *all* of our experiences, so that all experience is in varying degrees "experiencing-as" or inherently interpretive.[16]

According to Hick, not only is all of our experience interpretive but also there is a pervasive and irreducible ambiguity in the world such that the world can be experienced rationally in either religious or nonreligious ways. There are strong arguments for Christian theism as well as persuasive arguments for naturalism; the evidence is not such that a conclusive case can be made for either position. Given the conflicting nature of the evidence and philosophical arguments, the determinative factor is the nature of one's experience. The person who experiences God interprets the totality of life theistically; the one who fails to experience God interprets life naturalistically. Either response *can* be rational, depending upon one's particular set of circumstances and experiences.

The interpretive element in "experiencing-as" is greatest in the religious dimension, and the exercise of it is what Christians mean by "faith." The physical environment can be somewhat ambiguous at points, but it is more coercive than the other dimensions in that there is a fairly narrow range of acceptable interpretations (if you fail to interpret fire appropriately, you get burned). But God has granted a much greater degree of "cognitive freedom" in the religious dimension so that, although he has created us with a "religious bias" in our nature, religious belief and behavior are not coerced but are to be freely developed in response to God. Faith, then, is the uncoerced interpretive element within the believer's religious experience. It is "an uncompelled mode of 'experiencing-as'—experiencing the world as a place in which we have at all times to do with the transcendent God."[17] Hick argues that "this innate religious bias of our nature, inclining but not determining us to interpret our world religiously, is an essential precondition of any truly personal relationship between God and man."[18] In order to preserve the freedom of response in a personal relationship with God, there must be a measure of

---

[15]Ludwig Wittgenstein, *Philosophical Investigations*, trans. G. E. M. Anscombe, 3rd ed. (New York: Macmillan, 1958), pp. 193-95. The second edition was published in 1953.

[16]Hick, *Faith and Knowledge*, p. 142. For Hick's use of these themes in his later model of religious pluralism, see his *An Interpretation of Religion: Human Responses to the Transcendent* (New Haven, Conn.: Yale University Press, 1989), chapters 8-10.

[17]Hick, *Faith and Knowledge*, p. 151. See also John Hick, "Religious Faith as Experiencing-As," in *Talk of God*, ed. G. N. A. Vesey (London: Macmillan, 1969), pp. 20-35.

[18]Hick, *Faith and Knowledge*, p. 139.

ambiguity in God's presence and activity in the world. "In order to be cognitively free in relation to God we must possess an innate *tendency* to recognize his presence behind the phenomena of life, and yet a tendency which is not irresistible but which we may repress without doing manifest violence to our nature."[19]

The notions of "experiencing-as," the religious ambiguity of the universe, the importance of "cognitive freedom," and faith as "the interpretive element within religious experience" all contribute to a weak sense of rationality according to which it can be rational for the Christian to interpret life as the gift of God's grace, while also allowing for the rationality of the atheist who experiences life as merely the product of strictly natural processes. Much later, in the 1980s and 1990s, Hick was still writing on the rationality of religious belief, but by then the options were no longer simply Christian theism or atheism but included a bewildering variety of other religious alternatives as well. By then Hick was immersed in the discussion of Christian faith and other religions, but even as he developed his model of religious pluralism, he continued to operate largely within the epistemological framework initially put forward in *Faith and Knowledge*. What became apparent in his later work, however, was that some of the earlier epistemological assumptions that he had used so effectively in defending Christian belief against attacks from atheism could also be used, when modified slightly, to argue in a more general way for the rationality of non-Christian religious beliefs on the basis of religious experiences within other religious traditions.

Transition: Exploring Theological Alternatives

The second stage of Hick's career began with his move in 1964 from Princeton to Cambridge University, and it continued until the publication of *God and the Universe of Faiths* (1973).[20] This period saw Hick struggle increasingly with Christian orthodoxy on a number of fronts and consider seriously the implications of other religions for Christian theology. For example, in his classic work on theodicy, *Evil and the God of Love* (1966),[21] Hick argued that a successful theodicy must affirm a clear soteriological universalism in which ultimately all people will be reconciled to God. But the greatest tensions for Hick at this time were in Christology. Although he had been a staunch defender of traditional Chalcedonian two-nature Christology,[22] in the 1960s he was increasingly uncomfortable with the language

---

[19]Ibid. Emphasis in the original.

[20]John Hick, *God and the Universe of Faiths* (New York: St. Martin's, 1973). A second edition of the book was published in 1988.

[21]John Hick, *Evil and the God of Love* (New York: HarperCollins, 1966). The revised edition was published in 1977.

[22]One of his first published articles was a critique of D. M. Baillie's Christology for being insufficiently orthodox. See John Hick, "The Christology of D. M. Baillie," *Scottish Journal of Theology* 11 (March 1958): 1.

and metaphysical assumptions of Chalcedon and began searching for alternative ways to understand the significance of Jesus Christ.

In a significant article, "Christology at the Crossroads" (1966), Hick was still unwilling to abandon the traditional doctrine of the incarnation, but he was clearly troubled by the implications of the doctrine for other religions. He began the essay by noting that the "most disturbing theological problem" Christianity would face in the coming century would arise from "the communicational unification of the world and the consequent emergence of a common human history," with much greater awareness of other religions.

> In this new situation the old issue of the uniqueness of the Christian revelation, and of the nature of the Christian claim over against other religions, has become urgent and may become obsessive. At its heart lies the question of the uniqueness of Christ. It is on this central and most crucial issue that Christology stands today at the cross-roads.[23]

Throughout the article Hick was concerned to retain what he saw as the heart of the Chalcedonian definition while restating it in more acceptable categories, not in terms of Jesus' "substance identity" with God but rather as "agape identity." But he recognized that even this restatement implies a unique relationship between God and Jesus, and thus he concluded by asking, "[W]hat does this claim imply concerning the other religions of the world? And do the facts of history permit us to believe what it implies?"[24] Hick clearly had his doubts.

In 1967 Hick moved to Birmingham, where he was appointed to the H. G. Wood Chair in Theology and Philosophy at Birmingham University. Here Hick was exposed to the ethnic and religious diversity of the city, and he became highly active in social issues, especially efforts to combat racial discrimination and prejudice. As one of the cofounders of All Faiths For One Race (AFFOR), Hick was involved regularly with Hindus, Muslims, Sikhs and Jews, providing not only sustained exposure to other traditions but also opportunities to develop personal relationships with intelligent and articulate followers of other faiths. Hick continued to publish widely in philosophy of religion and theology, and although many of his writings dealt with standard issues in the Western tradition, he also began to explore the implications of other religions for Christian theology.

In the final chapter of *Arguments for the Existence of God* (1971), for example, he recognized that the epistemological arguments he had advanced in support of the rationality of Christians believing as they do on the basis of experiences of God also apply in principle to followers of other religions.

---

[23]John Hick, "Christology at the Crossroads," in *Prospect for Theology*, ed. F. G. Healey (London: James Nisbett, 1966), p. 139.
[24]Ibid., p. 166.

The principle which I have used to justify as rational the faith of a Christian who on the basis of his own religious experience cannot help believing in the reality of "the God and Father of our Lord Jesus Christ", also operates to justify as rational the faith of a Muslim who on the basis of *his* religious experience cannot help believing in the reality of Allah and his providence; and the faith of the Buddhist who on the basis of *his* religious experience cannot help accepting the Buddhist picture of the universe; and so on.[25]

Hick did not resolve this problem here, nor did he yet move clearly down the path toward pluralism, but he was aware of the implications of his epistemology for followers of other religions. His growing interest in other religions at this time was also indicated by his publishing articles on the subject of reincarnation, a doctrine he did not accept but nevertheless treated with interest and respect.[26]

Hick's growing interest in other religions throughout the 1960s and 1970s coincided with his increasing dissatisfaction with orthodox Christology, yet even in 1970 he wrote that being open to other religions need not mean watering down traditional understandings of Christ. "[C]ould it not be that Christ is indeed the incarnation of God as personal love; but that this fact does not preclude an equally valid awareness of other aspects of the divine in other religions"?[27] In terms of the threefold taxonomy of exclusivism, inclusivism and pluralism, at this stage Hick was operating within a broadly inclusivist paradigm. He acknowledged that other religions do encounter the divine reality in profound and important ways and that ultimately all people will in fact be reconciled to God, but he still maintained the distinctiveness of Jesus as the one in whom God was most fully revealed.

Pluralism

With the publication of *God and the Universe of Faiths* (1973), however, Hick spoke of undergoing a "Copernican revolution" in theology that involved "a shift from the dogma that Christianity is at the centre to the realization that it is *God* who is at the centre, and that all religions of mankind, including our own, serve and revolve around him."[28] The following year he edited *Truth and Dialogue in World Religions: Conflicting Truth Claims,* a collection of essays from a conference at the University of Birmingham on the views of Wilfred Cantwell Smith, whose *The*

---

[25]Hick, *Arguments for the Existence of God*, pp. 117-18. Emphasis in the original.

[26]See John Hick, "Reincarnation: A Critical Examination of One Form of Reincarnation Theory," *Journal of Religious Studies* (Punjabi University) 3, no. 1 (1971): 56-59; and John Hick, "The Idea of Rebirth—A Western Approach," *Indian Philosophical Annual* (1970): 89-101.

[27]John Hick, "The Reconstruction of Christian Belief for Today and Tomorrow: 2," *Theology* 73 (September 1970): 404.

[28]Hick, *God and the Universe of Faiths,* p. 131. Emphasis in the original.

Meaning and End of Religion had a significant impact on Hick.[29] Although adopting a broadly pluralist paradigm, Hick was still at this point thinking in largely theistic terms, so that it is *God,* a personal being, who is at the center of the religious universe and to whom all of the religions respond.

Hick's growing interest in other religions resulted in several extended visits to India and Sri Lanka from 1974 to 1976, culminating in the publication of *Death and Eternal Life* (1976), a remarkable work that draws upon Hindu and Buddhist traditions in addition to Christianity in constructing a global theological eschatology.[30] In 1980 Hick moved to Claremont Graduate School in California, placing him at the center of a highly eclectic and pluralistic environment in which to work out systematically his model of religious pluralism. Hick remained at Claremont until his retirement in 1992.

A significant meeting of theologians and philosophers was held at Claremont in 1986, with the major papers of the conference later published as *The Myth of Christian Uniqueness,* coedited by John Hick and Paul Knitter. The book was intended by the contributors to serve as a kind of "crossing of a theological Rubicon," or a public rejection of both exclusivism and inclusivism and acceptance of a genuinely pluralistic view of religions. Contributors to the volume included some of the most influential figures in contemporary theology, such as Gordon Kaufman, John Hick, Langdon Gilkey, Wilfred Cantwell Smith, Raimundo Panikkar, Rosemary Radford Reuther and Paul Knitter. Knitter stated, "Through this collection of essays we hope to show that such a pluralist turn is taking shape, that it is being proposed by a variety of reputable Christian thinkers, and that therefore it represents a viable, though still inchoate and controversial, option for Christian believers."[31] Hick continued to develop his model, presenting it in its most complete form in *An Interpretation of Religion* (1989), which was based upon the 1986 Gifford Lectures. Later discussions of pluralism include his *The Metaphor of God Incarnate: Christology in a Pluralistic Age* (1993); *A Christian Theology of Religions: The Rainbow of Faiths* (1995); and *The Fifth Dimension: An Exploration of the Spiritual Realm* (1999).[32]

John Hick's model of religious pluralism has developed over several decades,

---

[29]See John Hick, ed., *Truth and Dialogue in World Religions: Conflicting Truth-Claims* (Philadelphia: Westminster Press, 1974); and Wilfred Cantwell Smith, *The Meaning and End of Religion* (New York: Harper & Row, 1962).

[30]John Hick, *Death and Eternal Life* (San Francisco: Harper & Row, 1976).

[31]John H. Hick and Paul F. Knitter, eds., *The Myth of Christian Uniqueness* (Maryknoll, N.Y.: Orbis, 1987), p. viii.

[32]John Hick, *The Metaphor of God Incarnate: Christology in a Pluralistic Age* (Louisville: Westminster John Knox, 1993); John Hick, *A Christian Theology of Religions: The Rainbow of Faiths* (Louisville: Westminster John Knox, 1995); and John Hick, *The Fifth Dimension: An Exploration of the Spiritual Realm* (Oxford: Oneworld, 1999).

moving away from an earlier Christian inclusivism, which regarded the divine in Christian trinitarian terms and regarded other religions as somehow related to the Christian God, to a more vague theism (the "Eternal One") around which the various religions revolve, and then to an explicit pluralism that abandons most vestiges of theism (the "ineffable Real").[33] Applying his earlier epistemological framework to religious experiences within the many religions, Hick developed a sophisticated model that holds that "the great world faiths embody different perceptions and conceptions of, and correspondingly different responses to, the Real [the religious ultimate] from within the major variant ways of being human."[34] The various religions, then, are the product of a complex interplay between divine and human initiatives, the Real "revealing" itself to humankind and humankind in turn responding in historically and culturally conditioned ways to the Real. Diversity among religions is explained in terms of the contingent historical and cultural factors; commonalities are used to justify postulation of the Real as the ultimate reality behind all religious traditions. Soteriological transformation—salvation, enlightenment or liberation—is said to be a reality roughly equally available in all religions, so that no single tradition can legitimately claim to be the one true religion.

The move away from theistic understandings of the religious ultimate to an explicitly nontheistic model was prompted in part by Hick's desire to produce a framework that could accommodate nontheistic traditions (certain schools of Buddhism, Hinduism and Jainism) as well as theistic ones. One factor in this change from a theistic pluralism to a nontheistic understanding of the religious ultimate, transcending both personal and nonpersonal categories, was the ongoing conversation between Hick and his colleague at Claremont, the Japanese Buddhist Masao Abe. Abe was heavily involved in Buddhist-Christian dialogue and, although always gracious, he was uncompromising in his Buddhist convictions, regularly challenging Christian theologians to reinterpret ontology in terms of the ultimacy of *sunyata,* or "emptiness," rather than "being."[35] Significantly, in Hick's later model of

---

[33]The development in his model can be traced through the following writings: John Hick, *Christianity at the Center* (London: Macmillan, 1968); *God and the Universe of Faiths* (1973); *Death and Eternal Life* (1976); *The Center of Christianity* (San Francisco: Harper & Row, 1978); *God Has Many Names* (1980); *Problems of Religious Pluralism* (1985); *An Interpretation of Religion* (1989); *Disputed Questions in Theology and Philosophy of Religion* (1993); *The Metaphor of God Incarnate* (1993); and *A Christian Theology of Religions* (1995).

[34]Hick, *Interpretation of Religion*, p. 240.

[35]See, for example, Masao Abe, "A Dynamic Unity in Religious Pluralism: A Proposal from the Buddhist Point of View," in *The Religious Experience of Diversity*, eds. John Hick and Hasan Askari (Brookfield, Vt.: Gower, 1985), pp. 163-90; Masao Abe, "Kenotic God and Dynamic Sunyata," in *The Emptying God: A Buddhist-Jewish-Christian Conversation*, ed. John B. Cobb Jr. and Christopher Ives (Maryknoll, N.Y.: Orbis, 1990), pp. 3-65; and Masao Abe, "Two Types of Unity and Religious Pluralism," *Eastern Buddhist* 26, no. 2 (1993): 76-85.

religious pluralism the Real seems to be very much what Buddhists speak of as *sunyata*—something that Hick himself acknowledges.[36] At this point one might well object that Hick has not produced a genuinely pluralistic understanding of the different religions (a model that explains the diversity of the religions without privileging any of them in a special way) but in fact has adopted the framework of one of the religious traditions, Zen Buddhism, for his model.

As a result of religious pluralism, Hick significantly modified his understanding of the person and significance of Jesus. By 1973 Hick made explicit what he had only hinted at earlier, namely that the incarnation should be reinterpreted in terms of "myth," or a "story . . . which is not literally true . . . but which invites a particular attitude in its hearers."[37] The notions of "myth" and "metaphor" were to become increasingly dominant in Hick's thought, and the idea of the incarnation as "myth" received extensive publicity with the 1977 publication of the highly controversial *The Myth of God Incarnate,* edited by John Hick. In his contribution to the volume, "Jesus and the World Religions," Hick argued that the incarnation should not be understood as affirming that Jesus Christ is literally God and man but rather in a mythological or metaphorical sense as holding that God was present and active in Jesus in a manner similar to the ways in which he is present in other religious leaders.[38] Jesus, then, is simply a human being who was open to the presence and reality of God to such an unprecedented degree that he dramatically impacted everyone with whom he came in contact.

> I see the Nazarene, then, as intensely and overwhelmingly conscious of the reality of God. He was a man of God, living in the unseen presence of God, and addressing God as *abba,* father. His spirit was open to God and his life a continuous response to the divine love as both utterly gracious and demanding. He was so powerfully God conscious that his life vibrated, as it were, to the divine life; and as a result his hands could heal the sick, and the "poor in spirit" were kindled to new life in his presence. . . . Thus in Jesus' presence, we should have felt that we are in the presence of God—not in the sense that the man Jesus literally *is* God, but in the sense that he was so totally conscious of God that we could catch something of that consciousness by spiritual contagion.[39]

According to Hick, the language of incarnation need not be abandoned, but it should be reinterpreted. The incarnation "is a mythological idea, a figure of speech,

---

[36]See Hick, *A Christian Theology of Religions*, pp. 60-61; and John Hick, "The Meaning of Emptiness," in *Masao Abe: A Zen Life of Dialogue*, ed. Donald W. Mitchell (Boston: Tuttle, 1998), pp. 143-50.

[37]Hick, *God and the Universe of Faiths*, pp. 166-67.

[38]See John Hick, "Jesus and the World Religions," in *The Myth of God Incarnate*, ed. John Hick (Philadelphia: Westminster Press, 1977).

[39]Ibid., p. 172. Emphasis in the original.

a piece of poetic imagery. It is a way of saying that Jesus is our living contact with the transcendent God. In his presence we find that we are brought into the presence of God."[40] Hick developed the metaphorical understanding of incarnation within a pluralistic context more fully in *The Metaphor of God Incarnate* (1993). "We see in Jesus a human being extraordinarily open to God's influence and thus living to an extraordinary extent as God's agent on earth, 'incarnating' the divine purpose for human life."[41] Hick raises the question of plural incarnations, asking whether "epoch-making spiritual leaders such as Moses, Gautama, Confucius, Zoroaster, Socrates, Mohammed, Nanak may not in fact have been such divine incarnations." Responding affirmatively, Hick says that if we understand incarnation metaphorically, "it becomes entirely natural to say that all the great religious figures have in their different ways 'incarnated' the ideal of human life in response to the one divine Reality."[42]

Hick is not calling for Christians to abandon their loyalty and commitment to Christ. He allows that it is entirely appropriate that Christians have an "absolute" commitment to Jesus Christ as *their* Lord and Savior, so long as they recognize that followers of other religious traditions have *their own* equally legitimate objects of ultimate devotion and commitment. Jesus may be the Savior for Christians, but he is not necessarily Lord and Savior for all persons in all cultures.

There are three main reasons for Hick's rejection of the traditional understanding of the incarnation. First, Hick is clearly bothered by implications of the orthodox doctrine: If Jesus really was God become man, then it becomes difficult indeed to treat Jesus, the New Testament and Christian faith as essentially the same as phenomena from other religious traditions. There would be something inherently superior, to say the least, about Jesus and the Christian faith.

> Traditional orthodoxy says that Jesus of Nazareth was God incarnate—that is, God the Son, the Second Person of a divine Trinity, incarnate—who became man to die for the sins of the world and who founded the church to proclaim this to the ends of the earth, so that all who sincerely take Jesus as their Lord and Savior are justified by his atoning death and will inherit eternal life. It follows from this that Christianity, alone among the world religions, was founded by God in person. God came down from heaven to earth and launched the salvific movement that came to be known as Christianity. From this premise it seems obvious that God must wish all human beings to enter this new stream of saved life, so that Christianity shall supersede all the other world faiths. . . . Christianity alone is God's own religion, offering a fullness of life that no other tradition can provide; it is therefore divinely intended for all men and women without exception.[43]

---

[40]Hick, *God Has Many Names*, p. 74.
[41]Hick, *Metaphor of God Incarnate*, p. 12.
[42]Ibid., pp. 96, 98.
[43]Hick, "Pluralist View," pp. 51-52.

Hick assumes that this entails that the vast majority of humankind throughout history have not been saved and that this in and of itself is sufficient to discredit the traditional interpretation.

A second reason for Hick's rejection of the traditional view is what Hick regards as the failure of orthodoxy to give any identifiable meaning to the formula "truly God and truly man." He asserts, "That Jesus was God the Son incarnate is not literally true, since it has no literal meaning." To affirm that the historical Jesus of Nazareth was also literally God "is as devoid of meaning as to say that this circle drawn with a pencil on paper is also a square."[44] It is not clear whether Hick believes that the traditional formula actually entails a logical contradiction, so that it is logically impossible for it to be true, or whether it simply is so muddled and unclear that it conveys no clear meaning.

Third, although there is little evidence of skepticism about the historical Jesus in his earlier writings, Hick's treatment of Christology since 1973 relies heavily upon the more radical and skeptical wing of New Testament scholarship. He maintains that whereas Jesus did not regard himself as in any sense divine, over a period of time the early church came to interpret his significance in such categories and attributed deity to him. Hick is remarkably skeptical about the possibility of any significant knowledge of the historical Jesus. For example, he begins his essay "Jesus and the World Religions" by pointing to what he sees as the "confusion and uncertainty which assail us when we try to speak of Jesus. For New Testament scholarship has shown how fragmentary and ambiguous are the data available to us as we try to look back across nineteen and a half centuries, and at the same time how large and how variable is the contribution of the imagination to our 'pictures' of Jesus." It is hardly surprising, then, that he later refers to Jesus as "the largely unknown man of Nazareth."[45]

Reflections on Hick's Journey
In Hick's journey from orthodoxy to pluralism we find several themes that are common among those attracted to religious pluralism. First, it is significant that Hick's earliest published work embraced a moderately skeptical religious epistemology holding that the universe is sufficiently ambiguous that alternative worldviews, both religious and nonreligious, cannot be ruled out as rationally untenable. Hick did not try to demonstrate the truth of Christianity through the classical arguments for God's existence. Rather, he adopted the more modest approach of trying to show that it can be rational for those who experience God in their lives to believe in God on that basis. This was a brilliant move that helped to shift the focus in the

---

[44]Hick, "Jesus and the World's Religions," p. 21.
[45]Ibid., pp. 167-68.

debate over the rationality of Christian belief, but it has some clear limitations.

On a positive note, success is more likely with Hick's approach, since it is more difficult to demonstrate the truth of Christianity than it is merely to show that a Christian can be rational in accepting Christian beliefs. Negatively, the more modest expectations of this approach also affect how we think of success here. For while on Hick's premises it becomes easier to conclude that Christians are rational in believing as they do, it also becomes more difficult to hold that Christian theism is in an epistemically privileged position—that atheists or Buddhists, for example, rationally ought to change their beliefs and accept Christianity. Given the religious ambiguity of the world and the inherently interpretive nature of all experience, the same principles used to support Christian belief can also be used to justify alternative perspectives.

The notion of rationality bristles with controversy, but we can distinguish weak and strong senses of rationality. Although there is clearly a relation between the two concepts, rationality is not the same thing as truth. Truth is a property of statements or propositions such that a statement is true if and only if the state of affairs to which it refers is as the statement asserts it to be; otherwise it is false.[46] Rationality, by contrast, is a feature of persons when they adopt beliefs in appropriate circumstances or for appropriate reasons. Although we like to think that there is a correlation between rationality and truth, so that what is rational to believe is also true, in principle it is possible for it to be rational to believe something that is in fact false.

A strong notion of rationality carries with it rationality norms and expectations that make acceptance of the relevant belief *(p)* obligatory. To fail to accept *p* is then irrational. For example, belief in the reality of the external world or the general reliability of memory is usually regarded as eminently rational, and indeed failure to accept these beliefs indicates cognitive malfunctioning or irrationality of some sort. It is not just that we are somehow *permitted* to believe in the reality of the external world; rather, the expectation is that people whose cognitive faculties are operating properly and are rational *will* believe in the reality of the external world.

But there is a weaker sense of rationality such that it can be rational for a person in a particular set of circumstances and with particular background beliefs to believe a proposition *p* even if others, in their circumstances, can also be rational in not believing *p*. This sense of rationality is thus person-relative and context-dependent. Whereas the stronger notion of rationality involves what we might call epistemic obligation, the weaker sense involves epistemic permission. The basic

---

[46]We will consider the concept of truth in religion further in chapter six.

idea is that one can be rational in believing *p,* given a relevant set of conditions, even if others are not necessarily obligated to also believe *p* in order to be rational. In this weaker sense, given appropriate circumstances and background beliefs, it can be rational for a person to believe *p* even if *p* is in fact false. For example, we can say that it was rational for people in Spain in the twelfth century to believe that the earth was flat even though that belief was false.

Applying this distinction between weak and strong rationality to the issue of Christian belief, then, it is easier to argue that a Christian can be rational in believing in God in the appropriate circumstances than to try to demonstrate the rationality of Christian theism in the stronger sense, so that non-Christians too are epistemically obligated to believe in God if they are to be rational. Not surprisingly, in recent years it has become common for defenders of Christian theism to argue in terms of a weaker notion of rationality, so that Christians are "within their epistemic rights" or "violate no norms of rationality" in believing as they do. While there are obvious advantages to this, the limitation of this move is that, although it can establish the rationality of the Christian's beliefs, it is very difficult to go beyond this to argue that those who hold different, even contradictory, beliefs are mistaken or irrational in their beliefs. Thus, according to the weaker notion of rationality, it can be rational for the Christian to accept Christian beliefs on the basis of experience of God, but it can also be rational for the Buddhist to hold Buddhist beliefs on the basis of the experience of *satori,* or even for the atheist to reject belief in God on the basis of his or her experiences.

Accepting the weaker notion of rationality, and combining it with Hick's other epistemological assumptions, results in a leveling of the playing field with respect to the rationality of religious beliefs. It becomes difficult to argue that one particular set of religious beliefs is more rational than other alternatives. If there is no way to move beyond the weaker sense of rationality to argue for the Christian set of beliefs as opposed to other alternatives, then we are left with a situation in which each group rationally believes as they do based upon their own respective experiences. We will return to this issue in chapter eight.

While we will critically examine Hick's model of religious pluralism in chapter seven, some brief comments on his treatment of Christology are in order here. Hick correctly recognizes that the central theological issue in the debate over pluralism is Christology. It would be inaccurate to assume that Hick's rejection of orthodox Christology in favor of a metaphorical interpretation of the incarnation was prompted merely by a desire to accommodate other religions. Careful reading of Hick's works in the 1960s indicates a genuine struggle over what he perceived to be insurmountable problems with the traditional view. Yet it is also clear that his growing exposure to other religions intensified his dissatisfaction with orthodoxy, so that the combined effect of skepticism on theological and philosophical grounds and greater appreciation of other religions heightened the plausibility of pluralism.

Hick's conclusions about Jesus and the New Testament, however, are controversial, and many critics have pointed out that he relies upon some dubious assumptions concerning the allegedly evolutionary development of early Christian beliefs. These assumptions, although popular in the earlier part of the century, have been shown in more recent literature to be untenable.[47] In particular, Hick's fundamental assumptions—for example, that early Christological understanding evolved in a linear fashion from a primitive devotion to Jesus as Master and Messiah into a more metaphysical conception of him as Son of God, or as God the Son, and eventually into the sophisticated trinitarian formula of the Second Person of the Trinity, and that neither Jesus himself nor his first followers thought of him as in any sense divine—have been shown by C. F. D. Moule of Cambridge, among others, to be highly problematic.[48] Moule persuasively argues that an evolutionary model holding that a "high" Christology evolved from a primitive "low" Christology by a process of borrowing from extraneous sources over a period of time simply does not fit the data of the New Testament. To the contrary, he maintains that the transition from invoking Jesus as a revered Master to the acclamation of him as divine Lord is better understood in terms of a model of development according to which "the various estimates of Jesus reflected in the New Testament [are], in essence, only attempts to describe what was already there from the beginning. They are not successive additions of something new, but only the drawing out and articulating of what is there."[49] Moule argues that "Jesus was, *from the beginning,* such a one as appropriately to be described in the ways in which, sooner or later, he did come to be described in the New Testament period—for instance, as 'Lord' and even, in some sense, as 'God.' "[50] Some of the most elevated Christology in the New Testament is present, either explicitly or implicitly, in the Pauline epistles—widely

---

[47]See, for example, Michael Green, ed., *The Truth of God Incarnate* (Grand Rapids, Mich.: Eerdmans, 1977); Michael Goulder, ed., *Incarnation and Myth: The Debate Continued* (Grand Rapids, Mich.: Eerdmans, 1979); Norman Anderson, *The Mystery of the Incarnation* (London: Hodder & Stoughton, 1978); Brian Hebblethwaite, *The Incarnation* (Cambridge: Cambridge University Press, 1987); Thomas V. Morris, *The Logic of God Incarnate* (Ithaca, N.Y.: Cornell University Press, 1986); and Richard Sturch, *The Word and the Christ: An Essay in Analytic Christology* (Oxford: Oxford University Press, 1991).

[48]See C. F. D. Moule, *The Origin of Christology* (Cambridge: Cambridge University Press, 1977). See also R. N. Longenecker, *The Christology of Early Jewish Christianity* (London: SCM Press, 1970); I. Howard Marshall, *The Origins of New Testament Christology* (Downers Grove, Ill.: InterVarsity Press, 1976); and Paul Barnett, *Jesus and the Rise of Early Christianity: A History of New Testament Times* (Downers Grove, Ill.: InterVarsity Press, 1999).

[49]Moule, *Origin of Christology*, pp. 2-3.

[50]Ibid., p. 4. Emphasis in the original.

accepted as the earliest documents in the New Testament.[51] Moule and Martin Hengel of Tübingen have demonstrated that the Christological titles are not later innovations but can be traced back to very early usage. Hengel, for example, holds that the title Son of God was applied to Jesus between A.D. 30 and 50.[52] Similarly, after a short but judicious summary of the New Testament data, I. Howard Marshall concludes, "We have found that the concept of incarnation, i.e. that Jesus Christ is the Son of God made flesh, is the principle of Christological explanation in the writings of John, the writings of Paul including the Pastoral Epistles, the Epistle to the Hebrews, and 1 Peter. The view that it is found merely on the fringe of the New Testament is a complete travesty of the facts."[53]

Moreover, Norman Anderson correctly points out that Hick "greatly exaggerates the paucity of positive evidence we have about the one to whom he refers as the 'largely unknown man of Nazareth.' "[54] Curiously, in spite of his professed skepticism about the historical Jesus, Hick makes some rather specific claims about what Jesus was like and about his relation to God and his immediate followers. Consider, for example, the following statement, summarizing Hick's metaphorical interpretation of the incarnation:

> In the case of the metaphor of divine incarnation, what was lived out, made flesh, incarnated in the life of Jesus can be indicated in at least three ways, each of which is an aspect of the fact that Jesus was a human being exceptionally open and responsive to the divine presence: (1) In so far as Jesus was doing God's will, God was acting through him on earth and was in this respect "incarnate" in Jesus' life; (2) In so far as Jesus was doing God's will he "incarnated" the ideal of human life lived in openness and response to God; (3) In so far as Jesus lived a life of self-giving love, or *agape,* he "incarnated" a love that is a finite reflection of the infinite love. The truth or the appropriateness of the metaphor depends upon its being literally true that Jesus lived in obedient response to the divine presence, and that he lived a life of unselfish love.[55]

But if this paragraph is informative at all, then clearly Hick is assuming that we have a good understanding of what Jesus of Nazareth was really like, that he exemplified obedience to God and agape in his life, and so on.

Hick, of course, is not the first person to question the intelligibility or coher-

---

[51]Ibid., pp. 2-7. See also C. F. D. Moule, "Three Points of Conflict in the Christological Debate," in *Incarnation and Myth,* p. 137.

[52]Martin Hengel, *The Son of God: The Origin of Christology and the History of the Jewish-Hellenistic Religion* (Philadelphia: Fortress, 1976), pp. 2, 10.

[53]I. Howard Marshall, "Incarnational Christology in the New Testament," in *Christ the Lord,* ed. H. H. Rowdon (Leicester, England: Inter-Varsity Press, 1982), p. 13. For a careful and responsible study of New Testament texts on the deity of Jesus Christ, see Murray J. Harris, *Jesus as God: The New Testament Use of* Theos *in Reference to Jesus* (Grand Rapids, Mich.: Baker, 1992).

[54]Anderson, *Mystery of the Incarnation,* p. 64.

[55]Hick, *Metaphor of God Incarnate,* p. 105.

ence of the Chalcedonian formulation of two-nature Christology. And if he is correct in charging that the formula "truly God and truly man" is incoherent—whether this be construed in terms of logical inconsistency or merely the absence of any significant identifiable meaning—it follows that the orthodox understanding of the incarnation cannot stand. But is the doctrine really incoherent? Certainly it is mysterious, even paradoxical. But it is far from obvious that it is logically inconsistent or devoid of any significant meaning. As Stephen Davis reminds us, millions of people throughout history have regarded the claims made by Chalcedon as not only coherent and meaningful but true.[56] Certainly the Chalcedonian formula does not explain how it is that Jesus can be both God and man and, given the limitations of human finitude, any attempt at such explanation inevitably runs into difficulty. Chalcedon simply defines the acceptable parameters within which we are to think of the person of Christ if we are to be faithful to the witness of the New Testament.

Finally, it is surely significant that Hick's shift to an explicit pluralism roughly coincided with his move to Birmingham, with its enormous ethnic, cultural and religious diversity. Here Hick encountered, among other things, the darker side of the legacy of British colonialism in the form of prejudice and discrimination against the many Muslim, Sikh and Hindu immigrants.[57] In joining the interfaith struggle against ethnic discrimination Hick developed close ties with leaders from the many different faith communities in Birmingham. This had profound implications for his view of other religions: "Occasionally attending worship in mosque and synagogue, temple and gurdwara, it was evident to me that essentially the same kind of thing is taking place in them as in a Christian church—namely, human beings opening their minds to a higher divine Reality, known as personal and good and as demanding righteousness and love between man and woman."[58] In this Hick speaks for many today who, through personal relationships with sincere and morally respectable followers of other faiths, find it difficult not to conclude that they too are properly related to the one divine reality. In these various ways, then, Hick's theological journey toward pluralism can be seen as representative of transitions that many in the West are undergoing as they reconsider the relationship between Christianity and other religions.

---

[56]Stephen T. Davis, "Critique of John Hick," in *Encountering Jesus*, ed. Stephen T. Davis (Atlanta: John Knox Press, 1988), p. 23. For further discussions of alleged logical problems with the orthodox view, see Stephen T. Davis, *Logic and the Nature of God* (Grand Rapids, Mich.: Eerdmans, 1983), chapter 8; Morris, *Logic of God Incarnate;* and Sturch, *Word and the Christ*.

[57]Hick explicitly makes the connection between the legacy of British colonialism and the problems of Muslim, Sikh and Hindu immigrants in *Problems of Religious Pluralism*, pp. 5-6.

[58]Hick, *God Has Many Names*, pp. 17-18.

PART 2
ENGAGING
RELIGIOUS PLURALISM

6
RELIGIONS & TRUTH

The different creeds are the historical formulations of the formless truth. While the treasure is one and inviolable, the earthen vessel that contains it takes the shape and the colour of its time and environment.

SARVEPALLI RADHAKRISHNAN, *Eastern Religions and Western Thought*

Of course religions make claims—if they asserted nothing, there would be no religions. . . . But it is clear that, in their traditional forms, religious traditions take as essential to salvation precisely matters on which there is deep disagreement among religious traditions.

KEITH YANDELL, *Philosophy of Religion*

I n formulating a response to religious pluralism we must begin by considering the nature of religious truth and the problem of conflicting truth claims. Even a cursory survey of the religions reveals important differences among them. Christians worship in churches; Sikhs pray in *gurdwaras;* Hindus have their temples; Muslims gather in mosques for prayer and worship. Some differences are incidental (the habit of Roman Catholic Franciscans is brown whereas the robes of Theravada Buddhist monks are saffron); other differences are more significant.

Diversity in appearance, behavior or belief often is rooted in fundamental differences in the respective religious worldviews. For example, differences between Christianity and Theravada Buddhism over what one ought to do in order to attain the desired goal—whether to follow the Noble Eightfold Path or repent of one's sin and follow Jesus as Lord and Savior—reflect not only diverse *means* but also different *ends* that are to be pursued. Such differences, in turn, are embedded in sharply contrasting understandings of the nature of reality, including what is religiously ultimate, the nature of the problem plaguing the universe, and the remedy for this predicament. On this level differences between religions can take the form of conflicts of belief, or contrasting visions of reality, resulting in opposition between at least some doctrines in the respective religions. And since each religion typically regards its own beliefs as true, such conflicts produce what is often called the problem of conflicting truth claims.

Conflicting Truth Claims

Some conflicts between claims of various religions are more significant than others. Judaism and Islam disagree, for example, over the identity of the son of Abraham who was to be sacrificed: the Hebrew Scriptures identify him as Isaac whereas Islamic tradition maintains it was Ishmael. But other disagreements are more fundamental, involving conflicting claims concerning what is central to a particular religion.

Although Jesus is held in great esteem in both Christianity and Islam, disagreement between them over his identity reveals the fundamental difference between the two monotheistic faiths. Christians accept Jesus as the unique incarnation of the eternal, infinite God—Jesus was fully God and fully man. Muslims, on the other hand, reject this claim as blasphemous. Although the Qur'an portrays Jesus as a great prophet, it indicates that he was still only a man.[1] Furthermore, Christians and Muslims disagree over the factual question of whether Jesus was actually crucified on the cross, for many Muslims interpret Surah 4:155-159 of the Qur'an to be explicitly ruling out the death of Jesus on the cross.[2] This cannot be dismissed as merely a minor disagreement over an obscure historical fact, for the atoning work of Jesus on the cross is central to the Christian message of salvation. Thus it has traditionally been maintained that Islam and Christianity cannot both be correct in their respective beliefs about the person and work of Jesus of Nazareth. The disagreement here is fundamental, and while it is logically possible for both Christians and Muslims to be wrong about the identity of Jesus (perhaps he was neither God incarnate nor a great prophet), both cannot be correct. At least one view of Jesus must be false.

Most religions presuppose that human beings, and in some cases the cosmos at large, are presently in some kind of undesirable predicament. Furthermore, they presuppose that, in contrast to this predicament, an ultimately good and desirable state can be achieved—either through one's own individual efforts or through the benevolent assistance of one or more higher beings or powers. Given this common structure, three questions naturally emerge that can profitably be put to the various religious traditions: What is the nature of the religious ultimate? What is the nature of the human predicament? What is the nature of salvation (or enlightenment or liberation)? The three questions are clearly interrelated, for one's views on the human predicament and the religious ultimate will have profound implications

---

[1]On the Islamic understanding of Jesus, see Geoffrey Parrinder, *Jesus in the Qur'an* (New York: Oxford University Press, 1977); Kenneth Cragg, *The Call of the Minaret*, 3rd ed. (Oxford: Oneworld, 2000); and Neal Robinson, *Christ in Islam and Christianity* (Albany: State University of New York Press, 1991).

[2]For a full discussion of issues involved in interpreting this text, see Parrinder, *Jesus in the Qur'an*, pp. 108-21.

for beliefs about salvation and how it is to be achieved. Just as in medicine the physician's prescription to the patient will largely be determined by the diagnosis of the problem and the available resources for treating that condition, so too in religion any prescription for the human predicament will presuppose a particular understanding of the nature of the problem and resources for its treatment.

How do the major religions answer the three questions above? Is it plausible to maintain, as many do today, that the different religions all make essentially the same claims and teach basically the same truth? Careful examination of the basic tenets of the various religions demonstrates that, far from teaching the same thing, they have radically different perspectives on the religious ultimate, the human predicament and the nature of salvation. Any attempt to produce an essential unity in outlook among the many religions will result in distorting at least some of the actual beliefs of followers of the various traditions. We cannot here consider in any depth how the religions deal with these questions, but even a brief summary of some perspectives within Hinduism, Buddhism, Islam and Shinto should indicate the difference on these issues.[3]

What is the nature of the religious ultimate? There is no question about what is ultimate in Islam: Allah, the one eternal Creator God, is the religious ultimate. Any attempt to blur the clear-cut distinction between the Creator and the creation is regarded by Muslims as *shirk,* or idolatry. Islam thus joins other monotheistic faiths, such as Christianity and Judaism, in ascribing ultimacy to the one eternal Creator God. The matter is not so unambiguous, however, in the case of three other religions: Buddhism, Hinduism and Shinto.

What, for example, are we to say of Buddhism? Theravada Buddhism does not acknowledge anything like a monotheistic God, and thus if we must speak in these terms at all, perhaps ultimacy should be identified with *nirvana,* since it alone is said to be unconditioned and permanent. But in doing so, of course, we must be careful not to think of *nirvana* as some kind of ultimate Being with personal characteristics. *Nirvana* is the condition of complete cessation of attachment, something that transcends both positive and negative predication. Mahayana Buddhists, on the other hand, might prefer to speak of the *Dharmakaya,* the ultimate, all-inclusive Law Body of the Buddha essence, as the religious ultimate. Zen Buddhists might ascribe ultimacy to *sunyata,* or emptiness.

---

[3]For a more complete discussion on this point, see Harold Netland, *Dissonant Voices: Religious Pluralism and the Question of Truth* (Grand Rapids, Mich.: Eerdmans, 1991), chapters 2-3. Good general introductions to the major religions include Roger Schmidt et al., *Patterns of Religion* (Belmont, Calif.: Wadsworth, 1999); Ninian Smart, *The World's Religions*, 2nd ed. (Cambridge: Cambridge University Press, 1998); Ninian Smart, *The Religious Experience of Mankind*, 3rd ed. (New York: Charles Scribner's Sons, 1984); and David S. Noss and John B. Noss, *A History of the World's Religions*, 9th ed. (New York: Macmillan, 1994).

And of course, Pure Land Buddhists will tend to think in quasi theistic terms of the Amida Buddha, a being with definite personal characteristics, as the religious ultimate. Obviously, there is not just one concept that functions as the religious ultimate for all Buddhists.

Among Hindus too we find a variety of possibilities for religious ultimacy. Followers of monistic Advaita Vedanta will regard the *nirguna* Brahman, absolutely nondifferentiated Being, as the religious ultimate. Philosophically less sophisticated Hindus might recognize a wide variety of deities, singling out one or more for special reverence and devotion. Thus some Hindus will think of Vishnu, Shiva or even Krishna in theistic terms, giving them ultimate devotion and reverence. By contrast, atheistic Hindus, rather than identifying ultimacy with any particular deity, will tend to regard the entire cosmic process as ultimate.

It is not clear that the notion of religious ultimacy is even applicable in the case of Shinto, for the *kami* (deities) are not regarded as ontologically transcendent, distinct from the phenomenal world. There is no room in Shinto for the monotheistic understanding of an ontologically distinct eternal Creator who brought into being from nothing all that exists. In Shinto the religious ultimate is not something located outside of the world but rather is in an important sense continuous with the world of our experience. And yet the difficulty we have in identifying religious ultimacy in Shinto is in itself instructive, for it underscores the great differences in worldview between polytheistic religious traditions such as Shinto and monotheistic faiths such as Christianity and Islam.

What is the nature of the human predicament? The various religions give quite different answers to the question of the human predicament as well. Hinduism and Buddhism largely accept the view that humankind is trapped within *samsara,* the cycle of rebirths through which one transmigrates in accordance with *karma.* Buddhism emphasizes that *samsara* is characterized by *dukkha,* pervasive suffering or dissatisfaction. The root problem of human existence is not sin (deliberate moral rebellion against a holy and righteous God) but rather a profound ignorance, blindness or confusion regarding the true nature of reality.

Unlike Christianity, Buddhism or Hinduism, Shinto does not seem to have a strong sense that the present order is somehow radically distorted or fallen. The human predicament (if this terminology is even adequate) is more a matter of cosmic imbalance or disharmony brought about through somehow offending the *kami.* Evil is rooted in defilement or contamination from association with what is impure. But contamination does not stem from sin (rebellion against a holy God) but rather from association with what is undesirable, especially death.

Islam, on the other hand, does have an understanding of sin, although not as clearly defined as one finds in the Christian tradition. The ultimate sin, of course, is *shirk,* associating anything created with the Allah. Islam unambiguously condemns idolatry. Conspicuously lacking in Islam, however, are concepts of the radical depravity of human nature, the pervasive impact of sin and the complete inability of humankind to redeem itself from the bondage of sin. Sin is more a weakness, a defect or an imperfection than a radical corruption of the nature and will. Thus, although Iblis (Satan) is said to be constantly tempting humans to disobey Allah, it is within their power to resist Iblis and to remain faithful to Allah. It is not that humankind stands in need of a Savior and Redeemer, someone who can transform the corrupted sinful nature into one that can be pleasing to God, but rather that human beings need to act in faithfulness and submission to the revealed will of Allah—something that is held to be within the grasp of disciplined and religiously sensitive persons.

What is the nature of salvation? Given the various understandings of the nature of the human predicament, it is to be expected that the religions would have different perspectives on how one is to attain salvation or liberation from the present predicament. Hindus generally regard the spiritual goal as *moksha,* complete release from the chains of *karma* and the cycle of rebirths. Such deliverance is said to be attainable through a variety of means: *karma marga,* the way of selfless or disinterested action, or the rigorous adherence to moral and ritual prescriptions; *jnana marga,* the way of liberating insight into the nature of reality; or *bhakti marga,* the way of devotion to a personal lord. Some Hindus consider all three ways to be equally legitimate, depending upon one's circumstances and abilities; others pick out one particular way, say *bhakti marga,* as the only legitimate way, or at least as superior to the others.

For Buddhists, release from *samsara* is generally thought of in terms of *nirvana,* the complete elimination of desire and the conditions producing rebirth. According to Theravada Buddhists, through a process of rigorous self-discipline focused upon the Noble Eightfold Path and encompassing numerous lives, one can attain *nirvana.* On the other hand, many Mahayana Buddhists, minimizing the notion of *samsara,* tend to think of salvation more in terms of enlightenment in this life. And Pure Land Buddhists generally equate salvation with rebirth in the Pure Land after death. Also within Buddhism are striking differences between those who insist that salvation or enlightenment is strictly the result of one's own individual efforts (Theravada Buddhists) and those who, calling all self-effort futile, maintain that only faith in the mercy and merit of another will bring about salvation (Jodo-Shinshu Buddhists).

Shinto has no explicit eschatology or soteriology. Salvation in Shinto is largely a matter of achieving a healthy and robust life in the present. A sincere heart that seeks to acknowledge the presence of the *kami* in all of life, and that carefully maintains the rituals of ceremonial purity, can expect the blessings of the *kami* in the daily affairs of life.

By contrast, salvation in Islam is primarily eschatological. On the Day of Judgment only those whom Allah declares worthy will be admitted to the delights of Paradise. Salvation is not so much a present reality that finds its culmination in the future but a glorious future awaiting those who prove to be faithful to the will of Allah.

It is evident, then, that Buddhism, Hinduism, Islam and Shinto provide quite different answers to the questions concerning the religious ultimate, the human predicament and the nature of salvation. Significantly, in some cases, the three questions themselves do not seem entirely appropriate. Thus, rather than regarding the various religions as providing different answers to common questions, it is better to think of them as responding to certain issues that arose within their own particular historical and cultural contexts. And while there may be some overlap in issues addressed (especially in the case of Hinduism and Buddhism), there is also considerable diversity, both in terms of questions posed and answers given.

What implications follow from this? First, while we must recognize that mere difference in perspective, in and of itself, does not entail opposition of beliefs, there are instances in which the various religions clearly do seem to be making mutually incompatible claims about the nature of reality. Is the religious ultimate personal or nonpersonal? Is there one God, many *kami* or no higher Being of any kind? Is the human predicament at root caused by human rebellion against a holy and righteous God, or is it the product of a cosmic illusion or ignorance? Is salvation a matter of the total transformation of one's nature, resulting in a restored relationship with God, or is it a matter of release from the cycle of rebirths? William Christian states that "two doctrines are opposed if they cannot be jointly accepted without absurdity."[4] It is difficult indeed to escape the conclusion that some of the central affirmations of Christianity, Hinduism, Buddhism, Islam and Shinto are opposed. So long as the meanings of the doctrines within the respective religious communities are preserved, they cannot be jointly accepted without absurdity.

There is a tendency to think of Asian religions as all basically the same, with different Indian, Chinese and Japanese traditions comprising just minor cultural variations on one common theme. In reality, of course, there is remarkable diversity, not only between, say, Indian and Japanese religious and philosophical traditions but also among Indian traditions themselves.[5] India gave birth to the three great

---

[4]William A. Christian, *Oppositions of Religious Doctrines: A Study in the Logic of Dialogue Among Religions* (London: Macmillan, 1972), p. 2.

[5]See Hajime Nakamura, *Ways of Thinking of Eastern Peoples*, trans. Philip P. Wiener, rev. ed. (Honolulu: University of Hawaii Press, 1964); Ninian Smart, *Doctrine and Argument in Indian Philosophy* (London: Allen & Unwin, 1964); and John M. Koller and Patricia Joyce Koller, *Asian Philosophies*, 3rd ed. (Upper Saddle River, N.J.: Prentice-Hall, 1998).

religions of Hinduism, Buddhism and Jainism, and yet there are striking differences—even incompatibilities—between them. They disagree fundamentally on the nature of what exists and what is ultimately real. For example, they provide very different answers to the question "Does an enduring person exist, and if so, what is its nature?" Keith Yandell states:

> Three views are relevant here: Advaita Vedanta's claim that (i) only Brahman without qualities exists, Jainism's contention that (ii) persons are inherently immortal and independently existing beings, and the typical Buddhist view that (iii) persons are composite entities, made up of other things that are not persons and that comprise the basic constituents of the universe. These are obviously logically incompatible claims; all could be false, but not more than one could be true.[6]

Incompatibilities exist among the orthodox schools of Hinduism as well. The Nyaya, Vaisheshika, Samkhya and Mimamsa schools of Hinduism agree that the world experienced through perception is real and exists independently of being perceived. They are ontologically dualistic or pluralistic in maintaining that reality is constituted by more than one kind of thing. But this is denied by the Advaita Vedanta school, which holds that there is only one reality, Brahman, and that what appears to be plural and changing—the realm of perception—is an illusion.[7]

Second, although our concern here is primarily with beliefs, we should observe that opposition takes place not only on the level of doctrine but also with respect to courses of action advocated by various religious communities. Fundamental beliefs about the nature of the religious ultimate and the human predicament call for certain appropriate patterns of behavior. Based upon their respective beliefs about reality, the Advaitin Hindu, Pure Land Buddhist and Muslim will advocate markedly different courses of action as appropriate.

Third, the common assumption that all religions ultimately teach the same thing in their own culturally conditioned ways is untenable. Not only are they not all saying the same thing but also the particular issues addressed in the various religions are not necessarily the same. William Christian observes that the views claiming that the beliefs of the major religions are all mutually consistent, and that all religions say basically the same thing, "seem very implausible, and certainly much current talk in aid of these views is loose and sentimental."[8] Surely the burden of proof rests with those who would maintain the contrary.

Not surprisingly, then, given the problem of conflicting truth claims, it has traditionally been held that the religions cannot all be true. While one religion (or

---

[6]Keith Yandell, *Philosophy of Religion: A Contemporary Introduction* (New York: Routledge, 1999), p. 241.
[7]See Koller and Koller, *Asian Philosophies*, chapters 5-8.
[8]Christian, *Oppositions of Religious Doctrines*, p. 5.

perhaps several closely related traditions) might be true, the others must in varying degrees be false. Accordingly, Christians have traditionally held that Christianity is true and that other religions, whatever merits they might have on other grounds, are in a profound sense mistaken or false. Thus Christian particularism, as we defined it in chapter one, holds that where the central claims of Christian faith are incompatible with those of other religious traditions, the latter are to be rejected as false.

But this way of thinking about religious differences is distasteful to many today, for it implies that large numbers of sincere, morally good, intelligent adherents of other religions are mistaken in some of their most fundamental beliefs. Religious belief and practice touch upon some of the deepest commitments of the heart, and there is something disturbing about saying that pious, learned and faithful practitioners of other religious ways are wrong. Many thinkers, desiring to avoid this conclusion, have suggested that there must be something mistaken about the way in which the problem of conflicting truth claims is typically understood. This response is particularly popular among those attracted to religious pluralism, for it becomes difficult indeed to embrace a thoroughgoing pluralism so long as we have the scandal of mutually incompatible truth claims. But perhaps the problem of conflicting truth claims is really a pseudoproblem that evaporates once the issues are reinterpreted properly. There are several ways in which one might try to redefine the issues. We will consider briefly some attempts that do so by challenging some traditional assumptions about religion and religious truth. According to these critics, when the problematic assumptions are abandoned, the "problem" of conflicting truth claims disappears as well.

As with most influential views, there is an element of truth here. But I will argue that, even when the legitimate points in these perspectives are acknowledged, the problem of conflicting truth claims remains. Religious traditions do make distinctive claims about reality, and these claims do at times conflict. There is an important sense in which traditional notions of propositional and exclusive truth do apply in religion, and to fail to recognize this is to ignore a central dimension of the religious traditions themselves. Moreover, as I will argue in chapter seven, the problem of conflicting truth claims presents a formidable obstacle to any genuinely pluralistic model of the religions.

The Reification of Religion

It has become popular in some circles to dismiss the problem of conflicting truth claims as merely the product of a faulty understanding of religion. The mistake, it is said, stems from an "essentialist" view of religions that considers religions such as Islam or Hinduism as autonomous, clearly defined entities defined by beliefs or doctrines. However, to think of religions in this manner is to engage in an illicit reification of religious phenomena, that is, taking the empirical patterns of the religious life of specific communities and treating them as objectified, abstract entities. Moreover, it mistakenly focuses upon belief or doctrine as what is most important in religion.

An especially influential expression of this critique is found in the writings of the historian and Islamist Wilfred Cantwell Smith, whose *The Meaning and End of Religion* (1962) has, as much as any other book in the past half century, shaped the academic study of religion.[9] Smith calls for a fresh way of understanding religion, one that does not reify religions by emphasizing beliefs but rather considers carefully the religious commitments of people. Smith argues that there is no such thing as "religion in general," nor are there distinct entities such as "Buddhism" or "Christianity" or "Islam." "Neither religion in general nor any one of the religions, I will contend, is in itself an intelligible entity, a valid object of inquiry or of concern either for the scholar or for the man of faith." In making this contention, Smith is not denying that religion is an important part of our world nor saying that people are not religious in different ways. "The phenomena that we call religious undoubtedly exist."[10] Religious phenomena in particular communities can be observed and studied, but Smith emphasizes that to identify such external patterns with different religions, as if we can pick out the essence of distinct religions on the basis of such observable features, is to engage in the reification of religion.

Smith distinguishes between what he calls the external "cumulative tradition" of religious communities and the inner faith of the religious believer. Instead of looking at external patterns of the cumulative tradition, we should be considering what it means for people in communities to be religious, or in Smith's terms, to "have faith."

> The proposal that I am putting forward can, at one level, be formulated quite simply. It is that what men have tended to conceive as religion, and especially as a religion, can more rewardingly, more truly, be conceived in terms of two factors, different in kind, both dynamic: an historical "cumulative tradition," and the personal faith of men and women.[11]

The cumulative tradition is formed by one or more communities over a period of time and includes the various external aspects of a religious tradition that give it its peculiar identity.

---

[9]Wilfred Cantwell Smith, *The Meaning and End of Religion: A Revolutionary Approach to the Great Religious Traditions* (San Francisco: Harper & Row, 1962, 1978). The work had a significant impact upon John Hick, who wrote the foreword to the 1978 edition of the book.
[10]Ibid., pp. 12, 17
[11]Ibid., p. 194.

By "cumulative tradition" I mean the entire mass of overt objective data that constitute the historical deposit, as it were, of the past religious life of the community in question: temples, scriptures, theological systems, dance patterns, legal and other social institutions, conventions, moral codes, myths, and so on; anything that can be and is transmitted from one person, one generation, to another, and that an historian can observe.[12]

Smith claims, however, that far more important than this external dimension is the inner faith of the religious believer.[13] Faith is intensely personal and is an expression of the individual within a community in his or her response to God. Although sharing common elements across traditions, faith can also take many different forms of expression. Thus in a later work Smith speaks of faith as "that propensity of man that across the centuries and across the world has given rise to and has been nurtured by a prodigious variety of religious forms, and yet has remained elusive and personal, prior to and beyond the forms."[14] Faith is not to be identified with belief, although it can be expressed in beliefs and doctrines. But faith is the primary phenomenon; belief is secondary and parasitic upon faith. Faith is inherently personal and is what gives rise to visible expressions of religious commitment. "'Faith', then, I propose, shall signify that human quality that has been expressed in, has been elicited, nurtured, and shaped by, the religious traditions of the world."[15]

According to Smith, to concentrate upon external factors—such as rituals, practices, beliefs, institutions and scriptures—is to ignore faith, the inner dynamic of religion, the personal response of the individual to God. What really matters as we look at religion is not "religion" as a generic category or even the separate "religions," understood in terms of their cumulative traditions. What is most significant is the personal faith of believers, regardless of their particular religious affiliation, and not the external trappings of various religious communities.

We cannot trace here the various reasons advanced by Smith in support of his claims, except to note that he makes much of the fact that the concept of "a religion" as a distinctive entity, and of the various religions as separate realities, is a relatively modern one that would have been confusing to premodern peoples.

The issues raised by Smith are important. We can readily admit that there has been a tendency to "essentialize" or "reify" religion, treating it as an autonomous, abstract entity somehow detached from the actual lives of religious persons. Furthermore, there can indeed be an excessive focus upon beliefs or doctrines so that

---

[12]Ibid., pp. 156-57.
[13]Ibid., chapter 7.
[14]Wilfred Cantwell Smith, *Faith and Belief* (Princeton, N.J.: Princeton University Press, 1979), p. 3.
[15]Ibid., p. 6.

religions are reduced to a set of propositions. Smith's discussion of the cumulative tradition and personal faith can be a helpful reminder that in religion we are dealing with much more than merely a tidy set of beliefs floating in a social and historical vacuum. Indeed, regardless of whether one accepts all the implications Smith derives from it, some such distinction between the inner, personal dimension of religious commitment and the external, cumulative tradition seems necessary.

Nevertheless, Smith's call for abandoning the notion of "the religions" is confused and unhelpful. Concepts and categories are to be assessed in terms of their capacity to elucidate the phenomena under consideration, and in this case the issue is whether the notion of distinctive religions (Islam, Hinduism, Buddhism and so on), when purged of the problematic elements noted above, is important for understanding the religious dimension of human experience. I think it is.[16]

As Smith himself recognizes, different peoples throughout history and in many cultures have "been religious" and expressed their religious commitments in identifiably distinct ways. This is not only a matter of those from the outside making judgments about the religious lives of others, so that we can distinguish the religious practices and beliefs of, say, the Mayan civilization of the eighth century from the Japanese Shinto traditions of the early twentieth century. It also involves those within a particular religious community making judgments about the beliefs and practices of others—in some cases judgments resulting in the rejection of particular beliefs or practices as incompatible with one's own tradition.

This, of course, introduces the category of heresy, which is normally associated with Christianity and the struggles between orthodox and heretical individuals within the Christian tradition. But similar distinctions between acceptable and unacceptable beliefs and practices are to be found among many religious traditions, including those of India, which are often regarded by Western scholars as almost limitlessly tolerant of diversity. Even Hindus have limits on what is to be accepted within the community, for as Wendy Doniger O'Flaherty remarks, "The contradiction of the Vedas remains the basic heresy in the Hindu viewpoint."[17] Jains, Buddhists and Sikhs, who all rejected the authority of the Vedas, were thus regarded as complete outcastes or heretics. From within the Hindu religious community, there was a clear distinction between those who accepted the Vedas and those who did not, and this distinction served as a boundary marker between those inside and those outside the tradition. Elimination of talk of "the religions" makes it difficult

---

[16]A balanced and perceptive assessment of Smith's proposals can be found in Robert D. Baird, *Category Formation and the History of Religions* (The Hague: Mouton, 1971), pp. 74-106, 126-42.

[17]Wendy Doniger O'Flaherty, "The Origin of Heresy in Hindu Mythology," *History of Religions* 10, no. 4 (1971): 272. See also Wilhelm Halbfass, *India and Europe: An Essay in Understanding* (Albany: State University of New York Press, 1988), chapter 11.

to treat the sense of common religious identity that particular groups of people have, marking them as distinct from others. The fact is that, for example, followers of Gautama the Buddha had a distinctive sense of common identity, expressed in certain beliefs (such as denial of an enduring *atman*) that both united them in their allegiance to the Buddha's teachings and separated them from other Indian religious communities that did believe in the *atman* and the authority of the Vedas. Even today followers of the Buddha are united in their commitment to the Buddha's teachings (regardless of how they might differ in interpretations of these teachings), and this sets them apart from the followers of Jesus Christ. Using the term *Buddhism* to refer to the ways in which followers of the Buddha express their religious commitments is a helpful way of speaking of this reality.

What Is Religion?

Before considering the place of belief and truth in religion, we must first have some idea of what we mean by *religion*. But defining *religion* is no easy task, for each proposed definition seems to privilege certain religious traditions at the expense of others.[18] Moreover, definitions tend to be either too broad, and thus include within religion things normally not regarded as religious, or too narrow, thereby excluding from the category of religion things normally accepted as religious.

It is helpful to distinguish between substantive and functional definitions. Substantive definitions characterize religion in terms of something—usually a belief—that is said to be intrinsic to religion and thus that all religions share. The nineteenth-century anthropologist Edward Tylor gave a famously concise definition of religion as "belief in Spiritual Beings."[19] The difficulty with substantive definitions, however, is finding any one significant feature, such as a major belief or practice, common to all religions. Although Tylor's definition (on a fairly broad interpretation of "Spiritual Beings") captures an essential element of many religious traditions, there are some major traditions (Theravada Buddhism, Jainism, some Confucian and Hindu traditions) that either are explicitly atheistic or are agnostic on the existence of any superhuman beings.

Functional definitions, by contrast, characterize religion in terms of its functions, that is, what it does for its adherents or society at large. Such definitions are generally linked to pragmatic or functionalist theories that understand religion primarily in terms of what it does, with special emphasis upon the social and psy-

---

[18]Our concern in this section is with definitions or characterizations of religion that accurately reflect the observable phenomena of religious communities. The question of the truth of specific religious claims is a separate issue, as is a Christian theological understanding of religions. Chapter ten puts forward a theology of religions based upon Christian assumptions.
[19]As quoted in Schmidt et al., *Patterns of Religion,* p. 6.

chological functions of religion.[20] Accordingly, Frederick Streng characterizes religion as "a means to ultimate transformation," defining ultimate transformation as "a fundamental change from being caught up in the troubles of common existence (sin, ignorance) to living in such a way that one can cope at the deepest level with those troubles."[21]

Substantive and functional definitions have both strengths and weaknesses, but as Eric Sharpe reminds us, "To *define* religion is . . . far less important than to possess the ability to *recognize* it when we come across it."[22] Characterizing religion involves having certain paradigm cases of what counts as religion and extrapolating from them typical patterns. Wittgenstein's famous discussion of "family resemblances" and games can be instructive here. Although there is no single feature shared by all games, there is a network of similarities and analogies among them, not unlike the resemblances among members of a natural family, such that we can identify various games when we encounter them.[23] Similarly, although there is no single feature essential to all religions, there are sufficient patterns of similarity such that, in spite of obvious differences, we can speak of various patterns of belief and behavior as constituting religions.[24] In this connection Roger Schmidt and his colleagues offer the following definition: "Religions . . . are systems of meaning embodied in a pattern of life, a community of faith, and a worldview that articulate a view of the sacred and of what ultimately matters."[25] Religions, on this understanding, include a pattern of life or way of living; a community of faith; and a worldview, or basic beliefs about what is ultimately real and of value.

Religion is thus a multifarious phenomenon, and Ninian Smart has helpfully suggested that we think of it in terms of seven distinct but interrelated dimensions.[26] What Smart calls the *ritual dimension* includes the visible rites, ceremo-

---

[20]See Donald Crosby, *Interpretive Theories of Religion* (The Hague: Mouton, 1981), p. 37.

[21]Frederick Streng, *Understanding Religious Life*, 3rd ed. (Belmont, Calif.: Wadsworth, 1985), p. 2. Similarly, the cultural anthropologist Clifford Geertz speaks of religion as "(1) a system of symbols which acts to (2) establish powerful, pervasive and long-lasting moods and motivations in men by (3) formulating conceptions of a general order of existence and (4) clothing these conceptions with such an aura of factuality that (5) the moods and motivations seem uniquely realistic" (Clifford Geertz, *The Interpretation of Cultures* [New York: Basic, 1973], p. 90).

[22]Eric J. Sharpe, *Understanding Religion* (New York: St. Martin's, 1983), p. 47. Emphasis in the original.

[23]Ludwig Wittgenstein, *Philosophical Investigations*, trans. G. E. M. Anscombe, 3rd ed. (New York: Macmillan, 1958), sec. 66, p. 31.

[24]This is the approach adopted by John Hick in *An Interpretation of Religion* (New Haven, Conn.: Yale University Press, 1989), pp. 3-5.

[25]Schmidt et al., *Patterns of Religion*, p. 10.

[26]Smart, *World's Religions*, pp. 11-22. Smart earlier used six dimensions for understanding religion, with the seventh, the material dimension, being added later. For the six dimensions, see Ninian Smart, *Worldviews: Crosscultural Explorations of Human Beliefs*, 2nd ed. (Englewood Cliffs, N.J.: Prentice-Hall, 1995).

nies and institutions that are used in a carefully prescribed manner by the religious believers. Religious services, prayers, offerings, baptisms, sacrifice and so on are thus part of this dimension. The collection of myths, images and stories through which the invisible, transcendent world is symbolically expressed is called the *mythological* or *narrative dimension*. (Smart is not using the term *myth* to imply that the content is necessarily false. What he means by *myth* is similar to a story, whether true or false.) The *doctrinal dimension* includes the systematic attempt to clarify and integrate the central beliefs of a religious tradition. Yet another aspect is the *ethical dimension,* which includes the moral teachings of a tradition that bear directly upon the manner in which the believer is to live his or her life. Closely related to the ethical is the *social* or *institutional dimension,* which reflects the patterns and mores that dictate desirable relationships among the believers in the religious community. This dimension also includes the institutions that provide necessary structure and organization to the tradition. The *experiential dimension* is that part in which the religious believer participates actively in the various rites and patterns of the religious tradition (for example, through worship, prayer and meditation). Finally, the *material dimension* refers to the material forms identified with a religion—magnificent buildings, works of art, gardens, sacred sites and so on. A genuinely comprehensive understanding of religion will include appreciation of all seven dimensions.

One implication of this multidimensional view of religion is the close link between culture and religion. The ritual, ethical and social dimensions in particular find expression in broader cultural institutions and practices. Religious festivals (Ramadan in Islam, Christmas in Christianity) combine religious commitment with cultural celebration. Religious beliefs, such as those associated with the ancestors in many religions, carry with them deeply rooted social and cultural implications, as the ancestors are regarded as part of the community and thus must be properly cared for, fed and placated through appropriate sacrifices. The particular relation between the religious and cultural domains varies greatly, depending upon both the religion and the society in question. In cases where one religion has been socially dominant for a long time (Theravada Buddhism in Thailand), it can be difficult to distinguish the religious from the cultural dimensions. By contrast, where a religion is a minority tradition (Christianity in Japan), the distinction between the two is more pronounced.

Finally, we must make a basic distinction between what is often called formal or "high" religion and "folk" religion.[27] Formal religions are what one tends to encounter in textbooks about religion—highly systematized and institutionalized

---

[27]See Paul G. Hiebert, R. Daniel Shaw and Tite Tiénou, *Understanding Folk Religion* (Grand Rapids, Mich.: Baker, 1999).

religions with clearly defined doctrines, often with authoritative sacred scriptures and recognized doctrinal experts or intellectual elites. Thus, when studying Christianity, Buddhism or Hinduism as formal religions, one must give special attention to the doctrinal or philosophical framework of each. Formal religions generally have carefully prescribed boundaries to protect the orthodoxy of the traditions.

But if one's understanding of Buddhism is restricted to the formal religion of the philosophical schools, one is likely to be quite surprised by the actual beliefs and practices of Buddhists in a mountain village in Thailand. Among the villagers, there is apt to be little understanding of, or interest in, philosophical Buddhism, and their beliefs and practices will probably include many animistic and shamanistic influences that are frowned upon by the more philosophically minded. What one observes among the common people is the folk religion, the practices and beliefs that shape their lives and that typically focus upon the practical, existential concerns of everyday life (health, power, marriage, bountiful harvest, fear of death, the afterlife, the spirits and so on). In thinking of religious traditions, then, we must keep both the formal and the folk dimensions in view, recognizing that each is important in its own way for understanding religious life.

Religion and Belief

The preceding discussion makes it clear that religion cannot be identified simply with a set of beliefs or doctrines. But neither can one ignore the central place of beliefs in religion. The major religious communities characteristically teach their members to live in certain ways, to adopt particular values and to regard all of life from certain perspectives.[28] The distinctive religious perspective of a tradition is articulated in terms of basic beliefs about the cosmos and humankind's place within the cosmos. It is helpful in this connection to think of a religious tradition as embracing a particular religious worldview. A worldview, in turn, can be thought of as a comprehensive set of basic beliefs and values regarding reality that regulate characteristic patterns of behavior.[29] Following Smart, we might use *worldview* in a general sense to include both religious traditions, such as Islam or Buddhism, and secular ideologies, such as Marxism or secular humanism.[30] Religions such as Christianity, Judaism, Shinto and Buddhism would then exemplify different religious worldviews.

It seems clear that each religious tradition demands from its adherents a particular religious way of life that accords with its particular religious worldview. And

---

[28]William Christian, *Doctrines of Religious Communities: A Philosophical Study* (New Haven: Yale University Press, 1987), p. 5.
[29]See Paul Hiebert, *Cultural Anthropology,* 2nd ed. (Grand Rapids, Mich.: Baker, 1983), chapter 18.
[30]Smart, *Worldviews,* pp. 1-5.

undergirding this religious way of life are fundamental assumptions about the nature of the cosmos, the religious ultimate, the place of the human person in the cosmos, the relation of the person to the religious ultimate, the human predicament and the possibility of deliverance from this predicament. The importance of such basic beliefs must not be minimized, for as Smart observes, "The world religions owe some of their living power to their success in presenting a total picture of reality, through a coherent system of doctrines."[31] These fundamental beliefs about reality, particularly those concerning the religious ultimate and its relation to human beings, are what William Christian calls the "primary doctrines" of a religious community.[32] We might also think of them as the defining beliefs of a given religious tradition, in that they define the acceptable parameters of that tradition and help to determine the nature of the tradition's other dimensions (ritual, ethical, experiential and so on).

In passing on its primary doctrines to new members, a religious community does not merely suggest them as possible options for acceptance. Primary beliefs (defining beliefs) are not up for grabs. The religious community fully expects new members of the community to embrace them. And accepting the doctrines involves, among other things, taking what is asserted by them as true. Thus the fundamental assumptions about reality that define the worldview of a given religious community are (implicitly if not explicitly) accepted by that community as true.[33] Furthermore, as Paul Griffiths reminds us, there is a quality of absoluteness, or definitiveness, about basic religious claims.

> Religious claims to truth are typically absolute claims: claims to explain everything; claims about the universal rightness and applicability of a certain set of values together with the ways of life that embody and perpetuate them; and claims whose referent possesses maximal greatness. These tendencies to absoluteness, although they have certainly been typical of Christian doctrines, are not typical only of them; they are characteristic also of many of the most interesting claims made by the religious virtuosi of non-Christian traditions.[34]

In other words, while we can readily admit that there is much more to a religious tradition than simply its beliefs or doctrines, it should be clear that fundamental beliefs defining the worldview of a religious community are of great significance for that tradition.

Therefore, Wilfred Cantwell Smith's insistence that we concentrate upon the

---

[31]Smart, *Religious Experience of Mankind*, p. 8.
[32]Christian, *Doctrines of Religious Communities*, pp. 1-2, 5-11.
[33]Ibid., p. 42.
[34]Paul J. Griffiths, *An Apology for Apologetics: A Study in the Logic of Interreligious Dialogue* (Maryknoll, N.Y.: Orbis, 1991), pp. 2-3.

inner faith of religious believers, and not upon the external cumulative tradition, is misguided to the extent that it minimizes the central place of belief in religion. Even if we grant that an essentialist notion of "a religion" is in some sense misleading, the problem of the status of religious beliefs and their truth value remains. For we would still have particular individuals who accept and propagate certain beliefs, dogmas, teachings and so on, and presumably these are accepted by the believers as true. We would still have, for example, the Christian theologian Augustine asserting that an omnipotent God created the universe *ex nihilo* and the Buddhist Nagarjuna maintaining that the universe is the product of *pratityasamutpada,* or dependent origination. So merely shifting the focus from religions as such to the religious faith of believers will not rid us of the question of the truth value of the beliefs accepted by the various traditions, nor of the accompanying problem of conflicting truth claims.

Religions and Truth

I have argued that the religions do include fundamental beliefs about the nature of reality and that at least some of these beliefs do differ from one another, resulting in the problem of conflicting truth claims. Implicit in the discussion so far has been a realist and propositional concept of truth. Since the idea of propositional truth is frequently depicted through caricature and then summarily dismissed as irrelevant to religion, some clarification of the concept is necessary. In particular, it is often said that, while propositional truth might be applicable in domains such as biology or mathematics, it is not appropriate in religion. Religious truth is said to be qualitatively different from propositional truth, and to think of it in the latter sense is to misconstrue what religion is all about.

Truth theory is both complex and controversial, and the issues concerning religious truth involve contested questions about the nature of religious discourse, epistemology and ontology. To be sure, religion is not the same thing as chemistry or history, and religious statements do function differently than assertions in geology or medicine. Truth in religion is not something one can accept or reject in a personally detached manner; rather, religious truth, when properly grasped, demands an existential response that profoundly affects the individual. Thus Frederick Streng delineates three aspects of religious truth: "(1) the character of accurate knowing, (2) the nature of the reality known, and (3) the formation of value as the power to actualize this reality in authentic living. As a general concept, religious truth can be defined as the knowledge and expression of what-is for the purpose of achieving the greatest well-being possible (i.e. salvation, absolute freedom, or total harmony)."[35]

---

[35]Frederick Streng, "Truth," in *The Encyclopedia of Religion*, ed. Mircea Eliade (New York: Macmillan, 1987), 15:63.

However, when due allowance has been made for the distinctiveness of religion, the notion of propositional truth remains crucial to religious truth. The central features of propositional truth have been explicated recently by William Alston in his excellent discussion of "alethic realism," or a realist conception of truth.[36] The heart of a realist understanding of truth is the idea that "a statement (proposition, belief . . .) is true if and only if what the statement says to be the case actually is the case."[37] Alethic realism is closely related to what is often called the correspondence theory of truth, which holds that "for a statement to be true, there must be some appropriate *correspondence* between true statements and actual features of the world."[38] A realist understanding of truth must be distinguished from epistemic conceptions of truth, which maintain that truth is a function of evidence in favor of a statement or some other epistemic feature relative to the subject.

> What it takes to make a statement true on the realist conception is the actual obtaining of what is claimed to obtain in making the statement. If what is stated is that grass is green then it is grass's *being* green that is both necessary and sufficient for the truth of the statement. Nothing else is relevant to its truth value. This is a *realist* way of thinking of truth in that the truth *maker* is something that is objective vis-à-vis the truth *bearer*.[39]

What makes a statement true, then, is the special relation between what the statement asserts and the way reality actually is, and not something about the epistemic condition of the one asserting the statement. Whether one knows that the statement is true, or is justified or rational in believing the statement, are matters quite distinct from what constitutes the truth or falsity of the statement.

To clarify what is meant by propositional truth, we must make a basic distinction between sentences and statements or propositions. The distinction is essentially that between "what is said (or written)" and "what is used to say what is said." *What is said* is said through the use of a sentence, but it is not identical with the sentence. Sentences are always in a given language (such as English, German, Spanish, Hindi and so on) whereas *what is expressed* by the sentence is not con-

---

[36]William P. Alston, *A Realist Conception of Truth* (Ithaca, N.Y.: Cornell University Press, 1996). Other helpful treatments of truth include Paul Horwich, *Truth* (Oxford: Blackwell, 1990); and Michael Devitt, *Realism and Truth*, 2nd ed. (Oxford: Blackwell, 1991). For a good discussion of various views on the nature of truth in religion, see Hendrick M. Vroom, *Religions and the Truth: Philosophical Reflections and Perspectives* (Grand Rapids, Mich.: Eerdmans, 1989).

[37]Alston, *Realist Conception of Truth*, p. 5.

[38]Paul K. Moser, Dwayne H. Mulder and J. D. Trout, *The Theory of Knowledge: A Thematic Introduction* (New York: Oxford University Press, 1998), p. 65. Alston's discussion of alethic realism, however, is primarily concerned with the concept of truth itself and not with providing a theory about the nature of the relation between a true statement and the reality in virtue of which the statement is true. See Alston, *Realist Conception of Truth*, chapter 1.

[39]Alston, *Realist Conception of Truth*, p. 7. Emphasis in the original.

fined to a particular language, for the same content expressed in a sentence in English can also be expressed in sentences in many different languages. Indeed the same content can be expressed in different sentences within the same language. This has led many philosophers to make a basic distinction between sentences and statements or propositions. For our purposes we can regard "statements" and "propositions" as virtually synonymous. We can then roughly define a proposition as the meaning expressed by a declarative sentence, or *what is conveyed* by a sentence that makes an implicit or explicit assertion. Propositions are logically basic to beliefs and assertions. "For *what* is asserted or *what* is believed, the *content* of an assertion or a belief, *is* a proposition."[40] There is considerable debate among philosophers over the ontological status of propositions—just what are they and what is their relation to the mind? There is no need to enter into that technical discussion here, although we should emphasize that propositions cannot be identified with mental acts such as believing, judging, asserting and so on.[41] Strictly speaking, propositions are not "in the mind," although the mind does apprehend them.

To say that truth is propositional, then, is to recognize that, although "true" and "truth" can be used in a variety of ways, in the logically basic sense, truth is a property of propositions such that a proposition is true if and only if the state of affairs to which it refers obtains; otherwise it is false. Propositions can thus be thought of as the minimal vehicle of truth. Thus "John failed the math exam last Tuesday" is true if and only if John did in fact fail the math exam last Tuesday. "God was in Christ reconciling the world to himself" is true if and only if God was in Christ reconciling the world to himself. "Attachment to the notion of an enduring self prevents attainment of *nirvana*" is true if and only if attachment to the notion of an enduring self does prevent attainment of *nirvana*.

Religious Truth as Personal Truth

We have already encountered Wilfred Cantwell Smith's call for less focus in religious studies upon beliefs and doctrines and greater appreciation for the inner, subjective faith of persons. It comes as no surprise, then, that Smith is also a vigorous critic of the idea of propositional truth in religion. To think in terms of propositional truth in religion, he asserts, is to give undue emphasis to beliefs and doctrines and to be restricted by an idea that, although perhaps of value in other domains, is inappropriate in religion. Thus Smith argues that religious truth should be understood as "personal truth" since in religion "one has to do not with religions, but with religious persons."[42]

---

[40]Ibid., p. 15. Emphasis in the original.
[41]Ibid., pp. 15-22.
[42]Smith, *Meaning and End of Religion,* p. 153.

In other words, religious truth is different from concepts of truth found in ordinary life or in the sciences, and it is best understood as something other than propositional truth. "Truth, I submit, is a humane, not an objective, concept. It does not lie in propositions."[43] Smith states, "Truth and falsity are often felt in modern times to be properties or functions of statements or propositions; whereas the present proposal is that much is to be gained by seeing them rather, or anyway seeing them also, and primarily, as properties or functions of persons."[44]

Religious truth, then, is not a property of beliefs or doctrines as such but rather a function of the inner person. "Human behavior, in word or deed, is the nexus between man's inner life and the surrounding world. Truth at the personalistic level is that quality by which both halves of that relationship are chaste and appropriate, are true."[45] This notion of personal truth is less than entirely clear, but what Smith has in mind seems to be, first, the idea that truth applies not to propositions, statements or beliefs but rather to persons, and second, the idea that religious truth does not reflect correspondence with reality so much as it signifies integrity, sincerity, faithfulness, authenticity of life and the existential appropriation of certain beliefs in one's life and conduct. Thus religious traditions "can be seen as more or less true in the sense of enabling those who look at life and the universe through their patterns to perceive smaller or larger, less important or more important, areas of reality, to formulate and to ponder less or more significant issues, to act less or more truly, less or more truly to be."[46] Truth is not an abstract, static property of propositions or doctrines but rather is a dynamic product of human involvement with what is said to be true. Personal truth is not something detached from actual life; it demands existential appropriation. "No statement might be accepted as true that has not been inwardly appropriated by its author."[47] Thus personal truth is a transforming, life-changing truth.

Furthermore, Smith claims that personal truth is not unchanging. Statements, beliefs and even religious traditions can become true or might be true for me but false for you. A religious tradition "becomes more or less true in the case of particular persons as it informs their lives and their groups and shapes and nurtures their faith."[48] Applying this viewpoint to Christianity in particular, Smith says, "Christianity, I would suggest, is not true absolutely, impersonally, statically;

[43]Wilfred Cantwell Smith, *Towards a World Theology: Faith and the Comparative History of Religion* (Maryknoll, N.Y.: Orbis, 1989), p. 190.
[44]Wilfred Cantwell Smith, "A Human View of Truth," in *Truth and Dialogue in World Religions: Conflicting Truth Claims*, ed. John Hick (Philadelphia: Westminster Press, 1974), p. 20.
[45]Ibid., p. 26.
[46]Smith, *Towards a World Theology*, p. 94.
[47]Smith, "Human View of Truth," p. 35.
[48]Smith, *Towards a World Theology*, p. 187.

rather, it can *become* true, if and as you or I appropriate it to ourselves and interiorize it, insofar as we live it out from day to day. It becomes true as we take it off the shelf and personalize it, in actual existence."[49]

Obviously, acceptance of the notion of personal truth will have far-reaching consequences for the way in which we regard the relation among different religions. Instead of considering truth and falsity as properties of propositions (or beliefs) that are accepted by believers in their respective traditions, we will view truth as a changing, dynamic product of the faith of religious individuals. The assumption that religious beliefs are central to religious traditions, that they have objective truth value and that on occasion beliefs from different religions conflict with each other will have to be discarded as misleading at best. No longer will it make sense to speak of, say, the truth of the doctrine of the incarnation without also making reference to the personal response of faith to the doctrine. The doctrine could not be said to be true or false in and of itself. We could only say that it is true for someone, and it would be true only to the extent that someone existentially appropriated belief in the doctrine. Thus, while the doctrine of the incarnation might be "true for Joe," it could simultaneously be "false for Linda," insofar as she failed to appropriate existentially belief in the doctrine. We could no longer speak of a particular religion, such as Christianity, as being true in and of itself. It would be "true" only to the extent that individual Christians appropriate its teachings and traditions and are significantly impacted by it in their lives. Similarly it would make little sense to speak of one religion being true and others false, for presumably there are devout believers in all religions who are transformed existentially by their respective traditions. In this sense, all religions could be considered "true"—or at least true for those believers who happen to appropriate the beliefs and practices of their respective religions. It is evident, then, that Smith's proposal is a radical reinterpretation of the concept of truth in religion.

Although Smith's notion of personal truth contains an important insight, if it is meant to exclude the concept of propositional truth, it is seriously confused. Certainly the personal dimension is important in religion, and Smith rightly emphasizes that religious faith cannot be reduced to intellectual assent to a set of propositions. Integral to religious faith is the idea that one must appropriate certain beliefs so that one's conduct and character are significantly altered—we are to be doers of the Word and not hearers only!

But critics of propositional truth often set up the issues in terms of a misleading exclusive disjunction: either one has propositional truth about God or one has an existential encounter with God, but not both. In reality, not only is it possible to

---

[49]Wilfred Cantwell Smith, *Questions of Religious Truth* (London: Victor Gollancz, 1967), pp. 67-68. Emphasis in the original.

have both, but in fact one cannot respond appropriately to God without first having some knowledge about God. The believer can only respond personally to God as Lord and Savior if he or she already knows something about what God is like and what he expects from humankind. The more one knows about God, the more one will be able to know God personally and respond appropriately to him. As Nash puts it, "Personal encounter cannot take place in a cognitive vacuum."[50] Furthermore, we must reject the assumption, implicit in much contemporary theology and religious studies, that propositional truth is abstract, detached, cold and incapable of eliciting more than a bland intellectual response of mental assent from believers. There is no reason to suppose that true propositions about God cannot prompt powerful and moving personal responses from believers. Propositions may indeed be "response evoking," as Paul Helm puts it, particularly if the propositions have to do with the nature of God (for example, his love) and what he has graciously done for humankind.[51]

In sorting through Smith's proposal it is helpful to distinguish among three frequently conflated concepts—faith, belief and truth. "Faith" can be used in two distinct senses, the difference between the two being indicated by the Latin words *fiducia* and *fides,* both of which are translated into English as "faith." *Fiducia* refers to faith as trust in, or commitment to, God; *fides* signifies belief that certain propositions about God are true.[52] It is important to see that faith as *fiducia* is logically dependent upon faith as *fides.* As Roger Trigg puts it, "In any sphere the fact of commitment logically entails certain beliefs and precludes certain others. One must believe in the truth of what one is committed to."[53] Trust in God presupposes that certain propositions about God (that he is reliable, trustworthy and so on) are true. Although there is some overlap in the meanings of "faith" and "belief," for our purposes it will be helpful to restrict use of "faith" to indicate *fiducia,* or the personal response of trust and commitment to God. "Belief" should then be used to mean faith as *fides,* or the acceptance of certain propositions about God as true. "Truth" should not be used to mean faith in either of these senses but, as noted above, should be understood primarily as a property of propositions or statements. With these distinctions in mind, let us return to Smith's proposal of personal truth.

A pervasive ambiguity in Smith's discussions of personal truth allows for at least

[50]Ronald Nash, *The Word of God and the Mind of Man* (Grand Rapids, Mich.: Zondervan, 1982), p. 46-47.

[51]Paul Helm, *Divine Revelation* (London: Marshall, Morgan & Scott, 1982), p. 27.

[52]See John Hick, *Faith and Knowledge,* 2nd ed. (Ithaca, N.Y.: Cornell University Press, 1966), pp. 3-4. See also H. H. Price, "Belief 'In' and Belief 'That,' " in *The Philosophy of Religion,* ed. Basil Mitchell (Oxford: Oxford University Press, 1971), pp. 143-67; and Paul Helm, *Faith and Understanding* (Grand Rapids, Mich.: Eerdmans, 1997), chapter 1.

[53]Roger Trigg, *Reason and Commitment* (London: Cambridge University Press, 1973), p. 44.

three possible interpretations: (1) Personal truth can legitimately be applied to religion whereas propositional truth cannot. (2) Both personal truth and propositional truth can be applied to religion, but personal truth is somehow more fundamental than propositional truth. (3) Both personal truth and propositional truth can be applied to religion, but propositional truth is more basic than personal truth.

Smith's proposal seems to entail (1) or (2), but both of these formulations are untenable. The major difficulty with both (1) and (2) is the fact that logically the most basic notion of truth in any realm whatsoever is propositional truth. To be sure, "truth" and "true" have a wide variety of meanings in ordinary discourse, so that we can say "the purse is true alligator," "he is a true Democrat," "Jesus is the Truth," "her music is full of truth" or "his presentation this morning just didn't have the ring of truth." And in religion "truth" is often used to mean something like "ultimate significance," "ultimate meaning or purpose," "that which radically transforms one" or "authenticity."

The inadequacy of (1) and (2) can be demonstrated as follows. Let P stand for the statement of Smith's theory of personal truth, as understood in (1) or (2):

P: In religion, truth is primarily personal, not propositional, and is attributed to persons who satisfactorily appropriate religious beliefs.

It is crucial to see that, if P is offered as something we should accept as true (and surely this is Smith's intention), then it is itself dependent upon the notion of propositional truth. For P expresses a proposition that makes a claim about reality: it asserts that reality is such that truth is primarily personal and is attributed to persons who satisfactorily appropriate religious beliefs. Thus, in proposing P for acceptance, Smith is suggesting that we accept it because it is true, that is, that reality actually is as the proposition expressed by P asserts it to be. Now clearly the sense in which P is presumed to be true is *not* that of personal truth. For if P were said to be true only in the sense of personal truth, then it would be true only in so far as you or I appropriate it and allow it to impact significantly upon our lives. Therefore, P might be true for Smith but false for me, or true for me but false for you. But obviously this is not what Smith has in mind. In advancing his theory he is assuming that it is true in the logically basic sense of propositional truth.

We can observe the inadequacy of the concept of personal truth from a different perspective as well. Smith's suggestion that religious beliefs *become* true to the extent that they are internalized and appropriated, if meant to exclude the notion of propositional truth, is misguided. A believer will appropriate such beliefs only if he or she already accepts them as true in a propositional or nonpersonalistic sense. For example, the belief that Allah is a righteous judge will "become true" in a personal sense only if the Muslim first accepts the proposition expressed by the statement "Allah is a righteous judge" as true in a nonpersonalistic, propositional sense.[54] We can readily admit that "true" can be used to mean something like "authentic," "genuine," "faithful" or "sincere." When used in this sense, "religious truth" would be a quality of life in the believer such that there are no glaring inconsistencies between what one professes and the manner in which one lives. To affirm that the statement "Allah is a righteous judge" is true, on this understanding of "true," would then be to recognize that a particular Muslim's life is congruous with belief that Allah is a righteous judge. But this presupposes that the Muslim accepts and appropriates not only a certain set of values, practices and manner of life but also a set of beliefs about reality, including the existence and nature of Allah. And the Muslim will accept such basic beliefs in the first place because he or she regards them as accurately portraying the way reality actually is. Thus the fundamental beliefs defining the Muslim's worldview (for example, "Allah is a righteous judge") are accepted as true not in a personal but in a propositional sense. But if so, personal truth cannot be regarded as an alternative to propositional truth, for it actually presupposes propositional truth. Wilfred Cantwell Smith has confused the question of truth with that of the believer's response to the truth. But the truth value of a belief and the degree to which one allows that belief to impact one's life are two very different matters.[55]

William Wainright summarizes nicely the implications of this for the issue of conflicting truth claims:

> It is a mistake . . . to argue that doctrinal conflicts are unimportant because truth as authenticity or truth as reality are more important than propositional truth. Genuine authenticity presupposes that one possesses propositional truth. Ultimate reality is the truth (more than anything else) only if certain propositions are true. If doctrinal conflicts can't be rationally resolved, then there is no rational way of determining which lives are more authentic, or whether God or Nirvana or Brahman are the truth. Beliefs, and the truth of what one believes, are important.[56]

Religious Truth as Ineffable

An influential objection to the idea that propositional truth is inescapable in religion comes from those who argue that religious beliefs are really just inadequate attempts to express what is inexpressible. Beliefs and doctrines are merely inadequate pointers toward what cannot be clearly articulated. Religious truth is ineffa-

---

[54]See William J. Wainwright, "Wilfred Cantwell Smith on Faith and Belief," *Religious Studies* 20 (September 1984).

[55]See Donald Wiebe, *Truth and Religion: Towards an Alternative Paradigm for the Study of Religion* (The Hague: Mouton, 1981), p. 213.

[56]William J. Wainwright, *Philosophy of Religion*, 2nd ed. (Belmont, Calif.: Wadsworth, 1999), p. 206.

ble and cannot be captured in neat propositions; it can only be intuited. What is important is not the beliefs themselves but rather what they point toward. This situation is like pointing a finger toward the moon: if you concentrate on the finger itself, instead of on what it is pointing at, you will never see the moon. Focusing upon doctrine, then, is like mistaking the finger for the moon.

The incomprehensibility of God is, of course, a major theme in the history of Christian thought. God is an infinite Being far exceeding human concepts and language. The early church father Chrysostom is typical of many writers through the centuries who have emphasized God's incomprehensibility:

> [W]e call Him the inexpressible, the unthinkable God, the invisible, the incomprehensible, the inapprehensible; who quells the power of human speech and transcends the grasp of mortal thought; inaccessible to the angels, upheld by the Seraphim, unimagined of the Cherubim, invisible to principalities and authorities and powers, and, in a word, to all creation.[57]

Similarly Gregory of Nyssa stated that God is "incapable of being grasped by any term, or any idea, or any other device of our apprehension."[58]

Christian theology includes the long and venerable tradition of the *via negativa*, the negative way, in thinking about God. Dionysius the Areopagite, Meister Eckhart and Nicholas of Cusa, among many others, emphasized the way of negation in speaking of God. But probably the most sophisticated argument for the *via negativa* is found, not in a Christian theologian, but in the thirteenth-century Jewish philosopher Moses Maimonides.[59] Maimonides claimed that, although we can know of the acts of God, we can make no positive statements at all about the nature of God, unless we give the predicate terms (for example, "wise," "good") meanings entirely different from the meanings of those terms when predicated of finite creatures. We cannot speak positively of what God is; we can only speak negatively of what God is not. No human concepts or linguistic terms can be applied to God since God utterly transcends all human categories.

The idea that the religious ultimate is beyond any possible description, and cannot be expressed in language, is a pervasive theme in Eastern religions as well. The Tao (Way) of Taoism is said to be indescribable, indefinable, incapable of being grasped by human thought. The Taoist classic *Tao Te Ching* begins with the enigmatic statement "The way [Tao] that can be spoken of is not the constant way; The

---

[57]Chrysostom, third discourse of *De incomprehensibili*, as quoted in Rudolf Otto, *The Idea of the Holy*, trans. J. Harvey (1917; reprint, New York: Oxford University Press, 1950), p. 180.

[58]Gregory of Nyssa, "Against Eunomius," in *A Select Library of Nicene and Post-Nicene Fathers of the Christian Church*, ed. Philip Schaff, 2nd series (Grand Rapids, Mich.: Eerdmans, 1954), 5:99.

[59]Moses Maimonides, *Guide for the Perplexed*, trans. M. Freidlander, 2nd ed. (London: Routledge & Sons, 1940).

name that can be named is not the constant name."[60] The Tao is said to be "forever nameless." Suspicion of words finds classic expression in the cryptic statement "One who knows does not speak; one who speaks does not know."[61] Zen Buddhism, heavily influenced by Taoism, similarly rejects the idea that the Buddhist dharma, or ultimate Truth, can be expressed in language; it is passed on directly from master to disciple. The core of Zen teaching is expressed in a poem attributed to the legendary fifth-century patriarch Bodhidharma:

Not relying on words or letters,
An independent self-transmitting apart from the doctrinal teaching,
Directly pointing to one's mind,
Awakening to one's original Nature, thereby actualizing his Buddhahood.[62]

The Zen master Daiei claimed that "Zen has no words: when you have *satori* [enlightenment] you have everything."[63]

Given this emphasis across religions that the religious ultimate cannot be captured in conceptual and linguistic categories, one might well conclude that it is a serious error to concentrate upon the truth value of beliefs and doctrines. After all, beliefs are no more than inadequate pointers toward that which ultimately is inexpressible. There is an important point here, for humans are finite and the religious ultimate far exceeds the grasp of the human intellect. The problem, however, is how to understand divine transcendence in such a way that the "otherness" of the religious ultimate is preserved while also maintaining the possibility of genuine knowledge of this ultimate.

Thinking in terms of Christian theism, there certainly is a sense in which God can be said to be beyond the scope of human conceptual and linguistic categories. But it does not necessarily follow from this that *none* of our concepts and linguistic terms can be applied meaningfully to God. The question is how we are to understand God's transcendence. W. D. Hudson points out that there are two distinct senses in which we can say that God is "wholly other," incomprehensible and beyond the grasp of our intellect.[64] The difference between the two can be seen in the ways in which they respectively answer the question "Can God coherently be described in human language as ordinarily used?" On the one hand, there is the

---

[60]*Lao Tzu: Tao Te Ching*, trans. D. C. Lau (New York: Penguin, 1963), p. 57.

[61]Ibid., pp. 91, 117.

[62]Cited in Masao Abe, *Zen and Western Thought*, ed. William R. LaFleur (Honolulu: University of Hawaii Press, 1985), p. 23.

[63]Quoted in D. T. Suzuki, *Essays in Zen Buddhism: Second Series*, ed. Christmas Humphreys (New York: Samuel Weiser, 1953), p. 31.

[64]W. Donald Hudson, "The Concept of Divine Transcendence," *Religious Studies* 15 (June 1979): 198. A helpful discussion of ineffability can also be found in Keith Yandell, *The Epistemology of Religious Experience* (Cambridge: Cambridge University Press, 1993), chapters 3-5.

ineffability thesis, which claims that no coherent descriptions of God can be formulated in language. On the other hand, there is the tradition maintaining that coherent descriptions of God's nature and activity can be formulated in human language, although such descriptions have their limitations and must be interpreted appropriately. The latter position has been characteristic of most Protestant and Catholic theology.

The major problem with the ineffability thesis is the difficulty of stating it in such a way that it is coherent and preserves the possibility of knowledge about God. A strict formulation of the ineffability thesis is as follows:

I: No concepts or linguistic terms can be meaningfully applied to God.[65]

Ineffability can be construed as either an epistemological or a metaphysical thesis, although the two senses are often conflated. The epistemological claim is that concepts, categories and linguistic terms with which we are familiar cannot be applied to God at all because we simply do not grasp what God is really like. The metaphysical claim is that God is such that no properties of any kind pertain to God, and therefore no concepts or propositions apply to God. Thus language, which inevitably makes use of concepts, is inapplicable to God. In the former case, ineffability stems from the limitations of our intellectual processes; in the latter case, ineffability is due to the nature (or lack thereof) of the religious ultimate itself. Either way, however, the result is the same: nothing meaningful can be said—even metaphorically—about God.

The ineffability thesis expressed in *I* has some disastrous consequences. First, it follows from *I* that we can have no knowledge of God, for if no concepts at all can be applied to God, then no true or false statements about God can be made. To have a concept of some entity x is, roughly, to know the meaning of the word "x," to be able to pick out and recognize an instance of x and to have a grasp of the properties that distinguish x. Concepts are essentially linked to properties, attributes or qualities. To ascribe a property to an object (for example, "The ball is red") is to apply a concept, or a collection of concepts, to that object. Now if concepts are essentially linked to properties, and if no concepts at all can be applied to God, then it follows that no properties at all can be ascribed to God. It would further follow that no truths about God could be known. For to know a truth about God is to know that some proposition *p* about God is true, and if *p* is true, then it will attribute some property to God. To say "God is merciful" is to ascribe the property of being merciful to God. But according to *I,* since no concepts can be applied to God, no proper-

---

[65]The discussion on ineffability here is in terms of theism. Appropriate modifications can be made for nontheistic traditions by substituting *"nirguna* Brahman" or "the Tao" or "emptiness" for "God."

ties can be ascribed to him either. It follows, then, that no truths about God can be known.

Paradoxically, if *I* were true, we could never know that it is true. If true, *I* would express a true proposition about God. But as we have seen, *I* entails that no truths about God can be known. Thus, if *I* is true, we could never know that it is true. It is possible also to argue that *I* is self-refuting, since it ascribes a concept (the concept of "being unconceptualizable") to God. But if even one concept is applicable to God, then *I* cannot be true. Thus the assertion of *I* actually falsifies *I*. If, on the other hand, *I* is interpreted as not applying any concept to God, then it is hard to see how it can be a meaningful and informative statement. Advocates of ineffability some-times modify *I* in various ways, claiming, for example, as John Hick does, that only formal concepts (such as "x having the property of being referred to") and no sub-stantial properties ("being good" or "being greedy") can be applied to the religious ultimate.[66] We will consider Hick's version of ineffability further in chapter seven.

Yet another move is to consider ineffability in terms of the *via negativa,* so that no terms signifying positive attributes can be applied to God; only terms signifying what God is not can be used in divine predication. The *via negativa,* or apophatic theology, has a long and distinguished history in Jewish, Christian and Islamic the-ologies. But to be informative, the *via negativa* must be supplemented with some positive knowledge of God.[67] If we have some positive knowledge of God, or at least what is taken to be knowledge of God, then we can apply negative predication in order to purify our understanding of God. For example, if we know that God is an incorporeal being, then we can deny that he is tall, short or even a physical being at all. But if we have absolutely no positive knowledge of God, on what basis could we say that certain properties cannot be ascribed to God? Simply to say that God is not a physical object or not mortal or not evil, with no corresponding positive affirma-tion, is hardly informative. The same could be said of numbers or riddles. Effective use of the *via negativa* presupposes that at least some positive knowledge of God is available and that at least some positive predication about God is legitimate.

If one modifies *I* further by saying that since God is transcendent, beyond human comprehension and therefore incapable of being captured by concepts and words, then we have an important truth. But this is no longer ineffability. There is nothing here that rules out the possibility of partial, but nevertheless informative, communication of truth about God. To be sure, concepts and linguistic terms with

---

[66]See John Hick, *A Christian Theology of Religions: The Rainbow of Faiths* (Louisville: Westminster John Knox, 1995), pp. 61-62.

[67]This was clearly recognized by Thomas Aquinas. See *Summa theologica* 1.q.13.a.2., in *Basic Writings of Saint Thomas Aquinas*, ed. Anton C. Pegis (New York: Random House, 1945), 1:114-16.

which we are familiar cannot exhaustively "capture" God. Such concepts and terms have limitations and must therefore be interpreted carefully. The question, then, is not *whether* we can apply certain concepts and terms to God but *how we are to understand them* when we do so, and there is a rich and sophisticated tradition within Christian theology devoted to precisely this question.[68]

Some religious traditions present special challenges in that they advance the claim that the religious ultimate transcends all duality and thus has no distinguishing properties at all. Thus any application of concepts or properties to the ultimate is inappropriate. An influential example of this theme is found in the Hindu tradition of Advaita Vedanta, derived from Shankara (A.D. 788–820). According to Advaita Vedanta, there is only one reality, *nirguna* Brahman, or Brahman without qualities or attributes.[69]

The distinction between two levels of reality and two levels of truth is fundamental to Advaita Vedanta.[70] Shankara accepted the distinction between the realm of ordinary phenomenal reality, or appearance, and that of Brahman, absolute, undifferentiated Being. Truth on the level of appearance is important—the phenomenal reality of the appearances is not to be denied. However, there is a higher Reality and Truth—that of absolutely undifferentiated Being. The person who transcends the ordinary realm and realizes that he or she is in fact identical with Brahman sees the provisional nature of ordinary reality and truth. From the perspective of ultimate Truth, the highest Reality, ordinary reality is illusion *(maya)* and the "truth" attained on this level no more than cosmic ignorance *(avidya).* The highest form of spiritual knowledge or Truth *(para vidya)* relegates all other kinds of

---

[68]For good introductions to some of the issues, see Michael Peterson, William Hasker, Bruce Reichenbach and David Basinger, *Reason and Religious Belief: An Introduction to the Philosophy of Religion*, 2nd ed. (New York: Oxford University Press, 1998), chapter 8; Patrick Sherry, *Religion, Truth, and Language Games* (London: Macmillan, 1977); and William P. Alston, *Divine Nature and Human Language* (Ithaca, N.Y.: Cornell University Press, 1989).

[69]Helpful discussions of Shankara and Advaita Vedanta include Eliot Deutsch, *Advaita Vedanta* (Honolulu: University of Hawaii Press, 1969); John M. Koller and Patricia Joyce Koller, *Asian Philosophies*, chapter 8; and Arvind Sharma, *The Philosophy of Religion and Advaita Vedanta: A Comparative Study in Religion and Reason* (University Park: Pennsylvania State University Press, 1995).

[70]Something like this distinction is also found in the perennial philosophy tradition, and it finds classic expression in Fritjof Schuon's *The Transcendent Unity of Religions*, trans. Peter Townsend, rev. ed. (New York: Harper & Row, 1975). Schuon distinguishes between *exoteric* and *esoteric* truth in religion. Exoteric truth is that truth that followers of religions generally are able to apprehend. It is subject to rational analysis and can be expressed propositionally. The highest form of religious truth, however, is esoteric truth, and it is on this level that one discovers the ultimate unity among religions. Esoteric truth cannot be expressed propositionally, nor can it be assessed by rational and logical criteria applicable to exoteric truth. It can only be experienced by direct intuition or "faith." See also Aldous Huxley, *The Perennial Philosophy* (New York: Harper & Brothers, 1945); and Huston Smith, *Forgotten Truth: The Primordial Tradition* (New York: Harper & Row, 1976).

knowledge and truth to lower levels of reality. Such Truth is entirely self-certifying; no criteria, arguments or experience from the lower level of reality and truth can either confirm or refute it.[71]

Let us note briefly two problems with Advaita Vedanta or any similar perspective. First, it is far from clear that the notion of *nirguna* Brahman—Brahman without attributes or properties, pure undifferentiated Being—is even coherent. Keith Yandell states, "It looks as if Advaita wants to hold all of a set of logically inconsistent theses. In particular, it begins with the claim that something exists but altogether lacks properties, and that something that altogether lacks properties can be identical to a variety of things that have properties and are distinct from one another."[72] Yandell expresses concisely a criticism of Shankara's position that was actually made by the eleventh-century Vedantin theologian Ramanuja: "[I]t is logically impossible that there be anything that lacks all qualities; *X exists but for every property P, X lacks P* is simply a contradiction."[73] Thus the charge of incoherence is made not only by Western philosophers but also has found powerful expression by Hindu thinkers.[74] Ramanuja agreed with Shankara that the only reality is Brahman, but unlike Shankara, he held that Brahman includes within his being real distinctions and attributes. The universe, including individual selves and things, are real and exist as the "body" of Brahman. Ramanuja maintained that Shankara's views on Brahman not only were logically incoherent but also undermined the meaningfulness of the language of the Vedic scriptures.

Second, we must ask why we should accept the doctrine of two levels of truth in the first place. Is there a compelling reason to do so? If consistent, the advocate of the doctrine will not present carefully reasoned arguments for the distinction, for to do so would be to appeal to rational and logical criteria in support of a doctrine holding that such criteria are legitimate only on the lower level of reality. It would be inconsistent to appeal to such criteria in order to justify the assertion that ultimate Truth transcends ordinary reality and truth.

---

[71]The idea of two levels of reality and truth is also central to certain forms of Buddhism, especially those influenced by the second-century Indian Buddhist Nagarjuna and the Madhyamaka school. It was also emphasized by the sixth-century Chinese Buddhist Chi-tsang. See Paul Williams, *Mahayana Buddhism: The Doctrinal Foundations* (London: Routledge, 1989), pp. 69-72, 75-76. The distinction is also central to the Zen tradition and is given contemporary expression in Abe, *Zen and Western Thought*, especially chapters 1, 2 and 5.

[72]Yandell, *Philosophy of Religion*, p. 242.

[73]Yandell, *Epistemology of Religious Experience*, p. 299. Emphasis in the original. Yandell's discussion in chapter 13 explores the difficulties of Advaita Vedanta in detail and deserves careful study.

[74]On Ramanuja, see John Braisted Carman, *The Theology of Ramanuja: An Essay in Interreligious Understanding* (New Haven, Conn.: Yale University Press, 1974); and Julius Lipner, *The Face of Truth: A Study of Meaning and Metaphysics in the Vedantic Theology of Ramanuja* (Albany: State University of New York Press, 1986).

Advocates of the doctrine might respond by saying that the distinction is somehow self-evident or self-certifying. The person who is fortunate enough to have the experience of grasping the nature of ultimate Reality simply knows that the distinction is legitimate. Those who do not have this experience cannot be persuaded by rational argument that the distinction is sound. It would seem, then, that those without the experience must simply accept the testimony of the one claiming to have had the experience. His or her authority justifies accepting the distinction.

But why should we accept the word of someone claiming to have had such an experience? The simple claim to have had such an experience, in and of itself, cannot be regarded as determinative. Appeal to authority in and of itself settles nothing. There are always competing claims based upon authority, and the question then becomes which (if any) authority or testimony is to be accepted, and on what basis. Nor will it help here to appeal to the sacred scripture of some tradition, for one can always ask why those particular writings should be accepted as divinely revealed truth.

Advocates of the doctrine of two truths thus face a dilemma: any attempt to provide reasons for accepting the testimony of someone claiming to have had the experience will make appeal to criteria and principles that are said to be applicable only on the lower level of reality and truth. And one cannot consistently appeal to such criteria in an effort to justify the basic distinction between levels of truth. However, failure to provide such reasons results in a situation in which one simply makes an arbitrary choice to accept or not to accept the testimony. It would seem that the one without the experience, then, could never be in a position in which the most reasonable thing to do is to accept the testimony.

7

THE PROBLEMS
OF PLURALISM

Let us consider, that, in matters of religion, whatever is different is contrary; and that it is impossible the religions of ancient Rome, of Turkey, of Siam, and of China should, all of them, be established on any sound foundation.

DAVID HUME, An Enquiry Concerning Human Understanding

It is by no means unusual in these days to find students (and others) occupying a position which is at one and the same time positive toward religion-in-general and negative toward religion-in-particular, especially when the latter has anything to do with traditional Christianity. (The traditional religions of the geographical East, on the other hand, fare much better.)

ERIC J. SHARPE, Understanding Religion

A traditional Japanese saying—"Although the paths to the summit may differ, from the top one sees the same moon"—when applied to religion suggests that, although there are different religious paths, ultimately each way is in touch with the same divine reality and will reach the same goal.[1] This is a recurring theme in Asian cultures and religions. In the Hindu scripture Bhagavad-Gita Lord Krishna proclaims, "Whatever path men travel is My path; No matter where they walk it leads to Me."[2] Commenting on this verse, the Hindu philosopher Sarvepalli Radhakrishnan says, "The same God is worshipped by all. The

---

[1]This is not to suggest that traditional Japanese attitudes have been accepting of all religious options. The idea that there can be different, alternative ways of responding to the religious ultimate has usually been tempered by an emphasis upon ethnicity and culture, so that Buddhism and Shinto, along with their syncretistic offspring, are regarded as legitimate options for Japanese while Christianity is valid for Europeans and Americans. Religious diversity in the Japanese context is tolerated only as long as carefully defined social parameters, including participation in the ancestral cult and acceptance of a common sense of religious identity rooted in myths of ethnicity, are preserved. Once these boundaries are crossed—as when Japanese acknowledge Jesus Christ as the one Lord and Savior for all humankind—there can be significant opposition.

[2]*Bhagavad-Gita*, trans. Swami Prabhavananda and Christopher Isherwood (New York: Mentor, 1972), p. 51.

differences of conception and approach are determined by local colouring and social adaptations. All manifestations belong to the same Supreme."[3]

As we have seen, the idea that the religions are culturally and historically conditioned human responses to the same divine reality is increasingly popular in the West as well. The pluralist intuition is prompted by the desire to affirm cultural and religious diversity along with the conviction that large numbers of sincere, morally good and intelligent people simply cannot be mistaken about their basic religious beliefs. Religious pluralism is found both among ordinary persons who have never given the question much thought and among academics who have developed quite sophisticated models for understanding the relations among the religions. In this chapter we will consider the most rigorous and influential model of pluralism to date, that of John Hick, but first we must consider some approaches that initially appear to be pluralistic but in fact are not.

Pseudopluralisms

The attraction of pluralistic views lies in the perception that pluralism is genuinely accepting of other religions whereas particularism and inclusivism are not. After all, pluralism affirms the major religious traditions as all equally legitimate ways of responding to the one divine reality, and pluralists appear to be nonjudgmental about the beliefs and practices of the religions.

But appearances can be deceiving. As we shall see, it is difficult to come up with a genuinely pluralistic model that is coherent and does not privilege any particular religious perspective. What sometimes seems to be an open pluralism can in reality be a covert kind of inclusivism, so that what initially appears to be a very accepting posture toward other religions really involves understanding and accommodating religious others within the framework of one's own tradition, which remains normative. As Langdon Gilkey observes, "This has been an extremely impressive attitude in which all other religions are accepted, tolerated and even admired—but still interpreted as to their worth and validity according to the criteria, the consequently absolute criteria, of the interpreting faith."[4] This is not really pluralism but merely an especially generous form of inclusivism.

Interestingly, some of the leading non-Western spokespersons for religious diversity and tolerance, persons who are often perceived in the West as advocates of radical pluralism, are actually very sophisticated and open inclusivists. Despite

---

[3]Sarvepalli Radhakrishnan, *The Bhagavadgita: With an Introductory Essay, Sanskrit Text, English Translation and Notes* (New York: Harper Colophon, 1973), p. 159.

[4]Langdon Gilkey, "The Pluralism of Religions," in *God, Truth and Reality: Essays in Honour of John Hick*, ed. Arvind Sharma (New York: St. Martin's, 1993), p. 112. See also Keith Yandell, "Some Varieties of Religious Pluralism," in *Inter-religious Models and Criteria*, ed. James Kellenberger (New York: St. Martin's, 1993), pp. 190-91.

impressions to the contrary, they do not regard all religions as more or less equally salvific; they remain firmly committed to a particular tradition, whether Hindu or Buddhist, and their tolerance and openness to others grows out of their religious worldview.

For example, in the earlier part of the twentieth century Sarvepalli Radhakrishnan (1888-1975) exercised unparalleled influence in the West as an advocate for religious tolerance and diversity.[5] Educated in mission schools, including Madras Christian College, Radhakrishnan had early exposure to Christianity, but rather than foster an appreciation for Christian faith, this experience stimulated in him a deeper interest in his own Indian culture and Hindu traditions. After several professorial posts in India, Radhakrishnan went on to become the first Spalding Professor of Eastern Religions and Ethics at Oxford University (1936-1952), where he was widely recognized as the leading interpreter of Hinduism to the West. He also was active in politics, serving as ambassador for India to the Soviet Union, then as vice president of India and finally as president of India (1962-1967). Radhakrishnan lectured widely, was a prolific writer and became a highly visible symbol of the struggle for world unity and religious tolerance. But he was an uncompromising and often bitter critic of religious conversion and what he perceived to be the dogmatism and intolerance of monotheistic religions such as Judaism and Christianity.

There is much to suggest that Radhakrishnan was a religious pluralist who held that all religions are equally legitimate ways of responding to the divine. A common theme in his writings is that the various religions are different paths leading to the same goals, that doctrinal differences are merely culturally conditioned ways of affirming the same basic insight and that at the heart of the many religions lies a common mystical core.

> The name by which we call God and the rite by which we approach Him do not matter much. . . . Toleration is the homage which the finite mind pays to the inexhaustibility of the Infinite. . . . There are many possible roads from time to eternity and we need to choose one road. . . . The doctrine we adopt and the philosophy we profess do not matter any more than the language we speak and the clothes we wear.[6]

---

[5] A helpful account of Radhakrishnan's life is K. Satchidananda Murty and Ashok Vohra, *Radhakrishnan: His Life and Ideas* (Albany: State University of New York Press, 1990). Among Radhakrishnan's major works are *Eastern Religions and Western Thought* (Oxford: Clarendon, 1939); *Indian Philosophy*, rev. ed., 2 vols. (New York: Macmillan, 1927); *An Idealist View of Life* (London: Allen & Unwin, 1957); and *Religion in a Changing World* (London: Allen & Unwin, 1967). See also Robert A. McDermott, ed., *Radhakrishnan: Selected Writings on Philosophy, Religion, and Culture* (New York: E. P. Dutton, 1970); and Paul Arthur Schilpp, ed., *The Philosophy of Sarvepalli Radhakrishnan* (New York: Tudor, 1952).

[6] Radhakrishnan, *Eastern Religions and Western Thought*, pp. 317-18.

And yet this apparent generosity of spirit was not really a genuine pluralism that places all of the religions on a level playing field. Radhakrishnan was unequivocally a Hindu, and he interpreted not only other Hindu traditions but also other religions through his particular understanding of Advaita Vedanta Hinduism. Ninian Smart correctly states, "His neo-Hinduism . . . forms the basis of an attempt to reconcile the teachings of the different world religions. He interprets these as essentially affirming, or reaching toward, what is to be found in Vedanta, and is critical of dogmatic, and therefore divisive, attitudes in religion: they are a main cause of conflict between faiths."[7] Thus the unity of religions Radhakrishnan advocated was based upon what he perceived as the inner core of all true religion, the kind of mysticism that finds its highest expression in Advaita Vedanta Hinduism. While Advaita Vedantins acknowledge a personal deity, they see this deity as really but one aspect of the Absolute, *nirguna* Brahman, which transcends all duality, and they accommodate the teachings and founding figures of other religions within a Vedantin framework as lesser approximations of what is most fully available in Advaita Vedanta. In other words, Radhakrishnan's acceptance of other religious traditions was strictly on the terms of his prior commitments to the epistemology and ontology of Vedanta Hinduism.

Radhakrishnan's critics were quick to point out that his Hindu commitments often caused him to seriously distort the data from other traditions. Jesus becomes an Eastern holy man; a *sannyasi,* or wandering ascetic; an *avatar* of Vishnu; a mystic whose teachings, far from being original, were already anticipated in the Upanishads.[8] Likewise, Gautama the Buddha is depicted, in spite of consistent Buddhist testimony to the contrary, as not really denying the existence of the *atman* (self) and as not rejecting the authority or teachings of the Upanishads.[9] Moreover, Radhakrishnan's eloquent calls for religious tolerance and respect did not always find expression in his own life, for he was a bitter critic of Christianity. Stephen Neill comments that "much of what [Radhakrishnan] writes is the expression of a dislike, amounting at times to a passionate hatred, of Christianity. Christianity must not be allowed to score a single point; all the trumps must be in the hands of the Eastern thinker."[10] Vinoth Ramachandra perceptively observes:

> Radhakrishnan's "comprehensive and synthetic spirit of Hinduism" does on the level

[7]Ninian Smart, "Radhakrishnan," in *The Encyclopedia of Philosophy*, ed. Paul Edwards (New York: Macmillan, 1967), 7:62.

[8]On Radhakrishnan's views on Jesus, see Ishwar Harris, "Radhakrishnan's View of Christianity," in *Neo-Hindu Views of Christianity*, ed. Arvind Sharma (Leiden, Holland: E. J. Brill, 1988), pp. 156-81.

[9]For a perceptive critique of Radhakrishnan's interpretation of Buddhism, see T. R. V. Murti, "Radhakrishnan and Buddhism," in *Philosophy of Sarvepalli Radhakrishnan*, pp. 567-605.

[10]Stephen Neill, *Christian Faith and Other Faiths* (London: Oxford University Press, 1961), p. 82.

of thought what the ranking of caste distinctions does on the level of Indian society. "Hinduism", he writes, "insists on our working steadily upwards and improving our knowledge of God. The worshippers of the Absolute are the highest in rank, second to them are the worshippers of the personal God, then come the worshippers of the incarnations like Rama, Krishna, Buddha, below them are those who worship ancestors, deities and sages, and lowest of all are the worshippers of the petty forces and spirits." This is simply religious imperialism masquerading as tolerance. Pluralism is ultimately undermined, because the "Other" is never taken seriously as a challenge to the entire framework of discourse.[11]

Radhakrishnan, in other words, was not really a pluralist but rather a modern Hindu who understood religious diversity in terms of a modified Advaita Vedanta framework.

More recently the Dalai Lama, Tenzin Gyatso (b. 1935), has assumed the role of Eastern spokesman for religious tolerance and diversity. The Dalai Lama is not only the exiled leader of Tibetans and the spiritual leader of the Geluk (dGe lugs) school of Tibetan Buddhism but is also regarded as an incarnation of the *bodhisattva* of compassion, Avalokitesvara. Through his many writings (including several recent bestsellers), his extensive lecture tours in the West and especially his humble and gracious public demeanor, the Dalai Lama has become a powerful symbol of religious harmony.

As with Radhakrishnan, there is much in what the Dalai Lama says that suggests religious pluralism. He too is a strong critic of religious dogmatism and proselytization, although one does not find in the Dalai Lama the bitter antagonism toward Christianity so evident in Radhakrishnan. He states, "All of the different religious faiths, despite their philosophical differences, have a similar objective. Every religion emphasizes human improvement, love, respect for others, sharing other people's suffering. On these lines, every religion has more or less the same viewpoint and the same goal." Much of the attraction of the Dalai Lama consists in his call for people to cultivate spirituality within their own traditions while respecting the differences of others. "I am not interested in converting other people to Buddhism but in how we Buddhists can contribute to human society, according to our own ideas."[12] In his address to the 1993 Parliament of the World's Religions the Dalai Lama said, " Each religion has its own philosophy and there are similarities as well as differences among the various traditions. What is important is what is suitable for a particular person. . . . Everyone feels that his or her form of religious practice

---

[11]Vinoth Ramachandra, *Faiths in Conflict? Christian Integrity in a Multicultural World* (Leicester, England: Inter-Varsity Press, 1999), p. 74. The quotation from Radhakrishnan is from his *The Hindu View of Life* (London: Macmillan, 1969), p. 24.

[12]His Holiness the Dalai Lama, "Religious Harmony," in *Christianity Through Non-Christian Eyes*, ed. Paul J. Griffiths (Maryknoll, N.Y.: Orbis, 1990), pp. 163, 165.

is the best. I myself feel that Buddhism is best for me. But this does not mean that Buddhism is best for everyone else."[13]

All of this might suggest that the Dalai Lama is a pluralist, but this would be to misunderstand his position. As Jane Compson persuasively argues, "Whilst his tolerance is entirely genuine, it arises from prioritizing Buddhist ideas over those of other faiths, and in this respect the apparent pluralism is deceptive."[14] There is no question that the Dalai Lama is a convinced Buddhist, accepting the basic epistemology and ontology of the Geluk tradition, which in turn is heavily influenced by the Madhyamaka ("Middle School") tradition of Nagarjuna. All religious perspectives are not equally acceptable. As Paul Williams observes, "In terms of reasoning to find the ultimate truth, if carried out correctly and without bias, the Dalai Lama holds as himself a Buddhist, in common with all dGe lugs practitioners, that only Buddhism will be found to make final sense."[15]

Two features of the Dalai Lama's Buddhist worldview enable the positive approach to other religions. First, Buddhism adopts a pragmatic, functional view of belief that minimizes the place of doctrine. Doctrines are means toward an end; the desired end is liberation or enlightenment, and teachings and doctrines are only tools that help us achieve this goal. Buddhism developed the notion of *upaya-kausalya,* or "skillful means," according to which doctrines can be adapted to fit the level of the audience's present state of comprehension. Since not everyone at present is capable of grasping the higher truths of Buddhism, other teachings, even false teachings, can be useful in helping some people along the path. Thus, even though strictly speaking Buddhism rejects as false the Christian belief in an eternal Creator God, theism can be useful for some people. As the Dalai Lama said:

> [T]he variety of the different world religious philosophies is a very useful and beautiful thing. For certain people, the idea of God as creator and of everything depending on his will is beneficial and soothing, and so for that person such doctrine is worthwhile. For someone else, the idea that there is no creator, that ultimately one is oneself the creator—in that everything depends upon oneself—is more appropriate. . . . For such persons, this idea is better and for the other type of person, the other idea is more suitable.[16]

---

[13]Dalai Lama, "The Importance of Religious Harmony," in *The Community of Religions: Voices and Images of the Parliament of the World's Religions*, eds. Wayne Teasdale and George Cairns (New York: Continuum, 1996), pp. 17-18.

[14]Jane Compson, "The Dalai Lama and the World Religions: A False Friend?" *Religious Studies* 32 (June 1996): 271.

[15]Paul Williams, "Some Dimensions of the Recent Work of Raimundo Panikkar: A Buddhist Perspective," *Religious Studies* 27, no. 4 (1991): 519.

[16]Dalai Lama, "The Bodhgaya Interviews," in *Christianity Through Non-Christian Eyes*, pp. 167-68.

Yet ultimately for the Dalai Lama Christian theism is false, for there is no God.

The second aspect of Buddhism that encourages a positive view of other religions is belief in rebirth. Spiritual maturation takes place over many lives, and very few will be in a position in this life to comprehend the Buddhist *dharma*. For the rest, the most that can be expected is some progress in understanding and action, so that eventually, in some future life, they can recognize the truth of Buddhism. Paul Williams says:

> From a Buddhist perspective there is no hurry. The ultimate truth can wait—it is not necessarily of such immediate importance, there are many future lives and very few of us, Buddhists included, will attain enlightenment in this life, or even the next. Moreover the Dalai Lama holds that just as the Buddha taught many teachings within Buddhism to suit those at different levels, it is appropriate for a Buddhist (and may be true) to see other religions as teachings of the compassionate Buddha for those in different circumstances and situations.[17]

However much the teachings and practices of other religions might be useful in helping people on the path toward enlightenment, the Dalai Lama is clear that ultimately liberation is attained only within the framework of Buddhism. In an interview he stated, "Liberation in which 'a mind that understands the sphere of reality annihilates all defilements in the sphere of reality' is a state that only Buddhists can accomplish. This kind of *moksha* or *nirvana* is only explained in the Buddhist scriptures, and is achieved only through Buddhist practice."[18] This is hardly religious pluralism. It is a clear Buddhist inclusivism that, while sincerely respectful and tolerant of religious differences, is so on Buddhist grounds that in no way compromises the distinctive truth of Buddhism.

This raises an important question: Can there be an explanatory model of the religions that is both coherent and genuinely pluralistic? Or does every attempt to formulate one inevitably privilege a particular religious perspective at the expense of others? It would seem that a truly pluralistic framework for understanding the religions should do the following: (1) recognize the clear differences in beliefs and practices among the religions, (2) affirm the different religions as more or less equally effective ways of responding to the one ultimate reality, so that no single religious tradition is granted normative or privileged status, and (3) provide a coherent explanation for how (1) and (2) can be simultaneously embraced. The explanatory framework for accepting (1) and (2) cannot itself come from one of the religions, or what we have is no longer pluralism but rather inclusivism.

Assumptions Behind John Hick's Model

The most rigorous and philosophically sophisticated attempt to provide a model of

---

[17]Williams, "Some Dimensions," p. 520.
[18]Dalai Lama, "Bodhgaya Interviews," p. 169.

religious pluralism that does not privilege any particular tradition is that of John Hick. His proposal is based upon a number of significant assumptions, many of which are controversial. Hick's epistemological framework was outlined in chapter five, so here we will just briefly mention several key themes that shape his views on pluralism.

Hick's epistemological assumptions were set out in *Faith and Knowledge* (1957) and have not changed significantly since then.[19] Hick has consistently held that the universe is "religiously ambiguous" in that it is not possible, on the basis of careful analysis of the universe and experience alone, to determine definitively whether there is a God.[20] The universe can rationally be interpreted in either religious or nonreligious ways. In *An Interpretation of Religion* (1989), after reviewing traditional arguments used to support religious and nonreligious interpretations, Hick concludes:

> It seems, then, that the universe maintains its inscrutable ambiguity. In some aspects it invites whilst in others it repels a religious response. It permits both a religious and a naturalistic faith, but haunted in each case by a contrary possibility that can never be exorcised. Any realistic analysis of religious belief and experience, and any realistic defence of the rationality of religious conviction, must therefore start from this situation of systematic ambiguity.[21]

Furthermore, if the universe is interpreted religiously, one cannot, by philosophical analysis alone, determine whether the religious ultimate is the monotheistic God of the Semitic tradition or the monistic *nirguna* Brahman of Hinduism. Which is more likely to be true, Christian theism or the monism of Advaita Vedanta? Religious ambiguity prevents us from being able to answer this question definitively, so that it can be rational to interpret the universe as a Christian theist or a Vedantin Hindu or a Theravadin Buddhist or any of a number of other kinds of religionists, depending upon one's experiences.[22]

Moreover, in his later writings Hick continues to hold that all experience, including religious experience, is inherently interpretive, or "experiencing-as." But religious experience is distinctive in that the interpretive element in religious experience is faith, or "that uncompelled subjective contribution to conscious experi-

---

[19]John Hick, *Faith and Knowledge* (Ithaca, N.Y.: Cornell University Press, 1957). The second edition was published in 1966.
[20]See, for example, John Hick, *Arguments for the Existence of God* (New York: Herder & Herder, 1971), chapter 7; John Hick, *Philosophy of Religion*, 4th ed. (Englewood Cliffs, N.J.: Prentice-Hall, 1990), chapter 7; and John Hick, *An Interpretation of Religion* (New Haven, Conn.: Yale University Press, 1989), chapters 5-7, 10.
[21]Hick, *Interpretation of Religion*, p. 124.
[22]See John Hick, "On Grading Religions," *Religious Studies* 17, no. 4 (1981): 451-67; and Hick, *Interpretation of Religion*, especially chapters 10, 13, 17 and 20.

ence which is responsible for its distinctively religious character."[23] Given the pervasive religious ambiguity of the world and the inherently interpretive nature of all experience, Hick regards religious faith as an exercise of "cognitive freedom."

Although it can be rational to interpret reality in various ways, the choice of one perspective over others need not be arbitrary. The decisive element in the epistemological equation is religious experience. Those who experience God in their lives can be rational in believing in God; those without the requisite experience can be rational in not believing in God. Religious experience in general cannot be ruled out as delusory, and in many cases it is perfectly reasonable to conclude that religious experiences are reliable. "It is as reasonable for those who experience their lives as being lived in the presence of God, to believe in the reality of God, as for all of us to form beliefs about our environment on the basis of our experience of it."[24] Thus, although philosophical reflection alone cannot settle the question of the reality of God, it is rational for those who experience the universe religiously to believe in the reality of God. This, of course, applies not merely to the Christian theist but to religious believers in other traditions as well.

In terms of theology, Hick recognizes that Christology is central to the issues of religious pluralism, for if Christian orthodoxy is correct on this point, then it becomes impossible to maintain genuine pluralism. But as we have seen, Hick rejects the orthodox view and regards Jesus as "unambiguously a man, but a man who was open to God's presence to a truly awesome extent and was sustained by an extraordinarily intense God-consciousness."[25] Jesus, then, should be regarded as one among many great religious leaders in whom the religious ultimate—God, for Christians—has been especially present.

> We can see Jesus as the one who has made God real to us, who has shown us how to live as citizens of God's kingdom, who is our revered spiritual leader, inspiration, and model. We can do this without having to deny that other spiritual leaders and other revelatory histories function in the same way and to the same extent (so far as we can tell) for other people within other religious traditions.[26]

These assumptions concerning religious epistemology and Christology are crucial to Hick's thesis, but they are also highly controversial and contested. If the world is not as ambiguous as Hick claims, so that a strong case can be made for one religious worldview over others, or if religious experience is not the determinative fac-

---

[23]Hick, *Interpretation of Religion*, pp. 140-41, 160.

[24]Ibid., p. 210.

[25]John Hick, *A Christian Theology of Religions: The Rainbow of Faiths* (Louisville: Westminster John Knox, 1995), pp. 91-92. See also John Hick, *The Metaphor of God Incarnate: Christology in a Pluralistic Age* (Louisville: Westminster John Knox, 1993).

[26]John Hick, "A Pluralist View," in *Four Views on Salvation in a Pluralistic World*, ed. Dennis L. Okholm and Timothy R. Phillips (Grand Rapids, Mich.: Zondervan, 1996), p. 59.

tor in the rationality of religious belief, or if the orthodox view of Jesus as God incarnate is correct, then a pluralistic model for understanding the religions becomes much more difficult to sustain. Although I will not argue the point here, each of Hick's assumptions faces some significant problems.

Hick's Model of Religious Pluralism

The most complete expression and defense of Hick's model of religious pluralism is in *An Interpretation of Religion* (1989). In several books and many articles since then, Hick has responded to his critics and continues to refine his views. At the heart of his model are three claims: (1) that there is an ultimate reality to which the different religions are legitimate responses, (2) that the various religions are historically and culturally conditioned interpretations of this reality, and (3) that soteriological transformation is occurring roughly to the same extent within the major religions. Therefore, the various religions are to be affirmed as equally legitimate religious alternatives, with preferences among them largely being functions of individual characteristics and social and cultural factors. Consider the following statements of his thesis, taken from writings spread over two decades:

- The basic hypothesis which suggests itself is that the different streams of religious experience represent diverse awarenesses of the same transcendent reality, which is perceived in characteristically different ways by different human mentalities, formed by and forming different cultural histories. (1980)[27]

- I want to say that the noumenal Real is experienced and thought by different human mentalities, forming and formed by different religious traditions, as the range of gods and absolutes which the phenomenology of religion reports. And these divine *personae* and metaphysical *impersonae*, as I shall call them, are not illusory but are empirically, that is experientially, real as authentic manifestations of the Real. (1989)[28]

- The hypothesis to which these analogies point is that of an ultimate ineffable Reality which is the source and ground of everything, and which is such that in so far as the religious traditions are in soteriological alignment with it they are contexts of salvation/liberation. These traditions involve different human conceptions of the Real, with correspondingly different forms of experience of the Real, and correspondingly different forms of life in response to the Real. (1995)[29]

- This means that the different world religions—each with its own sacred scriptures, spiritual practices, forms of religious experience, belief systems, founder or great exemplars, communal memories, cultural expression in ways of life, laws and customs, art forms and so on—taken together as complex historical totalities, constitute differ-

---

[27]John Hick, *God Has Many Names* (Philadelphia: Westminster Press, 1980), p. 83.
[28]Hick, *Interpretation of Religion*, p. 242.
[29]Hick, *Christian Theology of Religions*, p. 27.

ent human responses to the ultimate transcendent reality to which they all, in their different ways, bear witness. (1999)[30]

Hick's proposal, then, is that "the great religions are all, at their experiential roots, in contact with the same ultimate divine reality."[31]

Before examining Hick's thesis in greater detail, we should clarify the nature of his proposal. Hick's proposal is intended as an explanatory model for understanding religious diversity in our world, that is, a second-order explanation of first-order data that we observe in the various religions.[32] In other words, Hick's theory should not be seen as the introduction of a new global religion but rather as a fresh way of understanding existing religions, an explanatory framework for making sense of the relationships among religious traditions.

As such, Hick's model includes both a descriptive and a prescriptive, or normative, component. On one level, he is suggesting a theory about existing religions and thus is concerned to describe phenomena from the religions accurately. Descriptively, his model should be able to account for both the commonalities and differences across religions. But clearly Hick is up to much more than merely the careful phenomenology of religion. He is unhappy with traditional ways of understanding the relations among religions and thus is arguing for what he regards as the preferred alternative, and this prescriptive dimension of the model requires rejecting or reinterpreting significant aspects of existing religions (such as the orthodox understanding of the incarnation in Christianity). Obviously, there is a certain tension between the two aspects of Hick's model, for on the descriptive level he is concerned to portray other religions accurately, just as they are, while on the prescriptive level some modification of existing beliefs is called for. This is an issue to which we will return in due course.

We should also note that, although the effect of Hick's proposal is to relativize particular religions, so that none can legitimately claim to be the one true religion for all humankind, he is not a relativist in the sense of denying that there is such a thing as truth that transcends particular contexts. To the contrary, Hick holds that there *is* truth that applies to everyone, and he believes that his model is the correct way to understand the religions, or at least that it is much closer to the truth than existing alternatives. So it will not do to criticize his position as merely another expression of relativism. Moreover, as the above quotations indicate, Hick does not claim to *know* that his model of religious pluralism is true. Rather, his views are

---

[30]John Hick, *The Fifth Dimension* (Oxford: Oneworld, 1999), p. 77.

[31]John Hick, "The Outcome: Dialogue into Truth," in *Truth and Dialogue in World Religions: Conflicting Truth-Claims*, ed. John Hick (Philadelphia: Westminster Press, 1974), p. 151.

[32]See John Hick, "The Possibility of Religious Pluralism: A Reply to Gavin D'Costa," *Religious Studies* 33 (June 1997): 163.

presented as a working hypothesis that, he thinks, accounts for the relevant data better than other alternatives.

Hick is very much aware of the enormous diversity among religions. His proposal differs, then, from the views of some in the "perennial philosophy" movement who maintain that there is in all religions an identifiable esoteric core, a unifying essence, usually identified as some form of mysticism.[33] Hick recognizes that the ontologies of, for example, orthodox Christianity and Theravada Buddhism are incompatible. Even among the mystical traditions, he acknowledges that there are irreducible differences between the claims made by the Zen Buddhist and the Advaita Vedantin Hindu.[34] On one level, then, Hick is clearly aware of the incompatible differences between religious traditions, and his model attempts to account for such conflicting truth claims. However, as we shall see, his proposal minimizes such differences by reinterpreting the more problematic beliefs in ways unacceptable to the believers themselves.

But if the various religions all are in contact with the same divine reality, as Hick claims, why the bewildering diversity in conceptions of this one reality? Why is there not greater uniformity of belief among the many religions? Hick presents a comprehensive theory that accounts for diversity in belief and practice by appealing to historical and cultural factors. Thus the varying religious expressions can be regarded as historically and culturally conditioned human responses to the same ultimate reality, the Real. While the major religions can be regarded as different responses to the same religious ultimate, Hick says:

> [W]e always perceive the transcendent through the lens of a particular religious culture with its distinctive set of concepts, myths, historical exemplars and devotional or meditational techniques. And it is this inexpungible human contribution to religious awareness that accounts for the fascinating variations of religious thought, experience, and practice around the globe and down through the centuries, in all their rational and irrational, profound and shallow, impressive and absurd, morally admirable and morally reprehensible features.[35]

Drawing an analogy to Immanuel Kant's epistemology of perception, in which the categories of the understanding give conceptual shape to the input of the sensible representations, resulting in our knowledge of the world, Hick suggests that cultural variables function as conceptual lenses through which different peoples

---

[33]Such views are found in Aldous Huxley, *The Perennial Philosophy* (1945; reprint, London: Triad Grafton, 1989); Fritjof Schuon, *The Transcendent Unity of Religions* (New York: Harper & Row, 1975); Huston Smith, *Forgotten Truth* (New York: Harper & Row, 1976); Wilfred Cantwell Smith, *The Meaning and End of Religion* (1962; reprint, New York: Harper & Row, 1978); and Wilfred Cantwell Smith, *Towards a World Theology* (Philadelphia: Westminster Press, 1980).

[34]See Hick, *Interpretation of Religion*, pp. 165-69; and Hick, *Fifth Dimension*, chapters 12-16.

[35]Hick, *Interpretation of Religion*, p. 8.

understand and respond to the religious ultimate.[36] One difference between Kant and Hick, however, is that whereas for Kant the categories are a priori and thus universal and necessary, resulting in a certain consistency in human experience, with Hick the cultural variables are contingent and relative, thereby producing differences in religious experience and belief.

In sum, although ultimately the various religious traditions encounter the same divine reality, historical and cultural factors shape both the awareness of and the response to this reality. These factors form a kind of grid, or filter, through which individuals perceive and understand the Real.

The Real

Hick maintains that there is a religious ultimate, a divine reality, and thus he is an ontological realist with respect to religion. But this religious ultimate is not the direct object of our religious experiences. Borrowing again from Kant's famous distinction between the noumenon and the phenomenon in the epistemology of perception, Hick distinguishes between the religious ultimate as it is in itself and the religious ultimate as experienced by historically and culturally conditioned persons. He refers to the former by the term "the Real." But the Real as it is in itself is never the direct object of religious experience. Rather, it is experienced by finite humankind in one of any number of historically and culturally conditioned manifestations of the Real—either as personal (for example, Yahweh, Allah, Krishna) or as nonpersonal (*Dharmakaya, sunyata, nirguna* Brahman). Hick calls the various personal conceptions, or manifestations, of the Real *personae* of the Real; he refers to conceptions of the Real as nonpersonal as *impersonae* of the Real.

> [F]or Kant God is postulated, not experienced. In partial agreement but also partial disagreement with him, I want to say that the Real *an sich* is postulated by us as a pre-supposition, not of the moral life, but of religious experience and the religious life, whilst the gods, as also the mystically known Brahman, Sunyata and so on, are phenomenal manifestations of the Real occurring within the realm of religious experience. Conflating these two theses one can say that the Real is experienced by human beings, but experienced in a manner analogous to that in which, according to Kant, we experience the world: namely by informational input from external reality being interpreted by the mind in terms of its own categorial scheme and thus coming to consciousness as meaningful phenomenal experience. All that we are entitled to say about the noumenal source of this information is that it is the reality whose influence produces, in collaboration

---

[36]Ibid., pp. 243-45. On Kant's influence upon Hick, see Paul Eddy, "Religious Pluralism: Another Look at John Hick's Neo-Kantian Proposal," *Religious Studies* 30, no. 4 (1994): 467-78. This article was reprinted in Philip L. Quinn and Kevin Meeker, eds., *The Philosophical Challenge of Religious Diversity* (New York: Oxford University Press, 2000), pp. 126-38.

with the human mind, the phenomenal world of our experience.[37]

The Real, then, is the "divine noumenon" that is encountered within the various religious traditions as the range of "divine phenomena" exemplified in the religious history of humankind.

We have, then, the Real as it is in itself, the postulated ground of all religious experience, and the Real as it is perceived by finite humankind—the *personae* of the theistic faiths and the *impersonae* of certain strands of Hinduism, Buddhism and Taoism. The distinction is intended to enable affirmation of both the undeniable diversity in conceptions of the religious ultimate and the unity of religions in their varying responses to the same religious ultimate. Whether it is in fact able to do so depends largely upon the manner in which the relation between the Real and the various *personae/impersonae* is formulated, a question to which we shall turn shortly.

It is significant that Hick uses the rather bland term "the Real" to denote the religious ultimate. His earlier discussions of pluralism portrayed the religious ultimate in theistic terms, but Hick came to see that such language privileged theistic traditions over nontheistic ones, and thus with the Gifford Lectures (1986–87) he adopted "the Real" as a supposedly neutral term. As we shall see, there is good reason to think that this designation is hardly neutral, for it is similar to some Buddhist depictions of the religious ultimate. It is also interesting that, as Hick has moved successively away from a theistic view of the religious ultimate to one that supposedly transcends both theistic and nontheistic categories, he has given greater emphasis to the notion of ineffability.

> The distinction between the Real as it is in itself and as it is thought and experienced through our human religious concepts entails . . . that we cannot apply to the Real *an sich* the characteristics encountered in its *personae* and *impersonae*. Thus it cannot be said to be one or many, person or thing, conscious or unconscious, purposive or non-purposive, substance or process, good or evil, loving or hating. None of the descriptive terms that apply within the realm of human experience can apply literally to the unexperienceable reality that underlies that realm.[38]

There is a certain ambivalence in Hick's writings. He affirms that "the noumenal Real is such as to be authentically experienced as a range of both theistic and non-theistic phenomena." Yet he quickly qualifies this by adding, "We cannot, as we have seen, say that the Real *an sich* has the characteristics displayed by its manifestations, such as (in the case of the heavenly Father) love and justice or (in the case of Brahman) consciousness and bliss." Thus, "whilst there is a noumenal

---

[37]Hick, *Interpretation of Religion*, p. 243.
[38]Ibid., p. 350.

ground for the phenomenal divine attributes, this does not enable us to trace each attribute separately upwards into the Godhead or the Real." It is hardly an exaggeration, then, for Hick to state that "the Real *an sich* is the ultimate Mystery."[39]

Soteriological Transformation

Given the clear differences in conceptions of the religious ultimate found in the religions, why should we postulate the Real as the common ground of the religions? One factor is Hick's contention that we cannot dismiss religious experience in general as delusory. He recognizes that this presents an epistemological parity among religious traditions, so that the arguments used to show that it is rational for Christians to believe in God on the basis of their religious experiences also apply in principle to practitioners of other traditions, granting their experiences prima facie validity as well.

But a crucial reason for postulating the Real is what Hick sees as a common soteriological structure to the major religions, producing within the lives of religious believers the "transformation from self-centredness to Reality-centredness."

> My reason to assume that the different world religions are referring, through their specific concepts of the Gods and Absolutes, to the same ultimate Reality is the striking similarity of the transformed human state described within the different traditions as saved, redeemed, enlightened, wise, awakened, liberated. This similarity strongly suggests a common source of salvific transformation.[40]

The teachings of the various religions concerning the human predicament and the nature of salvation (or liberation or enlightenment) constitute "variations within different conceptual schemes on a single fundamental theme: the sudden or gradual change of the individual from an absorbing self-concern to a new centring in the supposed unity-of-reality-and-value that is thought of as God, Brahman, the Dharma, Sunyata or the Tao. Thus the generic concept of salvation/liberation, which takes a different specific form in each of the great traditions, is that of the transformation of human existence from self-centredness to Reality-centredness."[41]

Understood as the transformation from self-centeredness to Reality-centeredness, salvation is said to be evident in all the major religions. But from our present perspective, it is impossible to rank religions according to their soteriological effectiveness. "It may be that one [religion] facilitates human liberation/salvation more than the others, but if so this is not evident to human vision. So far as we can tell, they are equally productive of that transition from self to Reality which we see in the saints of all traditions."[42]

---

[39]Ibid., pp. 246-47, 349.
[40]Hick, *Christian Theology of Religions*, p. 69.
[41]Hick, *Interpretation of Religion*, p. 36.
[42]John Hick, *Problems of Religious Pluralism* (New York: St. Martin's, 1985), pp. 86-87.

Not only does what Hick sees as a common soteriological structure in the great religions provide a reason for postulating the Real as the transcendent ground of different religious images but also it provides the criterion for discriminating between responses to the Real that are legitimate and those that are not. No one supposes that all religious leaders or teachings are equally valid or equally in touch with the Real. There is a substantial difference between Jim Jones or Bhagwan Shree Rajneesh and St. Francis of Assisi or Mahatma Gandhi. Likewise, there is a difference between child sacrifice to Molech and the Muslim practice of *zakat* (giving alms). How is one to distinguish between what is and what is not an authentic response to the Real? Hick contends that "the basic criterion must be soteriological." Religious traditions "have greater or less value according as they promote or hinder the salvific transformation."[43]

But how do we know when such transformation has taken place? This too requires identifiable criteria. And Hick suggests that criteria for making that judgment lie in the spiritual and moral fruit found in the lives of exemplary believers in the religions. Those whose lives have been authentically transformed, who no longer are controlled by "self-centredness" but live according to "Reality-centredness"—the "saints" of the great traditions—manifest certain qualities in their lives. Among these qualities are compassion and love for all humankind, indeed all of life; strength of soul; purity; charity; inner peace and serenity; and radiant joy.[44]

> The production of saints, both contemplative and practical, individualistic and political, is thus one valid criterion by which to identify a religious tradition as a salvific human response to the Real. In the light of this criterion we can readily see that each of the great world faiths constitutes a context for salvation/liberation: for each has produced its own harvest of saints. . . . The salvation/liberation which it is the function of religion to facilitate is a human transformation which we see most conspicuously in the saints of all traditions. It consists, as one of its aspects, in moral goodness, a goodness which is latent in the solitary contemplative and active in the saint who lives in society, serving his or her fellows either in works of mercy or, more characteristically in our modern sociologically-conscious age, in political activity as well, seeking to change the structures within which human life is lived.[45]

The presence of saints in each of the major religions, then, is said to be compelling evidence of the religions being authentic responses to the one divine reality, the Real.

Myth, Metaphor and Truth
In Hick's later writings on religious pluralism we find increasing tension between

---

[43]Hick, *Interpretation of Religion*, p. 300.
[44]Ibid., pp. 301-2. In his most recent work Hick gives considerable attention to examples of saints from various traditions, including three chapters on Mahatma Gandhi. See Hick, *Fifth Dimension*, chapters 19-23.
[45]Hick, *Interpretation of Religion*, pp. 307, 309.

his commitment, on the one hand, to critical realism and the "fact-asserting," or cognitively informative, nature of religious language, and on the other hand, to the prominent role that myth and metaphor play in his model of pluralism. Hick's commitment to ontological realism and the factually informative nature of religious discourse, which was evident in his early writings against the challenges of logical positivism, continues into his discussions of pluralism.[46] However, although his commitment to critical realism remains, his views on the nature of religious truth have changed, and it is not clear whether his model of pluralism can consistently maintain both religious realism in ontology and the centrality of myth and metaphor.[47]

Hick has consistently been critical of religious nonrealists and noncognitivists, who wish to retain the language of Christian theism while abandoning the ontological realism that grounds it.[48] Hick notes that just as in epistemology "realism is the view that material objects exist outside us and independently of what we take to be our perceptions of them," so too "religious realism is the view that the objects of religious belief exist independently of what we take to be our human experience of them." With respect to religious language, "what I am calling the realist option understands such language in a basically realist way as referring to an object that is 'there' to be referred to."[49] Nonrealism denies the objective, extramental existence of such objects, whether physical or religious. Religious nonrealists, such as R. M. Hare, D. Z. Phillips and Don Cupitt, interpret religious language "not as referring to a transcendent reality or realities, but as expressing our emotions, or our basic moral insights and intentions, or our way of seeing the world, or as referring to our moral and spiritual ideals."[50]

A further distinction can be made between naive realism and critical realism. Just as in the epistemology of perception naive realism assumes that the world is just as we experience it to be, so in religion naive realism takes it for granted that "what is spoken about in the religious language that one has learned is just as described in this language, understood literally." And by "literally" Hick means "straightforwardly, rather than as metaphor or myth."[51]

---

[46]See John Hick, *Faith and Knowledge*, 2nd ed. (Ithaca, N.Y.: Cornell University Press, 1966), chapters 7-8; and Hick, *Interpretation of Religion*, chapters 11-13.

[47]See Brian Hebblethwaite, "John Hick and the Question of Truth in Religion," in *God, Truth and Reality: Essays in Honour of John Hick*, ed. Arvind Sharma (New York: St. Martin's, 1993), pp. 124-34.

[48]Hick, *Interpretation of Religion*, chapter 11.

[49]Ibid., pp. 172-73.

[50]John Hick, *Disputed Questions in Theology and the Philosophy of Religion* (New Haven, Conn.: Yale University Press, 1993), p. 7.

[51]As an example, Hick suggests that a Christian naive realist would understand the Genesis 3 narrative to be speaking about a literal Adam and Eve as the first human beings, specially created by God. Ibid., p. 6.

By contrast, critical realism in perception recognizes that, although the objects of our experience exist independently of our awareness of them, nevertheless there is a significant human contribution to our perception and thus understanding of such objects. Similarly critical realism in religion holds that, although the referents of religious discourse exist apart from our awareness of them, our understanding of them is shaped to some extent by factors internal to the subject, and our language about such objects reflects this subjective contribution. Thus, to pick an example from Christianity, to speak of God as "Father" is to adopt a concept and language from human discourse and apply it metaphorically to God, but what is signified by doing so is a reality that exists in its own right and cannot be reduced merely to human projection. "Thus a critical realism affirms the transcendent divine reality which the theistic religions refer to as God; but is conscious that this reality is always thought of and experienced by us in ways which are shaped and coloured by human concepts and images." Hick accepts critical realism and claims that "the debate between realist and nonrealist understandings of religious language exposes the most fundamental of all issues in the philosophy of religion today."[52] The dispute between the religious believer and the naturalist is a real one, as is that between the religious realist and the religious nonrealist, and it concerns the nature of the universe and of the religious ultimate, if any.

Despite his commitment to religious realism, Hick's later thought gives much greater emphasis to metaphor and myth, and this in turn affects his understanding of religious truth. Brian Hebblethwaite locates the shift in emphasis in Hick's contribution to the 1970 conference on conflicting truth claims held at the University of Birmingham.[53] From that point on, the concept of myth became increasingly prominent in Hick's writings, first in relation to Christology and the incarnation and then more generally to religious beliefs.

By "myth" Hick means "a story or statement which is not literally true but which tends to evoke an appropriate dispositional attitude to its subject matter." Hick notes that some religious questions can in principle be answered, but we are unable to do so at present because of insufficient data. But other questions are in principle unanswerable for us as humans, since they point to realities that cannot be expressed in human terms. In response to questions in the first category we formulate theories; in dealing with those in the second we develop myths. There are also two kinds of myths. Expository myths "say something that can also be said non-mythologically, though generally with markedly less imaginative impact"

---

[52]Ibid., pp. 7, 3.
[53]Hebblethwaite, "John Hick and the Question of Truth," pp. 125-28. Hick's contribution was published as "The Outcome: Dialogue into Truth," in *Truth and Dialogue in World Religions,* pp. 140-55.

whereas "myths as mystery" address issues "to which no answer is possible in a literal use of language."[54] Myths as mystery deal with realities that transcend human conceptual and linguistic categories and thus cannot be expressed in nonmythological language.

Hick then applies his discussion of myth to the notion of truth, distinguishing "literal truth" from "mythological truth," with the latter taking priority within his model.

> The literal truth or falsity of a factual assertion (as distinguished from the truth or falsity of an analytic proposition) consists in its conformity or lack of conformity to fact: "it is raining here and now" is literally true if and only if it is raining here and now. But in addition to literal truth there is also mythological truth. A statement or set of statements about X is mythologically true if it is not literally true but nevertheless tends to evoke an appropriate dispositional attitude to X. Thus mythological truth is practical, or in one sense of this much abused word, existential. For the conformity of myth to reality does not consist in a literal conformity of what is said to the facts but in the appropriateness to the myth's referent of the behavioural dispositions that it tends to evoke in the hearer.[55]

Literal truth, then, is roughly equivalent to what we spoke of in chapter six as a realist conception of truth, or truth as correspondence. Mythological truth, by contrast, is pragmatic in the sense that the truth value of a statement or story does not depend upon an objectively existing state of affairs but rather upon the effect it has upon individuals or communities. And thus "true religious myths are accordingly those that evoke in us attitudes and modes of behaviour which are appropriate to our situation in relation to the Real."[56] On this understanding, the doctrines concerning various *personae* or *impersonae* within the religious traditions, while not applying literally to the Real, can be said to express mythological truth about the Real in so far as they evoke in the believers appropriate dispositional responses.

> And our concepts—such as personality, consciousness, goodness, love, justice, power, unity, plurality, substantiality—apply literally, in either the univocal or the analogical mode, to these manifestations. But in speaking literally in these ways about a manifestation of the Real we are at the same time speaking mythologically about the Real in itself. . . . If this is so, the different conceptions of the Real, in terms of which the different forms of religious experience and response have developed, are not literally true or false descriptions of the Real but are mythologically true in so far as they are soteriologically effective.[57]

---

[54]Hick, *Interpretation of Religion*, pp. 248, 347-49.
[55]Ibid., p. 348.
[56]Ibid., p. 248.
[57]Hick, *Disputed Questions*, pp. 116-17.

The biblical story of the fall of Adam and Eve, the story of the flight of the Buddha through the sky to Sri Lanka, the belief that the Qur'an was dictated by the archangel Gabriel—all these are examples of "true myths" in that, although not literally true, they tend to evoke in Christians, Buddhists and Muslims appropriate dispositional responses to the Real.

What are the implications of this for the problem of conflicting truth claims? Hick argues that the doctrinal differences among religions stem from different responses, prompted by different historical and cultural patterns, to the unanswerable questions. He distinguishes three levels of such disagreements: first, disagreements over matters of historical fact (did Jesus really die on the cross or not?); second, disputes over matters of "transhistorical" fact (is reincarnation true or not?); and third, different conceptions of the ultimate reality (is the religious ultimate personal or nonpersonal?).[58] When the claims giving rise to such disagreements are understood, not in terms of literal truth, but rather as mythological truth, then the traditional problem of conflicting truth claims disappears. Disagreements on all three levels are, for different reasons, unanswerable for us at present, but this is not significant since such disputes do not affect soteriology.[59]

But an obvious question here is what it means for human attitudes, emotions or modes of behavior to be "appropriate dispositional responses to the Real." Hick responds by saying:

> We can only answer within the circle of the hypothesis. It is for the god or the absolute to which we relate ourselves to be an authentic manifestation of the Real and for our practical response to be appropriate to that manifestation. In so far as this is so, that *persona* or *impersona* can be said to be in soteriological alignment with the Real.[60]

To love God and one's fellow human beings is an appropriate response to God as understood within the Christian tradition. To the extent that Christian doctrines and stories tend to evoke this dispositional response in Christians, they can be regarded as "true myths." And as noted earlier, it is the soteriological criterion—the evidence for the transformation from self-centeredness to Reality-centeredness— that discriminates between authentic and inauthentic manifestations of the Real.

Evaluating Hick's Model

In a world torn apart by religious strife and competition, Hick's suggestion that the

---

[58]Hick, *Interpretation of Religion*, chapter 20.
[59]Indeed Hick adopts the Buddhist notion of *upaya,* or "skillful means," suggesting that different religions, with their doctrinal disagreements, might be "skilful [*sic*] means to a radically new or transformed state of being—a state which is intrinsically desirable and which is believed both to depend upon and to manifest the ultimately real" (Hick, *Disputed Questions*, p. 133).
[60]Hick, *Interpretation of Religion*, p. 353.

major religious traditions are all culturally and historically conditioned human responses to the same ultimate Reality has an enormous attraction. With the exception of certain aberrant forms of religious expression, all religions are to be accepted, for all provide effective paths in which the transition from self-centeredness to Reality-centeredness takes place. One is left with a parity among religions so that no single tradition is definitive or normative for everyone.

The issue, however, is not whether Hick's thesis is attractive but rather whether it is warranted by the data from the various religions and is likely to be true. Hick's theory can be challenged at a number of key points. As noted earlier, one might well question some of his basic assumptions, such as the following: that *all* experience, including religious experience, is inherently interpretive and involves "experiencing-as"; that the universe is as "religiously ambiguous," as he contends; that religious experience is epistemologically determinative for religious belief. His assumptions about the New Testament and Jesus are debatable as well.

But rather than pursue these issues here, I will concentrate upon some other difficulties with Hick's model. Given that his proposal is a second-order theory intended to account for the first-order data from the religions, the adequacy of his theory depends largely upon two factors: (1) the accuracy with which his theory reflects, and the ease with which it can accommodate, the data from various religious traditions, and (2) the internal consistency of the theory itself. I will argue that Hick's model is fatally flawed on both counts.

The Reinterpretation of Beliefs and Reductionism

Hick's treatment of beliefs from different religions is frequently reductionistic, and he freely reinterprets troublesome doctrines so as to accommodate them within his theory. But to the extent that major religious traditions do not find their beliefs— as they are understood within the respective traditions—adequately accounted for by Hick's analysis, his model as a general theory about the religions is called into question.

In an earlier article I argued that Hick's model is problematic because, although it purports to be an explanatory model that accounts for the data from the various religious traditions, it does so by reinterpreting the actual beliefs and practices of the religions in ways unacceptable to orthodox practitioners of the religions themselves.[61] But in response Sumner Twiss defended Hick's model by distinguishing between "descriptive reductionism" and "explanatory reductionism," maintaining that while Hick does engage in the latter, this is inevitable with any second-order

---

[61]Harold Netland, "Professor Hick on Religious Pluralism," *Religious Studies* 22 (June 1986): 249-61.

model and thus not especially problematic.[62] Descriptive reductionism occurs when one describes first-order religious phenomena in terms that are unacceptable to religious insiders. For example, if one were to describe the Christian doctrine of the atonement in a way that does not accurately reflect what Christians mean by the doctrine, this would be descriptive reductionism, and clearly this is inappropriate in a model explaining what Christians believe. Explanatory reductionism, on the other hand, is when one offers a second-order theory that explains first-order phenomena in terms and categories that are somewhat different from those of the religious tradition in which the phenomena appear, and Twiss holds that this is not only appropriate but often inevitable in second-order explanatory models. And Twiss is surely correct in this.

Nevertheless, the distinction does not do away with the problem of inappropriate reductionism in Hick's model, and to see this we must distinguish between explanatory reductionism that occurs from within the conceptual framework of a particular religion and the kind of reductionism operative in Hick's model of religious pluralism. Each religion will be able to offer some general explanation for other religious traditions from within its own framework. Thus Advaita Vedantin Hindus can account for other religions in terms of the assumptions and categories of Advaita Vedanta Hinduism, orthodox Christians can do so from within the perspective of Christian theism, and so on. When done properly, such accounts— whether Islamic, Buddhist, Hindu, Christian or whatever—will avoid descriptive reductionism in their portrayal of other religions, but they will adopt explanatory reductionism in that they account for the beliefs and practices of other religions in terms and categories alien to the religions themselves. This is inevitable and need not be problematic. Let us call such explanations of other religions from the perspective of a particular religious tradition "religion-specific explanations" (RSEs). It is crucial to see that the adequacy of any RSE depends upon the logically prior issue of the acceptability of the religious framework from within which the explanation emerges. The adequacy of the Vedantin Hindu account of other religions, for example, depends upon the general adequacy of the Advaita Vedantin worldview.

It is here that differences between RSEs and Hick's pluralistic model are significant. Typically, an RSE will account for the beliefs and practices of other religions by maintaining that at least some of the central affirmations of other religions are false or otherwise inadequate. This is true even of the most apparently tolerant and

---

[62]Sumner B. Twiss, "The Philosophy of Religious Pluralism: A Critical Appraisal of Hick and His Critics," *Journal of Religion* 70 (October 1990): 533-68, reprinted in Philip L. Quinn and Kevin Meeker, eds., *The Philosophical Challenge of Religious Diversity* (New York: Oxford University Press, 2000), pp. 67-98. The distinction between descriptive and explanatory reductionism is on pages 74 and 75 in the latter volume. It comes from the discussion by Wayne Proudfoot, *Religious Experience* (Berkeley: University of California Press, 1985), chapters 2 and 5.

"inclusivistic" perspectives in Buddhism or Hinduism. While on the level of mere description an RSE can agree with what adherents of other religions say about their beliefs and practices, on the level of explanation the RSE will reject their understanding of such beliefs and practices. These will be reinterpreted in accordance with the assumptions of the religion providing the RSE. Thus a Christian explanation for Zen meditation and *satori* (enlightenment) will be quite different from that of a Zen practitioner.

However, Hick's model of religious pluralism is usually presented as a preferred alternative to RSEs because it supposedly allows us to accept the major religions as they are without necessarily concluding that some religious practitioners are mistaken in their basic beliefs. Hick wants to hold the following three assumptions to be true: (1) The major religions have very different, even incompatible, beliefs and practices. (2) No single religious tradition can legitimately be regarded as superior or uniquely true. (3) All of the major religious traditions can be regarded as more or less equally "true" or "valid" or "effective" responses to the one divine reality. And yet, despite appearances to the contrary, one of the implications of Hick's model is that, while each of the major religions is "acceptable" in one sense, each religion is also fundamentally mistaken about its central affirmations in another sense.[63] In other words, Hick's model entails a fourth assumption: (4) At least some of the basic beliefs of each of the major religions, as these are understood by orthodox adherents of the religions themselves, cannot be accepted as true; they must be reinterpreted mythologically when understood in relation to the Real.

In other words, in offering general explanations of other religions, both RSEs and Hick's model are "reductionistic" in that (a) they account for the first-order data of the other religions in terms that are alien to the other religions themselves, and (b) the explanations entail the fact that at least some of the basic beliefs of the other religions are false or otherwise unacceptable.

But here a crucial difference between RSEs and Hick's model must be noted. As mentioned earlier, the adequacy of an RSE as a general explanation of other religions will depend upon the justification one has for accepting the religious worldview from which the RSE emerges. This must be established on other, independent grounds apart from the RSE itself. But we do not have an analogous case with Hick's model. One does not first establish the justification for his proposal and then from within the theory provide an explanation for other religions—Hick's proposal *is* that explanation. As such, the adequacy of his model is in large measure a function of its internal consistency as a theory and its capacity to account for the first-

---

[63]See Philip Quinn, "Towards Thinner Theologies: Hick and Alston on Religious Diversity," *International Journal for Philosophy of Religion* 38 (December 1995): 145-64, reprinted in Quinn and Meeker, *Philosophical Challenge of Religious Diversity*, pp. 226-43.

order data of the major religions without distorting them in the process. Thus the fact that Hick's model "accounts for" basic beliefs of the religions by reinterpreting them in significant ways counts against its plausibility as a general theory about the religions.

We will note several examples of reductionism in Hick's discussion. First, Hick's theory fails to account satisfactorily for the fact that each tradition ascribes ultimacy to its own particular conception of the religious ultimate. Hick is well aware that the notion of Yahweh is ontologically ultimate for Christians, as is Allah for Muslims, Brahman for Hindus, the Tao for Taoists and so on. Orthodox followers of each of these traditions would vigorously resist the suggestion that *their* particular conception of the ultimate is in fact merely a penultimate manifestation of what is truly ultimate—the Real. Nevertheless, this is precisely what Hick argues. As humanly experienced, *personae* or *impersonae* of the Real, images such as Yahweh, Allah, Shiva, Vishnu, Amida, *Dharmakaya, sunyata* or Brahman, are not themselves the religious ultimate but are merely penultimate manifestations of the Real. Yet careful attention to what the believers within the respective religious traditions mean when using these terms reveals that in each case they accord religious and ontological ultimacy to the referent of the particular concept.

Similarly, Hick contends that religious experience is never direct experience of the Real in itself but is always experience of one of the *personae* or *impersonae*. There is no direct, unmediated experience of the Real. Many would immediately object that mysticism in its varying forms presents an obvious counterexample to Hick's assertion. Particularly illuminating examples come from the traditions of Advaita Vedanta Hinduism and Zen Buddhism. It is significant that both Advaita Vedanta and Zen claim direct, unmediated access to the ultimate nature of reality, although their respective understandings of this reality are not only radically different but incompatible. But if the claims by either Zen or Advaita Vedanta were accepted, then religious pluralism would be unacceptable, for we would have one religious tradition that is privileged in that it has direct access to ultimate reality in a way that others do not.

Although Hick is well aware of these mystical traditions, he nevertheless rejects their claims and argues that even in these cases "that which is being directly experienced is not the Real *an sich* but the Real manifested respectively as Sunyata and Brahman."[64] In other words, even mystical experience involves interpretive activity and thus does not provide privileged, direct access to ultimate reality. Now I suspect that Hick is basically correct in his analysis of mystical experience. It is far from clear that the notion of *satori* (enlightenment) in Zen is even coherent. But

---

[64]Hick, *Interpretation of Religion*, p. 294.

this is largely beside the point. The problem here is that the notions of *satori* and *para vidya* (the higher knowledge) as they are understood in Zen and Advaita Vedanta respectively, cannot be accounted for neatly by Hick's thesis, and thus he reinterprets them as highly unusual cases of "experiencing-as." But Hindus and Buddhists are unwilling to concede their privileged access to ultimate reality, and they have accordingly criticized Hick's model.[65]

Further examples of Hick's reinterpretation of troublesome doctrines include his treatment of the incarnation in orthodox Christianity and the divine inspiration of the Qur'an in Islam. In both cases he calls for reinterpreting what orthodox believers in the two traditions accept.[66] But perhaps nowhere is Hick's reductionism more evident than in his treatment of soteriology. Hick correctly observes that the major traditions are all concerned in some sense with the theme of salvation (or liberation or enlightenment). He claims to discern a common soteriological structure within the great religions—"the transformation of our human situation from a state of alienation from the true structure of reality to a radically better state in harmony with reality," or "the transformation of human existence from self-centredness to Reality-centredness."[67]

It may well be that "the transformation from self-centeredness to Reality-centeredness" is part of a common structure of the religions. But as it stands, this is merely a formal expression lacking specific content, and each religious tradition would provide strikingly different meanings to this formula. What does it mean to be transformed from self-centeredness to Reality-centeredness? What does "self-centeredness" mean? The mistaken belief in a substantial, enduring ego, as Buddhists argue? Or the sinful tendency of individual human beings to regard themselves—and not God—as the object of ultimate concern, as Christians maintain? What does "Reality-centeredness" mean? For Advaita Vedantins this will mean recognizing one's own essential identity with Brahman. For Theravada Buddhists it

---

[65]For a Vedantin Hindu perspective on Hick's treatment of mysticism, see Arvind Sharma, *The Philosophy of Religion and Advaita Vedanta: A Comparative Study in Religion and Reason* (University Park: Pennsylvania State University, 1995), pp. 221-22. From a Zen Buddhist perspective, Jung H. Lee criticizes Hick for failing to take into account Zen understandings of enlightenment and for a "theistic bias" in his conception of religious experience. See Jung H. Lee, "Problems of Religious Pluralism: A Zen Critique of John Hick's Ontological Monomorphism," *Philosophy East and West* 48, no. 3 (1998): 453-77.

[66]It is remarkable that the notion of God's special revelation to humankind—a central tenet in orthodox Judaism, Christianity and Islam, and present in varying forms in certain streams of Hinduism, Baha'i and Sikhism—is virtually ignored in Hick's discussion of the religions. To be sure, the idea that God has definitively revealed himself in any one tradition is ruled out by Hick's theory. But again, the fact that a significant aspect of major traditions must be ruled out or radically reinterpreted in order to fit his theory prima facie counts against the theory as a comprehensive explanation for religious phenomena.

[67]Hick, *Interpretation of Religion*, pp. 10, 36.

will mean recognizing the ultimacy of *nirvana*. For Jodo Shinshu Buddhists it will mean responding appropriately to Amida Buddha by proper recitation of the *nembutsu*. For orthodox Christians it will mean acknowledging Jesus Christ as the one Lord and Savior.[68] Hick greatly minimizes soteriological differences by speaking as if all religions share a common goal and understanding of the nature of salvation. But surely this is misleading. Can the great Pauline theme of justification by faith or the Hindu understanding of *moksha* (liberation) or the Zen notion of *satori* (enlightenment) be reduced to "the transition from self-centredness to Reality-centredness"? Hick is adopting a kind of lowest-common-denominator soteriology resulting in a strictly formal formula that ignores central aspects of the soteriology of the various religions.[69]

The Real and the *Personae/Impersonae*

Central to Hick's model is the distinction between the Real as it is in itself and the various conceptions of the Real in the religions. The Real in itself is said to be the divine noumenon, the ground of all authentic religious experience, with the various culturally conditioned conceptions of the religious ultimate being the divine phenomena. Conceptions of the religious ultimate in personal terms (Yahweh, Allah, Krishna, Shiva, Ahura Mazda) are the divine *personae,* and images of the religious ultimate in nonpersonal terms (the Tao, *nirguna* Brahman, *sunyata, nirvana, Dharmakaya*) are the divine *impersonae,* through which the Real is manifest.

Hick correctly observes that the distinction between the divine reality as it is in

---

[68]Wolfhart Pannenberg states, "If salvation is taken to refer to some 'actual transformation of human life from self-centredness to Reality-centredness,' then there is no reason to deny that such transformation occurs in various cultures and in many forms of authentic religious experience. But this is not the New Testament concept of salvation" ("Religious Pluralism and Conflicting Truth Claims," in *Christian Uniqueness Reconsidered: The Myth of a Pluralistic Theology of Religions*, ed. Gavin D'Costa [Maryknoll, N.Y.: Orbis, 1990], p. 101).

[69]When Hick spells out what he means by the "transition from self-centredness to Reality-centredness," it is clear that what he has in mind is a moral transformation of the person. As he puts it, "The transformation of human existence which is called salvation or liberation shows itself in its spiritual and moral fruits" (Hick, *Interpretation of Religion*, p. 301). This transformation produces "saints" who are characterized by moral purity, charity, strength of soul, compassion, inner peace and radiant joy, and whose lives are marked by selfless giving of themselves for others. But we are tempted to ask, what is distinctively *religious* about this transformation? Is this not a goal that any morally sensitive person would embrace? Is not this transformation also a reality among those who are explicitly not religious, agnostics and atheists? Hick admits that this is indeed the case (ibid., p. 306). But if so, then what is it about the Real, as the postulated ground of different forms of religious experience, that distinguishes "Reality-centredness" from, say, "morally acceptable behavior"? One suspects that soteriology comes close to being reduced to morality, but surely this is something that a host of religious figures from many traditions would emphatically reject.

itself and the divine reality as it is perceived by humans has a long and distinguished history. Examples of the distinction can be found in the major traditions.[70]
And if the transcendence of God and the finitude of humankind are to be maintained, it seems that some such distinction is inevitable. But Hick's distinction is
intended to do more than merely remind us that the infinite God cannot be grasped
by human concepts. In his thought the distinction between the Real and the gods
and absolutes of the religions is supposed to enable us to maintain both that the
various manifestations of the Real are different, and even entail mutually incompatible beliefs and practices, and that beyond these conflicting pictures there is a
religious ultimate that gives rise to these different understandings.

But there just does not seem to be any satisfactory way to spell out the relationship between the Real and the *personae/impersonae*. There are two possible ways of
interpreting the relationship between the Real and the various conceptions of ultimacy in the religions. First, it is possible to maintain a strong element of continuity between the Real in itself and the various manifestations of the Real, so that in
their experiences of Yahweh, Allah, *sunyata* or Brahman the great religious figures
were indeed experiencing the Real, but always as mediated through a particular
persona or *impersona*. Some of Hick's statements lend themselves to this interpretation.

> I want to say that the noumenal Real is experienced and thought by different human
> mentalities, forming and formed by different religious traditions, as the range of gods
> and absolutes which the phenomenology of religion reports. And these divine *perso-*
> *nae* and metaphysical *impersonae,* as I shall call them, are not illusory but are empiri-
> cally, that is experientially, real as authentic manifestations of the Real.[71]

The *personae* of the theistic and polytheistic traditions, and the *impersonae* of the
monistic traditions, are the manifestations of the Real to culturally and historically
conditioned humans, the "images" or "grids" through which the Real is perceived
and experienced.

Now if the *personae* and *impersonae* are accurate reflections of the Real, there
must be significant continuity between them and the religious ultimate they
reflect. One way to put this is to say that the set of true propositions about a given
image (Amida, Allah, *nirvana*) must form a subset of the set of all true propositions
about the Real in itself. If this were not the case, it is difficult to see how the various
personae/impersonae could be regarded as genuinely informative of the Real.

But this interpretation of the relation between the Real and the *personae/imper-*
sonae runs into serious difficulty due to the undeniable differences among such

---

[70]See Hick, *Interpretation of Religion*, pp. 236-38; and John Hick, "Ineffability," *Religious Studies*
36 (March 2000): 35-40.
[71]Hick, *Interpretation of Religion*, p. 242.

images of the religious ultimate. Indeed use of the two terms—*personae* and *impersonae*—is Hick's way of acknowledging that there are fundamental differences between those traditions that regard the religious ultimate as personal and those that regard it as nonpersonal. On this interpretation, it is crucial to Hick's thesis that the Real can accurately be thought of in both personal and nonpersonal categories. Images from both traditions can legitimately be applied to the Real. As Hick says in an earlier work, "The divine nature is infinite, exceeding the scope of all human concepts, and is capable of being experienced both as personal Lord and as nonpersonal ground or depth of being."[72]

It is not just a question of whether the Real can be *experienced* as personal and nonpersonal but whether the Real can correctly be described as both personal and nonpersonal. It may be possible for the Real to be experienced as personal and nonpersonal without its necessarily being both. (Perhaps the Real is able to present itself in certain situations as a personal Lord and in others as a nonpersonal ground of being.) But since in talking about Brahman or Allah, for example, Hindus or Muslims are not simply talking about their respective experiences but intend to make ontological claims about the nature of reality, the Real must actually be both personal and nonpersonal. Thus, if this thesis is correct, it should be possible to speak informatively of the Real as Yahweh, Jesus Christ, Allah, Brahman, *sunyata*, the Amida Buddha and so on as these designations are understood within the respective traditions.

But is this plausible? Does it make sense to speak of the Real in personal and nonpersonal categories as these are understood within the various traditions? Can one seriously maintain that the ontological implications of the Judeo-Christian understanding of the divine as Yahweh, the ontologically independent personal Creator and righteous Judge are compatible with the monistic implications of the Hindu notion of *nirguna* Brahman or with the ontologically ultimate image of *sunyata* (emptiness) in Zen?

According to this interpretation, terms such as "Yahweh," "Allah," "Shiva," "*nirguna* Brahman," "*sunyata*" and "the Tao" should all ultimately have the same referent. To be sure, in one sense the terms do have different meanings; they do not all share the same connotations and they can be paraphrased in different ways. Perhaps here a distinction should be made between what we can call the direct or penultimate referent and the ultimate referent of a term. Thus the direct referent of "Allah" is not the same as that of "*sunyata*," for they refer to different manifestations of the Real. But if indeed they are reflections of the one religious ultimate, then it seems that they should have the same ultimate referent; they should all

---

[72]Hick, *God Has Many Names*, p. 38.

denote the same Reality. And yet when the meanings of these terms within their respective traditions are retained, it becomes absurd to suppose that they all denote the same religious ultimate.[73]

But although there are suggestions in Hick's writings that, taken by themselves, indicate strong continuity between the Real and the various *personae/impersonae*, careful reading of *An Interpretation of Religion* as well as later writings shows that Hick rejects this interpretation in favor of one that minimizes continuity between the Real and the *personae/impersonae*. This is the second way of interpreting the relationship between the Real and the various conceptions of ultimacy in the religions. The object of religious experience is never the Real in itself but always some particular image or manifestation of the Real. The distinction between the Real and the *personae/impersonae* takes on a strong Kantian tone: our religious experiences are limited to culturally conditioned experiences of certain images of the Real in itself. The Real—much like the noumenon in Kant's epistemology of perception—is never the direct object of experience but is postulated in order to make sense of the fact of religious experience in general.[74]

I am suggesting applying this insight to our awareness of the Real, by distinguishing between the noumenal Real, the Real *an sich,* and the Real as humanly perceived in

---

[73]It may be tempting at this point to recall mathematician and philosopher Gottlob Frege's classic discussion of identity statements, and his distinction between *Sinn* (sense) and *Bedeutung* (reference), in an effort to clarify Hick's thesis. See Gottlob Frege, "On Sense and Reference," in *Translations from the Philosophical Writings of Gottlob Frege,* eds. M. Black and P. Geach (Oxford: Oxford University Press, 1952). Frege observed that, although both of the following are similar identity statements, they differ in an important respect: (A) The morning star is identical with the morning star. (B) The morning star is identical with the evening star. Although we now know that both A and B are true and that in both cases it is the planet Venus that is being referred to, there is a significant difference between the two statements, for A expresses a tautology and is obviously and necessarily true, whereas B enunciates an astronomical discovery. In an important sense, then, the meanings of A and B are the same, but they are clearly different as well. Frege's solution to the puzzle was the well-known distinction between sense and reference. "The morning star" means the same thing as "the evening star" in that both expressions refer to the same thing: they both denote the planet Venus. But the two expressions mean different things in that they each have a different sense: their connotations differ and they can be paraphrased differently.

Similarly, it may be suggested that terms such as *Allah, Yahweh, Brahman* and *sunyata* all have the same *referent* (the Real) although they have different *senses*. It seems that some such distinction is inevitable if this interpretation of Hick's thesis is to have any plausibility. But notice that Frege's example has the force and charm that it does only because relevant astronomical data have already made it plausible to believe that the referents of "the morning star" and "the evening star" are identical, whereas this identity of referents is precisely what is at issue in the current debate over religious pluralism. Given the undeniable differences in connotation of terms such as *Shiva, Allah, the Tao, Yahweh* and *Brahman,* it does not seem plausible to maintain that they all denote the same reality. Surely the burden of proof rests with anyone claiming that the ultimate referent of each is the same.

[74]Hick, *Interpretation of Religion,* pp. 243-49.

different ways as a range of divine phenomena. . . . I am suggesting analogously that we are aware of our supernatural environment in terms of certain categories which the mind imposes in the formation of religious experience. The two basic categories are deity (the Real as personal) and the absolute (the Real as non-personal). Each of these categories is then made concrete, or in Kant's terminology "schematized"—not, however, (as in his system) in terms of abstract time but in terms of the filled time of history and culture as the experienced Gods and Absolutes of the various religious traditions.[75]

Hick does not hesitate to draw out the obvious implications from such a radical disjunction between the Real and the realm of our experience: none of our substantial categories or concepts can be applied to the Real in itself.

It follows from this distinction between the Real as it is in itself and as it is thought and experienced through our religious concepts that we cannot apply to the Real *an sich* the characteristics encountered in its *personae* and *impersonae*. Thus it cannot be said to be one or many, person or thing, substance or process, good or evil, purposive or non-purposive. None of the concrete descriptions that apply within the realm of human experience can apply literally to the unexperiencable ground of that realm.[76]

The Real is said to be "the ultimate ground, transcending human conceptuality, of the range of *personae* and *impersonae* through which humans are related to it."[77] But although the Real is the ground of both personal and nonpersonal conceptions of the religious ultimate, in itself it is neither personal nor nonpersonal, for it transcends such categories.

The difficulty of understanding the ontological status of the *personae/impersonae* in relation to the Real is brought out nicely by George Mavrodes, who suggests two possible models for this relationship.[78] One is the "disguise model," in which a prince, desiring to hear for himself the actual sentiments of his subjects, assumes the disguises of an itinerant monk and a stonemason and thus mingles freely with the common folk in the kingdom. Throughout, he is always the same prince, although he appears to the people as a monk or a stonemason. But there is always an identity relation between the prince and his appearances as monk or stonemason.

Another possibility is the "construct model," which involves several artists who all observe the same landscape (rolling hills, trees, a village church and so on) and

---

[75]Hick, *Christian Theology of Religions*, p. 29.
[76]Hick, *Interpretation of Religion*, p. 246. See also ibid., p. 350; and Hick, *Christian Theology of Religions*, p. 27.
[77]Hick, *Interpretation of Religion*, p. 266.
[78]George Mavrodes, "Polytheism," in *The Rationality of Belief and the Plurality of Faith: Essays in Honor of William P. Alston*, ed. Thomas D. Senor (Ithaca, N.Y.: Cornell University Press, 1995), pp. 273-76.

paint what they see. The resulting paintings are thus constructs in that they are the creative products of the artists. They will have some resemblances, since it is the same landscape being painted, but the particular perspectives, interests and styles of the artists produce significant differences as well. The paintings are thus products of both the creativity of the artists and what is given in the landscape itself.

Mavrodes observes that although there are passages in Hick that suggest the disguise model, so that the Real appears to us as the gods and absolutes of the religions, overall his discussion seems to reject this view. The construct model seems more promising, as it recognizes the creative contribution of religious believers without reducing the gods and absolutes of the religions to mere human projections. But Mavrodes then asks what kind of ontological reality the gods and absolutes have, given Hick's appeal to a Kantian epistemology and ontology. Hick, as we have seen, draws a parallel between the objects of our experience (the phenomena) in Kant and the gods and absolutes of the religions. But for Kant the phenomena have a kind of objective reality; they are not illusions or mere human projections. If the Kantian analogy is taken seriously, Mavrodes argues, then the various gods and absolutes of the religions "are real *in the same sense that cantaloupes are real on the Kantian view.*"[79] This, of course, would suggest an ontology heavily populated by various gods, Yahweh, Allah and Vishnu, and nonpersonal realities such as the Tao and *sunyata,* prompting Mavrodes to give Hick the dubious distinction of being "probably the most important philosophical defender of polytheism in the history of Western philosophy."[80]

Not surprisingly, Hick rejects the label, although he admits to being "polysomething, though not precisely a poly-theist" while on another level being a "mono-something, though not precisely a mono-theist."[81] Furthermore, although he admits that each model has a legitimate insight into his theory, Hick rejects both the disguise model and the construct model as inadequate for the relation between the Real and the *personae/impersonae,* leaving the ontological status of the gods and absolutes unresolved. Thus, in his further response to Hick, Mavrodes sounds bewildered: "[I]f Hick is not a polytheist then what is he?" Mavrodes concludes that despite his professed Kantianism, Hick "does not think that the gods, etc., of the actual religions—Allah, Shivah, Brahman, the Holy Trinity and so on— are real at all. . . . Hick may really think of the gods of *all* the religions as much more like fictional characters, illusions, etc., than like the Kantian phenomena."[82]

---

[79]Ibid., p. 272. Emphasis in the original.

[80]Ibid., p. 262.

[81]John Hick, "The Epistemological Challenge of Religious Pluralism," in *Faith and Philosophy* 14, no. 3 (1997): 283.

[82]George Mavrodes, "A Response to John Hick," *Faith and Philosophy* 14, no. 3 (1997): 289-90. Emphasis in the original.

William L. Rowe concurs, saying:

> I think that Hick's own view comes closest to the view that the gods are projections of
> the religious imagination, creations of the human mind through which we encounter
> what is truly ultimate reality. That is, although no such beings actually exist, they are
> not simply the mental products of inner psychological needs, as Freud and some reli-
> gious sceptics would say. They are mental products that are appropriate in view of
> human encounters with what is truly ultimate and beyond all literal descriptions of
> the Real itself.[83]

Strictly speaking, then, the Christian who believes in the existence of God the Holy
Trinity, Creator of the universe, is wrong, for *that* being does not exist, although
that particular conception of the ultimate can be one (among many) effective ways
of thinking about the religious ultimate.

Ineffability

Hick has given increasingly greater emphasis to the theme of ineffability, so that the
Real is said to be utterly beyond the range of human conceptual and linguistic categories. "By 'ineffable' I mean (with a qualification to be mentioned presently) having
a nature that is beyond the scope of our networks of human concepts. Thus the Real
in itself cannot properly be said to be personal or impersonal, purposive or non-purposive, good or evil, substance or process, even one or many."[84] Properties, concepts
and categories with which we are familiar cannot be ascribed to the Real. "The Real in
itself is thus, from our human point of view, totally transcategorial."[85] But of course,
to claim that literally *none* of the properties we can conceptualize apply to the Real is
self-referentially incoherent. If this were the case, then at the very least "the property
of being totally beyond all conceptual and linguistic categories" would apply to the
Real, thereby refuting the original claim. In order to avoid this absurdity Hick distinguishes between purely formal properties and substantial properties.

> There are what we can call substantial attributes, which would tell us something about
> what the Godhead in itself is like—for example, that it is personal or that it is imper-
> sonal. And there are what I have called formal attributes, which do not tell us anything
> about what the Godhead in itself is like. Thus for example, that it can be referred to
> does not give us any information about its nature. Formal attributes are thus trivial or
> inconsequential in that nothing significant follows from them concerning the intrin-
> sic nature of the Godhead.[86]

---

[83]William L. Rowe, "Religious Pluralism," *Religious Studies* 35 (June 1999): 142.
[84]Hick, *Christian Theology of Religions*, p. 27. See also pp. 60-65; John Hick, *Interpretation of Religion*, pp. 239, 246-49, 264, 266, 350; and John Hick, "Ineffability," *Religious Studies* 36 (March 2000): 35-46.
[85]Hick, "Ineffability," p. 41.
[86]Ibid.

No substantial properties can be predicated of the Real since it is beyond all such conceptual categories.

But even Hick's "modified ineffability" is untenable. First, it is not at all clear that the claim that there is a Real, but that no substantial properties apply to the Real, is even coherent.[87] What would it mean for an entity to exist without its having *any* substantial properties we can conceive of? Since no substantial properties could be ascribed to it, an agnostic silence concerning it would seem the only reasonable course. As Keith Ward puts it, "If the Real is ineffable, how can one know that it exists? If no truth-claim can apply to it, how can one be entitled to say anything of it? And if this reality is unknowable, how can we know that all claims about it are equally valid, except in the sense that all are completely mistaken?"[88] But in spite of his commitment to the ineffability of the Real, Hick clearly assumes that we do know some things about the Real and that some substantial properties can be ascribed to it. For example, Hick speaks of the Real as "the source and ground of everything," "a transcendent reality," "the necessary condition of our existence and our highest good," "that to which religion is a response" and so on.[89] As Mavrodes observes, postulating the Real as the most reasonable explanation for religious phenomena assumes a causal relationship between the Real and the *personae* and *impersonae* that his model will not permit.

> [Hick] postulates something which is neither good nor evil, neither purposive nor non-purposive. And of course Hick's Real is not loving, not powerful, not wise, not compassionate, not gentle, not forgiving. The Real does not know me (or anyone else), does not care about me (or anything else) and so on. The Real did not create the world, did not design the world, does not sustain the world, and will not bring the world to an end. What in the world does the Real have to do with anything which happens in the world? Why would anyone suppose that it "accounts" for any fact at all, religious or otherwise? Hick, I think, is himself unsatisfied with the ineffability which he professes. So he is continually drifting into causal, or quasi-causal, talk about the Real—that it is the "noumenal ground" of certain experiences, that there is a "transmission of information from a transcendent source to the human mind/brain," the Real has an "impact upon us," and so on. But this talk is either empty (though with the appearance of content) or else it violates the prohibition of applying to the Real any humanly conceivable, positive, substantial characteristics.[90]

Moreover, Hick's insistence that the Real itself transcends all substantial proper-

---

[87]See, for example, Rowe, "Religious Pluralism"; Mavrodes, "Response to John Hick," p. 291; and Alvin Plantinga, *Warranted Christian Belief* (New York: Oxford University Press, 2000), pp. 49-55.
[88]Keith Ward, "Truth and the Diversity of Religions," in *Philosophical Challenge of Religious Diversity*, p. 113.
[89]Hick, *Christian Theology of Religions*, pp. 27, 60, 63, 67. On this point, see Keith Yandell, *Philosophy of Religion: A Contemporary Introduction* (New York: Routledge, 1999), pp. 71-72.
[90]Mavrodes, "Response to John Hick," pp. 292-93.

ties means that the moral categories of good or evil cannot be predicated of the Real. Hick repeatedly acknowledges this: the Real cannot be said to be good or evil.[91]

> "Good" and "benign"—together with our other value terms—are human conceptions. They apply within human life, and they apply to the range of divine phenomena which we have ourselves partially constructed; but not to the ultimate noumenal reality in itself. Our human nature, with its range of concepts and languages, is such that *from our point of view* the Real, experienced in a variety of divine phenomena, is benign and good.[92]

So although the language of good and evil is informative, and although moral categories can be applied within the realm of human experience, we cannot apply such language and categories to the Real itself, which transcends all such categorial distinctions.[93]

But here we confront a fundamental inconsistency at the heart of Hick's model. An essential component of his theory is the soteriological or moral criterion (the moral transformation from self-centeredness to Reality-centeredness) that performs two critical functions. First, it provides a justification for postulating the Real as the noumenal ground for the various religions. That is, it is the supposed fact that moral transformation and the production of saints take place on roughly an equal basis across the major religions that entitles us to postulate the Real as the ground of the religions.[94] Second, Hick is not willing to recognize just any religious tradition as being in "soteriological alignment" with the Real. Thus traditions such as Nazism and Satanism, and leaders such as Jim Jones, David Koresh and Shoko Asahara of the Aum Shinrikyo sect, are not to be regarded as providing legitimate responses to the Real.[95] And it is the moral criterion that supposedly enables us to discriminate between legitimate and illegitimate religious teachings and practices. But here is the problem: If indeed the Real in itself is beyond moral categories, so that it is neither good nor evil, how can Hick use a *moral* criterion in this manner? Given Hick's ontology, why suppose that moral transformation within a given religion is at all informative about that tradition's relationship to the Real? Alvin Plantinga states the problem clearly:

---

[91]Hick, *Interpretation of Religion*, p. 246. See also p. 350; and Hick, *Christian Theology of Religions*, pp. 27, 60-62.

[92]Hick, "Ineffability," p. 44. Emphasis in the original.

[93]This sounds very much like what Buddhists say about *sunyata*, or emptiness, an analogy that Hick accepts: "If you understand the idea of *sunyata* as indicating that the ultimately real is completely and utterly empty of everything that the human mind projects in its activity of cognition, then this does indeed apply to what I mean by the Real" (Hick, *Christian Theology of Religions*, pp. 60-61).

[94]Ibid., p. 69.

[95]Ibid., pp. 44-45; Hick, *Fifth Dimension*, pp. 154-55.

[W]hy think some ways of behavior are appropriate to the Real and others are not? . . . If the Real has no positive properties of which we have a grasp, how could we possibly know or have grounds for believing that some ways of behaving with respect to it are more appropriate than others? . . . We can't have it both ways. If this being is really such that we literally know nothing positive about it (if it has no positive properties of which we have a grasp), then there is no reason to think self-centered behavior is less appropriate with respect to it (granting, indeed, that some modes of behavior *are* more appropriate with respect to it than others) than living a life of love.[96]

Despite his efforts to depict the Real in terms that do not privilege any particular religious tradition, Hick is operating on borrowed capital. That is, he is tacitly assuming certain theistic characteristics of the Real even as he states that no such attributes can be predicated of the Real. But he cannot have it both ways.

There is much more we could say in assessing Hick's proposal, but this should be sufficient to show that fundamental inconsistencies and epistemological problems vitiate his model of religious pluralism. In conclusion, we might note a remarkable irony in the entire effort. One of the more significant motivations for pluralists is the desire to avoid the implication of particularism and inclusivism, namely that large numbers of morally good, sincere, intelligent people are simply wrong in their basic religious beliefs. And so they enthusiastically put forward pluralism as the preferred alternative to such judgmental views. However, as we have seen, the clear implication of pluralism is that orthodox Jews, Christians, Muslims, Advaita Vedantin Hindus, Pure Land Buddhists and Mormons are all wrong in their basic beliefs. To be sure, the pluralist is quick to add that, despite their mistaken beliefs, they are all in *some* way responding appropriately to the religious ultimate; it is just that they are not doing so in the manner in which the believers themselves think they are. But it is hard to see why this way of rejecting their beliefs as mistaken is any more tolerant than that of the particularist or inclusivist.

---

[96]Plantinga, *Warranted Christian Belief*, pp. 57-58. For similar criticism, see also Wainwright, *Philosophy of Religion*, 210-11.

8

APOLOGETICS & RELIGIOUS PLURALISM

To show that one (logically) may be holding a true belief does not suffice in cases of extreme epistemic pressure; not only the publicans and tax collectors, but also the racists and the flat earthers can do as much. . . . There are situations in which it is not possible for a religious community to fulfill its epistemic duties without entering into positive apologetics. . . . This is because, in such a situation, a religious community is typically presented with the realization that its own absolute answers to the mysteries of human existence and human salvation are directly challenged by an incompatible set of answers given by another community, and that typically, this opposed set of answers provides an existence apparently as meaningful and ordered for its adherents as does the set adhered to by members of the first religious community for its.

PAUL GRIFFITHS, *An Apology for Apologetics*

We had just moved from the lovely city of Kyoto, Japan, to the sprawling megalopolis of Tokyo. I was engaged in language study and my wife, Ruth, was expecting our first child. On one of her regular visits to the maternity clinic Ruth happened to meet an American woman, married to a Japanese and living in Tokyo. Since we did not often encounter Americans, Ruth invited the woman to our home. Expecting a casual visit full of small talk about things back home, Ruth was shocked by what followed. After exchanging pleasantries, the guest launched into an impressive and moving testimony of how she had "found peace and true meaning to life" in Nichiren Buddhism. The woman, it turned out, was an American convert to Soka Gakkai Buddhism and was now a regional director of Soka Gakkai in Tokyo. In recounting the incident to me later, Ruth said it was one of the most impressive testimonies she had heard—change a few key terms here and there and it could have been a beautiful Christian testimony.

This incident illustrates some of the new realities in the twenty-first century. No longer is it a matter of the "Christian West" taking the gospel to the "pagan East"; the East has come West. Furthermore, this encounter illustrates graphically the bankruptcy of any approach to Christian witness that is limited to "sharing our story," refusing to support personal testimony with other corroborating factors.

Christian witness based merely upon personal experience or the pragmatic benefits of conversion would have little to say concerning *why* the woman ought to abandon Buddhism and embrace Christian faith.

We noted in chapter four that the culture of modernity presents some distinctive challenges to Christian faith. The idea that we can know religious truth, especially concerning the truth claims of orthodox Christianity, is rejected by many today. But paradoxically, along with skepticism about traditional beliefs, we also have remarkable credulity when it comes to alternative religious movements, leading to the challenges of religious pluralism. Many enthusiastically embrace the possibility of multiple saviors and religious paths, while they dismiss as religious imperialism the Christian insistence upon just one Savior and one correct religion. And even if in principle they grant that one religious tradition might be superior to the rest, and that one religious figure might be universally normative, why should we assume that Christianity and Jesus Christ are in these privileged positions? Why Jesus and not the Buddha?

Christian Apologetics

Attempts to respond to these challenges are normally regarded as part of the discipline of apologetics. The term *apologetics* itself is today rather pejorative, so that, for example, to call someone an apologist for the tobacco industry is actually to call into question the objectivity of his or her testimony. This is unfortunate, for apologetics is integral to Christian theology and historically has had a distinguished place in the Christian tradition.

But just what is apologetics, and what place—if any—should it have in Christian witness in a multicultural and pluralistic world? Within the Christian community there have been vigorous, and at times highly polemical, debates over the nature of apologetics and its place in responsible witness. There is no need for us to rehearse these intramural discussions.[1] Our concern is with the implications of religious pluralism for apologetics, and so after considering briefly the nature of apologetics and some historical instances of interreligious apologetics, we will look at implications of some recent work in the epistemology of religion for apologetics in contexts of pluralism.

The Christian faith includes some profound and far-reaching claims about the nature of the universe, God, the human predicament and salvation. But part of the price of making such claims is the exposure of such statements to the inevitable questions about their justification. We normally do not blindly accept just any

---

[1] For good introductions to the issues and approaches, see Gordon R. Lewis, *Testing Christianity's Truth Claims* (Chicago: Moody Press, 1976); and Steven B. Cowan, ed., *Five Views on Apologetics* (Grand Rapids, Mich.: Zondervan, 2000).

claim to truth, nor should we expect others to do so. We are confronted today by a bewildering assortment of religious claims, ranging from amusing but relatively harmless promises of the benefits of crystals to the disastrous claims of Jim Jones and the Peoples Temple, David Koresh and the Branch Davidians, or Shoko Asahara and the Aum Shinrikyo. We do not accept at face value just any religious assertion; we expect adequate evidence or proper grounds for a claim if we are to accept it. Although notoriously difficult to formulate precisely, there is a direct correlation between the proper acceptance of a particular belief and the warrant or justification for that belief. The more significant and controversial the claim, the greater our expectation for its justification. The central truth claims of the Christian faith are significant and controversial indeed, and thus those who proclaim the gospel today should be prepared to respond in an appropriate and informed manner to questions that naturally arise.

Christian apologetics has been defined by Mark Hanna as "a systematic response of the reflective and culturally informed Christian to attacks that inevitably come upon the truth claims of the Christian faith."[2] Although the nature of the critiques may vary with time and culture, the church in every generation, in each culture, faces intellectual challenges of one kind or another, and it is the task of apologetics to respond appropriately to them. Hanna's definition underscores the importance of understanding the cultural context in which particular critiques emerge and gain their plausibility, and this is especially significant when considering the challenges posed by religious pluralism.

Much of the confusion over approaches in apologetics stems from failure to distinguish between what we might call theoretical apologetics and applied apologetics. Theoretical apologetics is concerned with the objective justification of the Christian faith irrespective of any particular context or how any given audience might respond to the issues.[3] It is concerned with problem solving, and its purpose is to answer satisfactorily certain questions about the acceptability of Christian truth claims, including the following: Can we know whether God exists, and if so, how? Did Jesus actually rise from the dead, and if so, what is the significance of this? Is the Islamic understanding of Jesus compatible with that of the New Testament? Is the biblical understanding of God compatible with Buddhist claims about the ultimacy of *sunyata* (emptiness)? Theoretical apologetics tends to be a highly rigorous and specialized endeavor, incorporating a variety of disciplines, although

---

[2]Mark M. Hanna, *Crucial Questions in Apologetics* (Grand Rapids, Mich.: Baker, 1978), p. 63.
[3]By "objective," I mean having a reality or validity independent of individual or collective states of consciousness. "Objective justification" refers to the processes and principles according to which a belief is properly acceptable, regardless of whether any individual or group happens to accept the belief. While these principles are influenced by particular social, cultural and linguistic factors, they cannot be reduced to such factors.

epistemology is central. Applied apologetics, or context-specific apologetics, by contrast, takes place within a particular sociocultural context and is very much concerned with human response to the gospel. It is the use of appropriate justification procedures and relevant data in the actual presentation and defense of the gospel to a particular person or group. Its purpose is to elicit a favorable response from the audience—it actively seeks to persuade. Both the methodology and the level of sophistication of applied apologetics will vary greatly, depending upon the audience and relevant cultural context.

The distinction here is essentially that between uncovering the answers to certain questions and persuading others that one has indeed found the answers. It is one thing to ascertain the answers; it is something else again to persuade others that you have done so. It is important to see that answers to questions on the applied level are logically dependent upon answers to corresponding questions on the theoretical level. For example, the appropriate response to an inquiring university student in Singapore who asks, "How can I be sure that Jesus really did rise from the dead?" is logically dependent upon the answer to the (theoretical) question "Did Jesus actually rise from the dead, and if so, how can we know this?"

Furthermore, applied apologetics is both person- and culture-specific in a way that theoretical apologetics is not. On the theoretical level, there is one correct answer to the question "Did Jesus really rise from the dead?" If Jesus really did rise from the dead, then this remains true regardless of the culture in which related questions emerge. On the applied level, however, apologetics should adapt to varying contexts, both with respect to the nature of the questions addressed and the manner in which they are engaged. The issues will vary from culture to culture—the question of God's existence is not likely to be a pressing concern among Muslims in Pakistan (although the deity of Jesus Christ certainly will be), whereas this will be a significant issue for university students in a Buddhist society in Thailand. Furthermore, the manner in which one responds to issues and attempts to persuade is also to some extent relative to cultures. What is appropriate and effective in Kyoto may not be acceptable in Mexico City or Cairo. Sharp confrontation and aggressive debate are not appropriate in Japan, where harmony and the appearance of accord are highly valued, but they might be effective elsewhere. Thus considerable creativity and variety in approach are essential in applied apologetics.[4]

We must, of course, resist the temptation to turn applied apologetics into mere technique, assuming that skillful argumentation alone will change hearts and produce conversion. Apologetics in and of itself will not save anyone. Nobody is argued

---

[4]On the importance of cultural sensitivity in effective apologetics, see David Clark, *Dialogical Apologetics: A Person-Centered Approach to Christian Defense* (Grand Rapids, Mich.: Baker, 1993), chapter 8.

into the kingdom. Apologetics—just as evangelism or any other activity—is ineffective apart from the power and work of the Holy Spirit on the heart. Saving faith is a gift of God's grace (Eph 2:8-10), and ultimately it is the Holy Spirit who brings about conviction of sin (Jn 16:8-11), liberates the spiritually blind from the grasp of the Adversary and gives new birth in Christ (Jn 3:5; 1 Cor 2:14-16; Tit 3:5). But of course, this does not make apologetics unnecessary any more than it renders evangelism optional. We must carry out both evangelism and apologetics with much prayer and conscious dependence upon the power of God.

Moreover, God's grace reaches people where they are, with their particular dispositions and characteristics, rooted in their social and cultural environments with all of the attendant influences. Within such matrices sinful human beings are called by God's grace to believe and accept the gospel of Jesus Christ. Thus, in our witness to an unbelieving world, we must always give primacy to the simple, direct, Spirit-anointed proclamation of the gospel (Rom 1:16; Heb 4:12). But where appropriate, we should also supplement such witness with informed and sensitive responses to questions, showing why one should accept the claims of Christian faith (1 Pet 3:15). Properly construed, then, apologetics is ancillary to evangelism and discipleship and is concerned to lead others into a direct encounter with the risen Lord Jesus Christ.

Interreligious Encounters and Apologetics

Many think of apologetics as a distinctively modern response to the challenges posed by the Enlightenment to the church. But this is not the whole picture, for Christian apologetics goes back to the early church and indeed is a significant part of the New Testament writings.[5] The second century, in particular, produced remarkable Christian apologists such as Aristides, Justin Martyr, Claudius Apollinaris, Athenagoras, Tatian, Theophilus of Antioch and Clement of Alexandria, followed in the third century by Origen and Tertullian.[6] The subject matter of their writings varied, with some apologists addressing the political authorities in an effort to win official recognition of the Christian religion. Others responded to attacks from pagan Greco-Roman thinkers. Still others tried to persuade Jews to accept Jesus as the Messiah.

Because second-century apologists such as Justin Martyr, Theophilus of Antioch, Athenagoras and Clement of Alexandria were concerned about the relationship

---

[5]See F. F. Bruce, *The Defense of the Gospel in the New Testament* (Grand Rapids, Mich.: Eerdmans, 1959).

[6]See Robert M. Grant, *Greek Apologists of the Second Century* (Philadelphia: Westminster Press, 1988); Mark Edwards, Martin Goodman and Simon Price, eds., *Apologetics in the Roman Empire* (Oxford: Oxford University Press, 1999); and Avery Dulles, *A History of Apologetics* (Philadelphia: Westminster Press, 1971), chapter 2.

of God's revelation in Christ to the surrounding Greek intellectual tradition and were quite positive about aspects of some Greek philosophers, they are sometimes held up as early advocates of inclusivism who recognized God's presence and activity in non-Christian religious traditions.[7] We must not, however, read back into their discussions the specific issues of pluralism today. It would be anachronistic to regard them as addressing today's questions or fitting neatly into current paradigms. Moreover, although some church fathers could be remarkably positive in what they had to say about Socrates and Plato, they consistently rejected popular Hellenistic and Roman religious practices as idolatry and insisted unequivocally upon the uniqueness of God's incarnation in Jesus of Nazareth.[8]

The apologists of the first four centuries were concerned largely with responding to issues arising from Judaism or the surrounding Greco-Roman cultures. But in the Middle Ages attention shifted to a distinctively new religious and cultural challenge—Islam.[9] The medieval church produced some perceptive and sensitive apologists with respect to Islam. In the eighth century John of Damascus, who held an administrative post under the Umayyad caliphs in Damascus, wrote *A Dialogue Between a Saracen and a Christian,* and his disciple Theodore Abu Qurrah wrote *God and the True Religion* in Arabic. Avery Dulles describes Abu Qurrah's approach:

> In this treatise Abu Qurrah confronts squarely the problem of choosing among the various religions that claim to be revealed: Zoroastrianism, the Samaritan religion, Judaism, Christianity, Manichaeism, and the sects of Marcion, Bardesanes, and Mohammed. After examining the points of similarity and difference, Abu Qurrah proposes an allegory. A certain king, he narrates, had a son who had never seen him. In a foreign land the son fell ill and sent to his father for medical advice. Several messages came, one from the father, the others from the latter's enemies. The son, assisted by the advice of a doctor, scrutinized each message from the point of view of what it indicated about the author, the understanding of the disease, and the reasonableness of the proposed remedy, and accepted the prescription that best satisfied all three crite-

---

[7]See, for example, Jacques Dupuis, *Toward a Christian Theology of Religious Pluralism* (Maryknoll, N.Y.: Orbis, 1997), pp. 53-83; and Richard Henry Drummond, *Toward a New Age in Christian Theology* (Maryknoll, N.Y.: Orbis, 1985), pp. 25-35.

[8]See Gerald Bray, "Explaining Christianity to Pagans," in *The Trinity in a Pluralistic Age: Theological Essays on Culture and Religion,* ed. Kevin J. Vanhoozer (Grand Rapids, Mich.: Eerdmans, 1997), pp. 9-25; and Bruce W. Winter, "In Public and in Private: Early Christians and Religious Pluralism," and Graham A. Keith, "Justin Martyr and Religious Exclusivism"—both in *One God, One Lord: Christianity in a World of Religious Pluralism,* ed. Andrew D. Clarke and Bruce W. Winter, 2nd ed. (Grand Rapids, Mich.: Baker, 1992).

[9]See Dulles, *History of Apologetics,* chapter 3; Tibor Horvath, "Apologetics as 'Dialogue' in the Western Church from the Classical Period of Scholasticism to the Beginning of the Reformation," *Asia Journal of Theology* 4, no. 1 (1990): 136-61; and William Montgomery Watt, *Muslim-Christian Encounters: Perceptions and Misperceptions* (London: Routledge, 1991).

ria. Applying the allegory to the choice of a religion, Abu Qurrah tries to show that Christianity presents the most plausible idea of God, exhibits the fullest understanding of man's actual religious needs, and prescribes what appear to be the most appropriate remedies.[10]

In Abu Qurrah, then, we have a premodern example of a thoughtful Christian response to the plurality of religious claims, arguing that Christianity makes sense of the relevant data in a way that other religious traditions do not.

Under the shadow of the Crusades in the twelfth century, Peter the Venerable, abbot of Cluny, undertook a careful study of Islam and became disillusioned with the violence of the Crusades, concluding that "the avowed purposes and goals of the Crusade had omitted entirely what should have been the most central Christian concern, namely, the conversion of the Moslems."[11] In *A Book Against the Sect or Heresy of the Saracens* Peter tried to reassure Muslims, saying that he approached them not "as our people often do, by arms, but by words; not by force, but by reason; not in hatred, but in love."[12]

The outstanding medieval apologist was, of course, St. Thomas Aquinas, one of the great intellects of Western history.[13] Thomas lived and wrote in the thirteenth century, when Islamic influence was keenly felt in Europe. Arabic contributions to literature, philosophy and science were abundant, and thinkers such as the Spanish Muslim Ibn Rushd, known in the West as Averroes, introduced Aristotelian philosophy to Europe. Recognizing the need to interact with this powerful new perspective, Thomas responded by formulating a Christian theological system in Aristotelian categories. Thomas's most complete work in apologetics is the masterful *Summa contra Gentiles,* composed in part as a work that could be used for training Christian missionaries to Muslims in Spain.[14]

One of the earliest accounts of a Christian encounter with Buddhism is provided by the thirteenth-century Franciscan friar William of Rubruck, who reached the Mongol court at Karakorum in central Mongolia in 1253.[15] In his diaries William provides us

---

[10]Dulles, *History of Apologetics*, pp. 73-74.

[11]James Kritzeck, *Peter the Venerable and Islam* (Princeton, N.J.: Princeton University Press, 1964), p. 23; as quoted in Watt, *Muslim-Christian Encounters*, p. 84.

[12]Quoted in Dulles, *History of Apologetics,* p. 82.

[13]For a summary of Thomas's contribution in apologetics, see Dulles, *History of Apologetics,* pp. 85-94. For an excellent introduction to Thomas's thought, see Brian Davies, *The Thought of Thomas Aquinas* (Oxford: Clarendon, 1992).

[14]See Dulles, *History of Apologetics*, p. 87. See also James Waltz, "Muhammad and the Muslims in St. Thomas Aquinas," *Muslim World* 66 (1976): 81-95.

[15]See Richard Fox Young, *"Deus Unus* or *Dei Plures Sunt?* The Function of Inclusivism in the Buddhist Defense of Mongol Folk Religion Against William of Rubruck (1254)," *Journal of Ecumenical Studies* 26, no. 1 (1989): 100-135; and Samuel Hugh Moffett, *A History of Christianity in Asia* (New York: HarperCollins, 1992), 1:409-14. I am especially indebted to Professor Young's fine analysis of the debate.

with the records of a debate between a Buddhist and himself, held in 1254 before Mongke Khan, grandson of the great Mongol ruler Genghis Khan. Mongke Khan had invited representatives of various traditions (Manichaeism, Islam, Christianity, Chinese Buddhism and Mongol folk religion) to argue the merits of their respective traditions, ostensibly so that he might decide which religion was true. Our only access to the content of the debates is through William's diaries, but from this it is clear that William and the Buddhist engaged in a vigorous debate, an exchange indicating how little each really understood of the other's perspective and yet how, in spite of such misunderstandings, each could nevertheless discern certain weaknesses in the other's worldview. The Buddhist, for example, picking up on William's uncompromising monotheism, raised the perennial problem of evil: "If your God is as you say, why does he make the half of things evil?" When William protested that all that proceeds from God is good, the Buddhist then demanded, "Whence then comes evil?"[16]

After listening to the presentations, Mongke Khan summoned William and said, "As God gives us the different fingers of the hand, so he gives to men diverse ways. . . . Eternal heaven gave us diviners [shamans]; we do what they tell us, and we live in peace." The khan then ruled in favor of Buddhism as more compatible with Mongol folk religion, and thus acceptable to the empire, and William was informed that he must leave the court. William, it seems, was perceived in the debate as having ridiculed the beliefs and practices of Buddhists and followers of Mongol folk religion, thus inviting Mongke Khan's parting rebuke: "God gives you the Scriptures, and you Christians keep them not. You do not find in them that one should find fault with another, do you?"[17] It is, of course, impossible to know all that was involved in this encounter between William and the Buddhist, but it appears that the khan, concerned with what would prove beneficial for his kingdom, sensed that the rigidity and exclusivism of Christianity were not conducive to his social and political agendas.

In the sixteenth century the Jesuit Matteo Ricci, one of the most extraordinary missionaries of any era, journeyed to the imperial court in China.[18] Ricci saw clearly that the long-term success of Christian missions in China depended upon the gospel being expressed in authentic Chinese idiom and the Christian worldview being accepted by the cultural elite, the Confucian literati. Ricci embarked upon a serious and in-depth encounter between Christianity and the Confucian worldview. Without the aid of

---

[16]Young, *"Deus Unus,"* p. 115.

[17]Ibid., p. 116.

[18]For discussions of Ricci and his impact in China, see Ralph Covell, *Confucius, the Buddha, and Christ: A History of the Gospel in Chinese* (Maryknoll, N.Y.: Orbis, 1986), chapter 3; Andrew Ross, *A Vision Betrayed: The Jesuits in Japan and China, 1542-1742* (Maryknoll, N.Y.: Orbis, 1994), chapters 6-7; Charles E. Ronan and Bonnie B. C. Oh, eds., *East Meets West: The Jesuits in China: 1582-1773* (Chicago: Loyola University Press, 1988); and Jonathan Spence, *The Memory Palace of Matteo Ricci* (New York: Viking Penguin, 1984).

grammars or dictionaries, Ricci mastered not only contemporary but also classical Chinese and adopted the dress of the Confucian literati. Andrew Ross observes, "He had become such a master of Chinese and the Confucian Classics that the literati as a class could treat him as if one of themselves."[19] Ricci was convinced that original Confucianism had been monotheistic and that the classical deity, Tian (Heaven) or Shangdi (Lord on High), was indeed the transcendent Creator God of the Bible. Later generations, he claimed, had corrupted this original monotheism with a more ambiguous metaphysic. Just as Thomas Aquinas had used Aristotelian philosophy to articulate Christian truth for Europeans, so too, thought Ricci, might Chinese Christians use Confucian thought in the expression of Christian faith.

In 1603 Ricci published *On the True Meaning of the Lord of Heaven,* a creative and influential work of Christian apologetics.[20] According to Ross, "Ricci was setting out to show that there was a belief in a transcendent God contained in what he insisted was original Confucianism, and that this transcendent Lord of Heaven and the God of the Bible were the same. What is so extraordinary was that in the eyes of a large number of literati he succeeded in proving his point."[21] Even those scholars who disagreed with him treated him as an intellectual equal and recognized his interpretation as a legitimate possibility. Ricci's apologetic method was essentially an exercise in what is sometimes called "natural theology," or the attempt to establish truths about God apart from recourse to special revelation in Scripture. Drawing upon natural theology and the "natural law" tradition,[22] Ricci felt that some common ground with Confucianism could be established. Ricci believed that classical Confucianism, in line with the natural theology tradition of Christianity, recognized that "human beings are able to reason from human nature and from the nature of the universe to the existence and nature of God and the kind of moral life pleasing to God."[23] Contemporary Confucians were highly critical of Taoism and Buddhism, and Ricci skillfully used this to his advantage. Thus in establishing the existence of a personal Creator God, distinct from the creation, Ricci argued against the Taoist notion of "nothingness" and Buddhist "emptiness" *(wu)* as well as the Neo-Confucian notion of "Supreme Ultimate" *(taiji)* and "Principle" *(li).*[24]

---

[19]See Ross, *Vision Betrayed,* p. 135.

[20]See Matteo Ricci, *The True Meaning of the Lord of Heaven,* trans. Douglas Lancashire and Peter Hu Kuo-chen (St. Louis: Institute of Jesuit Sources, 1985).

[21]Ross, *Vision Betrayed,* p. 147.

[22]"Natural law" refers to the general awareness of an objective and universal moral order that is in principle accessible to all persons, apart from recourse to special revelation. For a good discussion of the historical tradition and contemporary issues, see J. Budziszewski, *Written on the Heart: The Case for Natural Law* (Downers Grove, Ill.: InterVarsity Press, 1997).

[23]Covell, *Confucius, the Buddha, and Christ,* p. 46.

[24]Ricci, *True Meaning of the Lord of Heaven,* chapters 1-2. However, it is generally recognized that Ricci did not accurately understand the Taoist and Buddhist notions of nothingness and emptiness.

Ricci had an enormous impact upon the cultured elite, and a number of significant Confucian literati became Christians through his ministry.[25] His achievements were monumental, for, as Ross observes, "Ricci's interpretation of Confucius was accepted as a valid form of Confucian discourse by the literati of late Ming China," whether they ultimately accepted his views or not.[26] However, the early Jesuit experiment with contextualization was short-lived. The "Rites Controversy"—a complex set of disputes over translation of Christian terms into Chinese, Chinese ancestral rites and Confucianism in general—called into question the Jesuits' rather accommodating approach to Chinese culture. After a prolonged dispute between the Jesuits and their critics (the Franciscans and Dominicans), the Vatican eventually ruled against the Jesuits, thus ending their mission in China.[27]

We cannot here pursue the story of Christian apologetics in the modern era, except to note that with the social, cultural and intellectual transformations in the West during the past several centuries Christian apologetics has become increasingly preoccupied with the challenges of secularism, agnosticism and atheism.[28] While gifted and effective apologists in Christian missions remained active—for example, Henry Martyn, Karl Pfander and Samuel Zwemer with Islam; Bartolomaeus Ziegenbalg, William Hodge Mill and John Muir with Hinduism; James Legge, William A. P. Martin and Karl Reichelt with Confucian, Taoist and Buddhist thought—apologetics has had a diminishing role in Christian missions in the modern era. Chief among the many reasons for this must be the growing dissatisfaction among Christian theologians with apologetics, both for theological and for philosophical reasons; the political and cultural realities of a postcolonial world that make interreligious apologetics especially controversial; and profound theological shifts within the missiological community itself, resulting in greater emphasis upon interreligious dialogue rather than evangelism.

Religious Polemics Against Christianity

It is often assumed that the attempt to defend the truth of one's own religious commitments, and to persuade others to accept them as well, is a uniquely Western (if not Christian) phenomenon that is largely unknown in other religious traditions. Whereas other religions are content to live and let live, it is the Christians who insist upon intellectual confrontation and conquest. Buddhism and Hinduism, in particular, are frequently thought of as highly inclusive and tolerant religions that do not

---

[25]See Willard J. Peterson, "Why Did They Become Christians? Yang T'ing-yün, Li Chih-tsao, and Hsü Kuang-ch'i," in *East Meets West*, pp. 129-52.

[26]Ross, *Vision Betrayed*, p. 149.

[27]On the Rites Controversy, see Ross, *Vision Betrayed*, chapters 8-9; and Covell, *Confucius, the Buddha, and Christ*, pp. 61-67.

[28]See Dulles, *History of Apologetics*, chapters 4-6.

reject other religious perspectives. By contrast, the tendency to argue that one's own religious perspective is preferable to others is often dismissed as post-Enlightenment Christian rationalism that is not only without parallel in the East but is also ineffective outside the West. But these common assumptions are at best misleading.

Although Buddhism and Hinduism are in many ways more accommodating of other traditions than Christianity or Islam, even in these traditions apologetics has had its place. Not only have there been vigorous, and at times vicious, debates among competing schools *within* Hinduism or Buddhism but also there is a long history of intellectual debate *between* various Asian religions—Hindus disputing with Buddhists or Jains, Taoists against Confucians, Buddhists against Taoists and Confucians, Shintoists against Buddhists and so on.[29] In his excellent study Richard Fox Young observes:

> Hindu apologists did not defend Hinduism as such, but proponents of the great *darsanas,* philosophical views or systems, endeavored to brace their own ideas or doctrines by exposing the fallacies of others. To cite only one instance, Sankara's commentary on the Brahmasutras refuted, in turn, each of the major theories, cosmological, metaphysical, soteriological, etc., to which other Hindu thinkers, Buddhists, Jains, and materialists subscribed. Apologetics was so much a part of classical works on religion and philosophy that a text without at least an adumbration of the standard criticisms of its rivals would surely seem incomplete.[30]

Furthermore, the introduction of Christianity to Asian cultures was characteristically perceived by Muslims, Hindus and Buddhists as a direct threat, not only to their cultural practices but also to their basic beliefs about reality. Proclamation of the Christian message, with its competing truth claims, often precipitated a crisis in religious authority. In many cases Christian missions provoked vigorous intellectual responses by Muslims, Hindus and Buddhists intended to demonstrate the falsity and unreasonableness of Christianity.[31]

The vigorous Jesuit missionary activity in Japan during the sixteenth and seventeenth centuries, for example, stimulated some influential polemical writings against Christianity. Francis Xavier introduced Christianity to Japan in 1549, and

---

[29]On the very different philosophical and religious perspectives throughout East Asia, see Hajime Nakamura, *Ways of Thinking of Eastern Peoples: India, China, Tibet, Japan,* ed. Philip P. Wiener (Honolulu: University of Hawaii Press, 1964). For the diverse movements originating in India, see Ninian Smart, *Doctrine and Argument in Indian Philosophy* (London: Allen & Unwin, 1964).

[30]Richard Fox Young, *Resistant Hinduism: Sanskrit Sources on Anti-Christian Apologetics in Early Nineteenth-Century India* (Vienna: Institut für Indologie der Universität Wien, 1981), p. 13.

[31]See especially Young, *Resistant Hinduism;* and R. F. Young and S. Jebanesan, *The Bible Trembled: The Hindu-Christian Controversies of Nineteenth-Century Ceylon* (Vienna: Institut für Indologie der Universität Wien, 1995). Also helpful are Kenneth W. Jones, ed., *Religious Controversy in British India: Dialogues in South Asian Languages* (Albany: State University of New York Press, 1992); Harold Coward, ed., *Hindu-Christian Dialogue: Perspectives and Encounters* (Maryknoll, N.Y.: Orbis, 1989); and Paul J. Griffiths, ed., *Christianity Through Non-Christian Eyes* (Maryknoll, N.Y.: Orbis, 1990).

the church grew dramatically, so that by the end of the century there were some three hundred thousand baptized believers out of a total population of 20 million.[32] The remarkable "Christian century" in Japan came to a bitter end in 1639, however, when Christianity was formally banned and Japanese Christians were severely persecuted and martyred.

Fabian Fucan (Fukansai Habian) was a Buddhist monk who converted to Christianity and entered the Society of Jesus in 1586 to prepare for the priesthood.[33] However, for reasons unknown, the Jesuits refused to admit him into the priesthood and, disillusioned and resentful, Fabian not only left the Society but abandoned the Christian faith as well. While with the Jesuits, Fabian had written *Myotei Mondo [Myotei Dialogue],* a work in Christian apologetics demonstrating the falsehood of Buddhism, Confucianism and Shinto and arguing for a personal Creator. Now an apostate, Fabian in 1620 used his knowledge of both Buddhism and Christianity to write a diatribe against Christianity, *Ha Daiusu [Deus Destroyed].* In his superb study George Elison notes that Fabian's attack upon Christianity was constructed as a systematic refutation of his earlier work in Christian apologetics. The earlier *Myotei Mondo* had attempted to establish the necessity of an eternal personal Creator, to demythologize Buddhist and Shinto teachings and to demonstrate the moral superiority of Christian values and teachings. The agenda of *Ha Daiusu* was precisely the opposite: to affirm "the logical primacy of immanent, apersonal explanations of the source of order in the universe," to demythologize Christianity and to demonstrate the socially disruptive nature of Christian teachings.[34]

There were at this time numerous debates between Christians and Japanese Buddhists, and we have several writings in addition to those of Fabian intended to demonstrate the falsity of Christianity and the superiority of Japanese religious traditions. Among them are the anonymously written *Kirishitan Monogatari [Stories About the Christians]* (1639), *Ha Kirishitan [Against the Christians]* (1662) by the Buddhist Suzuki Shosan, and *Kengiroku [Deceit Disclosed]* (1636),[35] written by Christovao Ferreira, the Jesuit Mission Superior who apostatized and became an influential critic of Christianity in

---

[32]George Elison, *Deus Destroyed: The Image of Christianity in Early Modern Japan* (Cambridge, Mass.: Harvard University Press, 1973), p. 397.

[33]Little is known of Fabian's early life, including his original Japanese name. But we do know that he had trained to be a Zen monk prior to his conversion to Christianity. See Elison, *Deus Destroyed,* chapter 6; and Neil S. Fujita, *Japan's Encounter with Christianity: The Catholic Mission in Pre-Modern Japan* (Mahwah, N.J.: Paulist, 1991), pp. 203-22.

[34]Elison, *Deus Destroyed,* p. 166.

[35]English translations of *Ha Daiusu, Kirishitan Monogatari, Ha Kirishitan* and *Kengiroku* are included in George Elison's *Deus Destroyed.*

Japan.[36] Much later, in the nineteenth century, when Christian missionaries again were permitted in Japan, Buddhism countered with a vigorous anti-Christian apologetic that attacked the idea of an eternal Creator, the divine inspiration of the Bible and, due to the influence of German intellectuals upon Japanese education, the apparent incompatibility of the biblical account of creation with Darwinian science.[37] In the nineteenth century there were also vigorous polemical exchanges between Hindus and Christians in India and Ceylon, as well as between Christians and Muslims in India, so that vigorous intellectual engagement was something that leading thinkers within Hinduism, Buddhism and Islam saw as vital to the preservation of their own traditions in the face of challenges posed by Christian missions.

Negative Apologetics and Positive Apologetics

Apologetics, then, has been a part of Christian witness among religious others throughout the history of the church. In spite of this, however, Christians remain ambivalent about apologetics, often sensing that changing cultural dynamics at the beginning of the twenty-first century demand fresh ways of engaging in apologetics.[38] Some critics of traditional apologetics argue that, for a variety of reasons, the attempt to somehow demonstrate that Christianity is true and other religions are false, or even that Christianity is somehow rationally preferable to other alternatives, cannot succeed. Whatever their differences in other areas, atheists and pluralists both agree, for very different reasons, that what the apologist wants to do cannot be done. For atheists, there is no true religion, thus any attempt to show that Christianity is uniquely true must fail. Pluralists, on the other hand, hold that all religions are more or less true, so the apologist cannot succeed. Curiously, however, some theologically orthodox Christian theologians and missiologists also vehemently reject any attempt to demonstrate the truth of Christianity over opposing religious and secular worldviews. This might be because they believe either that on epistemological grounds it *cannot* be done or that on theological grounds one *ought not* attempt to do so.

Here it is helpful to make a distinction between negative apologetics and posi-

---

[36]The haunting novel *Silence*, by Shusaku Endo, is based upon the apostasy of Christovao Ferreira in 1633 and the intense persecution of Japanese Christians during this time. See Shusaku Endo, *Silence*, trans. William Johnston (New York: Taplinger, 1980).

[37]See Notto R. Thelle, *Buddhism and Christianity in Japan: From Conflict to Dialogue, 1854-1899* (Honolulu: University of Hawaii Press, 1987), chapter 2.

[38]See, for example, John W. Cooper, "Reformed Apologetics and the Challenge of Post-Modern Relativism," *Calvin Theological Journal* 28 (April 1993): 108-20; David Clark, "Narrative Theology and Apologetics," *Journal of the Evangelical Theological Society* 36, no. 4 (1993): 499-515; and *Christian Apologetics in the Postmodern World*, ed. Timothy R. Phillips and Dennis L. Okholm (Downers Grove, Ill.: InterVarsity Press, 1995).

tive apologetics.[39] The distinction in the names of these kinds of apologetics has nothing to do with the style or demeanor of the apologist but rather with two very different sets of expectations concerning what can be accomplished through apologetics. Negative apologetics is concerned with responding to direct attacks upon the truth or rationality of Christian faith, trying to show that such criticisms are unjustified. The objective here is to show that the believer is justified or is not violating any rationality norms or is within his or her "epistemic rights" in accepting Christian beliefs. The operative notion here is that of epistemic permission. But there is no attempt to go beyond this to demonstrate that the unbeliever ought to accept the Christian claims as well. Positive apologetics, on the other hand, goes beyond merely responding to critiques and is concerned to show, in an appropriate manner, that non-Christians too ought to accept the truth claims of Christianity. Rationality is understood in terms of epistemic obligation, so that the apologist attempts to demonstrate that there is an important sense in which unbelievers are epistemically obligated to accept Christian faith, or that it is unreasonable or irrational for them not to do so.

Negative apologetics has always been an integral part of Christian witness, and few Christian thinkers would hesitate to affirm its importance for the church today. Positive apologetics, however, is more controversial. Some Christians question its value because of the enormous difficulty in meeting the expectations it raises. How can anyone familiar with the epistemological controversies of the past four centuries presume that we can demonstrate in any appropriate manner the superiority of Christian theism to alternative worldviews? Surely this is naiveté in the extreme! Others, out of a desire to uphold the sovereignty and authority of God against the tendency of sinful humanity to assert its own autonomy, hold that attempts to support Christian faith through reasoned argumentation are not only ineffective but also manifest a form of idolatry. These are important issues, but it is impossible for me to pursue them in the depth they deserve here. However, I will argue that responding properly to the challenges of religious pluralism today requires going beyond negative apologetics to engage in appropriate forms of positive apologetics.

Self-Authenticating Experiences

Challenges to Christian faith in the West over the past few centuries have been understood largely in terms of agnosticism or atheism, and thus Christian apolo-

---

[39]The distinction is made by Alvin Plantinga, "Augustinian Christian Philosophy," *Monist* 75 (July 1992): 292-93; Paul J. Griffiths, *An Apology for Apologetics: A Study in the Logic of Interreligious Dialogue* (Maryknoll, N.Y.: Orbis, 1991), p. 14; and Dewey J. Hoitenga Jr., *Faith and Reason from Plato to Plantinga: An Introduction to Reformed Epistemology* (Albany: State University of New York Press, 1991), p. 203.

getics has characteristically focused upon issues such as God's existence, the possibility of miracles, the historicity of the resurrection and so on. Certainly these issues remain formidable obstacles to faith for many today. But it is also important to see that the challenges posed by the culture of modernity go far beyond atheism, for in our pluralistic world the choice is not simply between theism and atheism or between Christian faith and secular humanism. Increasingly, whether in New York, Bangkok, Paris or Rio de Janeiro, the issue may be expressed like this: Given the many alternative worldviews available today, both secular and religious, why should one become (or remain) a Christian? On what basis should one choose among religious perspectives?

Clearly there is an important sense in which we might answer this question from within the Christian worldview. Christians hold that God has revealed himself definitively in the incarnation and the written Scriptures, and if indeed the Bible is the very Word of God, true and fully authoritative, then we must reject anything incompatible with the Scriptures. Thus there is a significant sense in which the Christian is entitled—indeed is obligated—to reject as false any teachings incompatible with Scripture. But this response, legitimate as far as it goes, hardly settles the matter. For although from within the Christian worldview one can evaluate competing perspectives on the basis of principles and values internal to the Christian faith, there is a logically more basic question that must be addressed: On what basis should one accept the Christian perspective as true in the first place?

A popular way of dealing with this issue is simply to appeal to authority of one kind or another, whether the authority of a sacred scripture, religious experts, tradition or one's own experience. The problem, of course, is that each religious tradition assumes that it has privileged access to truth not available to outsiders. Christians appeal to the Bible as the definitive authority for religious matters; Muslims reject the Bible in favor of the Qur'an; Zen Buddhists claim to have direct access to ultimate reality through the experience of *satori,* or enlightenment; Advaita Vedanta Hindus rest upon the authority of the Upanishads and the experience of *samadhi* to validate their claims to truth; and of course, Shirley MacLaine has her own direct channel to religious truth. Merely resorting to divine authority in and of itself settles nothing, for each tradition has its own privileged authority structure. The question remains: Which "authority" is in fact ultimately authoritative?

Some, at this point, appeal to the allegedly self-authenticating nature of certain experiences as the way to validate one's commitments. We find in the major religions variations on this theme. Buddhists would hold that the following statement is known to be true through the self-authenticating experience of enlightenment: "There are no enduring, substantial egos; ultimate reality is *sunyata* (emptiness)." Hindus might appeal to the self-authenticating experience of *samadhi,* or existential union, for the truth of this statement: "I am ultimately identical with Brahman." Similarly Jains will base the truth of the following statement upon the self-authenticating experience of *kevala* (liberating knowledge): "The soul *(jiva)* is an enduring mental substance that is immortal."

It is not unusual to find appeals to self-authentication among Christians as well, with such self-authentication usually linked to the inner witness or testimony of the Holy Spirit to the believer.[40] Thus it is sometimes said that the believer can immediately know, through the witness or testimony of the Holy Spirit alone, certain truths about God. Due to the work of the Spirit, the believer has a much greater certainty about these truths than is otherwise available. Indeed, inherent in the concept of self-authentication is the idea that one *cannot* be mistaken about what one knows through the experience. Therefore, the attraction of self-authenticating experiences is their apparent immunity to criticism or contrary evidence. If you have the relevant experience, you just *know* that it is reliable and that claims flowing from it are true; appeals to evidence or arguments are irrelevant. If one has a self-authenticating experience of the inner witness of the Holy Spirit, then one simply knows—immediately, noninferentially and with complete certainty—that the central claims of the Christian faith are true.

There is much here that is controversial and deserves extended discussion, but I will restrict my focus to the question of the Christian's allegedly self-authenticating experience of the inner witness of the Holy Spirit. I suggest that the strong notion of self-authentication is not the best way to understand biblical teaching on the role of the Holy Spirit in bringing assurance to the believer and that it does not help us resolve the issues raised by religious pluralism.

To be sure, according to Scripture, the Holy Spirit is intimately involved in the process of the unbeliever coming to understand what Scripture says about God, seeing the truth of such claims and accepting them. Scripture teaches that the minds of unbelievers are "blinded," so that "they cannot see the light of the gospel of the glory of Christ" (2 Cor 4:4). Apart from the work of the Holy Spirit, we do not accept the things of God (1 Cor 2:14). So coming to understand and accept truths about God involves, in a profoundly mysterious way, the supernatural, illuminating work of God the Holy Spirit upon one's heart. With the new birth and the indwelling presence of the Holy Spirit (Jn 3:5-8, 16; Rom 8:9; Gal 4:6; Tit 3:4-7), the believer is able to understand, to some extent, spiritual truths. Moreover, in a remarkable text the apostle Paul says, "The Spirit himself testifies with our spirit

---

[40]For a robust defense of the self-authenticating nature of the inner witness of the Holy Spirit for the believer, see William Lane Craig, "Classical Apologetics," in *Five Views on Apologetics*, pp. 29-36. For a contrasting perspective in the same volume, see Paul Feinberg, "A Cumulative Case Apologist's Response" and "Cumulative Case Apologetics," pp. 69-73, 160-66.

that we are God's children," thus granting the believer confidence and assurance about belonging to God (Rom 8:16; see also 1 Jn 3:24). But does it follow from this that the experience of the Holy Spirit's inner witness is self-authenticating? What would this mean?

When one says that an experience is self-authenticating, he or she is making two claims: First, the experience is recognized immediately as reliable and, without argument, conclusions properly grounded in the experience are seen to be true. Second, one is claiming such a high degree of certainty that he or she cannot be mistaken about the nature of the experience or the conclusions that flow from it. Self-authentication is thus the ultimate trump card, for no amount of contrary evidence can defeat it. Keith Yandell defines self-authentication as follows: "Chandra's experience E is self-authenticating regarding proposition P if and only if Chandra has experience E, it is logically impossible that Chandra have E and proposition P be false, and Chandra rests his acceptance of P on his having had E."[41]

There is obvious appeal to the notion of self-authentication. Nevertheless, while I think that Scripture is clear about the role of the Holy Spirit in bringing unbelievers to faith in Christ and also in granting to the believer a sustained confidence in the truth of Scripture and of one's acceptance by God, I do not think that self-authentication is the right way to characterize these experiences.[42]

It is significant that we find appeals to self-authenticating experiences in the various religions, with both the nature of the experiences and the claims based upon them differing widely. Yet in each case the relevant experience is said to produce an immediate and certain knowledge of the reliability of the experience and the truth of propositions that follow from it. Furthermore, in each case the subject is said to have the kind of certainty about the experience guaranteeing immunity from error. But reports of allegedly self-authenticating experiences by Christians, Buddhists, Hindus and Jains reveal strikingly different ontological claims based upon the experiences. Not only are the claims different but they often have mutually incompatible entailments. For example, Christian theism entails the existence of individual souls or persons, but this is flatly incompatible with many forms of Buddhism, which explicitly deny the existence of individual, enduring persons. Assuming that contradictory states of affairs cannot obtain simultaneously, it seems clear that at least some of the claims to self-authenticating experiences are mistaken. Not every claim to self-authentication is to be taken at face value; what

---

[41]Keith Yandell, *Philosophy of Religion: A Contemporary Introduction* (New York: Routledge, 1999), p. 271. For a full discussion of self-authentication, see Keith Yandell, *The Epistemology of Religious Experience* (New York: Cambridge University Press, 1993), pp. 163-82.

[42]See William J. Abraham, "The Epistemological Significance of the Inner Witness of the Holy Spirit," *Faith and Philosophy* 7, no. 4 (1990): 434-50.

seems to be self-authenticating may in fact not be so. However, once we admit that claims to self-authenticating experiences may be mistaken, it is not clear—apart from arguing for the truth of Christian theism on other grounds—why one should accept Christian claims to self-authenticating experiences as opposed to others. But of course, if one *argues* for the reliability of Christian self-authenticating experiences, then one is no longer basing the truth of Christian theism upon the self-authenticating experience of the Holy Spirit but is in fact appealing to reason in support of Christian belief.

More significantly, I see nothing in Scripture demanding such a strong notion of the self-authenticating witness of the Holy Spirit. Paul's statement in Romans 8:15-16 speaks of the assurance the Spirit gives to the believer about his or her acceptance by God. As William Abraham says, "The claim it embodies refers to an experience of the Holy Spirit in which the believer experiences the testimony or witness of the Holy Spirit that he or she is a child of God."[43] What Paul speaks of here is not just the so-called "peak experiences" of the saints, with their extraordinary awareness of the presence and reality of God. The assurance of the Spirit is available to all believers in the proper circumstances. But Scripture nowhere provides an epistemological account of this activity of the Spirit, and it seems that at least three things should be borne in mind in developing epistemological conclusions from Paul's statement.

First, it is compatible with Scripture to maintain that the activity of the Spirit can result in varying degrees of confidence on the part of believers. The text does not promise incorrigibility in our beliefs. The psychology of belief (or unbelief) is complex, with degrees of certitude that one experiences being in part a function of a person's dispositions and inner constitution. Some Christians go through life with remarkably few doubts. Others, equally devout and committed to the Lordship of Jesus Christ, continually struggle with uncertainty about their faith. It would be simplistic to hold that those in the former group resist doubt through the self-authenticating inner witness of the Holy Spirit while those in the latter category fail to appropriate the testimony of the Spirit. Both Scripture and the phenomenology of Christian experience indicate that the assurance of the Holy Spirit comes in varying degrees, stronger in some persons than in others, and can be called into question on occasion by external factors.

Second, the inner testimony of the Holy Spirit is best understood not as a one-time, private experience that occurs in a cognitive or social vacuum. Rather, as Abraham reminds us, it is an experience—or rather, an ongoing series of experiences—that occurs within the matrix of the Christian worldview and communal

---

[43]Abraham, "Epistemological Significance," p. 437.

life, and thus a conjunction of broader factors render the experiences understandable and give them their plausibility. For example, discerning the testimony of the
Spirit is directly related to the cultivation of moral qualities associated with Chris-
tlikeness, or the fruit of the Spirit. Ongoing sin in one's life dulls the sense of confidence available through the Spirit. The teachings of Scripture provide the context
within which to understand the experiences of the Spirit as well as the criteria for
discriminating between genuine and spurious experiences of the Spirit. Furthermore, the assurance of which the Spirit speaks tends to be stronger as one participates actively in the communal life of the church, rather than in isolation.

Finally, it is surely significant that serious doubt about one's faith often occurs
after conversion. Many people do, of course, go through times of extensive questioning prior to conversion, considering carefully the rational grounds for faith.
Others live their whole lives, before and after conversion, with remarkably little
struggle against doubt. For still others, however, serious struggles with their faith
emerge after coming in faith to Christ. The phenomenology of Christian belief,
then, suggests that for many Christians the inner witness of the Holy Spirit is not
self-authenticating but rather is something that works in conjunction with a variety of other factors—including careful consideration of the reasons for Christian
belief—in sustaining faith and producing assurance of salvation.

Belief in God as Properly Basic

Dissatisfaction with positive apologetics is often linked to a powerful movement in
recent epistemology of religion associated primarily with the Christian philosopher
Alvin Plantinga. One of the most respected and influential philosophers today,
Plantinga has significantly altered the terms of the debate over religious epistemology through what is often called "Reformed epistemology." Although Plantinga's
work affects a broad range of significant issues, I will focus upon his notion of belief
in God as properly basic and explore some implications of this for religious pluralism.

Ever since the time of John Locke, David Hume and Immanuel Kant, it has been
widely accepted that one cannot be rational in Christian belief unless he or she is
able to demonstrate that such belief is justified. The burden of proof rested with the
theist, who was judged irrational unless he or she could demonstrate the rationality of Christian belief. This assumption is part of a broader perspective often called
"evidentialism" and results in the evidentialist objection to Christian belief,
expressed by Nicholas Wolterstorff as follows:

> The challenge can be seen as consisting of two contentions. It was insisted, in the first
> place, that it would be wrong for a person to accept Christianity, or any other form of
> theism, unless it was rational for him to do so. And it was insisted, secondly, that it is

not rational for a person to do so unless he holds his religious convictions on the basis of other beliefs of his which give to those convictions adequate evidential support.[44]

The basic idea here is that the strength of one's commitment to a belief should be proportional to the evidence for that belief, and the evidence for Christian theism is insufficient for rational belief.

But beginning with a seminal essay in 1983, "Reason and Belief in God," and culminating in a magisterial trilogy on epistemology, Plantinga has called into question the evidentialist framework.[45] Plantinga observed that the evidentialist challenge to Christian belief has been linked to what he calls "classical foundation-alism." Foundationalist epistemologies in general distinguish between two kinds of beliefs we hold. In one class are those beliefs we accept on the basis of, or derived from, other beliefs we hold. For example, my belief that *The faculty meeting this afternoon will be postponed* is an inference from my beliefs *If the dean is not present, then there will not be a faculty meeting* and *The dean is unable to attend the meeting because he is detained in Toronto due to bad weather.* But there are also beliefs that we accept but that are not derived from, or supported by, other beliefs we hold. Among such noninferential beliefs are simple arithmetical truths $(2 + 2 = 4)$, beliefs about the reality of other minds, the general reliability of memory, awareness of one's own existence and so on. Such beliefs are "basic" or "given" in that they are not derived from other more basic beliefs, and they form the foundation upon which the structure of knowledge rests. That there is such a distinction between basic and nonbasic beliefs is widely acknowledged, but there is considerable disagreement over how we are to construe the relation between these beliefs as well as how we are to identify basic beliefs.

A further distinction is necessary. The above definition of basic beliefs is descriptive in that it tells us that, for a given individual, certain beliefs are not inferred from other beliefs. But surely not just *any* belief someone holds in this manner is to be regarded as acceptable. This leads to the notion of properly basic beliefs, or beliefs that are basic in the above sense and that it is entirely reasonable or rational

[44]Nicholas Wolterstorff, introduction to *Faith and Rationality: Reason and Belief in God*, eds. Alvin Plantinga and Nicholas Wolterstorff (Notre Dame, Ind.: University of Notre Dame Press, 1983), p. 6.

[45]See Alvin Plantinga, "Reason and Belief in God," in *Faith and Rationality*, pp. 16-93; and Alvin Plantinga, "Justification and Theism," *Faith and Philosophy* 4 (October 1987): 403-26. Plantinga's general epistemological framework is found in his *Warrant: The Current Debate* (Oxford: Oxford University Press, 1993); and *Warrant and Proper Function* (Oxford: Oxford University Press, 1993). Application of the preceding discussion to the Christian faith is found in *Warranted Christian Belief* (Oxford: Oxford University Press, 2000). A helpful introduction to Plantinga's Reformed epistemology can be found in Michael Peterson, William Hasker, Bruce Reichenbach and David Basinger, *Reason and Religious Belief: An Introduction to the Philosophy of Religion*, 2nd ed. (Oxford: Oxford University Press, 1998), chapter 7.

to accept as basic. Classical foundationalism accepts this general structure but greatly restricts what can count as properly basic beliefs, holding that only beliefs that are such that it is impossible, or nearly impossible, to be mistaken about them fall into this category.[46] Properly basic beliefs are beliefs that are evident to the senses, or reports of immediate sense experience; beliefs that are self-evident, so that upon understanding them one sees them to be true; or incorrigible beliefs, that is, beliefs about which one cannot be wrong ("I seem to have pain"). According to classical foundationalism, then, all rational beliefs will be either properly basic beliefs, falling into one of the three classes above, or beliefs derived through proper methods of inference from such properly basic beliefs.

Plantinga's critique of classical foundationalism is twofold.[47] First, he claims that the statement of classical foundationalism itself is self-referentially incoherent in that it does not meet the conditions it stipulates for all rational belief. Thus on its own terms classical foundationalism should be rejected as irrational. Second, Plantinga notes that classical foundationalism is far too restrictive in its criteria for properly basic beliefs, for it rules out many beliefs that we normally accept as perfectly reasonable but that are neither properly basic in the stipulated sense nor derived from such properly basic beliefs.

What makes Reformed epistemology especially controversial, however, is not its rejection of classical foundationalism but its insistence that Christians do not need evidence to support their Christian beliefs in order to be reasonable or epistemically justified. Rejecting evidentialism, Plantinga states that belief in God apart from evidence can be entirely proper.

> [T]here is no reason at all to think that Christian belief requires argument or propositional evidence, if it is to be justified. Christians—indeed, well educated, contemporary, and culturally aware Christians—can be justified . . . even if they don't hold their beliefs on the basis of arguments or evidence, even if they aren't aware of any good arguments for their beliefs, and even if, indeed, there aren't any.[48]

The reason Christian beliefs can be rational apart from any appeal to evidence is because for Christians belief in God—or more accurately, certain beliefs that entail God's existence, such as *This vast and intricate universe was created by God*—can be properly basic.[49] As a basic belief, then, belief in God need not be inferred from, or supported by, evidence. But neither is it arbitrary, for according to Plantinga,

---

[46]See Plantinga, "Reason and Belief in God," pp. 55-59; and Plantinga, *Warranted Christian Belief*, pp. 82-85.

[47]Plantinga, "Reason and Belief in God," pp. 59-63; Plantinga, *Warranted Christian Belief*, pp. 94-99.

[48]Plantinga, *Warranted Christian Belief*, p. 93.

[49]Plantinga, "Reason and Belief in God," p. 80.

there are appropriate *grounds* (as distinct from evidence) for the belief. The grounds for belief in God are the conditions or circumstances that give rise to belief in God when the relevant noetic faculties are functioning properly. Just as it is the experience of perceiving a tree that provides the grounds for the belief that I see a tree, so too it is the experience of sensing God's reality as I stare at the heavens above that provides the grounds for the belief *This vast and intricate universe was created by God.* Thus "the belief that God exists, and other beliefs about God, are rightly and reasonably held in a basic way by one who finds that she *experiences* God's presence and activities."[50]

Reformed epistemology has met with a mixed reception from theologians and philosophers. Many embrace it enthusiastically as a wonderfully liberating alternative to the modern burden of having to justify Christian commitments on terms set by David Hume and Bertrand Russell. For those who have struggled within the strictures set by the evidentialist challenge it can be intellectually intoxicating to hear someone with the academic credentials of Alvin Plantinga proclaim that it can be "entirely right, rational, reasonable, and proper to believe in God without any evidence or argument at all."[51]

There is much to praise in Plantinga's Reformed epistemology. In particular, Plantinga and others correctly point out the significant difficulties in classical foundationalism. They rightly remind us that we do accept many beliefs in a basic way and that in many cases this is entirely reasonable. No doubt some people accept belief in God in a similar manner; for them belief in God is not something consciously inferred from other beliefs or evidence. Surely Kelly Clark's grandmother, to use an example he introduces in one of his writings, is fully rational in her Christian beliefs even though she has never heard of the theistic arguments or carefully examined the relevant Christian evidences.[52] And this undoubtedly is the case for many others as well, although I suspect that Reformed epistemologists tend to underestimate the extent to which people actually do consciously consider reasons, with varying degrees of sophistication and cogency, for belief.

In spite of its considerable appeal, however, Reformed epistemology has its critics, with some of the most trenchant critiques coming from other Christian philosophers.[53] Our concern here is not with the adequacy of Reformed epistemology in

---

[50]Peterson et al., *Reason and Religious Belief*, p. 156.

[51]Plantinga, "Reason and Belief in God," p. 17.

[52]Kelly James Clark, *Return to Reason: A Critique of Enlightenment Evidentialism and a Defense of Reason and Belief in God* (Grand Rapids, Mich.: Eerdmans, 1990), p. 157.

[53]See the essays in Linda Zagzebski, ed., *Rational Faith: Catholic Responses to Reformed Epistemology* (Notre Dame, Ind.: University of Notre Dame Press, 1993); Gary Gutting, *Religious Belief and Religious Skepticism* (Notre Dame, Ind.: University of Notre Dame Press, 1982), pp. 79-92; Philip Quinn, "In Search of the Foundations of Theism," *Faith and Philosophy* 2, no. 4

general but with its implications for the issues of religious pluralism we have been addressing. I will argue that, despite its appeal and important insights in some areas, it does not help us in resolving basic issues arising from religious pluralism. Let us assume that Reformed epistemologists are correct in saying that it can be entirely reasonable for belief in God to be a basic belief for a Christian in the appropriate circumstances. Thus it can be rational for someone in the right circumstances to believe in God without appealing to evidence to support that belief.

In saying that it can be rational for a Christian to regard belief in God as properly basic we are once again working with a fairly weak sense of rationality, that of "epistemic permission," or the idea that one is rational in believing *p* so long as he or she violates no relevant epistemic norms in doing so. But as we saw in the case of John Hick, there is an asymmetry between this weak sense of rationality and truth, so that in the appropriate circumstances it can be rational to believe what is in fact false.[54] In this sense it can be rational, in the appropriate circumstances, for people in different religious traditions to accept mutually incompatible beliefs. This has significant implications for debates over religious pluralism, as we shall see.

Critics of Reformed epistemology often argue that the fact of widespread disagreement undermines the appropriateness or significance of the claim that belief in God is properly basic.[55] Some, for example, question the appropriateness of placing belief in God in the class of properly basic beliefs, since this belief seems to be different from other beliefs that we normally accept as properly basic. Whereas no one (apart from the odd philosopher) seriously questions the reality of other minds or the general reliability of memory, and hence the inclusion of these beliefs in the set of properly basic beliefs is noncontroversial, many intelligent and sincere people do question the existence of God. Thus phenomenologically there seems to be a difference between the beliefs.

Moreover, once we move beyond the obvious and noncontroversial cases, there is no agreed-upon procedure or criteria for determining what is acceptable as a properly basic belief. Plantinga admits this but does not regard it as especially problematic.

(1985): 469-86; Stephen J. Wykstra, "Toward a Sensible Evidentialism: On the Notion of 'Needing Evidence,' " in *Philosophy of Religion: Selected Readings*, eds. William L. Rowe and William J. Wainwright, 3rd ed. (Fort Worth: Harcourt Brace, 1998), pp. 481-91; William Hasker, "Proper Function, Reliabilism, and Religious Knowledge: A Critique of Plantinga's Epistemology," in *Christian Perspectives on Religious Knowledge*, ed. C. Stephen Evans and Merold Westphal (Grand Rapids, Mich.: Eerdmans, 1993), pp. 66-86; and Roger Trigg, *Rationality and Religion* (Oxford: Blackwell, 1998), pp. 127-28.

[54]See George Mavrodes, "Jerusalem and Athens Revisited," in *Faith and Rationality*, pp. 193-211; Peterson et al., *Reason and Religious Belief*, pp. 152-53.

[55]See Quinn, "In Search of the Foundations of Theism"; Peterson et al., *Reason and Religious Belief*, pp. 153-56; Gutting, *Religious Belief and Religious Skepticism*, pp. 83-92.

Criteria for proper basicality must be reached from below rather than from above; they should not be presented *ex cathedra* but argued to and tested by a relevant set of examples. But there is no reason to assume, in advance, that everyone will agree on the examples. The Christian will of course suppose that belief in God is entirely proper and rational; if he does not accept this belief on the basis of other propositions, he will conclude that it is basic for him and quite properly so. Followers of Bertrand Russell and Madalyn Murray O'Hair may disagree; but how is that relevant? Must my criteria, or those of the Christian community, conform to their examples? Surely not. The Christian community is responsible to *its* set of examples, not theirs.[56]

Thus a Christian can be fully justified in accepting belief in God as properly basic even if others, with a different set of criteria for proper basicality, disagree.

But this leads to the question of the significance of affirming belief in God as properly basic. In a perceptive critique Philip Quinn notes that this move comes with a price, for "this is a game any number can play. Followers of Muhammed, followers of Buddha, and even followers of the Reverend Moon can join the fun."[57] Rhetoric aside, Quinn's point is an important one. It is difficult to see why belief in God can be accepted as properly basic by Christians but fundamental beliefs of other religions cannot also be properly basic for their adherents. For example, the central insights of Zen Buddhism are said to be perceived directly in the experience of *satori,* or enlightenment. They are not the product of rational argument; indeed, evidence and argument are not only irrelevant but are counterproductive in attaining enlightenment. Moreover, the experience of *satori* grounds the relevant claims. Thus belief in emptiness as the ultimate reality is a basic belief for Zen Buddhists. Is it also properly basic for Buddhists? Nothing in the discussions of Reformed epistemology shows why this could not be the case. Similar examples could be cited from other religious traditions as well, so that while it may be difficult to conclude that the Christian *cannot* rationally accept belief in God as properly basic, it seems that the same considerations that allow this also permit adherents of other religions to make similar claims for some of their central beliefs. But if so, this has the unsatisfying consequence of there being mutually incompatible beliefs within different religions, each of which can be regarded as properly basic by insiders to the relevant traditions.

Now there is a possible response to this problem. In his recent trilogy Plantinga has developed a positive account of epistemology, central to which are the notions of "warrant" and "proper function." Warrant is "that property—or better, *quantity*—enough of which is what makes the difference between knowledge and mere

---

[56]Plantinga, "Reason and Belief in God," p. 77. Emphasis in original.
[57]Quinn, "In Search of the Foundations of Theism," p. 473. See also Paul Helm, *Faith and Understanding* (Grand Rapids, Mich.: Eerdmans, 1997), p. 187; and Wainwright, *Philosophy of Religion*, pp. 167-70.

true belief." Plantinga also says, "A belief has warrant just if it is produced by cognitive processes or faculties that are functioning properly, in a cognitive environment that is propitious for that exercise of cognitive powers, according to a design plan that is successfully aimed at the production of true belief."[58] In other words, a belief is warranted only if it is produced by our epistemic faculties (our noetic structure, epistemic dispositions and inclinations) when they are operating properly, in accordance with their design plan, in appropriate contexts. By "design plan" Plantinga means the way that human beings are supposed to function: "Human beings and their organs are so constructed that there is a way that they *should* work, a way they are *supposed* to work, a way they work when they work right; this is the way they work when there is no malfunction."[59] As a Christian, Plantinga naturally understands the design plan in accordance with God's intentions for humankind in creation. Those who in the appropriate circumstances come to believe in God are thus following the divine design plan, and their epistemic faculties can be said to be functioning properly. Since a true belief is warranted when it is produced by our epistemic faculties functioning properly in the appropriate circumstances, then those who believe in God in this way are not only rational but also are warranted in so believing. So the Reformed epistemologist might respond by saying that the Christian and the Zen Buddhist are not really in similar situations with respect to proper basicality since belief in God can be warranted according to the design plan in a way that belief in emptiness cannot. The Buddhist who forms belief in the ultimacy of emptiness would then *not* be exercising his or her cognitive faculties properly in accordance with the design plan, and thus belief in emptiness would not be warranted.

There is much in Plantinga's discussion of warrant and proper function that is eminently plausible, especially as a Christian model of epistemology. But it is crucial to see that this account presupposes precisely what is at issue in the challenges from pluralism, for Plantinga understands "proper function" in terms of God's purposes in creating humankind.[60] But of course, alternative views of normal and proper functioning of the cognitive faculties abound, as Plantinga himself acknowledges. Not only the Freudian and Marxist but also the Theravada Buddhist and Advaita Vedantin Hindu offer accounts that depict belief in a personal Creator God as both false and the product of malfunctioning cognitive faculties. The purpose of meditation in Zen is precisely to obtain release from the cognitive obstructions (including belief in enduring persons and attachment to dualistic thinking) preventing the realization of *sunyata,* emptiness. The issue, then, between the Chris-

---

[58]Plantinga, *Warranted Christian Belief,* p. xi. Emphasis in original.
[59]Ibid., p. 154. Emphasis in original.
[60]Ibid., especially chapters 5-8.

tian and Buddhist is not merely a disagreement over what beliefs can be properly basic; it also concerns what constitutes proper function of the cognitive faculties. And settling *that* question requires determining the truth value of some of the claims of the Christian or Buddhist traditions. Plantinga himself acknowledges the importance of the truth question:

> Here we see the ontological or metaphysical or ultimately religious roots of the question as to the rationality or warrant or lack thereof for belief in God. What you properly take to be rational, at least in the sense of warranted, depends on what sort of metaphysical and religious stance you adopt. It depends on what kind of beings you think human beings are, what sorts of beliefs you think their noetic faculties will produce when they are functioning properly, and which of their faculties or cognitive mechanisms are aimed at the truth. Your view as to what sort of creature a human being is will determine or at any rate heavily influence your views as to whether theistic belief is warranted or not warranted, rational or irrational for human beings. And so the dispute as to whether theistic belief is rational (or warranted) can't be settled just by attending to epistemological considerations; it is at bottom not merely an epistemological dispute, but an ontological or theological dispute.[61]

I think Plantinga is right here. Unfortunately, he is not optimistic about prospects for settling disputes over the truth question. Speaking of his "Aquinas/Calvin models" for Christian epistemology, Plantinga says, "To show that these models are true, therefore, would also be to show that theism and Christianity are true; and I don't know how to do something one could sensibly call 'showing' that either of these is true."[62]

Pluralism also raises a somewhat different issue. Let us assume that belief in God can be properly basic for Christians in the appropriate circumstances. Proper basicality is person- and circumstance-relative. "[C]ertain beliefs are properly basic in certain circumstances; those same beliefs may *not* be properly basic in other circumstances."[63] Does exposure to widespread religious diversity alter the relevant circumstances, so that the Christian who is aware of religious others is under epistemic obligations not necessarily operative where such awareness is absent? Perhaps it can be perfectly acceptable for belief in God to be properly basic for a Christian who has been reared in a Christian home, who has lived in a community where most people share basic values and commitments, and who has no particular interest in theological or philosophical questions. But what about the university student who lives in Chicago, with its remarkable religious diversity, and who is confronted on a regular basis with religious beliefs and practices incompatible with

---

[61]Ibid., p. 190.
[62]Ibid., p. 170. Elsewhere he states, "I don't know of an argument for Christian belief that seems very likely to convince one who doesn't already accept its conclusion" (ibid., p. 201).
[63]Plantinga, "Reason and Belief in God," p. 74. Emphasis in the original.

Christianity? Can belief in God be properly basic for the Christian in these circumstances, or is the student under some obligation to justify his or her Christian beliefs by appeal to evidence or argument?

Interestingly, Plantinga does address this issue, and while he admits that awareness of religious diversity *can* serve as an initial defeater for some Christians, reducing confidence in their beliefs, it need not do so.[64] While for some Christians confronted by pluralism it will be important to consider arguments for and against Christian faith, Christians are not *required* by the fact of religious diversity alone to reassess or justify their beliefs. Others disagree and claim that awareness of intelligent and sincere adherents of other religions does place the believer under certain epistemic obligations. As Gary Gutting puts it, "Isn't it just common sense to admit that, when there is widespread disagreement about a claim, with apparently competent judges on both sides, those who assert or deny the claim need to justify their position?"[65]

Two questions need to be distinguished here. One is the empirical question of whether, when faced with intelligent, sincere and morally good people who embrace different religious commitments, Christians do in fact experience "cognitive dissonance," a reduction in confidence in their own beliefs, and sense the need to justify their beliefs. The second question is whether they *ought* to justify their own beliefs in an appropriate manner in order to be rational in continuing to hold them. Now it certainly seems that many people, including Christians, sense that religious diversity *does* challenge some of their beliefs, especially those that are more controversial and conflict with beliefs held by others. Others, of course, do not seem particularly bothered by such factors. Critics such as Quinn and Gutting, however, point out that Reformed epistemologists tend to minimize the degree to which individuals, including Christians, undergoing normal educational and socialization processes in the West, struggle with basic Christian beliefs, intuitively sensing the need of justification.[66] I think they are right. While it may be possible for belief in God to be properly basic for a given individual in the appropriate situation (it is difficult to see why this could *not* be the case), I suspect that for most people today belief in God is held and sustained by a variety of factors, including

---

[64]A defeater is a proposition that we know or believe to be true and that makes Christian theism irrational or unjustified. See Alvin Plantinga, "Pluralism: A Defense of Religious Exclusivism," in *The Rationality of Belief and the Plurality of Faith: Essays in Honor of William P. Alston*, ed. Thomas D. Senor (Ithaca, N.Y.: Cornell University Press, 1995), especially pp. 201-15; Plantinga, *Warranted Christian Belief*, pp. 357-73, 437-57.

[65]Cited in Peterson et al., *Reason and Religious Belief*, p. 153.

[66]See Quinn, "In Search of the Foundations of Theism," p. 481; Philip L. Quinn, "The Foundations of Theism Again: A Rejoinder to Plantinga," in *Rational Faith*, pp. 35-45; and Gutting, *Religious Belief and Religious Skepticism*, pp. 83-84.

appeal at some level to reasons, however unformed, for such belief.[67] For them, central Christian beliefs are what Stephen Wykstra calls "evidence essential" and stand in need of appropriate evidential support.[68]

Thus, while in principle it is possible for belief in God to be properly basic in the appropriate circumstances, the believer, when confronted with rival religious claims, is placed in a situation in which some justification for his or her beliefs is needed. David Basinger, for example, claims that "the undeniable existence of pervasive religious pluralism places knowledgeable theists under a prima facie obligation to do more than engage in negative apologetics. It requires such theists to *attempt* to produce positive evidence for their religious beliefs."[69] Although it is difficult to specify precisely the conditions under which a challenge to one's beliefs demands such justification, it certainly seems that sustained exposure to intelligent and sincere practitioners of religious traditions incompatible with one's own presents such a challenge.

Two qualifiers should be noted. First, the degree of sophistication of the response will vary according to the individual and the challenge. Someone with minimal education and interests in religious studies can hardly be expected to produce a rigorous refutation of Buddhist metaphysics in order to remain rational in believing in God. Nor can one be expected to investigate and respond to every rival claim on the table; resources (intellectual and otherwise) are limited, and there is much more to life than merely defending one's beliefs. Second, the epistemic challenge should be understood as applying to the community of faith, not necessarily to every individual believer equally. Challenges to faith come to the Christian community as a whole, and while it is unreasonable to expect every Christian to take up the issues and respond appropriately, *someone* within the community should do so. As Paul Griffiths observes, "A community may have epistemic duties that need not be fulfilled by every individual member of it."[70] The burden of responding to the challenges of religious pluralism, then, falls primarily upon the leaders of the Christian community, the intellectuals and the theologians.

---

[67]Part of the dispute between Reformed epistemologists and their critics might be due to the distinction between evidence and grounds, and to the fairly restrictive notion of evidence as inferential evidence, which is operative in the debate. It is not clear that evidence should be construed in such a narrow manner, nor is it clear that the distinction between grounds and evidence can be sustained. See Helm, *Faith and Understanding*, pp. 188-89; and Wykstra, "Toward a Sensible Evidentialism," pp. 483-84.

[68]Wykstra, "Toward a Sensible Evidentialism," p. 482.

[69]David Basinger, "Plantinga, Pluralism and Justified Religious Belief," *Faith and Philosophy* 8, no. 1 (1991): 69. See also David Basinger, "Religious Diversity: Where Exclusivists Often Go Wrong," *International Journal for Philosophy of Religion* 47 (February 2000): 43-55.

[70]Griffiths, *Apology for Apologetics*, p. 70. See also Wykstra, "Toward a Sensible Evidentialism," pp. 485-88.

Much of what we believe, and are justified in believing, we accept on the basis of authority or testimony. Thus for many ordinary Christians who become aware of religious diversity and the ensuing challenges it can be sufficient merely to know that leading Christian thinkers have carefully considered the relevant issues and responded appropriately to them. They can be justified in their beliefs by relying upon the authority of others who are more knowledgeable and have studied the issues. Others, however, will find that they need to work through the issues for themselves. Either way, it is crucial that responsible thinkers within the community respond to the challenges, and doing so will involve not only negative but also positive apologetics.

Religious Experience and Negative Apologetics

We saw in chapter five that John Hick's *Faith and Knowledge* was an influential attempt to defend the rationality of religious belief by grounding it in religious experience.[71] Hick regarded the world as religiously ambiguous and thus he adopted the rather modest constraints of epistemic permission, arguing that the believer who has religious experiences can be rational in believing in God on the basis of such experiences. But religious belief is not obligatory for those lacking the requisite experiences.

This move has been adopted by recent defenders of religious belief, with its most rigorous and sophisticated expression to be found in William P. Alston's *Perceiving God.*[72] Alston's achievement is impressive by any standards, and he persuasively argues that the believer can be entirely justified in his or her religious beliefs based upon experiences of God. But the limitations of this move with respect to religious pluralism are also apparent. As with John Hick, the same arguments that support the rationality of Christians believing as they do on the basis of their experiences of God are also in principle applicable in other religious contexts as well, thereby supporting the rationality of Muslims or Hindus believing as they do.

Alston's central thesis is "that experiential awareness of God, or as I shall be saying, the *perception* of God, makes an important contribution to the grounds of religious belief. More specifically, a person can become justified in holding certain

---

[71]John Hick, *Faith and Knowledge*, 2nd ed. (Ithaca, N.Y.: Cornell University Press, 1966).

[72]William P. Alston, *Perceiving God: The Epistemology of Religious Experience* (Ithaca, N.Y.: Cornell University Press, 1991). Alston credits Hick's *Faith and Knowledge* as having had a significant impact upon his own approach to religious epistemology. "From the first edition, [*Faith and Knowledge*] made a profound impression upon me, primarily for its insistence on the point that theistic faith, when live and fully formed, rests on the experience of the presence and activity of God in our lives" (William P. Alston, "John Hick: Faith and Knowledge," in *God, Truth and Reality: Essays in Honour of John Hick*, ed. Arvind Sharma [New York: St. Martin's, 1993], p. 25). Nevertheless, Alston's discussion of religious experience differs from Hick's at several key points. See Alston, *Perceiving God*, pp. 27-28, 264-66.

kinds of belief about God by virtue of perceiving God as being so-and-so." In another place Alston says, "The chief aim of this book is to defend the view that putative direct awareness of God can provide justification for certain kinds of belief about God."[73]

We cannot rehearse Alston's meticulous and rigorous argument for this thesis, except to say that he proceeds by developing an argument for the acceptability of religious experience (perception of God) based upon relevant analogies with sense perception, which is generally accepted as a reliable means of belief formation about the world around us. In both sense perception and perception of God beliefs are formed by engaging in certain "doxastic practices," or socially established practices resulting in formation of appropriate beliefs. In neither case is it possible to justify the reliability of the doxastic practices in a strictly noncircular manner. Yet in both cases we have established procedures for distinguishing appropriate from inappropriate beliefs. Thus beliefs formed through the relevant doxastic practices can be granted prima facie justification, and if there are no sufficient "overriders" (factors that would rebut or undermine the beliefs), then they can be considered "unqualifiedly justified" as well.

> CMP [Christian mystical perceptual practice] is a functioning, socially established, perceptual doxastic practice with distinctive experiential inputs, distinctive input-output functions, a distinctive conceptual scheme, and a rich, internally justified overrider system. As such, it possesses a prima facie title to being rationally engaged in, and its outputs are thereby prima facie justified, *provided we have no sufficient reason to regard it as unreliable or otherwise disqualified for rational acceptance.*[74]

It seems to me that Alston's argument here is correct and that there is a prima facie justification for religious beliefs formed in accordance with established doxastic practices. This is not to say that such beliefs are necessarily true; beliefs can be justified in the appropriate circumstances and still be false. Nor is it to say that they are immune from challenge or refutation. The prima facie justification can be overridden by arguments calling into question the beliefs themselves.

My concern here, however, is not with the merits of Alston's argument itself so much as with the relationship between his argument and religious pluralism. The challenge from religious pluralism here is twofold: First, while Alston's argument, as an exercise in epistemic permission, supports the rationality of Christian beliefs about God, based upon Christian experiences of God, it also supports the rationality of beliefs held by practitioners of other religions, based upon *their* respective religious experiences. So, in and of itself, it offers little help in answering the question

---

[73]Alston, *Perceiving God*, pp. 1, 9. Emphasis in the original.
[74]Ibid., p. 225. Emphasis in the original.

"Why should someone be a Christian instead of a Hindu or Buddhist?" Second, Alston is well aware that the fact of religious diversity undermines his thesis about the general reliability of religious doxastic practices for religious belief formation. Here the differences between sense perception and religious perception are important. While the doxastic practices for sense perception produce similar beliefs about the external world among diverse peoples, the doxastic practices of different religious communities result in different and sometimes mutually incompatible beliefs. Thus the fact of religious diversity—the presence of multiple doxastic practices in various religions producing incompatible truth claims—calls into question the reliability of any single doxastic practice, including that of the Christian community. That is, *"even if some form of MP [mystical practice] is reliable,* we have no non-question-begging grounds for determining which one that is; and hence it cannot be rational for a person to suppose any particular form to be reliable." However, Alston does not feel that this objection is decisive. He concludes that even with this challenge it can be rational for the Christian to "sit tight with the practice of which I am a master and which serves me so well in guiding my activity in the world" and to continue to hold Christian beliefs on the basis of experiences of God.[75]

At this point, however, Hick criticizes Alston on the grounds that, if a Christian is justified in this manner in believing that Christianity is uniquely true, then it follows that the Christian should conclude that the beliefs of other religions, based upon their respective experiences, are false. But if this is so, then it also follows that most of the religious beliefs based upon religious experience are in fact false. And thus for one particular religious community to assume that *its* doxastic practices are reliable and that *its* beliefs are justified, when those of the other religious communities are not, is arbitrary unless this assumption can be justified on independent grounds.[76]

It is significant that Alston also recognizes that his argument for the place of religious experience in grounding religious belief is only one part of a much broader defense of Christian theism. Indeed the last chapter of his book calls for exploring natural theology, along with religious experience, in developing a comprehensive case for Christian theism.[77] William Wainwright also calls for supplementing Alston's argument with independent arguments for the truth of relevant metaphysical claims.

---

[75]Ibid., pp. 268-69, 274. Emphasis in original.
[76]See John Hick, "The Epistemological Challenge of Religious Pluralism," *Faith and Philosophy* 14, no. 3 (1997): 278.
[77]See Alston, *Perceiving God,* chapter 8; and William P. Alston, "Response to Hick," in *Faith and Philosophy*, pp. 287-88.

Whether one is committed to a mystical practice or not, metaphysical and empirical argumentation of a familiar sort (arguments for God's or Nibbana's existence, Christian or Buddhist "evidences," etc.) is probably needed to show that commitment to an MP [mystical practice] is fully rational. Alston's defense of CMP is impressive and, on the whole, convincing. To be fully successful, however, I believe it must form part of a persuasive cumulative case argument for the Christian world-view.[78]

In other words, while negative apologetics and arguments defending the rationality of Christian belief in terms of epistemic permission are significant as far as they go, they are of limited value in dealing with the distinctive challenges of religious pluralism. To answer the question why one should be a Christian instead of a follower of another religious tradition one must go beyond negative apologetics to engage in positive apologetics.

Cumulative Case Arguments and Interreligious Apologetics

On the theoretical level, positive apologetics is a difficult and complex endeavor, as it seeks to show, in appropriate ways, that Christian theism is true or is rationally preferable to alternative worldviews. Dissatisfaction with positive apologetics is often due to the manner in which it is sometimes carried out and the unrealistic expectations raised by some apologists. Overly optimistic apologists sometimes promise such conclusive arguments for the Christian faith that any reasonable person should immediately recognize the truth of Christianity—five easy steps to proving the existence of God, the deity of Christ and the inspiration of Scripture. John Hick's discussion of the religious ambiguity of the universe can be a helpful corrective to such naive optimism.

But Hick's assumption about epistemic parity across worldviews should not be accepted uncritically. Hick gives the impression that the ambiguity is such that the major worldviews—religious and nonreligious—can be regarded as more or less equally rational. But is this really so? Is the case for theism really no stronger than the case for atheism? Is the rational or evidential support for Christian theism really no greater than that for Islam or Theravada Buddhism? This is an enormous assumption that many would reject.

Throughout history, of course, many have concluded that the universe is not so ambiguous and that a compelling case can be made for Christian theism. One thinks here of the long tradition of natural theology and the classical theistic arguments. The attraction of the theistic arguments is that, if successful, they settle the question of theism once and for all; atheism and nontheistic religious worldviews would then be falsified and theism would be firmly established. But the theistic

---

[78]William J. Wainwright, "Religious Language, Religious Experience, and Religious Pluralism," in *Rationality of Belief and the Plurality of Faith*, p. 188.

arguments have fallen into intellectual disrepute in recent times and they are often dismissed today as unsound and irrelevant. To be sure, no single argument is broadly accepted today, as each argument has at least one questionable premise.[79] The standards a successful deductive argument must meet are almost impossibly high, so it is hardly surprising that virtually no significant intellectual issue is resolved satisfactorily through a deductive proof. Yet we should also remember that many of the brightest minds throughout the centuries have been convinced that one or more of the arguments is sound, and even today formulations of theistic arguments have their able defenders.[80]

But positive apologetics need not be limited to deductive theistic arguments. Much more promising is what is often called a cumulative case approach to establishing the truth of Christian theism. Many distinguished apologists—such as Joseph Butler, John Henry Newman, F. R. Tennant, Elton Trueblood, G. K. Chesterton and C. S. Lewis—have adopted this approach, and in recent years this kind of justification of Christian faith has been given careful philosophical attention by Christian philosophers such as Basil Mitchell, Richard Swinburne and William Abraham.[81] The work of Richard Swinburne, in particular, provides an impressive sustained argument for the claim that Christian theism is more likely to be true than atheism.

The cumulative case approach is based upon the idea that a reasonable case for the truth of Christian theism can be established through the careful accumulation and analysis of a wide variety of data from various dimensions of our experience and the world. Several things distinguish this approach. First, rather than trying to establish just one belief in isolation—for example, God's existence or the historicity of the resurrection of Jesus—a cumulative case approach deals with "a whole cluster of beliefs which hang together and which need to be evaluated not just in isolation but as a whole."[82] Thus factors relevant in considering the historicity of the resurrection of Jesus, for example, also have broader implications for the question

---

[79]For a good discussion of the theistic arguments and their place in defending theism, see Stephen T. Davis, *God, Reason and Theistic Proofs* (Grand Rapids, Mich.: Eerdmans, 1997).

[80]One of the more widely discussed recent arguments is the so-called Kalam cosmological argument, as formulated by William Lane Craig. See William Lane Craig, *The Kalam Cosmological Argument* (London: Macmillan, 1979); and Davis, *God, Reason and Theistic Proofs*, pp. 150-55.

[81]See Basil Mitchell, *The Justification of Religious Belief* (Oxford: Oxford University Press, 1981); Richard Swinburne, *The Existence of God*, 2nd ed. (Oxford: Oxford University Press, 1991); William J. Abraham, "Cumulative Case Arguments for Christian Theism," in *The Rationality of Religious Belief: Essays in Honour of Basil Mitchell*, eds. William J. Abraham and Steven W. Holtzer (Oxford: Clarendon, 1987), pp. 17-37; Caroline Franks Davis, *The Evidential Force of Religious Experience* (Oxford: Clarendon, 1989), especially chapter 9; and Paul D. Feinberg, "Cumulative Case Apologetics," in *Five Views on Apologetics*, pp. 148-72.

[82]Abraham, "Cumulative Case Arguments," p. 23.

of God's existence, just as data relevant to the issue of God's existence have implications for how we look at evidence for the resurrection. Furthermore, this approach does not look at just one argument or at evidence from one domain but rather considers a wide constellation of evidential factors, all of which demand some explanation, and argues that Christian theism provides the most reasonable explanation for all of the data. Thus a cumulative case argument might appeal to certain aspects of the physical universe itself (its contingency or indications of design inherent in the physical order), to the marvelous capacities of human beings (the mind, the ability to understand and communicate meanings, creativity, self-consciousness and intentionality), to our deeply rooted awareness of moral obligation and the distinction between good and evil, to factors from history (the remarkable nature of the writings comprising the Old and New Testaments, the history of the Jewish people, the reports of the resurrection of Jesus, the sudden emergence and growth of the Christian church) and so on.

Cumulative case arguments contend that these (and many other) phenomena are all part of the world we know and experience and that they need some explanation, both for there being a world in the first place (why is there something instead of nothing?) and also for *this* world existing, with all of its marvelous features. The point is not that these data, individually or collectively, entail the truth of Christian theism; it is always logically possible that Christian theism is false, and alternative explanations for the data are available. But cumulative case arguments maintain that Christian theism provides a coherent and reasonable explanation for the data—indeed a more satisfying and plausible explanation than other alternatives.

Obviously there is an inescapable element of personal judgment in such arguments, as one considers the totality of the evidence and tries to come to the most reasonable explanation. To be sure, the criteria for a good explanation are far from precise, and part of the discussion inevitably concerns just what constitutes the most reasonable explanation. But this is how it is with most significant issues in nonreligious domains as well. This does not mean that such judgments are purely subjective or arbitrary or that there are no legitimate criteria for making such assessments, for as William Abraham notes, "Personal judgment simply means the ability to weigh evidence without using some sort of formal calculus."[83] In this sense, as Mitchell reminds us, we use personal judgment all of the time, not only in routine, everyday decisions but also in more specialized domains such as law, history, the sciences, literary theory and so on.[84]

In contexts of religious pluralism, then, positive apologetics should seek to show not merely that Christians can be rational in believing as they do but also that

---

[83]Ibid., p. 34.
[84]See Mitchell, *Justification of Religious Belief.*

Christian theism is preferable to other alternatives. We might do this by arguing for the truth or plausibility of certain core Christian beliefs or by arguing that there are compelling reasons for concluding that certain central beliefs of other religions are false. For example, in the context of Christianity and Buddhism the following two propositions will be central: (1) An eternal Creator God, who is morally good and omnipotent, exists. (2) There are no enduring, substantial persons or egos. Christians will affirm (1), but Buddhists will argue against it; Buddhists will defend (2), while Christians will argue against it.[85]

But the idea of positive apologetics among devout and sincere adherents of other religions strikes many today, especially those heavily involved in interreligious dialogue, as particularly distasteful. Many would insist that interreligious encounter should be characterized by the search for mutual understanding and an attempt to establish common ground, not polemics. In response Paul Griffiths provides a trenchant critique of "an underlying scholarly orthodoxy on the goals and functions of interreligious dialogue" that maintain that "understanding is the only legitimate goal; that judgment and criticism of religious beliefs and practices other than those of one's own community is always inappropriate; and that an active defense of the truth of those beliefs and practices to which one's community appears committed is always to be shunned."[86] Griffiths rightly argues that, to the contrary, in certain situations religious communities have an obligation to engage in interreligious apologetics.

> If representative intellectuals belonging to some specific religious community come to judge at a particular time that some or all of their own doctrine-expressing sentences are incompatible with some alien religious claim(s), then they should feel obliged to engage in both positive and negative apologetics vis-à-vis these alien religious claim(s) and their promulgators.[87]

Interestingly, Griffiths construes this obligation in both epistemic and ethical terms.[88] Religious communities characteristically hold that their central religious beliefs are true, and thus when a community is confronted by other beliefs challenging its own, it has an epistemic duty to consider whether the challenge makes it improper for the community to continue believing as it does. But there is an ethical imperative for apologetics as well. Most religious traditions maintain not only that their religious perspective is true but also that there is significant salvific value

---

[85]For a fascinating example of how Christian and Buddhist apologists might interact over the question of the existence of the person or soul, see Griffiths, *Apology for Apologetics*, chapter 6. An interesting Buddhist critique of Christian theism is found in Gunapala Dharmasiri, *A Buddhist Critique of the Christian Concept of God*, 2nd ed. (Antioch, Calif.: Golden Leaves, 1988).
[86]Griffiths, *Apology for Apologetics*, p. xi.
[87]Ibid., p. 3.
[88]Ibid., pp. 15-16.

in accepting their beliefs as true. Obviously this is developed in different ways within various traditions, but certainly many religions share the position that certain beliefs are to be accepted as true, and be appropriately acted upon, if one is to attain salvation or liberation or enlightenment. Thus, if a religious community is convinced that humankind suffers from some general malady, that its central beliefs are indeed true and that accepting and acting appropriately upon these beliefs can bring about the benefits of salvation, then the community has an ethical obligation to share this good news with those outside the tradition, trying to persuade them of the truth of the community's beliefs.

We must emphasize that apologetics within interreligious contexts is a difficult and sensitive matter that must be conducted with wisdom, tact and genuine respect for religious others. Interreligious encounters always occur in contexts shaped by history and culture, and the legacies of the past combine with present realities, sometimes helping and at other times hindering mutual understanding. Christians engaging in interreligious apologetics must be especially alert to several factors.

First, we must be careful to treat other religious traditions and worldviews with genuine respect and avoid simplistic caricatures that do not reflect other perspectives accurately. This will demand careful and responsible study of other traditions, mastering the languages necessary for study of their authoritative texts as well as undertaking careful ethnographic studies of relevant religious communities. Responsible interreligious apologetics will be fair in its treatment of other perspectives, willingly acknowledging what is true and good in them even as it seeks to point out what is problematic or false. The overriding concern is not to score easy points but to understand others, to be alert to strengths and weaknesses in their perspectives, encouraging them to consider what the Scriptures say about Jesus Christ.

Not only must Christians understand the theological distinctives of the other tradition but also they must be sensitive to the many cultural dynamics connected with the religion. Effective use of morally acceptable and culturally appropriate means of persuasion requires a mature understanding of the cultural context in which the interreligious encounter takes place. Christians must be especially sensitive to the use of symbolic power in the interreligious apologetic encounter. The search for truth, or the attempt to persuade others that one has found the truth, can easily deteriorate into a power game, with each party concerned to show its superiority over the other. As many apologists have discovered, one can win the debate but lose the person. Any activity that is manipulative or coercive, or otherwise infringes upon the dignity of the other, must be rejected. Certain historical, social and political contexts make interreligious apologetics especially difficult, if indeed it should be attempted in these contexts at all.[89] Situations in which Christianity is closely linked to political or military power, or where it is identified with cultural superiority, racism or economic exploitation, naturally make interreligious apologetics very sensitive.[90] Christians should be especially careful about apologetics encounters with religious communities, such as Jewish and Muslim communities, that have suffered greatly in the past at the hands of Christendom. Especially in these contexts Christian apologists must learn first to listen humbly in silence, cultivating relationships of trust before proceeding into encounters over truth.

Finally, we should reiterate the importance of treating religious others with respect and dignity. The haunting question of Mongke Khan to William of Rubruck—"God gives you the Scriptures, and you Christians keep them not. You do not find in them that one should find fault with another, do you?"—reminds us that there is no room in a genuinely Christian apologetic for ridicule of other religious figures, beliefs or practices. It is a reproach to the cause of Christ that Christians sometimes have been overly aggressive in evangelism and apologetics, subjecting other religions to caricature and ridicule. This is not only ineffective but, more importantly, fundamentally unchristian. One can engage in vigorous apologetics while simultaneously demonstrating genuine respect for opposing views and acceptance of religious others as fellow human beings created in God's image and the object of God's limitless love.

---

[89]Ibid., pp. 78-80.

[90]On the significance of these dynamics for interreligious apologetics in India, see Young, *Resistant Hinduism*.

9

EVALUATING ALTERNATIVE WORLDVIEWS

The Question of Criteria

"Father, we are not disputing about the right and wrong of your doctrine. In Spain and Portugal and such countries it may be true. The reason we have outlawed Christianity in Japan is that, after deep and earnest consideration, we find its teaching of no value for the Japan of today." . . .

"According to our way of thinking, truth is universal," said the priest, at last returning the smile of the old man. . . . "If we did not believe that truth is universal, why should so many missionaries endure these hardships? It is precisely because truth is common to all countries and all times that we call it truth. If a true doctrine were not true alike in Portugal and Japan we could not call it 'true.' " . . .

"All the fathers keep saying the same thing. And yet . . ." The interpreter slowly translated the words of yet another samurai. "A tree which flourishes in one kind of soil may wither if the soil is changed. As for the tree of Christianity, in a foreign country its leaves may grow thick and the buds may be rich, while in Japan the leaves wither and no bud appears. Father, have you never thought of the difference in the soil, the difference in the water?"

SHUSAKU ENDO, *Silence*

P ositive apologetics in interreligious contexts presupposes that nonarbitrary, rational assessment of alternative worldviews across cultural and religious boundaries is possible. But this assumption will be greeted with incredulity by many impressed with the culturally embedded nature of all thought and the deep differences among worldviews. According to these thinkers, trying to demonstrate that Christian theism is rationally preferable to, say, the Theravada Buddhist worldview is futile because of the constraining social and cultural influences upon all thought. Any judgments about the truth or falsity of alternative worldviews are necessarily biased in favor of the worldview within which they originate. Thus there is no nonarbitrary means for resolving basic cognitive disputes across religious worldviews.

Is it possible to resolve in a rational manner basic religious disagreements among diverse religious communities? Or are we all so shaped by our cultural and religious contexts that any judgment we make is of necessity merely the product of those influences? In other words, is there any nonarbitrary way in which alternative religious worldviews can be evaluated in terms of their truth or falsity? These are difficult and controversial questions, and we should not expect easy answers. But neither should we be unduly intimidated by the issues. While our expectations concerning what rational assessment across cultural and religious boundaries can accomplish must be appropriately modest, we should remember that people from many different cultures regularly do make these kinds of judgments. In this chapter we will look briefly at some issues involved in assessing perspectives across cultural and religious boundaries, and then we will consider how two criteria in particular might function in such assessment.

Understanding Across Cultural and Religious Boundaries

Resistance to the idea that we can evaluate truth claims from other religious traditions stems in part from the close relationship between religion and culture and the seemingly innocent observation that any evaluation we make is inescapably culturally conditioned. Many infer from this that there can be no "neutral" or "culture-independent" vantage point from which to settle disputes among alternative perspectives.[1] This assumption leads us into a deeper set of issues that go beyond simply religion and culture, that is, the epistemological difficulties involved in "crossing boundaries," or in moving from "the familiar" to "the unfamiliar." These

---

[1]In *Dissonant Voices: Religious Pluralism and the Question of Truth* (Grand Rapids, Mich.: Eerdmans, 1991), pp. 161-95, I concluded a discussion of relativism by suggesting some criteria that can be applied in the evaluation of alternative religious perspectives. Several writers (otherwise not unfavorable to the critique of relativism) strongly objected to my proposed criteria, claiming that this kind of assessment of alternative worldviews either cannot or should not be done. See Gavin D'Costa, "Whose Objectivity? Which Neutrality? The Doomed Quest for a Neutral Vantage Point from Which to Judge Religions," *Religious Studies* 29 (March 1993): 79-95; Vinoth Ramachandra, *The Recovery of Mission: Beyond the Pluralist Paradigm* (Grand Rapids, Mich.: Eerdmans, 1996), p. 169; T. S. Perry, "Are Harold Netland's Principles Universal and Neutral?" *Calvin Theological Journal* 31 (Novermber 1996): 487-94; and Lesslie Newbigin, "Truth and Authority in Modernity," in *Faith and Modernity*, ed. Philip Sampson, Vinay Samuel and Chris Sugden (Oxford: Regnum, 1994), pp. 85-86. Throughout his many writings Newbigin repeatedly rejects any attempt to demonstrate the "reasonableness" or "rationality" of Christianity by appealing to "neutral" or "objective" criteria to settle disputes over truth claims. See, for example, Lesslie Newbigin, *Truth to Tell: The Gospel as Public Truth* (Grand Rapids, Mich.: Eerdmans, 1991), pp. 27-28, 33-34; *The Gospel in a Pluralist Society* (Grand Rapids, Mich.: Eerdmans, 1989), pp. 8, 64; and "Truth and Authority in Modernity," pp. 80-81. While I cannot here address each of the specific points raised by these writers, this chapter is a general response to the kind of concerns found in their critiques. For my response to Perry's article, see Harold Netland, "The Question of Criteria: A Response to Mr. Perry," *Calvin Theological Journal* 31 (November 1996): 495-503.

issues are at the heart of a variety of disciplines, such as history, literary theory and hermeneutics, linguistics and translation theory. The importance of these issues for Christian theologians and missiologists can hardly be exaggerated. For if crossing historical, cultural or linguistic boundaries is impossible, or at least so problematical that nothing of significance can be achieved in so doing, then it follows that we have no access to God's special revelation, which was given in particular historical, cultural and linguistic contexts far removed from our own today.

Although we can understand the notion of "contextual boundaries" in various ways—as linguistic, intellectual, cultural, historical or social boundaries—the underlying issues are similar throughout. Our concern is primarily with cultural and religious boundaries and can be framed in terms of several questions. Since understanding logically precedes evaluation, the first issue concerns the possibility of *understanding* across boundaries. If we cannot understand what it means, for example, to be a Buddhist, then clearly we cannot make responsible judgments about the truth or falsity of Buddhist perspectives. Are we able to cross cultural and religious boundaries sufficiently so as to understand people from another religious tradition?

Those who deny that this is possible (though few go so far as to deny that *any* understanding across cultural or religious boundaries is possible) typically embrace some form of conceptual or cultural relativism. In the earlier twentieth century relativistic influences were entrenched in cultural anthropology, especially through the work of Franz Boas, Ruth Benedict, Melville Herskovits, Benjamin Whorf, Margaret Mead and others.[2] By the 1960s, discussions about rationality and understanding among philosophers, many of whom were influenced by the later writings of Ludwig Wittgenstein, began to draw explicitly upon work in the social sciences in support of relativistic theses. Peter Winch, for example, published a widely discussed article in 1964, "Understanding a Primitive Society," in which he responded to the anthropological ethnography of E. E. Evans-Pritchard among the Azande by questioning whether it makes any sense for us to make judgments about the rationality or irrationality of Azande beliefs about witchcraft.[3] Winch rejected the idea that there is a reality or set of norms independent of the "language games"

[2]See Elvin Hatch, *Culture and Morality: The Relativity of Values in Anthropology* (New York: Columbia University Press, 1983).

[3]Peter Winch, "Understanding a Primitive Society," *American Philosophical Quarterly* 1 (1964): 307-24. A collection of significant essays by philosophers and social scientists, including Winch's essay as well as several responses to Winch, is found in Bryan Wilson, ed., *Rationality* (Oxford: Blackwell, 1970). See also the essays in Martin Hollis and Steven Lukes, eds., *Rationality and Relativism* (Oxford: Blackwell, 1982); Michael Krausz and Jack W. Meiland, eds., *Relativism: Cognitive and Moral* (Notre Dame, Ind.: University of Notre Dame Press, 1982); and Paul K. Moser and Thomas L. Carson, eds., *Moral Relativism: A Reader* (New York: Oxford University Press, 2001).

or "forms of life" of a given community by which judgments of rationality can be made. Understandings of, and criteria for, rationality are strictly internal to worldviews, or language games or forms of life.[4] More recently, the work of thinkers such as Willard Van Orman Quine, Thomas Kuhn, Paul Feyerabend and Richard Rorty have supported relativistic theses by emphasizing the indeterminacy of translation among languages, incommensurability between paradigms or conceptual frameworks and our inability to transcend the limitations of time and place upon our experiences.

Now we should not minimize the difficulty of trying to understand across cultural boundaries. Anyone who has lived for a substantial period of time in a culture different from one's own, and has struggled to learn another language and way of life, will acknowledge that there are formidable obstacles to such understanding. Cultures are enormously complex and the potential for intercultural misunderstanding is great. Obviously we must first learn to listen and observe carefully before presuming to make judgments. Furthermore, difficulties in understanding are multiplied when the "others" are not only culturally different but are also deeply committed to different religious ways of life. The barriers to understanding religious others are very real and should not be dismissed casually.

Nevertheless, in spite of the difficulties, it seems clear that a measure of understanding across cultural, linguistic and religious boundaries is not only possible but occurs regularly. The strict "incommensurability thesis," which holds that terms or concepts used in culture A are so radically different that they cannot be equated with any terms or concepts in culture B, is simply unacceptable. Understanding is a matter of degree, not all or nothing. The difficulties involved should not obscure the fact that we do, on a regular basis, communicate more or less effectively with others in different linguistic, cultural and religious environments. The actual practice of cultural anthropologists (who are as responsible as any for the academic lure of relativism) is instructive. Ernest Gellner perceptively observes:

> It is an interesting fact about the world we actually live in that no anthropologist, to my knowledge, has come back from a field trip with the following report: their concepts are so alien that it is impossible to describe their land tenure, their kinship system, their ritual. . . . As far as I know, there is no record of such a total admission of failure. . . . What one does quite often hear is admission of partial failure of comprehension: "I simply cannot imagine what the so-and-so, a West African tribe, mean when they speak of washing their souls"; "I thought I knew the Himalayan hill folk well, having lived amongst them for a considerable time, but when a death occurred in

---

[4]In an earlier influential work Winch states, "Criteria of logic are not a direct gift of God, but arise out of, and are only intelligible in the context of, ways of living or modes of social life" (Peter Winch, *The Idea of a Social Science* [London: Routledge & Kegan Paul, 1958], p. 100).

the family, I saw from their reactions that I did not understand anything"; etc. Such partial incomprehensions are common, but they have not, to my knowledge, prevented the drawing-up of an account of at least large parts of the social life, language, etc., of the community in question.[5]

Nor should we be surprised by partial, but more or less adequate, understanding across cultures, for underlying the many differences between cultures are fundamental commonalities that all people share as human beings. In crossing cultural and religious boundaries, then, we are not moving among totally disparate, incommensurable frameworks, but rather we recognize and build upon certain commonalities in order to grasp what is unfamiliar. In the words of Stanley Tambiah, a cultural anthropologist from Sri Lanka, "An anthropologist's successful translation and account of another people's beliefs, norms, and actions implies that there is some shared space, some shared notions of intelligibility and reasoning (rationality) between the two parties."[6] Henry Rosemont Jr. makes the important point that the recognition of difficulties in understanding and translation itself indicates that the worlds being compared cannot be incommensurable:

> If someone had a view of the world altogether different from my own—if we shared, that is, no common perspectives—neither of us could ever come to know it. We must presuppose that we share some beliefs, assumptions, attitudes, and intentions—not an unreasonable presupposition, considering that we are both human—before either of us can begin to interpret any of the other's sentences and hence establish points of disagreement. Thus the possibility of a total failure of translation and interpretation—and consequently the possibility of radical conceptual relativism—is not one that should be entertained seriously by a rational person, for no rational arguments (in any language) or empirical (linguistic) evidence could ever be adduced to show that the possibility had been realized.[7]

In spite of clear differences among them, religious worldviews are not incommensurable and it is possible, with sufficient effort, to understand the beliefs, values and practices of other religious traditions. Tambiah provides a helpful illustration of how this takes place:

> To apply the same argument to a more complex example involving two cultures and two languages, it is possible to take the concept of "god" in the Bible and of "deva" in a Hindu text in Sanskrit, treat them as roughly parallel concepts and by recursive glossing and describing, delineate their different profiles, and from there by progressive

[5]Ernest Gellner, "Relativism and Universals," in *Rationality and Relativism*, p. 185.
[6]Stanley Tambiah, *Magic, Science, Religion and the Scope of Rationality* (New York: Cambridge University Press, 1990), p. 121.
[7]Henry Rosemont Jr., "Against Relativism," in *Interpreting Across Boundaries: New Essays in Comparative Philosophy*, ed. Gerald James Larson and Eliot Deutsch (Princeton, N.J.: Princeton University Press, 1988), p. 45.

expansion explain how the Christian God in a monotheistic religion is embedded in a conception of religion that is so different from a polytheistic Hindu conception. Now this whole operation is possible because although Christian "god" and Hindu "deva" are not the same concepts, we can still compare and plot their distinctive features because they share, or we assume they share, *some* commensurabilities, some amount of base agreement. Ultimately then the anthropological project of translation of cultures is committed to the maxim of interpretive charity which commits us "to treating not just our present time-slices, but also our past selves, our ancestors, and members of other cultures past and present, as persons; and that means . . . attributing to them shared references and shared concepts, however different the *conceptions* that we attribute."[8]

We must also remember that cultures have seldom been totally isolated, autonomous entities. There has always been some interaction among peoples resulting in mutual influence, so that cultures are continually undergoing change in response to encounters with others. Cultures, languages and religious traditions today, of course, have more extensive contact with other traditions, resulting in even greater "shared space" than was the case at earlier times.

Context-Independent Criteria

Some understanding across cultural and religious boundaries, then, is not only possible but occurs regularly. Does such understanding enable us to make legitimate judgments about the truth or falsity of beliefs from other worldviews? Can we evaluate claims to truth across cultural and religious boundaries? To make such assessments in a nonarbitrary manner presupposes that we have access to some context-independent criteria for evaluation, that is, criteria that are not relative to particular cultural or religious contexts. But this is precisely what is denied by many impressed by the diversity of opinion or disagreement across cultures and religions. Given such diversity, it is said, no single perspective can be regarded as normative. The sheer fact of cultural and religious diversity is taken as sufficient grounds for rejecting any attempt to demonstrate the truth of one perspective over against another. Moreover, since inescapably we are all contextually conditioned, any judgment we make inevitably is contextually conditioned as well, so that there cannot be any nonarbitrary or context-independent standpoint from which to evaluate alternative perspectives.[9]

It is clear that we are all contextually situated and are thus significantly influ-

---

[8]Tambiah, *Magic, Science, Religion and the Scope of Rationality*, p. 125. The quote from Hilary Putnam is from Putnam's *Reason, Truth and History* (Cambridge: Cambridge University Press, 1981), p. 119. Emphasis in the original.

[9]Both of these themes are evident in Gavin D'Costa's essay "Whose Objectivity? Which Neutrality?" as well as in Perry, "Are Harold Netland's Principles Universal and Neutral?"

enced by a wide variety of factors—genetic, social, cultural, historical, economic, linguistic, religious and so on. We are in important respects products of time and place. The issue is not whether we are so influenced but rather the nature and extent of these cumulative influences. Are we able to transcend the cumulative effects of our particular contexts and thus apprehend to some extent truths that, while expressed in particular linguistic and cultural categories, nevertheless are themselves ontologically independent of all such contexts? In other words, are there any nonarbitrary principles or criteria for assessing alternative perspectives? Or are all criteria for evaluating perspectives *merely* products of particular social, cultural or religious contexts?

If one denies that any criteria transcend particular contexts, I see no way of avoiding some form of relativism. But of course, relativism comes at enormous cost. Not only does the relativist forfeit the epistemological right to make any claim to universal truth but in addition he or she can no longer legitimately reject any alternative perspective as false. The most one could claim would be "From my particular perspective, and given my assumptions, I reject *p.*" But it is hard to see why anyone who does not happen to share *that* particular perspective should be bothered by such rejection. On the other hand, any attempt to escape the implications of relativism by arguing that one's own perspective is somehow preferable or privileged over others will result in at least implicit acknowledgment of some criteria that are independent of particular contexts and thus normative.

Furthermore, the common move from the empirical observation of diversity and disagreement to the normative judgment that no single perspective can legitimately be considered true is an unwarranted leap unless supported by argument. William Wainwright states:

> Even if different traditions employ different standards of truth and rationality, it does not follow that there are no universally valid standards in terms of which the doctrines and arguments of those traditions can be assessed. From the fact that beliefs about values vary from culture to culture, it does not follow that values vary from culture to culture. Similarly, from the fact (if it is a fact) that beliefs about what is true or rational vary from tradition to tradition, it does not follow that what is true or rational varies from tradition to tradition.[10]

If we reject a thorough relativism holding that all judgments about the truth or falsity of alternative worldviews are merely the products of particular contexts, then there emerges at least the possibility of making responsible judgments on the basis of criteria that transcend particular contexts. The question, then, is one of

---

[10]William Wainwright, "Doctrinal Schemes, Metaphysics and Propositional Truth," in *Religious Pluralism and Truth: Essays in Cross-Cultural Philosophy of Religion*, ed. Thomas Dean (Albany: State University of New York Press, 1995), p. 78.

identifying such criteria and applying them responsibly in particular cases.

One of the more significant new interdisciplinary movements within religious studies is the cross-cultural philosophy of religion, which is concerned with examining epistemological issues in religion from cross-cultural perspectives. Ninian Smart, one of the pioneers in the field, states that a major task of the philosophy of religion in the coming years will be "to clarify the criteria for determining the truth as between worldviews."[11] An increasing number of thinkers are dissatisfied with a muddled relativism that refuses to confront questions of truth or criteria for assessing conflicting perspectives. Ninian Smart, William Wainwright, Keith Yandell and Paul Griffiths—each a significant philosopher who is also thoroughly conversant with a major non-Christian religious tradition—all recognize that there are indeed some objective or context-independent criteria for evaluating alternative religious worldviews.[12] A variety of criteria, some more precise than others, have been suggested, including criteria demanding internal consistency within a set of beliefs, freedom from ad hoc hypotheses, congruence with what is known to be true in other domains such as history and the sciences, explanatory power in accounting for fundamental aspects of human experience and so on. In their discussion of criteria for assessing worldviews, Michael Peterson and his colleagues also add the following moral criterion: "[An acceptable religion] should satisfy some basic moral and aesthetic intuitions and provoke and inspire persons to live more morally responsive and responsible lives."[13]

Recognizing that there are such criteria is one thing; applying them to specific cases is quite another matter. As Wainwright puts it, "While there is some agreement concerning the criteria which are to be used in assessing metaphysical systems, these criteria are vague, indeterminate and difficult to apply. . . . It is not, therefore, surprising that intelligent and informed people can employ these criteria and come to radically different conclusions."[14] But this is really not so different from other fields of inquiry in which intelligent and responsible thinkers also disagree. We live in a world in which most truly significant issues—whether in envi-

---

[11]Ninian Smart, "The Philosophy of Worldviews," in *Religious Pluralism and Truth*, p. 24.

[12]Ninian Smart, "Truth, Criteria, and Dialogue Between Religions," in *Religious Pluralism and Truth*, pp. 67-71; Wainwright, "Doctrinal Scemes, Metaphysics and Propositional Truth"; William Wainwright, "Worldviews, Criteria and Epistemic Circularity," in *Interreligious Models and Criteria*, ed. J. Kellenberger (New York: St. Martin's, 1993), pp. 87-105; William Wainwright, *Philosophy of Religion*, 2nd ed. (Belmont, Calif.: Wadsworth, 1999), chapter 7; Keith Yandell, *Christianity and Philosophy* (Grand Rapids, Mich.: Eerdmans, 1984), chapter 8; Keith Yandell, *Philosophy of Religion: A Contemporary Introduction* (London: Routledge, 1999), especially chapters 9-13; and Paul J. Griffiths, *An Apology for Apologetics* (Maryknoll, N.Y.: Orbis, 1991), chapters 2-4.

[13]Michael Peterson, William Hasker, Bruce Reichenbach and David Basinger, *Reason and Religious Belief: An Introduction to the Philosophy of Religion*, 2nd ed. (New York: Oxford University Press, 1998), p. 274.

[14]Wainwright, "Doctrinal Scemes, Metaphysics and Propositional Truth," p. 83.

ronmental policy, international politics, history, genetics or sociology—are contested and controversial. Disagreement in these areas does not mean that there are no acceptable criteria for resolving disputes, but rather it indicates the complexity of applying them to particular issues. It is hardly surprising, then, that there are similar disagreements in the analysis of worldviews.

There is no reason to suppose that identifying certain criteria as context-independent should result in a simple mechanical procedure for testing the truth of any given worldview. Responsible application of criteria to particular cases requires adequate understanding of the relevant religious traditions. We must be sensitive to the distinctives of each religious worldview, for they differ not only in their beliefs but also in the relative weight they give to various kinds of belief within the system. Consistency with known historical events will be crucial to some traditions, relatively unimportant to others. Or to take another example, while internal consistency can be a negative criterion for truth (a religion that includes among its central and defining beliefs a clear contradiction faces rather daunting obstacles in defending its claim to truth), in any given case it can be difficult to determine whether a given religious tradition is actually internally inconsistent. Here, as in so many other areas, we must simply do our best to understand the doctrines in question, clarify ambiguities, explore relationships among religious claims and what we know to be true in other domains and, taking all of the relevant data into account, make judgments about the acceptability of particular assertions.

Nor should we suppose that maintaining context-independent criteria commits one to the position that all "reasonable" persons, when presented with appropriate arguments, will be readily convinced. Few issues of any significance meet this expectation. Even in areas where fairly clear criteria for assessment are recognized—history, law, geology—there can be considerable disagreement in their application to particular cases. Much more is involved in belief, especially in religious matters, than simply recognition of the compelling force of reasoned argument. But as William Wainwright reminds us, this does not negate the value of reasoned reflection.

> Even if the relevant criteria are not fully adequate (and what counts as adequacy should be partly determined by the subject matter) and doctrinal disagreements cannot be resolved by reason alone, that is, even if the adoption of a worldview inevitably involves a decision to venture beyond the evidence, it does not follow that these disputes need be a-rational, or that anything goes. That reason is insufficient does not entail that reason is unnecessary or even that it should not largely determine one's decision to adopt a worldview.[15]

---

[15]Ibid., p. 84.

Logical Consistency

But surely, it might be objected, the criterion of consistency, dependent as it is upon the principle of noncontradiction, cannot be a context-independent criterion since there are respectable religious traditions that explicitly reject it. Gavin D'Costa, for example, objects to my use of this criterion in *Dissonant Voices* by pointing out that some established Buddhist traditions reject logical consistency. "Zen Buddhists accept such rules of logic only to show that *satori* [enlightenment] transcends logical conceptuality and definition."[16] The issue here is not whether any given religious tradition, such as Zen, actually is internally inconsistent by including among its claims two or more contradictory beliefs; the issue is whether consistency itself—the principle of noncontradiction—is a nonarbitrary criterion for assessing worldviews.

Now there is little question that Zen is often understood to be rejecting the normativity of the principle of noncontradiction, and this perception has been fostered in the West by the popular writings of D. T. Suzuki, Alan Watts, Masao Abe and others. Whether this perception is really fair to the Cha'an tradition in China or Zen in Japan, to say nothing of the many other Buddhist schools that employ rigorous rational analysis, is a separate issue that need not detain us here. Our concern here is with the view that, since some traditions do not accept it, the principle of noncontradiction cannot be a context-independent criterion. Let us formulate the criterion of consistency as follows:

> C: A statement that is self-contradictory is false. If two or more statements are mutually contradictory, or entail further statements that are contradictory, at least one of the statements must be false.

"Contradiction" must be distinguished from "paradox" and "mystery," for strictly speaking, a contradiction is the simultaneous affirmation and denial of the same meaning. Paradox involves two or more statements that we have good reason for accepting as true but that, while not strictly contradictory, are nevertheless in tension. There are certainly paradoxical elements in Christian theology—one thinks not only of the doctrine of the Trinity but also the tension between human freedom and divine sovereignty, or between human responsibility and God's foreknowledge and so on. And the Christian faith is surely mysterious in some respects. There is much about God and his dealings with humankind that we do not and undoubtedly could not know. But Christian theology has traditionally insisted that there is no contradiction entailed by central Christian doctrines; if any doctrine entails contradictions, it cannot be true.

Two issues must be distinguished with respect to the use of the principle of non-

---

[16]D'Costa, "Whose Objectivity? Which Neutrality?" p. 84.

contradiction. The first is the empirical question of whether significant traditions do in fact reject the principle. The second is whether, regardless of what people happen to think about it, the principle is in fact universally normative. Many regard the principle of noncontradiction as merely a Western assumption, invented by Aristotle, that, although influential in the West, is largely rejected by Eastern traditions.[17] It cannot be regarded as having universal validity since large numbers of people in the East reject it.

But surely this generalization is misleading at best. For example, anyone familiar with the so-called "postmodernism" of the West will see how inaccurate this depiction of Western thought is. Many in the West openly reject the principle, especially in religious matters. Wilfred Cantwell Smith speaks for many when he states, "Modern Western logic, I myself am pretty sure, though serviceable for computers, is in other ways inept and is particularly ill-suited, it seems, for thinking about . . . spiritual matters."[18] Smith claims that "in all ultimate matters, truth lies not in an either-or but in a both-and."[19] Furthermore, as recent scholars of Eastern traditions have emphasized, although there clearly are traditions that reject such logical principles, there are also rich and dominant traditions in the East that quite self-consciously acknowledge their normativity. Frits Staal, for example, in his seminal work *Universals: Studies in Indian Logic and Linguistics* states, "In Indian logic we find that 'p and not p' is always treated as false."[20] And Paul Griffiths, a Christian philosopher who is also a recognized authority on Buddhism, after comparing how followers of the Hindu thinker Ramanuja and the contemporary Christian Anglican community defend their respective views, observes that both communities, although different culturally, historically and religiously, nevertheless share basic logical principles (including the principles of identity, noncontradiction and excluded middle) and argument forms (material implication and contraposition).[21] Elsewhere, after examining Buddhist philosophical arguments, Griffiths states, "The empirical part of the cultural relativist's thesis is at least very dubious; it just isn't clear that as a matter of fact the criteria for rationality and truth are so different from culture to culture. I would argue that, as far as Indian Buddhism and Anglo-American analytic philosophy are

---

[17]The classic statement of the principle is Aristotle *Metaphysics* 1005b.15-1009a. See Richard McKeon, ed., *The Basic Works of Aristotle* (New York: Random House, 1941), pp. 736-43.

[18]Wilfred Cantwell Smith, "An Attempt at Summation," in *Christ's Lordship and Religious Pluralism*, ed. Gerald H. Anderson and Thomas F. Stransky (Maryknoll, N.Y.: Orbis, 1981), p. 201.

[19]Wilfred Cantwell Smith, *The Faith of Other Men* (New York: Mentor, 1965), p. 17.

[20]Frits Staal, *Universals: Studies in Indian Logic and Linguistics* (Chicago: University of Chicago Press, 1988), p. 8.

[21]Griffiths, *Apology for Apologetics*, pp. 28-29.

concerned, they are close to identical."[22] Thus, while clearly there are significant cultural differences between groups, these should not be exaggerated.
Stanley Tambiah reminds us that "the doctrine of the *psychic unity of mankind* or *human universals* and the doctrine of *diversity of cultures/societies*
are not contradictory dogmas. The doctrine of human universals is applicable
to certain basic human capacities and operations, both physical and mental."[23]

But even if the empirical thesis is correct, and if significant traditions in the
East as well as increasingly in the West do reject the principle of noncontradiction,
what follows from this? Does the mere fact that Zen Buddhists, for example, reject
it negate its status as a context-independent criterion? Surely not, for there is a significant distinction between *rejection* and *refutation*. All kinds of beliefs have been
rejected—atheists reject belief in God's existence; flat earthers reject the belief that
the earth is round; historical revisionists reject the idea that the Holocaust ever
occurred. This in itself hardly settles the matter. What is needed is an argument
that refutes the principle or shows that it is not normative in all cultural contexts.
And to refute a belief is to show that it is false or at least that there are compelling
reasons not to accept it as true.

In spite of repeated assertions to the contrary, no one has refuted the principle
of noncontradiction.[24] Nor can it be done. To see this, let "P" stand for a statement
representing a claim from the Zen tradition limiting the applicability of the principle:

P: Ultimate reality, or emptiness, transcends all dualities and dichotomies, including
logical principles such as the principle of noncontradiction. The principle of noncontradiction therefore does not apply to ultimate reality.[25]

Presumably, in asserting *P* the Zen Buddhist does so with the assumption that what
is expressed by *P* is true; that is, the state of affairs to which *P* refers is actually as *P*

---

[22]Paul J. Griffiths, "Philosophizing Across Cultures: Or, How to Argue with a Buddhist," *Criterion*
26 (winter 1987): 13. See also A. C. Graham, "Rationalism and Anti-Rationalism in Pre-Buddhist
China"; B. K. Matilal, *"Dharma* and Rationality"; and J. N. Mohanty, "Indian Philosophical
Traditions: The Theory of *Pramana*"—all in *Rationality in Question: On Eastern and Western
Views of Rationality*, ed. Shlomo Biderman and Ben-Ami Scharfstein (Leiden, Holland: E. J. Brill,
1989).
[23]Tambiah, *Magic, Science, Religion and the Scope of Rationality*, p. 112. Emphasis in the original.
[24]For a penetrating analysis and defense of the objectivity of logic, see Thomas Nagel, *The Last
Word* (New York: Oxford University Press, 1997), chapter 4.
[25]This is not to suggest that every Zen Buddhist would accept this formulation. Zen writings are
notoriously difficult to interpret. But the writings of D. T. Suzuki and Masao Abe are full of
statements indicating that *satori* (enlightenment) leads to ultimate reality or *sunyata*
(emptiness), which utterly transcends all dualities and logical principles. See Masao Abe, *Zen and
Western Thought* (Honolulu: University of Hawaii Press, 1985); and D. T. Suzuki, *Essays in Zen
Buddhism: First Series* (New York: Grove Wiedenfeld, 1949).

asserts it to be. If this is not the case, then there is little reason to be bothered by Zen's claims in the first place. But notice that in advancing *P* as true the Buddhist is implicitly rejecting what is incompatible with *P* as false. For example, *Q* below is incompatible with *P:*

> Q: Ultimate reality, or emptiness, does not transcend all dualities and dichotomies. Dualities and dichotomies such as that implicit in the principle of noncontradiction do apply on the level of ultimate reality.

Now suppose that the Zen Buddhist says that in affirming *P* one is *not* denying *Q*. To deny that in asserting *P* one is implicitly ruling out *Q* is to imply both that emptiness *does* transcend all dualities, and thus that the principle of noncontradiction does not apply on this level, and that emptiness *does not* transcend all dualities, and thus that the principle of noncontradiction does apply on that level. But it is difficult indeed to make any sense out of this position. If, on the other hand, in asserting *P* one is implicitly rejecting *Q* as false, then one is appealing to the principle of noncontradiction in the assertion of *P.* The principle is actually being presupposed in the denial of the principle. Or to put it another way, if emptiness is the ultimate reality, then the state of affairs in which emptiness obtains rules out any other state of affairs incompatible with emptiness as ultimate, such as the existence of an eternal Creator God as the ultimate reality. But this too implies the principle of noncontradiction in ontology.

It is simply impossible to refute the principle of noncontradiction, since any attempt at refutation necessarily appeals to the principle itself. Any meaningful affirmation about anything at all, regardless of how cryptic, vague, paradoxical or imprecise the statement might be, if intended as true, makes implicit appeal to the principle by ruling out its negation as false. The fact that a Greek, Aristotle, happens to have been the first person to formulate the principle explicitly is entirely irrelevant. The principle is binding upon all humans, Japanese, Chinese, Indians as well as Europeans and Americans. The unavoidable nature of the principle in religion is recognized by Raimundo Panikkar, who himself is highly sympathetic to pluralism:

> A believing member of a religion in one way or another considers his religion to be true. Now, the claim to truth has a certain built-in exclusivity. If a given statement is true, its contradictory cannot also be true. And if a certain human tradition claims to offer a universal context for truth, anything contrary to that "universal truth" will have to be declared false.[26]

On this criterion, then, if Zen entails statements that are contradictory, or if it entails denial of the principle of noncontradiction itself, then we have good reason

---

[26]Raimundo Panikkar, *The Intrareligious Dialogue* (New York: Paulist, 1978), p. xiv.

for rejecting at least part of its central affirmations as false. Whether Zen does in fact have these consequences is a matter to be decided only after carefully considering what Zen Buddhists actually affirm.

The Moral Criterion

A curious ambivalence concerning moral discourse and religion prevails. On the one hand, there is, at least on the surface level, widespread suspicion of any talk about "universal" or "absolute" moral principles, especially if this is embedded within religious discourse. Initial commitments to ethical relativism are common, and talk of universally normative moral principles for assessing beliefs or practices across cultures is often rejected as merely the imposition of one group's standards upon others. Thus Gavin D'Costa—hardly an ethical relativist—dismisses the possibility of a moral criterion to evaluate religious traditions by asserting, "There are no sets of basic moral values which are neutral and acceptable to all people, and as soon as one tries to specify some their historical and tradition-specific nature becomes evident."[27]

Yet on the other hand, even while rejecting the language of universality, many display a deeper commitment to at least *some* moral values and principles that are binding on people in various cultures. For example, there is the loud and persistent call (primarily by Western intellectuals) for respect for human rights worldwide—a cause that inevitably finds expression in strong moral language.[28] Apologists for universal human rights are not bothered by the fact that some cultures do not happen to agree with their principles or agenda. They hold the moral principles undergirding human rights to be universally binding, so that they expect cultures practicing female circumcision, capital punishment, discrimination against women or child prostitution to change and bring their practices into line with the apologists' moral expectations.

Furthermore, the intimate connection between religion and morality is, I think, more widely acknowledged on a popular level than is often assumed. Many people do recognize that religious truth is congruent with basic moral values, so that moral awareness serves as a criterion in assessing religious leaders and their claims. It is no accident that most people respond favorably to morally respectable religious figures such as Confucius, Jesus, the Buddha, Gandhi, the Dalai Lama and Mother Teresa, and that the plausibility of their religious claims is enhanced by the moral integrity of their lives. By contrast, the religious claims of Jim Jones, David Koresh and Shoko Asahara were widely dismissed, in part because they were rightly

---

[27]D'Costa, "Whose Objectivity? Which Neutrality?" p. 88.
[28]See *International Human Rights Instruments of the United Nations, 1948-1982* (Pleasantville, N.Y.: UNIFO, 1983).

perceived to be lacking in moral virtue. Implicitly, then, people *do* use a moral criterion in assessing claims from various religious traditions, and surely this is as it should be.

The common perception of a connection between moral virtue and religious truth is operative in John Hick's use of the moral criterion in his model of religious pluralism. The link between morality and religious truth is reflected in the soteriological transformation of individuals from self-centeredness to Reality-centeredness, producing the saints of the various religions. The moral criterion not only provides justification for postulating the Real as the religious ultimate to which the various religious traditions are responses, but also it provides a criterion for distinguishing between legitimate responses to the Real and those that are illegitimate. As we saw in chapter seven, however, he uses the moral criterion inconsistently. But it is important to see that, in spite of the internal problems within his model, Hick is correct in recognizing the close connection between religious truth and moral principles.

Dissatisfaction with attempts to apply a moral criterion to the assessment of worldviews or religious traditions is often rooted in the awareness of cultural and religious diversity. Given the obvious differences between cultures, and given the fact that each of us is thoroughly embedded in a particular social, linguistic and cultural framework, how can we claim to have access to a moral criterion that somehow stands apart from all such contexts and is normative for all people at all times? Many take the mere fact of diversity as sufficient to refute any presumption of universally binding moral values and principles.

Certainly cultures exhibit considerable diversity on moral issues. Basic moral disagreements are of course found within a culture as well, so that within American society today there are deep disagreements over issues such as abortion, euthanasia, the death penalty, homosexual practice, extramarital sex and so on. But differences sometimes seem even more pronounced when comparing cultures with each other. Human sacrifice was an accepted part of religious ritual in ancient Aztec civilization; it is widely rejected today as immoral. Polygyny (marriage of one man to several wives) is practiced in some West African tribes; it is rejected in many other cultures. Female circumcision is an important rite of passage in certain cultures of Africa; it is not practiced in the West. The elderly were left to die of starvation in traditional Eskimo culture; this would be regarded as highly immoral in most other cultures.

The observation of diversity often leads to an empirical thesis about cultures: both ethical practices and basic moral principles are so radically different across cultures that the cultures in fact have in common little that is of any moral significance. This empirical thesis then is used to support ethical relativism, which denies that there are any objective or universally normative moral principles that apply to all cultures. If this is the case, then clearly we cannot use a moral criterion in assessing various worldviews.

But the common move from the empirical observation of diversity and disagreement to the conclusion that no single perspective can be considered universally normative is unwarranted apart from supporting argument. Even if it were the case that there is widespread disagreement among cultures on basic moral principles, it does not necessarily follow that no single perspective is true or that there is no set of moral principles that are objectively valid for all people in all cultures. What is needed is an argument that shows that there are no, or at least that we have no access to, moral principles that are normative in all cultural contexts.

The empirical thesis itself is problematic and should not be accepted without significant qualification. Here we must distinguish fundamental moral values or principles from particular customs, cultural norms or rules. Specific practices and rules do vary with culture and religious tradition, but simply because two societies have different views on a given practice (polygamy or abortion), it does not follow that they have different underlying moral values and principles. It is possible, even likely, that such differences in practice are due in part to the different circumstances and beliefs about human beings and the world that each society brings to the issue. Ronald Green observes:

> While ethicists do acknowledge the truth of "cultural relativism," the view that accepted or prohibited modes of conduct vary among cultures, they have pointed out that this does not necessarily mean that fundamental principles are dissimilar. Different technical and social situations can cause common basic principles to yield different results in specific circumstances. For example, a general principle of respect for parents may produce a stringent ban on parricide in a technically advanced civilization but may lead to a custom of abandoning infirm or elderly parents in hunter-gatherer cultures where there is no provision for sustaining the disabled and where dependency is regarded by all as shameful.[29]

Many today greatly underestimate the degree of agreement on basic moral values and principles across cultural traditions. Those who have studied morality cross-culturally often are less hesitant to speak of commonalities. Green states,

> One of the most striking impressions produced by comparative study of religious ethics is the similarity in basic moral codes and teachings. The Ten Commandments of

---

[29]Ronald M. Green, "Morality and Religion," in *The Encyclopedia of Religion*, ed. Mircea Eliade (New York: Macmillan, 1987), 10:94. See also William K. Frankena, *Ethics*, 2nd ed. (Englewood Cliffs, N.J.: Prentice-Hall, 1973), pp. 109-10; Louis P. Pojman, *Ethics: Discovering Right and Wrong*, 3rd ed. (Belmont, Calif.: Wadsworth, 1999), chapter 2; and James Rachel, "The Challenge of Cultural Relativisim," in *Moral Relativism*, pp. 53-65.

Hebrew faith, the teachings of Jesus in the Sermon on the Mount and of Paul in his epistles, the requirements of *sadharana,* or universal *dharma,* in Hinduism *(Laws of Manu,* 10.63), Buddhism's Five Precepts, and Islam's decalogue in the Qur'an (17:22-39) constitute a very common set of normative requirements. These prohibit killing, injury, deception, or the violation of solemn oaths. C. S. Lewis has called basic moral rules like these "the ultimate platitudes of practical reason," and their presence and givenness in such diverse traditions supports his characterization.[30]

Agreement here includes recognition of a basic distinction between good and evil, along with the belief that certain things—for example, unjustified killing of other humans, injury to others, deception and inappropriate sexual relations—are wrong. That different groups have conflicting views on, for example, what constitutes inappropriate sexual relations does not alter the fact that all societies recognize that not just any sexual activity with anyone is permitted. A remarkable example of commonality in moral values across cultural and religious traditions can be found in the so-called Golden Rule, most familiar in the saying of Jesus in Matthew 7:12: "In everything, do to others what you would have them do to you." The moral principle underlying the Golden Rule is also expressed in the writings of rabbinic Judaism, Hinduism, Buddhism, Jainism and Zoroastrianism, with the clearest expression being found in Confucianism: "Do not impose on others what you yourself do not desire."[31]

The commonalities across religious traditions in basic moral principles is especially striking because of the very different religious beliefs and metaphysical frameworks within the religions. The metaphysical assumptions of Judaism, Christianity, the various schools of Hinduism and Buddhism, Islam, Jainism and Confucianism are quite different and on occasion mutually incompatible. As Green says, "It is sometimes assumed, because religious traditions hold widely different religious beliefs, that their ethics must correspondingly differ; what is remarkable, however, is that these great differences in beliefs apparently do not affect adherence to at least the fundamental moral rules."[32] Thus in the moral realm, as well as in other areas, we must retain a proper balance between commonalities and differences across cultural and religious boundaries.

---

[30]Green, "Morality and Religion," p. 99. The reference to C. S. Lewis is to his *Abolition of Man* (New York: Macmillan, 1947), pp. 56-57. See also Ronald M. Green, *Religion and Moral Reason: A New Method for Comparative Study* (New York: Oxford University Press, 1988), especially chapter 1; Bimal Krishna Matilal, "Ethical Relativism and Confrontation of Cultures," in *Relativism: Interpretation and Confrontation,* ed. Michael Krausz (Notre Dame, Ind.: University of Notre Dame Press, 1989), pp. 339-62.

[31]*Analects* 12:2, in *Confucius: The Analects,* trans. D. C. Lau (London: Penguin, 1979), p. 112. For examples of similar moral injunctions from Hinduism, Jainism, Buddhism and Zoroastrianism, see John Hick, *An Interpretation of Religion* (New Haven, Conn.: Yale University Press, 1989), pp. 313-14; and Lewis, *Abolition of Man,* pp. 95-121.

[32]Green, "Morality and Religion," p. 100.

Moral Awareness and Interreligious Apologetics

A potentially fruitful task for Christian apologetics is exploring the connection between morality and religion, making explicit some of the implications of this connection for various worldviews. The point here is not to try to show that one religious tradition has, over time, been morally superior to others. Surely each religion has a historical legacy that is mixed at best, with embarrassing gaps between ethical ideals and practice. Rather, the issue here is whether the metaphysical and epistemological commitments of a given religious tradition are consistent with, or permit, its ethical insights. We will consider this question below with a contemporary example from Zen Buddhism.

The phenomenon of moral awareness is a crucial part of a cumulative case argument for Christian theism. Moral awareness in general, and the apparently universal experience of moral awareness in particular, comprise part of the phenomena demanding explanation by any adequate worldview. A cumulative case argument would first analyze the nature of moral awareness across ethnic, cultural and religious boundaries and then argue that a theistic worldview provides the best explanation for the phenomena of moral obligation. This is not a matter of trying to produce a conclusive deductive argument to the effect that the phenomena of morality *entail* God's existence. The step from moral phenomena to Christian theism is an inference to the best explanation. The "most reasonable explanation" for certain irreducible features of moral obligation—what George Mavrodes has called the "queerness of morality"—is that the world was created by a God who is himself an inherently moral being.[33]

Clearly some significant and controversial issues here need to be defended. For example, for moral awareness to function in this manner, some form of moral objectivism or moral realism must be correct. Moral objectivism is the view that basic moral values and principles are objective in the sense that they are valid and normative regardless of whether any particular individual or group of people recognizes them as such. I believe that moral objectivism is both correct and defensible, although I will not argue for it here.[34] As such, moral objectivism is incompatible

---

[33]George Mavrodes, "The Queernesss of Morality," in *Philosophy of Religion: Selected Readings*, ed. William L. Rowe and William J. Wainwright, 3rd ed. (New York: Harcourt Brace, 1998), pp. 197-207. On moral arguments for theism, see H. P. Owen, *The Moral Argument for Christian Theism* (London: Allen & Unwin, 1965); R. M. Adams, "Moral Arguments for Theistic Belief," in *Rationality and Religious Belief*, ed. C. F. Delaney (Notre Dame, Ind.: University of Notre Dame Press, 1979), pp. 116-40; Stephen T. Davis, *God, Reason and Theistic Proofs* (Grand Rapids, Mich.: Eerdmans, 1997), pp. 146-50; Basil Mitchell, *Morality: Religious and Secular* (Oxford: Clarendon, 1980); and Linda Zagzebski, "Does Ethics Need God?" *Faith and Philosophy* 4, no. 3 (1987): 294-303. A form of the moral argument was used by C. S. Lewis in *Mere Christianity* (New York: Macmillan, 1960), book 1.

[34]For a good introductory discussion to the issues, see Pojman, *Ethics*, chapter 3.

with those views that reduce the phenomena of morality to subjective feelings or attitudes, to the products of centuries of social and cultural development or to strictly biological or genetic factors. Moral objectivism also rules out a radical cultural relativism that identifies the validity of moral values and principles simply with what any given group happens to accept as normative.

Effective use of moral awareness in a cumulative case argument would also need to develop careful ethnographic research across cultural boundaries, taking seriously the moral discourse and practice of various cultures. The widespread perception that there are no common moral values across cultures is due to both ignorance about commonalities and a prior commitment to relativism as much as it is to awareness of differences in belief and practice.[35] Responsible empirical research in this area should acknowledge clear commonalities as well as differences in moral beliefs and practices.

Significantly, after a century that witnessed unprecedented human cruelty and destruction, much of the earlier optimism about human nature and its potential for limitless perfectibility has evaporated. Many are sensitive to the need for the moral category of evil to describe not only Hitler and the Holocaust but the many other cases of genocide as well. Along with the strident rejections of "moral absolutism" are deep concerns for justice and the rights of the oppressed. The irreducibly moral categories implicit in such discourse provide unique opportunities for culturally sensitive Christian thinkers to probe the implications of moral awareness for worldview analysis. What is needed is an argument that (1) makes explicit, on the basis of responsible ethnographic research, the point that, despite obvious differences, there are significant commonalities across cultures and religions in moral values and principles, (2) demonstrates that such moral values and principles are objective in that they cannot

---

[35]Anthropologist Robert Priest, for example, chastises cultural anthropologists for systematically ignoring the study of morality crossculturally: "When anthropologists do fieldwork, they listen as people talk about moral rights and duties of husband and wife, father and son, mother's brother and sister's son. They listen to gossip about moral failings of others, about those who are stingy with food when they ought to be generous, of those who are lazy and do not contribute their share. They overhear parental admonitions, warnings, and moral harangues at youth whose transgressions threaten to dishonor their family's reputation. Sentiments of gratitude, of disapproval, of resentment, of love, of feeling hurt, and of obligation or responsibility are the stuff of day-to-day interactions and discourse. Interpersonal conflicts with their accusations, expressions of indignation, jealous defense of marital rights, and expressions of guilt, remorse, and shame are universally present. Yet anthropologists have fairly consistently refused to utilize an analytical vocabulary appropriate to the sociocultural interpersonal order as a moral order. They have borrowed concepts from physics, mathematics, and the biological sciences to the exclusion and neglect of other equally viable concepts, concepts that, if used, would call our attention to the moral dimensions of life. I suggest that the anthropological value commitment to relativism has served to block conceptual development in the direction of the ethico-moral dimensions of life cross-culturally" (Robert J. Priest, "Christian Theology, Sin, and Anthropology," in *Explorations in Anthropology and Theology*, ed. Frank A. Salamone and Walter Randolph Adams [New York: University Press of America, 1997], p. 27).

be reduced to, or accounted for, merely on the basis of social, cultural, historical or biological factors, and (3) recognizes that Christian theism provides a satisfying explanation both for there being moral awareness at all and for the distinctive moral beliefs and practices we see across cultures.

The Moral Criterion and Zen

I suggested earlier that the phenomenon of moral awareness can serve as a negative criterion in assessing religious worldviews. By this I mean that the adequacy of a worldview depends in part upon its capacity for accommodating and accounting for the basic features of moral experience. In other words, a worldview is called into question to the extent that it is unable to account for, or has commitments that are incompatible with, basic features of morality. In this connection Zen Buddhism (at least according to some influential interpretations of Zen) faces serious problems.

Zen Buddhism has a long history in China and Japan, and in many ways it seems an unlikely religious tradition to flourish in highly modernized societies. Yet it has attracted a significant following in the West as well as in Asia and has become well established among the academic and cultural elite as an alternative to traditional Western worldviews.[36] Undoubtedly the most influential spokesman for Zen in the West is the Japanese scholar Masao Abe (b. 1915). Abe has been associated with the Kyoto School of Buddhism, inspired by the Japanese Buddhist philosopher Kitaro Nishida. This school is a distinctive movement that has tried to develop a synthesis between traditional Western concerns (especially as expressed by Continental philosophers) and Zen Buddhism.[37] Abe has grappled with the implications of modern

---

[36]The definitive historical study is Heinrich Dumoulin, *India and China*, vol. 1 of *Zen Buddhism: A History*, trans. James W. Heisig and Paul F. Knitter (New York: Macmillan, 1988); and Heinrich Dumoulin, *Japan*, vol. 2 of *Zen Buddhism: A History*, trans. James W. Heisig and Paul F. Knitter (New York: Macmillan, 1990).

[37]Nishida's most significant work is *An Inquiry into the Good*, trans. Masao Abe and Christopher Ives (New Haven, Conn.: Yale University Press, 1987). On the Kyoto School and its significance, see Robert E. Carter, *The Nothingness Beyond God: An Introduction to the Philosophy of Nishida Kitaro* (New York: Paragon, 1989); *The Buddha Eye: An Anthology of the Kyoto School,* ed. Frederick Franck (New York: Crossroad, 1982); James Fredericks, "The Kyoto School: Modern Buddhist Philosophy and the Search for a Transcultural Theology," *Horizons* 15, no. 2 (1988): 299-315; and Thomas Kasulis, "The Kyoto School and the West," *Eastern Buddhist* 15 (autumn 1982): 125-44. Although Zen is often portrayed in the West as the quintessence of Buddhism (a perception carefully crafted by Japanese Zen apologists such as D. T. Suzuki and Masao Abe), Zen has had a rather ambivalent relationship with other Buddhist schools. There is a vigorous debate within Japanese Buddhism over the status of Zen and some other Japanese Buddhist traditions, including the Kyoto School, with critics charging that Zen is a distortion of authentic Buddhist teachings. See Paul L. Swanson, " 'Zen Is Not Buddhism': Recent Japanese Critiques of Buddha-Nature," *Numen* 40 (1993): 115-49; *Pruning the Bodhi Tree: The Storm over Critical Buddhism*, eds. Jamie Hubbard and Paul L. Swanson (Honolulu: University of Hawaii Press, 1997); and Robert H. Sharf, "The Zen of Japanese Nationalism," in *Curators of the Buddha: The Study of Buddhism Under Colonialism*, ed. Donald S. Lopez Jr. (Chicago: University of Chicago Press, 1995), pp. 107-60.

Western thought for classical Buddhist perspectives, demonstrating remarkable insight into Western philosophers and Christian theologians.[38] Yet throughout Abe retains a clear Buddhist ontology and epistemology.

Abe follows the third-century Buddhist Nagarjuna and the Madhyamaka tradition in positing a distinction between two levels of truth and reality: (1) a provisional level in which we normally live and in which distinctions and duality apply; and (2) ultimate Truth and Reality—*sunyata*, or emptiness—that transcends all such dualities and in which conceptual and logical categories do not apply. Abe is clearly uncomfortable with a tendency in Buddhist thought to minimize the value of the provisional realm in which we live, and he frankly acknowledges the need for Buddhism in the modern world to take much more seriously the domains of science, history and social ethics that are relegated to this provisional level.

This is not to suggest that Buddhism is amoral or has no interest in ethics. Far from it. Moral values and principles have been integral to Buddhism from its inception.[39] The Buddha's Fourth Noble Truth, leading to the cessation of suffering through following the Noble Eightfold Path, explicitly calls for cultivating moral virtues in right conduct, right speech and right livelihood. Buddhist laity are expected to adhere to the Five Precepts—not to take life, not to steal, not to speak falsely, not to engage in sexual misconduct and not to take intoxicating liquor. Monastic discipline presupposes the belief that cultivation of moral virtues and elimination of vices prepare one for higher levels of spiritual attainment. And with the emergence of the Mahayana traditions there is a strong emphasis upon *karuna*, or altruistic compassion for all sentient beings, exemplified in the *bodhisattva* ideal.

The issue, however, is not whether Buddhism manifests moral awareness, nor even whether individual Buddhists can be persons of outstanding moral character (undoubtedly many are); the issue is whether the metaphysical commitments of Buddhism, and Zen in particular, allow for the moral insights and imperatives we find within Buddhist traditions. There are two points in particular where Buddhist ontology and moral awareness are in tension. The first has to do with whether the Buddhist doctrine of *anatta* (no-self) allows for any meaningful sense of personal moral responsibility and, if not, what the implications of this for morality might be.

---

[38]See Masao Abe, *Zen and Western Thought*, ed. William R. LaFleur (Honolulu: University of Hawaii Press, 1985); Masao Abe, "Kenotic God and Dynamic Sunyata," in *The Emptying God: A Buddhist-Jewish-Christian Conversation*, ed. John B. Cobb Jr. and Christopher Ives (Maryknoll, N.Y.: Orbis, 1990); Masao Abe, *Buddhism and Interfaith Dialogue*, ed. Steven Heine (Honolulu: University of Hawaii Press, 1995); and Masao Abe, *Zen and Comparative Studies* (Honolulu: University of Hawaii Press, 1997).

[39]The definitive study is Peter Harvey, *An Introduction to Buddhist Ethics*, (Cambridge: Cambridge University Press, 2000). See also Frank E. Reynolds and Robert Campany, "Buddhist Ethics," *Encyclopedia of Religion*, ed. Mircea Eliade (New York: Macmillan, 1987), 2:498-504; and David J. Kalupahana, *Ethics in Early Buddhism* (Honolulu: University of Hawaii Press, 1995).

Although this is a significant issue, we will not pursue it here.[40] The second problem concerns the relativizing of moral values and principles that seems inevitable given Buddhist metaphysical commitments.

Abe is well aware of this problem and addresses it in several places.[41] He clearly wants to take moral issues seriously and to provide a Buddhist justification for a strong moral response to the many injustices in our world. But there is a tension here as Abe's Zen ontology makes its difficult to provide an adequate foundation for moral obligation. It will be helpful to contrast Christian theism with Zen, noting how the Zen ontology rules out an ultimate distinction between good and evil. On this point Zen ontological commitments conflict sharply with a basic moral intuition shared by many people in various cultures and religions, and this, I suggest, provides a good reason for rejecting the Zen worldview.

Abe is clear on the fact that in Zen there is no God who serves as the ontological ground or basis for reality. Ultimate reality is *sunyata,* or emptiness, a paradoxical notion transcending all objectification, conceptualization and duality. "In Buddhism *sunyata,* or emptiness as ultimate reality, is entirely unobjectifiable and nonsubstantial in that *sunyata* is neither immanent nor transcendent, being beyond even the one God."[42] Abe claims:

> Buddhism has no need of a notion of one God because the fundamental principle of Buddhism is "dependent origination." This notion indicates that everything in and out of the universe is interdependent and co-arising and co-ceasing: nothing whatever is independent and self-existing. . . . The universe is not the creation of one God, but fundamentally is a network of causal relationships among innumerable things which are co-arising and co-ceasing.[43]

This has significant implications for the distinction between good and evil. Abe continues:

> Good and evil are completely dependent on one another. They always co-arise and co-cease so that one cannot exist without the other. There is, then, no supreme good which is self-subsistent apart from evil, and no absolute evil which is an object of eternal punishment apart from good. To Buddhists both the supreme good and absolute evil are illusions.[44]

---

[40]See Paul J. Griffiths, "Notes Towards a Critique of Buddhist Karmic Theory," *Religious Studies* 18, no. 3 (1982): 277-91; and Griffiths, *Apology for Apologetics,* pp. 99-108.

[41]See, for example, Masao Abe, "The Problem of Evil in Christianity and Buddhism," in *Buddhist-Christian Dialogue: Mutual Renewal and Transformation*, ed. Paul Ingram and Frederick J. Streng (Honolulu: University of Hawaii Press, 1986), pp. 139-54; "Ethics and Social Responsibility in Buddhism," *Eastern Buddhist* 30, no. 2 (1997): 161-72; *Buddhism and Interfaith Dialogue*, chapter 17; *Zen and Comparative Studies*, chapters 3 and 15.

[42]Abe, "Ethics and Social Responsibility," p. 164.

[43]Abe, "Problem of Evil," p. 145.

[44]Ibid.

According to Zen, although the distinction between good and evil has its use on the level of provisional reality, ultimately, as one awakens to the true nature of things through enlightenment, one must transcend even this duality. Reynolds and Campany observe, "The experience of enlightenment, interpreted by some Mahayana schools as the recognition of an identity with the Absolute or 'unproduced,' transported one to a higher plane of awareness. From this plane of awareness ethical distinctions (e.g. good/bad, right/wrong) and moral rules and precepts all were seen to be not so much irrelevant as relative."[45] Abe draws the following soteriological implications from this: "In Buddhism . . . what is essential for salvation is not to overcome evil with good and to participate in the supreme Good, but to be emancipated from the existential antinomy of good and evil and to awaken to Emptiness prior to the opposition between good and evil."[46]

Abe participated in a fascinating discussion with several Christian and Jewish theologians, and not surprisingly, he was pressed on the question of an ultimate distinction between good and evil and the implications of this distinction for an event like the Holocaust.[47] In response Abe distinguished among three dimensions of reality according to which the question of evil must be addressed.[48] The first is the nonhuman, natural dimension in which evil and suffering can be experienced through the processes of nature. Earthquake, floods, disease and even killing within the food chain constitute suffering on this level. The second dimension is that of the "transnatural human dimension represented by individual morality, and collective social and historical ethics." On this level there is a distinction between good and evil, with honesty, kindness, integrity and courage being regarded as good whereas stealing, lying and killing are regarded as evil. So long as we are on this dimension, Abe maintains, the distinction between good and evil, right and wrong, is real enough and we must do our best to promote good and eradicate evil. Nevertheless, he says, "Ultimately the distinction between good and evil in the ethical dimension is relative, not absolute."[49]

Abe distinguishes the second dimension from what he calls "the fundamental reli-

---

[45]Reynolds and Campany, "Buddhist Ethics," p. 501.

[46]Abe, *Zen and Western Thought*, p. 133.

[47]See the essays in *The Emptying God*. On a personal note, I was privileged to participate in a doctoral seminar on the problem of evil at Claremont Graduate School during the spring of 1981, conducted jointly by professors John Hick and Masao Abe. At that time Hick still retained something of a Christian theistic ontology and held to a clear distinction between good and evil, with goodness being grounded in the nature of God. Abe held to an uncompromising Zen perspective that relativized the distinction between good and evil. The discussions were fascinating and brought into sharp relief the differences between the two worldviews on ontology as well as the question of evil and suffering.

[48]Abe, "Kenotic God and Dynamic Sunyata," pp. 46-50.

[49]Ibid., p. 47.

gious dimension," or the level of ultimate reality: *sunyata,* or emptiness. On this level all dualities and distinctions, including that between good and evil, are transcended. Abe made the point explicit with reference to what has become the definitive symbol of evil—the Holocaust. On the secondary level of human social interaction, Abe is willing to speak of the Holocaust as "a brutal, atrocious, historical evil," although even here he emphasizes that, since all events are interrelated and codependent, there is a sense in which the "root karma" that caused the Holocaust is "common to all human beings," with good and evil interrelated in this network of causal factors. Nevertheless, he adds, "While in a human, moral dimension the Holocaust should be condemned as an unpardonable, absolute evil, *from the ultimate religious point of view even it should not be taken as an absolute but a relative evil.*"[50] From the perspective of ultimate reality—that is, emptiness—we cannot condemn the Holocaust as evil, since moral categories do not apply on that level.

As one might expect, Abe's relativizing of the distinction between good and evil in his treatment of the Holocaust received less than enthusiastic responses from John Cobb, Shubert Ogden, Jürgen Moltmann, David Tracy and especially the Jewish theologian Eugene B. Borowitz.[51] Abe's distinction between the human and the religious dimensions, and his relegation of moral categories strictly to the former, is strikingly at odds with the insights of many religious traditions. Integral to many religions is the conviction that one cannot separate the moral dimension from the religious; this is central to theistic traditions that insist that God is righteous and morally pure. Ultimate reality is inherently moral, and the good/evil distinction cannot be relegated to a lower level of reality. The irreducible connection between the moral and religious dimensions is also implicit in the common perception, noted earlier, that religious truth will be congruent with basic moral principles.

In sum, the relativizing of the distinction between good and evil in Zen points to a fundamental twofold problem with Zen as a general worldview: First, it is unable to account for, or explain adequately, the phenomena of moral obligation. Second, Zen's ontology clashes sharply with a widely shared aspect of human experience, namely the awareness of a real and irreducible distinction between good and evil, right and wrong.

---

[50]Ibid., pp. 52-53. Emphasis is mine.
[51]See their respective essays in *The Emptying God.*

10

TOWARD AN EVANGELICAL THEOLOGY OF RELIGIONS

Religion is by its very nature a communion, in which man answers and reacts to God's revelation. This definition implies that there is a divine revelation, an act of self-disclosure on the part of God. It also implies that there is a human response to this self-disclosure, either in a negative or in a positive sense. Religion can be a profound and sincere seeking of God; it can also be a flight from God, an endeavor to escape from His presence, under the guise of love and obedient service. At the bottom of it lies a relationship, an encounter.

J. H. BAVINCK, *The Church Between Temple and Mosque*

The way of the Cross as the way of reconciliation between God and people may never be muted in interreligious encounter in a misguided attempt to "give no offense." The paramountcy of Jesus Christ the crucified and risen Lord may never be called into question. He may never be shunted aside, never be deposed from his position as the only Way leading to God's Kingdom.

JOHANNES VERKUYL, *"The Biblical Notion of Kingdom"*

I n spite of the prominence of religious pluralism within theological discussions of the past fifty years, evangelicals, with a few notable exceptions, have been reticent on the issues. Those who do address the subject usually focus upon the destiny of the unevangelized, as if a clear answer on this matter resolves all remaining problems. Veteran evangelical missiologist Ralph Covell is surely correct in his assessment of evangelical responses:

> [Evangelicals] are clear on the uniqueness of Christ and on God's will to save all humanity, but they face the dilemma that most of the people of the world are comfortable in the religion in which they are born. Christ is the unique, but apparently not the universal, savior. When crucial target dates appear—1900 and 2000, for example— they mount new crusades to spread Christ's message universally, but without giving any new, creative thought to the relationship of these efforts to the nagging questions posed by world religions. For the most part, evangelical scholars from the time of the Wheaton Congress on Evangelism (1966) to the Lausanne II International Congress on World Evangelization (Manila 1989) have been satisfied with predictably repeating their basic proof texts on the finality of Christ. Disturbing biblical texts which might

nuance their attitudes to other religious expressions are glossed over, put in footnotes, subsumed under traditional views, or placed in the last paragraph of an article.[1]

Similarly the late Harvie Conn remarked, "Affirming the finality of Christ does not relieve us of the responsibility to explain the relationship between Christianity and other religions. Sadly, the evangelical world seems almost silent on this crucial issue."[2] It is hardly surprising, then, that the eighty-five evangelical theologians from twenty-eight countries meeting in 1992 at Manila under the auspices of the World Evangelical Fellowship to address the theme "The Unique Christ in Our Pluralistic World" acknowledged, "We evangelicals need a more adequate theology of religions."[3]

Some evangelicals in the 1980s and 1990s began exploring issues in the theology of religions,[4] with Clark Pinnock giving the most controversial treatment of the subject.[5] Pinnock's theology of religions rests upon two axioms: First, God is a God of

---

[1]Ralph Covell, "Jesus Christ and the World Religions: Current Evangelical Viewpoints," in *The Good News of the Kingdom: Mission Theology for the Third Millennium,* ed. Charles Van Engen, Dean S. Gilliland and Paul Pierson (Maryknoll, N.Y.: Orbis, 1993), pp. 162-63.

[2]Harvie Conn, "Do Other Religions Save?" in *Through No Fault of Their Own? The Fate of Those Who Have Never Heard,* ed. William V. Crockett and James G. Sigountos (Grand Rapids, Mich.: Baker, 1991), p. 207.

[3]"The WEF Manila Declaration," in *The Unique Christ in Our Pluralistic World,* ed. Bruce J. Nicholls (Grand Rapids, Mich.: Baker, 1994), p. 15.

[4]See, for example, Christopher J. H. Wright, "The Christian and Other Religions: The Biblical Evidence," *Themelios* 9, no. 2 (1984): 4-15; Christopher J. H. Wright, *What's So Unique About Jesus?* (Eastbourne, England: Monarch, 1990); Klaas Runia, "The Gospel and Religious Pluralism," *Evangelical Review of Theology* 14 (October 1990): 341-79; Edward Rommen and Harold Netland, eds., *Christianity and the Religions: A Biblical Theology of World Religions* (Pasadena, Calif.: William Carey Library, 1995); Daniel B. Clendenin, *Many Gods, Many Lords: Christianity Encounters World Religions* (Grand Rapids, Mich.: Baker, 1995); Alister McGrath, *A Passion for Truth* (Downers Grove, Ill.: InterVarsity Press, 1996), chapter 5; D. A. Carson, *The Gagging of God: Christianity Confronts Pluralism* (Grand Rapids, Mich.: Zondervan, 1996); Charles Van Engen, *Mission on the Way: Issues in Mission Theology* (Grand Rapids, Mich.: Baker, 1996), chapters 9-10; Terry C. Muck, "Evangelicals and Interreligious Dialogue," *Journal of the Evangelical Theological Society* 36, no. 4 (1993): 517-29; Terry C. Muck, "Is There Common Ground Among Religions?" *Journal of the Evangelical Theological Society* 40, no. 1 (1997): 99-112; Ramesh Richard, *The Population of Heaven: A Biblical Response to the Inclusivist Position on Who Will Be Saved* (Chicago: Moody Press, 1994); *One God, One Lord: Christianity in a World of Religious Pluralism,* ed. Andrew D. Clarke and Bruce W. Winter, 2nd ed. (Grand Rapids, Mich.: Baker, 1992); Millard J. Erickson, *How Shall They Be Saved? The Destiny of Those Who Do Not Hear of Jesus* (Grand Rapids, Mich.: Baker, 1996); and Gerald R. McDermott, *Can Evangelicals Learn from World Religions?* (Downers Grove, Ill.: InterVarsity Press, 2000).

[5]See Clark H. Pinnock, "The Finality of Jesus Christ in a World of Religions," in *Christian Faith and Practice in the Modern World,* ed. Mark A. Noll and David F. Wells (Grand Rapids, Mich.: Eerdmans, 1988), pp. 152-68; Clark H. Pinnock, *A Wideness in God's Mercy: The Finality of Jesus Christ in a World of Religions* (Grand Rapids, Mich.: Zondervan, 1992); Clark H. Pinnock, "An Inclusivist View," in *Four Views on Salvation in a Pluralistic World,* ed. Dennis L. Okholm and Timothy R. Phillips (Grand Rapids, Mich.: Zondervan, 1995), pp. 93-148; and Clark H. Pinnock, *Flame of Love: A Theology of the Holy Spirit* (Downers Grove, Ill.: InterVarsity Press, 1996).

limitless love and mercy who has acted redemptively in Jesus Christ for the sake of all humankind. Second, Jesus Christ is the unique incarnation of God, the only Savior for all peoples. But contrary to most evangelicals, Pinnock argues that a "high Christology" is perfectly compatible with "an optimism of salvation" that expects that many people will be saved apart from actually hearing the gospel of Jesus Christ.

> What has to be said forthrightly is that a biblically based Christology does not entail a narrowness of outlook toward other people. The church's confession about Jesus is compatible with an open spirit, with an optimism of salvation, and with a wider hope. . . . There is no salvation except through Christ, but it is not necessary for everybody to possess a conscious knowledge of Christ in order to benefit from redemption through him.[6]

Pinnock is concerned to counter what he sees as the pernicious effects of the "fewness doctrine," which holds that the benefits of Christ's work of redemption will be experienced only by the relatively few who actually hear the gospel and respond in faith to Jesus Christ. Although he recognizes non-Christian religions as including much that is false and evil, Pinnock is open to the possibility of the presence and work of the Holy Spirit in other religions. While we cannot claim that God *does* use other religions to draw people to himself, Pinnock suggests that "God *may* use religion as a way of gracing people's lives and that it is *one* of God's options for evoking faith and communicating grace." Pinnock holds that "grace operates outside the church and *may be* encountered in the context of other religions."[7] Pinnock is to be commended for raising important issues and for the clarity and forthrightness with which he articulates his own position, although most evangelicals regard his views as going well beyond what the biblical data support.[8]

At least three issues demand attention in a theology of religions: (1) the soteriological question of the destiny of the unevangelized; (2) a theological explanation for the phenomena of human religiosity; and (3) the missiological question of the extent to which we can adapt and build upon aspects of other religious traditions in establishing the church in various cultural contexts. Evangelical theologians have generally focused upon the first issue, and missiologists have at least indirectly addressed the third in discussions of contextualization. But the second issue has been largely ignored. Although we cannot do justice in this chapter to any of the three questions, we will set out in rather broad strokes what an evangelical theology of religions might look like.

---

[6]Pinnock, *Wideness in God's Mercy*, pp. 74-75.
[7]Pinnock, "Inclusivist View," p. 100. Emphasis in the original.
[8]For critiques of Pinnock's views, see Carson, *Gagging of God,* especially pp. 278-314, 351-52, 518-36; Richard, *Population of Heaven*; and Erickson, *How Shall They Be Saved?*

What Is Theology of Religions?

Since theology of religions is a subcategory of theology, it is important to clarify what we mean by theology itself. David Wells helpfully suggests that we think of theology as comprising three elements: confession, reflection upon this confession, and cultivation of a set of virtues grounded in confession and reflection.[9] Confession involves "what the Church believes," namely, "the truth that God has given to the Church through the inspired Word of God." The Scriptures, then, determine what is acknowledged as normative by the church throughout the ages. "There may be disagreements about what the Bible teaches on any one subject, as well as how that teaching should be assembled, but there is unanimous agreement that this authoritative truth lies at the heart of Christian life and practice, for this is what it means to live under the authority of Scripture."[10]

Theology also involves reflection, or "the intellectual struggle to understand what it means to be the recipient of God's Word in this present world." Such reflection must be comprehensive in drawing upon the totality of God's revelation in Scripture, making responsible connections between the various parts of Scripture and central themes relating to God's nature and purposes. It must also be informed by the wisdom of the church in the past, learning from how the church in earlier times understood and applied God's Word in different contexts. And finally, "reflection must seek to understand the connections between what is confessed and what, in any given society, is taken as normative."[11]

The third element of theology "involves the cultivation of those virtues that constitute a wisdom for life, the kind of wisdom in which Christian practice is built on the pillars of confession and surrounded by the scaffolding of reflection." Although often neglected, this element is critical, for genuine theology cannot be merely an intellectual exercise but rather must include that growth in wisdom that transforms not only the understanding but our dispositions and conduct as well. In other words, theology should result in "the type of spirituality that is centrally moral in its nature because God is centrally holy in his being, that sees Christian practice not primarily as a matter of technique but as a matter of truth, and that refuses to disjoin practice from thought or thought from practice."[12] Cultivation of a spirituality rooted in God's holiness and moral character ought to be integral to an evangelical theology of religions, affecting not only how we *think* about other religions but also how we *relate* interpersonally to adherents of other traditions.

Developing an evangelical theology of religions is central to the task of theology

---

[9]David F. Wells, *No Place for Truth: Or, Whatever Happened to Evangelical Theology?* (Grand Rapids, Mich.: Eerdmans, 1993), pp. 97-103.
[10]Ibid., p. 99.
[11]Ibid., pp. 99-100.
[12]Ibid. p. 100.

today. Asking what it means to be the recipient of God's Word in this present world—a world characterized by bewildering religious diversity, by the resurgence of traditional religions as well as the appearance of many new religious movements, by religious syncretism and eclecticism and increasingly by the ideology of religious pluralism—will involve an in-depth theological engagement with the phemonena of religions. Understanding our present world theologically will include accounting for the religious dimension of human experience in all of its multifarious patterns. In developing a theology of religions, the Western church in particular should draw upon the resources of the global church in many cultures, for Christians in many non-Western cultures already have had to address both theological and practical issues about living in the midst of other religious traditions.

Theology of religions must be clearly distinguished from the discipline of comparative religion, and one way of doing this is to consider the matter of theological method: What is the source of our data for doing theology? Is it merely the observable phenomena of the various religious traditions that can be analyzed and cataloged, or do we have access to truth about God and the world that comes to us from outside of our particular sociocultural contexts? In other words, has God actually revealed himself to us, or is theology to be done by deriving generalizations from the collective religious experience of humankind in all of its irreducible diversity?

John Hick, along with most pluralists, engages in a kind of inductive global theologizing, drawing upon the resources and experiences of all the major religions yet denying any single tradition definitive authority and modifying key elements of the various traditions to suit his purposes. However, reducing theology to comparative religion raises some significant questions: If the particular views of any single tradition cannot be accepted just as they are, why should we assume that adopting modifications of various views from many different traditions will be any more accurate? What assurance do we have that such inference from religious experiences in general is at all reliable in depicting the religious ultimate?

On the other hand, if indeed God has spoken, we are to submit to his revelation as truth and to allow it to control our beliefs, even where this truth may not be particularly palatable to contemporary tastes. The Christian church, in line with the witness of Scripture, has consistently held that God has indeed taken the initiative and revealed himself in an authoritative manner to us.[13] What distinguishes an

---

[13]Karl Barth was certainly extreme in his rejection of any divine self-disclosure outside of Christ, including general revelation, and his strong condemnation of all religion (including empirical, institutional Christianity) as unbelief. But in so doing he correctly pointed to the sharp contrast between a Christian faith that accepts as its point of departure the revealed Word of God and a theology that builds inductively from the phenomena of the religions. See Barth's "The Revelation of God as the Abolition of Religion," in *Church Dogmatics* 1/2, trans. G. T. Thomson and Harold Knight (Edinburgh: T & T Clark, 1956), pp. 280-361.

evangelical theology of religions and separates evangelicals from pluralists, then, is not simply the conclusions of each but also the methods through which these conclusions are determined. A genuinely Christian theology of religions cannot be reduced to comparative religion or philosophy of religion. Methodologically, while drawing upon these ancillary disciplines, it must take as its point of departure the authoritative revelation of God in Scripture.

Developing a comprehensive theology of religions is an enormous task that will demand collaborative work from specialists in various disciplines. But an adequate evangelical theology of religions should meet at least the following two conditions: (1) It must be shaped by the teachings, values and assumptions of the Bible and be faithful to the central confession of the church throughout the centuries. (2) It must be phenomenologically accurate in how it depicts the beliefs, institutions and practices of other religious traditions.

Biblical Themes for Theology of Religions

Although nowhere does Scripture present a comprehensive theology of religions, there is much in both the Old and New Testaments that is directly relevant to the subject.[14] The Word of God came to the patriarchs, prophets and apostles in contexts in which other religious beliefs and practices were widespread. God's call to Abram, the establishment of his covenant with the Israelites, the ensuing history of the people of Israel and their struggle with idolatry—all this took place within the context of surrounding cultures and religious traditions. Thus the relation of the God of Israel, the one true God, to the deities of the Egyptians, Canaanites, Philistines or Babylonians is a recurring theme throughout the Old Testament. Similarly the early Christians in the New Testament era lived and worshiped within a Mediterranean world that was highly syncretistic and pluralistic. Christians in Corinth, Ephesus and Rome, for example, were very familiar with other religious practices and acknowledged that the Word of God as given in Christ Jesus stood in stark contrast to the casual syncretism and pluralism of the times.

Although the Scriptures contain much that is highly relevant to a theology of religions, we must also recognize that the Bible does not deal with every issue we face today, nor is it equally clear on everything that it does address. As the Westminster Confession puts it, "All things in Scripture are not alike plain in themselves, nor alike clear unto all."[15] And these truths, combined with our fallenness and finitude (and hence the possibility of our committing error in interpreting the

---

[14]See the essays in *One God, One Lord.*

[15]The Westminster Confession of Faith (1646) 1.7, in *Creeds of the Churches*, ed. John H. Leith (Chicago: Aldine, 1963), p. 196. See also Daniel B. Clendenin, "The Only Way," *Christianity Today*, January 12, 1998, p. 37.

Scriptures), should engender within us a healthy sense of theological humility or modesty.

In looking at the Scriptures, then, we must distinguish three sets of issues: (1) issues that are explicitly treated in Scripture and concerning which the biblical teaching is clear (for example, salvation is always only by grace), (2) issues that may be touched upon in Scripture but that cannot be completely resolved because either there is some uncertainty concerning the meaning of particular biblical passages relevant to the issue or we are simply not given enough data to formulate dogmatic positions (for example, eschatological scenarios, forms of church government), and (3) matters that are not explicitly addressed in Scripture, although there may well be broad principles there that are applicable (for example, whether to offer incense at Buddhist funerals, what kind of political government is best). We must embrace with confidence what the Scriptures clearly affirm, even when doing so puts us at odds with the reigning ethos of our time. But we must treat with greater tentativeness those matters on which the Bible is less clear and over which there can be responsible disagreement. Daniel Clendenin wisely observes:

> On the complex question of religious pluralism, confident optimism in the character of God and theological modesty about our conclusions will serve us well as we proclaim that Jesus Christ is the way, the truth, and the life (John 14:6). We must try to steer a path between saying too much, which could lead to a needlessly harsh position that drives people into radically pluralistic viewpoints, and saying too little, which could to our own peril slide into religious relativism. In the words of John Calvin (1509-64), we should leave alone what God has left hidden, but not neglect what he has brought into the open, so that we might not be guilty either of excessive curiosity on the one hand or of ingratitude on the other. In his *Enchiridion* Augustine (354-430) likewise encourages believers to do their best to seek answers to the most difficult questions, "as far as that is possible in this life." Having done that, we have no alternative but to "rest patiently in unknowing."[16]

Theological modesty in this sense is not an irresponsible agnosticism or a cowardly refusal to take a stand on controversial issues. Rather, it comes from a healthy recognition that God's ways and thoughts are higher than ours and that, although we are to use the minds he has given us as best we can to probe difficult issues by examining carefully his revealed Word and the world around us, there inevitably comes a point where we must be content with unanswered questions, trusting in the goodness and justice of our sovereign God.

Nevertheless, while recognizing the need for theological humility, we must also

---

[16]Clendenin, *Many Gods, Many Lords,* p. 33. The reference to Calvin is found in *Calvin: Institutes of the Christian Religion*, ed. John T. McNeill, trans. Ford Lewis Battles (Philadelphia: Westminster Press, 1960), 2:925. The reference to Augustine is found in *Augustine: Confessions and Enchiridion*, ed. and trans. Albert C. Outler (London: SCM Press, 1955), p. 346.

affirm that Scripture is sufficiently clear on the major issues for us to formulate a basic framework within which to understand human religiosity. A biblical theology of religions should be shaped by the clear and dominant themes of Scripture informing us of the nature of God, the created world, humanity, sin and redemption. Although by no means exhaustive, the following general themes are foundational to an evangelical theology of religions, with consideration of more specific issues disciplined by this thematic framework.

1. The one eternal God is holy and righteous in all his ways. Both the Old and New Testaments are unequivocal in portraying God as morally pure and free from all evil and corruption. God is holy and entirely separated from sin and moral defilement (Lev 11:44-45; 20:26; Ps 77:13; 99:3, 5; Is 6:1-4; 40:25; 57:15; 1 Pet 1:15-16; Rev 4:8). As morally pure, God is also completely righteous and just (Ps 7:9, 11; 103:6; 119:137; 145:17; Is 45:21; Jer 12:1; Jn 17:25; Acts 3:14; Rev 15:3; 16:5; 19:2). As the psalmist says, "The LORD is righteous, he loves justice" (Ps 11:7).

The fact of God's holiness and moral purity should give us confidence in the justice of God's ways. Anxiety over the implications of Christian teaching for sincere followers of other faiths is sometimes driven by the nagging fear that, when all is said and done, we will discover that God is *not* really fair in his treatment of all people. But how could this be? If indeed, as the Scriptures consistently affirm, God is righteous and morally pure, there *cannot* be any unfairness or moral impropriety in God's dealings with humankind. Daniel Clendenin reminds us:

> Christians can be absolutely confident about the character of God when we deal with the problem of religions. While denying that all religions are equally valid or that all people will be saved, we remain utterly confident that God will treat every person with perfect love and justice. . . . For the Christian, it is unthinkable that God will treat any person of any time, place, or religion unfairly.[17]

Although we may not be able always to discern God's righteous ways, we can rest in complete confidence that the Holy One, the Judge of all the earth, will do what is right (Gen 18:25).

2. God has sovereignly created all things, including human beings, who are made in the image of God. The Scriptures consistently affirm that only God is eternal and that God freely created our universe and all that is in it (Gen 1—2; Is 40:28; 42:5; 45:18; Eph 3:9; Col 1:16). There is thus a fundamental ontological distinction between the eternal Creator God and the creation. Contrary to the views of some religions, the universe is not an extension of God, nor did it naturally emanate out of God. Furthermore, the universe, as created by God, is good (Gen 1:31).

At the apex of God's creation are human beings, who are said to be created in

---

[17]Clendenin, "Only Way," p. 36.

God's image (Gen 1:26-27; 5:1-3). Although sin has marred or corrupted the image of God in humans, even sinful persons are said to bear that image (Gen 9:6; 1 Cor 11:7; Jas 3:9), and thus even sinful humankind in some sense reflects what God is like. Scripture further teaches that, with regeneration and God's work of sanctification within the believer, the image is being restored to what it should be (Rom 12:2; 2 Cor 3:18; Eph 4:22-24; Col 3:10).

The Bible nowhere spells out precisely what the image of God includes, but D. A. Carson calls attention to the distinctiveness of human beings, alone among God's creation, as divine image bearers:

> The least that "image of God" language suggests, in addition to human personhood, is that human beings are not simply hairless apes with cranial capacities slightly larger than those of other primates, but that we are accorded an astonishing dignity; that human beings are moral creatures with special privileges and responsibilities; that there is implanted within us a profound capacity for knowing God intimately, however much we have suppressed and distorted that capacity; that we have a hunger for creating things—not, of course, *ex nihilo,* but in art, building, expression, thought, joy of discovery, science, technology; that we have a capacity for personal relations with other persons.[18]

Anthony Hoekema has suggested that the image of God includes both structural and functional aspects of the person. Structurally it includes "the entire endowment of gifts and capacities that enable man to function as he should in his various relationships and callings," including such things as the capacities for intellectual and rational reflection, moral awareness, awareness of God and worship, communication with others, the establishment of relationships with others and creative expression. Functionally, the image of God involves the cultivation of true knowledge, righteousness and holiness as "man's proper functioning in harmony with God's will for him."[19] Hoekema notes that, although the structural aspect of the image of God remains operative to some extent after the Fall, the functional aspect has been lost and must be renewed through the supernatural work of God in regeneration and sanctification. The biblical teaching on creation is rich with implications for understanding religious others, some of which will be noted below.

3. God has graciously taken the initiative in revealing himself to humankind, and although God's revelation comes in various forms, the definitive revelation for us is the written Scriptures. It certainly was possible for God to create the world in such a way that human beings have no knowledge of him or his ways. The possibility of having knowledge of God is based upon our being created with the capacity to know him, at least to some extent, and God's actually revealing himself to us. God

---

[18]Carson, *Gagging of God,* p. 205.
[19]Anthony Hoekema, *Created in God's Image* (Grand Rapids, Mich.: Eerdmans, 1986), pp. 70-72.

has not left humankind in the dark but has revealed truth about himself to us in an intelligible manner. Thus, whenever and however it occurs, knowledge of God is never something humankind attains on its own; it is always a product of God's grace and self-revelation.

Christian theologians typically distinguish between general and special revelation. Bruce Demarest and Gordon Lewis speak of general revelation as "the disclosure of God in nature, in providential history, and in the moral law within the heart, whereby all persons at all times and places gain a rudimentary understanding of the Creator and his moral demands."[20] Scripture teaches that God has revealed truth about himself in a general manner through the created universe and through the human person, in particular through the human conscience (Ps 19:1-4; Acts 14:15-17; 17:22-31; Rom 1:18-32; 2:14-15). Through general revelation humanity can understand that God exists, that he is the eternal Creator, that he is righteous and should be worshiped and that we should do what is right and refrain from doing what is wrong (Rom 1:19-20; 2:14-15).

Special revelation, on the other hand, is revelation from God given to particular people at a particular point in time. Special revelation is today usually associated with God's written revelation, the Bible, so that by "special revelation" we normally mean the written Scriptures. This is, of course, perfectly acceptable, so long as we bear in mind that according to Scripture itself the highest and fullest revelation from God is Jesus Christ, the incarnate Word of God. Although God's revelation has come at various times and in diverse forms, it has taken definitive shape in the incarnation in Jesus. As the letter to the Hebrews puts it, "In the past God spoke to our forefathers through the prophets at many times and in various ways, but in these last days he has spoken to us by his Son, whom he appointed heir of all things and through whom he made the universe. The Son is the radiance of God's glory and the exact representation of his being, sustaining all things by his powerful word" (Heb 1:1-3). The incarnation of the Word and the testimony of Scripture are crucial for our understanding of God, for as Wolfhart Pannenberg observes:

> The Christian tradition affirms that it is precisely through the biblical witness and definitively through Jesus Christ that this God is known to us. It does not deny that there is some dim and provisional knowledge of God in all humankind, but even the fact that it is *this one* God who is also otherwise known in provisional ways can be stated only on the basis of his revelation in Christ.[21]

---

[20]Bruce Demarest and Gordon Lewis, *Integrative Theology* (Grand Rapids, Mich.: Zondervan, 1987), 1:61. See also Bruce Demarest, *General Revelation: Historical Views and Contemporary Issues* (Grand Rapids, Mich.: Zondervan, 1982).

[21]Wolfhart Pannenberg, "Religious Pluralism and Conflicting Truth Claims," in *Christian Uniqueness Reconsidered: The Myth of a Pluralistic Theology of Religions*, ed. Gavin D'Costa (Maryknoll, N.Y.: Orbis, 1990), p. 97. Emphasis in the original.

We must also remember that, according to the Scriptures, God at various times has revealed himself directly in special ways to specific people outside the covenant community of Israel. Thus God appeared to, or otherwise communicated with, not only the patriarchs, prophets and apostles but also Abimelech of Gerar (Gen 20:3-7), the Egyptian pharaoh (Gen 41), Balaam (Num 22), the Babylonian king Nebuchadnezzar (Dan 2, 4) and the Roman centurion Cornelius (Acts 10:3-5). There is also the case of Melchizedek, the mysterious king of Salem, who is identified in Genesis 14:18 as "priest of God Most High." It is clear that Melchizedek had an understanding of the one true God, but the text does not tell us how he received this knowledge of God.[22] But while recognizing the variety in God's special revelation to certain individuals, Christian theology has consistently maintained that God's special revelation to the patriarchs and prophets, in the incarnation and to the apostles is preserved for us in the written Scriptures, the divinely inspired Word of God. Thus it is the Bible that is ultimately authoritative for believers and must shape our understanding of religious others.

4. God's creation, including humankind, has been corrupted by sin. The major religions all begin with the assumption that there is something fundamentally wrong with our universe and that the evils and suffering we experience are due to this basic malady. The Bible teaches that the root problem is sin, stemming from the choice of the first humans to rebel against God, thereby introducing the cancer of sin into the human race (Gen 2:16-17; 3; Rom 5:12).

Sin is a pervasive condition of the heart that affects all aspects of our being, including the way we think, our desires and our external actions and relationships with others. Sin not only involves dispositions of the heart and explicit actions (Gen 6:5) but also includes a condition of alienation from God (Is 59:2). Scripture clearly teaches that sin is universal. All people are sinners. There is no one who is righteous and consistently does what is right (Ps 14:2-3; Is 53:6; Rom 3:10-18, 23). Sin is both personal and social in its manifestations, it is found both in the individual and collectively in human cultures and societies. Furthermore, all persons, unless saved by God's grace, face God's just wrath and eternal condemnation for sin (Jn 3:36; Rev 20:11-15).

It is crucial to grasp the seriousness of the biblical understanding of sin, for the Christian teaching on salvation makes sense only against the backdrop of sin. This

---

[22]Clark Pinnock appeals to these examples, as well as Jethro, Job, the queen of Sheba and Cornelius, as instances of "holy pagans" who came to a saving relationship with God apart from access to special revelation. See Pinnock, *Wideness in God's Mercy,* pp. 161-62. However, although these examples should make us cautious about claiming that God cannot or does not communicate directly with certain individuals even today, careful examination of these cases shows that they do not provide support for Pinnock's conclusion. See Carson, *Gagging of God,* pp. 249-52, 291-99; and Erickson, *How Shall They Be Saved?* pp. 121-58.

is a point often ignored in discussions of other religions. Chris Wright incisively observes, "I find it a frustrating exercise reading the work of religious pluralists because they tend to be so vague and inadequate on what salvation actually is. And that in turn seems to me largely because they ignore the Hebrew Bible's insight on the nature and seriousness of sin."[23] Any adequate understanding of human religiosity must take very seriously the biblical teaching on sin and its effects as well as God's terrible wrath against sin.

5. *In his mercy God has provided a way, through the atoning work of Jesus Christ on the cross, for sinful persons to be reconciled to God.* Here we confront one of the great mysteries in Scripture—the Creator is gracious and merciful, a God of love who deeply cares for all people (Jn 3:16; 1 Jn 4:8). God's terrible wrath against sin and unfathomable love for all persons come together in a marvelous way in the life, death and resurrection of Jesus of Nazareth. In the incarnation—an utterly unique, one-time event in which the eternal Creator became man and took upon himself the sins of the world (2 Cor 5:21)—God himself took the initiative, providing a way for sinful persons to be forgiven and reconciled with him (Jn 3:16-18; Eph 2:4-5; 1 Pet 3:18). God's love for all people is manifest most clearly in the cross, when he gave his own Son to suffer and die as our substitute to pay the penalty for our sin (1 Jn 4:9-10). Salvation is rooted in the sinless person and atoning work of Jesus Christ (Rom 3:25; 2 Cor 5:18-19, 21; Heb 2:17; 1 Jn 2:2; 4:10), and it is because of this that Jesus is the only Savior for all of humankind, including followers of other religions. No one is reconciled to God except through the cross of Jesus Christ.

Although it is the person and work of Jesus that provides the objective basis for our salvation, there is a subjective dimension to salvation as well. Salvation—the work of God's grace and not the result of human effort or good works—must be appropriated through an act of faith in God (Eph 2:8-10). Thus the Scriptures exhort us to repent and turn to God for forgiveness and salvation (Mt 4:17; Acts 2:38; 17:30). Those who repent and come in faith to God will find him merciful and abundantly willing to pardon.

> Let the wicked forsake his way
>   and the evil man his thoughts.
> Let him turn to the LORD, and he will have mercy on him,
>   and to our God, for he will freely pardon. (Is 55:7)

Although God detests sin and evil, he is also a God of love and mercy whose compassion extends to people in all cultures, including followers of other religions.

---

[23]Christopher J. H. Wright, "The Unique Christ in the Plurality of Religions," in *The Unique Christ in Our Pluralistic World*, ed. Bruce Nicholls (Grand Rapids, Mich.: Baker, 1994), p. 39.

Turn to me and be saved,
   all you ends of the earth;
   for I am God, and there is no other. (Is 45:22)

Here we must give brief attention to an issue that has generated considerable controversy, especially among North American evangelicals: What is the fate of those who never hear the gospel of Jesus Christ? Must one be confronted with the gospel and explicitly respond to Jesus Christ in order to be saved, or is it possible for some to be saved without their actually hearing and responding to the gospel? There has always been a measure of disagreement over the issue, but it is easy to forget that what evangelicals share by way of basic commitments is far more significant than any differences among them.

For example, all evangelicals agree that Scripture teaches that all people in all cultures, including practitioners of other religions, are sinners facing God's just condemnation for sin. They agree that salvation is available only on the basis of the person and atoning work of Jesus Christ, the only Savior for all humankind. And they agree that no one is saved by being sufficiently sincere, pious or good. Salvation is always only by God's grace and through personal faith in God. Furthermore, evangelicals hold that, although ultimately not everyone will be saved, God is entirely just and fair in his dealings with humankind. No one is condemned by God unfairly. And finally, evangelicals agree that, both out of a sense of obedience to her Lord and compassion for the lost, the church is to be actively engaged in making disciples of all peoples.

In spite of a consensus on these issues, however, evangelicals do not all agree on the question of the unevangelized. We cannot here explore the relevant issues in any detail, but we should note three major ways in which evangelicals have dealt with the question.[24] It is important to recognize that differences between the positions do not concern the *means* of salvation (for example, grace versus works) but rather the amount of knowledge necessary for a saving response of faith to God.

Many evangelicals, including John Piper, Ronald Nash, R. C. Sproul and Carl F. H. Henry, hold that only those who hear the gospel and explicitly respond in faith to Jesus in this life can be saved. Explicit knowledge of the gospel of Jesus Christ is thus essential for salvation, and there is no hope for those who pass from this life without having come into contact with the gospel.[25] The obvious

---

[24]For further discussion of these and other positions, see Carson, *Gagging of God*, and Erickson, *How Shall They be Saved?*

[25]See Richard, *Population of Heaven*; John Piper, *Let the Nations Be Glad!* (Grand Rapids, Mich.: Baker, 1993), chapter 4; Ronald Nash, *Is Jesus the Only Savior?* (Grand Rapids, Mich.: Zondervan, 1994); R. C. Sproul, *Reason to Believe* (Grand Rapids, Mich.: Zondervan, 1978), pp. 48-56; R. Douglas Geivett and W. Gary Phillips, "A Particularist View: An Evidentialist Approach," in *Four Views on Salvation in a Pluralistic World*, pp. 211-45; and Carl F. H. Henry, *God, Revelation, and Authority* (Waco, Texas: Word, 1983), 6:367-69.

implication of this position, often referred to as restrictivism or exclusivism, is that the majority of humankind will be forever lost. According to this view, the importance of missions and evangelism can hardly be exaggerated, for *only* if Christians go to other cultures and communicate the gospel can those who have yet to hear be saved.

On the other hand, there is the "wider hope" perspective of Clark Pinnock, John Sanders and others that insists that we can expect large numbers of those who never hear the gospel to be saved. Although Jesus Christ is the one Savior for all humankind, and although salvation is possible only because of Christ's work on the cross, one need not know about Jesus Christ in order to be saved.[26]

Many evangelicals, however, place themselves somewhere between these positions, rejecting each of the above views for going beyond what the biblical data allow. Some in this group adopt a modest agnosticism regarding the unevangelized, refusing to speculate about how God might deal with them and leaving the matter in the hands of God. Others are willing to admit in principle that God might indeed save some who have never explicitly heard the gospel but add quickly that we simply do not know whether this occurs at all or, if so, how many might be saved in this manner. This possibility is admitted by evangelicals such as J. I. Packer, John Stott, Chris Wright, Millard Erickson and others.[27]

We must be careful not to misunderstand this position, for it is not saying that one can be saved by being a sincere follower of another religion or by being sufficiently good. As John Stott puts it, on the basis of Scripture we can be sure that "Jesus Christ is the only Saviour, and that salvation is by God's grace alone, on the ground of Christ's cross alone, and by faith alone."

> The only question, therefore, is how much knowledge and understanding of the gospel people need before they can cry to God for mercy and be saved. In the Old Testament people were "justified by faith" even though they had little knowledge or expectation of Christ. Perhaps there are others today in a similar position, who know that they are guilty before God and that they cannot do anything to win his favour, but who in self-

---

[26]In addition to the works of Clark Pinnock mentioned in footnote 5 above, see John Sanders, *No Other Name: An Investigation into the Destiny of the Unevangelized* (Grand Rapids, Mich.: Eerdmans, 1992); and John Sanders, "Inclusivism," in *What About Those Who Have Never Heard?* ed. John Sanders (Downers Grove, Ill.: InterVarsity Press, 1995), pp. 21-55.

[27]See J. I. Packer, "Evangelicals and the Way of Salvation," in *Evangelical Affirmations*, ed. Kenneth S. Kantzer and Carl F. H. Henry (Grand Rapids, Mich.: Zondervan, 1990), pp. 121-23; J. I. Packer, *God's Words: Studies of Key Bible Themes* (Downers Grove, Ill.: InterVarsity Press, 1981), p. 210; John Stott, *The Authentic Jesus* (London: Marshall Morgan & Scott, 1985), p. 83; Runia, "Gospel and Religious Pluralism"; and Alister McGrath, "A Particularist View: A Post-Enlightenment Approach," in *Four Views on Salvation in a Pluralistic World;* Millard J. Erickson, "Hope for Those Who Haven't Heard? Yes, But . . . ," *Evangelical Missions Quarterly* 11 (April 1975): 122-26; Millard J. Erickson, *How Shall They Be Saved?* and Christopher J. H. Wright, *What's So Unique About Jesus?* (Eastbourne, England: Monarch, 1990), pp. 36-39 .

despair call upon the God they dimly perceive to save them. If God saves such, as many evangelical Christians believe, their salvation is still only by grace, only through Christ, only by faith.[28]

Commenting on this possibility, Packer states:

> We may safely say (i) if any good pagan reached the point of throwing himself on his Maker's mercy for pardon, it was grace that brought him there; (ii) God will surely save anyone he brings thus far (cf Acts 10:34f; Rom. 10:12f); (iii) anyone thus saved would learn in the next world that he was saved through Christ. But what we cannot safely say is that God ever does save anyone in this way. We simply do not know.[29]

One way to appreciate the differences among the three perspectives is to consider their views on the potential efficacy of general revelation. On the one hand, no one would say that one can be saved *through* general revelation, for strictly speaking neither general nor special revelation saves anyone. Salvation is always the gift of God's grace on the basis of Christ's atonement. But is it possible that some, by God's grace, understand enough about God through general revelation and respond to this knowledge with appropriate faith?

Restrictivists typically rule out this possibility. General revelation provides some knowledge of God, so that all people are without excuse before God, but this knowledge is nevertheless insufficient for saving faith. This, however, invites the question of what it could mean to be "without excuse" if indeed those without the gospel *could not* have responded appropriately to God on the basis of what they know. As Erickson puts it, "How can people who have not heard the gospel be without excuse if they could not possibly have believed and if such belief is indispensable to salvation?"[30] Similarly David Clark observes, "The claim that natural revelation renders

---

[28]Stott, *Authentic Jesus*, p. 83.

[29]Packer, *God's Words*, p. 210.

[30]Erickson, *How Shall They be Saved?* pp. 63-64. Erickson contrasts his position as follows: "A more helpful approach is to note that the responsibility was in relationship to the available understanding. Those who lived in the Old Testament were not held responsible for not knowing, believing, or responding to the fuller knowledge of God as found in Christ. . . . What renders problematic the position that persons cannot possibly be saved through implicit faith is Paul's statement about those who have general revelation being without excuse (Rom. 1:20). In other words, if they are condemnable because they have not trusted God through what they have, it must have been possible somehow to meet his requirements through this means. If not, responsibility and condemnation are meaningless. What therefore must be the case is not that, on the basis of the internal law persons actually fulfill that law. Paul seems to be saying more than that no one fulfills the laws given to Moses, but that no one *can* be thus saved (Gal. 2:16, 21). If this is the case, then we must ask how one is saved, and the answer is that the law serves to make people guilty, to make them realize their need of grace, thus, to bring them to Christ (Gal. 3:24-25). Similarly, if individuals, on the basis of the inner law, come to realize their own sinfulness, guilt, and inability to please God, then that law would also have the effect of bringing them to grace" (ibid., p. 194).

one without excuse but cannot save is not required by Romans 1:18-23, although it is consistent with it. Romans 1:18-23 is also consistent with the claim that natural revelation fails to bring salvation to those who are rebellious and wicked, but potentially leads to salvation for those who respond to it."[31]

The other two perspectives recognize in principle that the knowledge of God attained through general revelation might be sufficient for a response of faith to God, but they disagree on the extent to which we can expect that this occurs. The "wider hope" group is quite optimistic whereas the more "agnostic" group refuses to speculate on this point. A further difference between these groups is over the degree of specificity in the knowledge of God available through general revelation. Erickson, for example, is quite specific on what he thinks Scripture affirms as being available through general revelation and thus necessary for saving faith whereas Pinnock speaks much more generally about "the faith principle," without giving it specific content.[32]

It seems to me that the wisest response to this perplexing issue is to recognize that we cannot rule out the possibility that some who never hear the gospel might nevertheless, through God's grace, respond to what they know of God through general revelation and turn to him in faith for forgiveness. But to go beyond this and to speculate about how many, if any, are saved this way is to move beyond what the Scriptures allow. Erickson correctly notes, "There are no unambiguous instances in Scripture of persons who became true believers through responding to general revelation alone. Scripture does not indicate how many, if any, come to salvation that way."[33] Indeed the clear pattern in the New Testament is for people first to hear the good news of Jesus Christ and then to respond by God's grace to the gospel in saving faith.

6. *The community of the redeemed are to share the gospel of Jesus Christ and to make disciples of all peoples, including sincere adherents of other religious traditions, so that God is honored and worshiped throughout the earth.* Finally, any biblically acceptable view of other religions must reflect the strong sense of urgency for proclaiming the gospel that undergirds both the teaching of the New Testament and the example of the apostles. The New Testament writings emerged, under the inspiration of the Holy Spirit, in contexts of mission and witness, as the early Christians moved about the Mediterranean world, sharing the good news of Jesus Christ with all who would listen. David Bosch, drawing upon the work of

---

[31]David Clark, "Is Special Revelation Necessary for Salvation?" in *Through No Fault of Their Own?* pp. 40-41.

[32]See Erickson, "Hope for Those Who Haven't Heard?" pp. 124-25; and Pinnock, *Wideness in God's Mercy*, pp. 157-68.

[33]Erickson, *How Shall They be Saved?* p. 158.

Martin Hengel, observes that "the history and theology of early Christianity are, first of all, 'mission history' and 'mission theology.' "[34] From its inception Christianity has been a missionary religion, so that the church moved out from Jerusalem to Antioch, Rome and Alexandria within a matter of decades, establishing itself in north Africa and India by the second century, as well as in what are now Spain, France and Britain by the fourth century. From there Christianity has spread so that it is literally a global religion.

The Christian gospel is inherently missionary; it is good news of reconciliation with God that must be shared with a world that is desperately lost. Commitment to missions and evangelism should flow from various motives, including obedience to the explicit command of our Lord to "make disciples of all nations" (Mt 28:19; see also Mk 16:15-16; Lk 24:45-49; Jn 20:21; Acts 1:7-8). It should be prompted by compassion for the lost who need to hear the gospel (Jn 3:16, 18, 36; Rom 1:16-17), and it ought to follow the examples of the apostles and early Christians who shared the good news freely with others. The church should be actively involved in global missions so that all peoples will worship and give glory to the one God and acknowledge Jesus Christ as Lord and Savior (Phil 2:10-11). As John Piper reminds us, "Missions exists because worship doesn't."[35]

This emphasis upon the missionary nature of Christian faith is especially controversial in the context of religious pluralism, with some even within the church calling for elimination of the call for conversion to Jesus Christ. Many Christians are frankly quite embarrassed by Christian missions, viewing it as an outdated vestige of our colonialist past. Lesslie Newbigin has remarked on the irony of the fact that, although Western Christians are very happy about the fact of the global church today, "they are embarrassed about the thing that made it possible—namely, the missions of the preceding century."[36] Newbigin's comments on the lack of missions enthusiasm among Western Christians riddled by "postcolonialist guilt" are incisive:

> The contemporary embarrassment about the missionary movement of the previous century is not, as we like to think, evidence that we have become more humble. It is, I fear, much more clearly evidence of a shift in belief. It is evidence that we are less ready to affirm the uniqueness, the centrality, the decisiveness of Jesus Christ as universal Lord and Savior, the Way by following whom the world is to find its true goal,

---

[34]David Bosch, *Transforming Mission: Paradigm Shifts in Theology of Mission* (Maryknoll, N.Y.: Orbis, 1991), p. 15. Bosch is referring to Martin Hengel, "The Origins of the Christian Mission," in *Between Jesus and Paul: Studies in the Earliest History of Christianity* (London: SCM Press, 1983), p. 53.

[35]Piper, *Let the Nations Be Glad!* p. 11.

[36]Lesslie Newbigin, *A Word in Season: Perspectives on Christian World Missions* (Grand Rapids, Mich.: Eerdmans, 1994), p. 122.

the Truth by which every other claim to truth is to be tested, the Life in whom alone life in its fullness is to be found.[37]

Similarly, the Dutch missiologist Johannes Verkuyl perceptively remarks, "The subversion of the missionary mandate one encounters in various contemporary missiologies and models of theology of religion must simply be called what it is: betrayal of Jesus Christ."[38]

Accuracy in Portraying Other Religions

We noted earlier that an adequate theology of religions must be both faithful to the witness of Scripture and accurate in the ways in which it depicts the beliefs and practices of other traditions. We must now turn our attention briefly to this second requirement. It is easy enough to develop views based upon simplistic caricatures, but this hardly amounts to a responsible theology of religions. After reviewing Christian literature on other religions, Charles and Betty Taber point out the tendency to caricature:

> The Christian literature even more often displayed explicit or implicit a priori positions which prevented writers from seeing what they were looking at. We have found a plethora of sweeping generalizations about each religion, and about "the religions," as if they were all alike, and as if their adherents were self-evidently in the same situation in relation to God. In fact, in this century Christian stances toward "other" religions have tended, as on so many other subjects, to polarize, and so to become caricatures of responsible scholarship.[39]

This is unfortunate and unacceptable. An adequate theology of religions must accurately reflect the beliefs and practices of the religious traditions. We must avoid reductionistic and simplistic generalizations as we give due attention to the enormous variety among and within religions.

We must also acknowledge the diversity *across* religions, so that in addition to the "major" religions of Hinduism, Buddhism and Islam we include the data from less prominent traditions as well. This will require making careful empirical studies of shamanism, animism and polytheism in local traditions; exploring the bewildering array of new emerging religious traditions; studying complex syncretistic movements that combine elements of major religions with ancient indigenous traditions; learning about the endless variety of folk religious practices and so on.

But we must also be sensitive to the remarkable diversity *within* particular reli-

---

[37]Ibid., p. 115.

[38]Johannes Verkuyl, "The Biblical Notion of Kingdom: Test of Validity for Theology of Religion," in *Good News of the Kingdom*, p. 77.

[39]Charles R. Taber and Betty J. Taber, "A Christian Understanding of 'Religion' and 'the Religions,' " *Missiology: An International Review* 20, no. 1 (1992): 70.

gions so that, for example, we don't simply identify Hinduism with the philosophical monism of Advaita Vedanta but acknowledge the numerous theistic, as well as polytheistic and even atheistic, Hindu traditions. Similarly, we must take into account the enormous diversity within Buddhism, ranging from clearly nontheistic forms of Theravada Buddhism to more theistic forms of Pure Land Buddhism, as well as animistic strands of folk Buddhism. We should observe differences between "high religion" (the philosophical and theological traditions) and "folk religion" (which often bears little resemblance to the former) as well.

A concern for phenomenological accuracy also requires that we give proper attention both to similarities and to differences between Christian faith and other traditions. Too often Christian responses to other religions grow out of a one-sided cataloging of the sharp differences between, say, the ontologies of Vedanta Hinduism and Christianity, in this way reinforcing the uniqueness of Christianity. The distinctiveness of Christianity is obvious when it is contrasted with the philosophical monism of Advaita Vedanta, the atheism of Theravada Buddhism or the polytheism of Shinto. But what evangelicals often ignore are the striking similarities between aspects of Christianity and aspects of other religions. For example, evangelicals tend to ignore the theistic emphases of some forms of Hinduism, such as that of the Vishisht-Advaita Vedanta tradition of Ramanuja, or the monotheism of Islam. Similarly, evangelicals often emphasize the distinctiveness of the place of grace within Christianity while ignoring the fact that certain forms of Hinduism and Pure Land Buddhism also acknowledge human inability to "save" oneself and the need to rely totally upon the grace or merit of, for example, Vishnu or the Amida Buddha.[40] In his careful and important study, John Carman points out the remarkable similarities among aspects of the Srivaishnava tradition of Hinduism, the Pure Land Buddhism of Shinran and Protestant Christianity.[41] And as we saw in chapter nine, consideration of basic moral values and ethical teachings in the religions reveals some significant commonalities as well.

Obviously the phenomena from each tradition must be understood carefully within their own contexts, so that we are not misled by surface similarities that obscure deeper differences. Vishnu is not merely another name for Yahweh; *karuna* (compassion) in

---

[40]In an important work Galen Amstutz argues that in spite of the fact that the Pure Land Buddhist schools attract the largest following in Japan, Western scholars of Japanese religion, as well as some Japanese scholars, have largely ignored the Pure Land traditions in favor of more exotic traditions such as Zen. Ironically, the similarity of Pure Land Buddhism to Protestant Christianity reduced interest in it, as scholars were more attracted to what is novel and different. See Galen Amstutz, *Interpreting Amida: History and Orientalism in the Study of Pure Land Buddhism* (Albany: State University of New York Press, 1997).

[41]See John Carman, *Majesty and Meekness: A Comparative Study of Contrast and Harmony in the Concept of God* (Grand Rapids, Mich.: Eerdmans, 1994).

Buddhism is not identical with agape (love) in Christianity; grace in Christianity is not precisely the same thing as the transfer of merit in Pure Land Buddhism; Shinran is not Luther and so on. But the fact that these concepts are not identical does not negate the fact that there are significant similarities between them, and a comprehensive theological understanding of other religions must account for not only the many differences between Christian faith and other religions but the commonalities as well.

The issue of commonalities and differences is related to the question (much discussed in the earlier twentieth century) of continuity or discontinuity between Christianity and other religions. Rather than think of an exclusive disjunction— either complete discontinuity or continuity—we should recognize both continuities and discontinuities, depending upon the specific question and particular tradition at issue. Furthermore, we must be careful to strike the proper balance here, for focusing excessively upon commonalities between Christianity and other religions will produce a distorted picture not only of the religions but also of the teachings of Scripture. The more inclusivist theologies of religion stress continuity to such an extent that they end up with rather naive views of other religions and obscure the radical discontinuities between Jesus and other religious figures. And of course, with radical pluralism the obsession with continuity eliminates any real differences among religions in terms of truth and salvific efficacy.

However, one can also err at the other extreme by so emphasizing discontinuity that there is no real point of contact or commonality between Christianity and other religions. What *seem* to be similarities or aspects of truth and goodness in other religions are explained away as elaborate deceptions by the Adversary. Faithfulness to the biblical witness and the empirical realities, however, suggests that a careful recognition of both continuity and discontinuity should inform an evangelical theology of religions. Missiologist Gerald Anderson rightly states:

> In faithfulness to biblical revelation, both of these traditions [continuity and discontinuity] must be affirmed and maintained, but this is difficult to do when some persons affirm continuity with doubtful uniqueness and others affirm uniqueness without continuity. What is needed in our theology of religions is uniqueness *with* continuity.[42]

Recognition of significant similarities in no way detracts from the distinctiveness and unique truth of God's revelation in Christ or the finality of Jesus Christ as the one Lord and Savior for all humankind.

Theology of Religions and Culture

As we saw in chapter six, religions are complex realities comprising multidimen-

---

[42]Gerald H. Anderson, "Theology of Religions and Missiology: A Time of Testing," in *Good News of the Kingdom,* pp. 205-6. Emphasis in the original.

sional ways of understanding and responding to what is taken to be of ultimate significance. Following Ninian Smart, we noted that religious traditions include distinctive worldviews, kinds of experience, narratives, doctrines, ethical norms, rituals, institutions, material forms and social patterns.[43] When understood in this way, what we call "religious traditions" overlap significantly with what we refer to as "culture." Thus we cannot understand particular religious traditions adequately unless we take into account their relationship with culture.

It is helpful to think of culture as a historically transmitted pattern of meanings embodied in symbols that are reflected in behavior, values, ideas and institutions through which people understand the cosmos and their place in it, communicate with each other and structure communal life patterns. As such, culture includes the products of a wide variety of human activities—reflection upon life experiences and the world around us; communication with others; the establishment of normative patterns of individual and communal behavior; relationships with others; social and political institutions; artistic expressions and so on. Culture includes the many dimensions of social life through which people make sense of their experiences and pass on to succeeding generations the wisdom and expectations thus acquired. The link between religion and culture means that studying another religion is not something that can be done apart from considering the broader social and cultural contexts within which it finds expression.

The relation between religion and culture should affect our theological understanding of religion. Just as human cultures, as the product both of God's creative activity and of human sin, reflect a mixture of good and evil, so too we should expect that in the religious dimensions of human experience there exist elements of both good and evil, both truth and falsity. Moreover, just as there are both commonalities and differences across cultures, so that no two cultures are totally incommensurable, so too we should expect that there will be both commonalities and differences among the various religions. The complex realities suggested by the overlap of the religious and cultural dimensions are reflected in the WEF Manila Declaration (1992):

> The term "religion" refers to a complex phenomenon and it is important to distinguish between its various aspects. In many societies, religion forms an important part of their identity. As such, a diversity of religions—or, more accurately, a diversity of certain aspects of the religions—may be affirmed as part of the richness of God's good creation, although it must be immediately added that people have often sinfully used these religions, including Christianity, to create a false ultimacy and superiority for their own cultures and religious groups. Religions may also be understood as expres-

---

[43]Ninian Smart, *Worldviews: Crosscultural Explorations of Human Beliefs*, 2nd ed. (Englewood Cliffs, N.J.: Prentice-Hall, 1995).

sions of the longing for communion with God, which is an essential human character-istic since we are created in the image of God for the purpose of service to him, fellowship with him, and praise for him. Here also, while always corrupted by sin in practice, we may affirm in principle the goodness of a diversity of some aspects of the religions.[44]

Although religion and culture are closely interconnected, we must be careful not to reduce a religion to its particular cultural expression. It is as wrong, for example, to identify Islam with its cultural expression in Iran or Saudi Arabia as it is to identify Christianity with its cultural manifestation in the United States or Italy. In each case there is both the link between the religion and its surrounding culture as well as the gap between the religion's ideals and its empirical expression.

The connection between religion and culture has significant implications for mis-siology. A central concern of missiology is contextualization, which involves using forms or symbols that are sufficiently familiar to a particular culture and that ade-quately convey biblical meanings in an effort to maximize understanding and accep-tance of the gospel within that culture.[45] Since culture and religion are often so intertwined, serious consideration of contextualization inevitably leads to questions about the relation of Christian faith to indigenous religious beliefs and practices, affecting everything from translation of the Scriptures to how Christians should regard local customs. The line between cultural and religious issues can be imprecise.

In Japan, for example, it is often difficult to distinguish the religious from what is strictly cultural, as contemporary Japanese culture is permeated with concepts, practices and institutions that once were, and perhaps still are, deeply religious in nature. Is the tea ceremony, widely recognized as a symbol of traditional Japan, religious or cultural? Tea was first introduced into Japan from China by Buddhist monks, and until the sixteenth century it was used primarily by monks within the monasteries. The tea ceremony itself was introduced in the thirteenth century and was widely practiced by Zen monks, thereby becoming closely identified with Zen.[46] The simple elegance of the tea ceremony communicated Zen themes of stillness, emptiness and simplicity. But symbolic meanings change with time, and many would hold that the tea ceremony has outgrown its Zen framework and is now just a cultural symbol. Indeed some Christian pastors have adopted the tea ceremony,

---

[44]"WEF Manila Declaration," pp. 15-16.

[45]For good discussions of contextualization, see Darrell L. Whiteman, "Contextualization: The Theory, the Gap, the Challenge," *International Bulletin of Missionary Research* 21, no. 1 (1997): 2-7; Paul G. Hiebert, *Anthropological Reflections on Missiological Issues* (Grand Rapids, Mich.: Baker, 1994), chapters 4-5; and David J. Hesselgrave and Edward Rommen, *Contextualization: Meanings, Methods, and Models* (Grand Rapids, Mich.: Baker, 1989).

[46]D. T. Suzuki, *Zen and Japanese Culture* (Princeton, N.J.: Princeton University Press, 1959), p. 272.

infusing Christian meanings into the ceremony in an effort to link Christian faith with Japanese culture.

The blending of the religious and cultural can be seen in language, institutions and festivals as well. The Japanese language is full of expressions and proverbs reflecting Buddhist themes, such as rebirth and *karma*. For example, *"Sode furi-au mo tasho no en"* is a famous saying that roughly translates as "Even brushing sleeves with someone as you pass by is the result of a connection in a previous existence." What seems to be a chance encounter actually has its roots in *karma* and previous lives.[47] Or we might consider festivals, such as the *shichi-go-san* (seven-five-three) ceremony for children ages seven, five and three. The children are dressed up and taken to local Shinto shrines, where Shinto priests perform a ritual of purification and then report the names of the children to the *kami*. "This rite is performed to give thanks to the tutelary deities for having permitted the children to reach these ages safely and also to pray for continued growth and good health."[48] The religious meanings of the ritual are unmistakable, but it would also be fair to say that for many Japanese the ceremony is primarily a cultural rite of passage, in which religious meanings are irrelevant. Further examples of the inter-connectedness of religion and culture include ancestor veneration practices, the martial arts, funerals and the enormously popular sport of sumo wrestling, which is steeped in Shinto symbolism. In each case it can be difficult to draw a clear line between the "cultural" and the "religious."

Any serious Christian engagement with Japanese culture will involve struggling with questions about traditional Japanese religious values and beliefs. Further-more, the fact that religion and culture are so closely interconnected means that Japanese often understand rejection of traditional religious beliefs and practices as at least implicit rejection of Japanese culture. When a Christian insists that salva-tion is available only through Jesus Christ, and not through Pure Land Buddhism, this can be interpreted as not only rejection of Buddhist teaching but also of Japa-nese culture as somehow inadequate. Thus, not only in Japan but throughout Asia, the question of the relation of Christian faith to other religions is inseparable from broader issues of the relation of Christianity to local cultures.

How Should We Think of Other Religions?

A theology of religions should provide a theological explanation for the phenome-

---

[47]See Stuart D. B. Picken, *Buddhism: Japan's Cultural Identity* (Tokyo: Kodansha, 1982), p. 58. Similarly, Christianity has influenced the English language so that it includes many expressions and proverbs that come from the Bible: "you reap what you sow"; "an eye for an eye"; "do unto others what you would have them do to you"; "don't cast your pearls before swine" and so on.

[48]Momoo Yamaguchi and Setsuko Kojima, eds., *A Cultural Dictionary of Japan* (Tokyo: Kenkyusha, 1979), p. 265.

non of human religiosity itself. Why are human beings incurably religious? Are non-Christian religions nothing more than satanic deception and evil? Or are they merely benign expressions of humankind reaching out for God? Can other religions be regarded in some sense as forerunners or precursors of Christianity, so that Christianity is really the fulfillment of non-Christian religions? If so, in what sense? These are difficult questions, but I suggest that human religiosity, or religion in general, should be understood in terms of the following three interrelated biblical themes: (1) creation and revelation, (2) sin, and (3) satanic and demonic influence.

Creation and revelation. It is no accident that religious interest and expression are universal in human cultures. The capacity to reflect upon one's place within the cosmos, the awareness of a reality transcending the physical world, the yearning for the Creator and life beyond physical death, the recognition that the world as we experience it is not the way it is supposed to be, the search for ways in which to appease or propitiate God or the gods and to attain a better existence—all of this and more, which we identify with religion, is possible only because God has created humankind with particular abilities and dispositions.

The great Reformer John Calvin spoke of an immediate awareness of God's reality, the *sensus divinitatis,* that all people as God's creatures have: "There is within the human mind, and by natural instinct, an awareness of divinity." Drawing upon Cicero, Calvin states, "Yet there is, as the eminent pagan says, no nation so barbarous, no people so savage, that they have not a deep-seated conviction that there is a God."[49] Even idolatry, the perversion of worship, is taken to be evidence of this. However, for Calvin this inherent awareness of God does not lead to salvation, for people do not respond appropriately to what they know to be true about God. In line with the apostle Paul's argument in Romans 1—2, Calvin is concerned to establish a general awareness of God in order to underscore human responsibility before God. But in so doing he makes it clear that humankind in general does know something about God.[50] Calvin's point here is an important one and helps to explain human religiosity, for, however distorted or incomplete it might be in any

---

[49]Calvin *Institutes of the Christian Religion*, 1:43-44. Much earlier Cicero had said, "For what nation or what tribe of men is there but possesses untaught some 'preconception' of the gods?" (Cicero, *De natura deorum* I.xvi.43, trans. H. Rackham [New York: G. P. Putnam's Sons, 1933], p. 45).

[50]Calvin states, "Since, therefore men one and all perceive that there is a God and that he is their Maker, they are condemned by their own testimony because they have failed to honor him and to consecrate their lives to his will. . . . But upon his individual works he has engraved unmistakable marks of his glory, so clear and so prominent that even unlettered and stupid folk cannot plead the excuse of ignorance" (*Institutes of the Christian Religion* 1:44, 52). For a helpful discussion of some of the epistemological issues surrounding Calvin's *sensus divinitatis*, see Paul Helm, *Faith and Understanding* (Grand Rapids, Mich.: Eerdmans, 1997), chapter 8.

given case, the fact that there is any awareness of the divine at all is due to God's creating us with the capacity for *some* understanding of the divine realm. The religions, whatever else they might include, are testimony to this awareness.

Closely related to this is the notion of the *imago Dei*—the idea that human beings are created in God's image. In particular, if we understand the image of God to include the capacities for reflection, communication, relationships with others, creative self-expression and especially moral awareness, then it makes sense to think of the expression of these capacities in the religions as products of what God has given in creation. To be sure, with sin these capacities are not expressed as they should be, resulting in idolatry. But the *possibility* of such expression in the first place, however misguided in actual fact, is a gift of God's grace in creation.

The doctrine of general revelation is also crucial for understanding religion. This is closely related to the teaching on creation, as is evident in Calvin's notion of the *sensus divinitatis*. But what is especially emphasized here is God's self-revelation through the created order and human conscience, through which human beings are aware of some truths about God and our responsibility to him. While Scripture affirms a general awareness of God and our accountability before him, it nowhere suggests that this rudimentary understanding is equally clear and complete for all persons or among cultures. It is consistent with the biblical witness to hold that the degree of precision and fullness of understanding can vary from person to person and from culture to culture. Indeed we can expect variance in such understanding within a society, from one generation to the next, so that there is a measure of fluidity in the specific content available through general revelation. This diversity in awareness of truth about God is reflected in cultures and religious traditions, with theistic traditions such as Islam and Judaism being much closer to Christianity than, say, Theravada Buddhism. What is emphasized in Scripture, however, is that such awareness is sufficient to hold people morally accountable to God for how they respond to it.

Thought of in these terms, the religious dimension of human life is an expression of humanity as God's creation and can be regarded, in part, as a response to God's self-revelation. As Christopher J. H. Wright puts it, "The whole human race, therefore, has the capacity of being addressed by God and of making response to him. Man is the creature who is aware of his accountability to God."[51] Similarly, the Dutch missiologist J. H. Bavinck says, "Religion is the human answer to divine, or at least allegedly divine, revelation."[52]

The doctrines of creation and revelation have significant implications for how

---

[51]Wright, "Christian and Other Religions," p. 4.

[52]J. H. Bavinck, *The Church Between Temple and Mosque: A Study of the Relationship Between the Christian Faith and Other Religions* (Grand Rapids, Mich.: Eerdmans, 1966), p. 18.

we think of religious others.[53] For example, given God's general revelation and the fact that all people bear the divine image, we should not be surprised to find elements of truth and value in other religions. There is no reason to maintain that everything taught by non-Christian religions is false or that there is nothing of value in them. Not only is this not demanded by Scripture but in fact it is not consistent with what we see in other traditions. We can think of the religions as displaying, in varying degrees, a rudimentary awareness of God's reality through creation and general revelation. This is not to suggest that God directly revealed himself to, say, the Buddha or Muhammad, or that the sacred scriptures of the non-Christian religions are divinely inspired. Not at all. But it is to acknowledge that the founding figures of other religious traditions, as human beings created in God's image and recipients of general revelation, had varying degrees of understanding of God's reality that is reflected in their teachings and practices. But such understanding is partial and often distorted. For example, we noted in chapter eight that there are striking commonalities across religions in basic moral principles, exemplified in the numerous expressions of the Golden Rule. But this should not be unexpected. After all, given that all people have access to God's general revelation and are created in his image, we should expect to see fundamental moral principles such as the Golden Rule reflected in the various religions. It would be surprising if this were not the case.

Furthermore, the teaching on creation in particular has implications for how we think about religious others. Wright perceptively remarks:

> As the image of God, man still reflects the Creator, responds to Him, recognizes His hand in creation and, along with the rest of the animal creation, looks to the hand of God for the very supports of life itself (Ps 104:27f). God is involved in the whole life of man, for man is human only through his relationship to God. Man, therefore, cannot utterly remove God from himself without ceasing to be human. This fact about man is prior to any specifics of "religious" belief or practice. Our fellow human being is first, foremost and essentially one in the image of God, and only secondarily a Hindu, Muslim, or secular pagan. So, inasmuch as his religion is part of his humanity, whenever we meet one whom we call "an adherent of another religion," we meet someone who, in his religion as in all else, has *some* relationship to the Creator God, a relationship within which he is addressable and accountable.[54]

The unity of the human race as creatures bearing God's image means that the many differences among peoples are really secondary to what all human beings share in common. Commonalities across ethnic, cultural and religious boundaries

---

[53]For a creative treatment of the implications of the doctrine of revelation for other religions, see McDermott, *Can Evangelicals Learn from World Religions?*

[54]Wright, "Christian and Other Religions," p. 5. Emphasis in original.

are ultimately more significant than the differences that distinguish them.

This has powerful implications for how Christians should relate to followers of other religions. Unfortunately most of us understand and relate to other people on the basis of fixed categories that define the other in terms of ethnicity, class, gender and religion. Labels and categories can be useful, but they can also be distorting. If the primary category through which I understand a particular group is "Hindu," then to some extent the individuality and distinctiveness of the others are violated by my preconceptions of what a Hindu ought to be. I may well be blind to the fact that a given individual does not really fit my picture of a Hindu. Furthermore, in relating to others primarily through the category of "Hindus" I am emphasizing what sets them apart from me, namely different religious beliefs and practices. On the other hand, if I recognize others primarily as fellow creatures who bear God's image, and only secondarily as Hindus, then I deliberately acknowledge that we have more in common as human beings than what separates us in terms of religious affiliation. The differences are still there and should not be minimized, but when one looks first for commonalities, points of contact with the other can more easily be established. And from this bridges of communication and relationship will more easily follow.

From the biblical teaching on creation and revelation, then, we can think of religions as expressions of a genuine, although misguided, search and longing for God. Persons are created in the image of God, with a capacity for being addressed by God and responding to him. In spite of sin, there remains a rudimentary awareness of God's reality and of our accountability to God. The religious dimension of humankind, then, can be seen in part as an expression of the creature reaching out for that intimacy with the Creator for which we were made. This sense of longing for the divine was captured beautifully by the great North African theologian Augustine: "You [God] made us for yourself and our hearts find no peace until they rest in you."[55]

Sin. It would be misleading to think of religions as simply benign expressions of humanity reaching out for God. Sin has corrupted all aspects of the human person, including the capacities giving expression to human religiosity, and thus religion too manifests the ravages of sin. Scripture maintains that, although people have some awareness of God's reality and responsibility to him, they characteristically do not respond appropriately to this knowledge but rather suppress the truth and reject what they know to be right. This rebellion too finds expression in the religious dimension of human experience. Chris Wright states:

[W]e have to add at once that his relationship has been corrupted by sin so that in his

---

[55]Augustine, *Confessions*, trans. R. S. Pine-Coffin (London: Penguin, 1961), p. 21.

religion, as in all else, man lives in a state of rebellion and disobedience. Indeed, if religion is "man giving account of his relation to God," it will be in the religious dimension of human life that we would expect to find the clearest evidence of the radical fracture of that relationship. If the immediate response of the fallen Adam in us is to hide from the presence of the living God, what more effective way could there be than through religious activity which gives us the illusion of having met and satisfied him? "Even his religiosity is a subtle escape from the God he is afraid and ashamed to meet." The fallen duplicity of man is that he *simultaneously* seeks after God his Maker and flees from God his Judge. Man's religions, therefore, simultaneously manifest both these human tendencies. This is what makes a simplistic verdict on other religions— whether blandly positive or wholly negative—so unsatisfactory and indeed unbiblical.[56]

Here, then, is the paradox of humankind: On the one hand, persons are created in the image of God and thus long for a proper relationship of the creature to the Creator. On the other hand, they are rebels and sinners and thus try desperately to hide from God. While religion can be a way of reaching out to God, it can also be a means of hiding from him. Significantly, Jesus directed his harshest comments against the Pharisees and other leaders of Jewish religion—those who would have been regarded by their contemporaries as the most religious, the most pious and the best that Judaism had to offer (Mt 23:1-36). It is often our religiosity (even "Christian" religiosity)—our attempts to try to impress God or to earn his favor through following carefully prescribed religious rituals and rules—that keeps us furthest away from him.

Satanic influence. Finally, a genuinely biblical perspective on other religions should recognize that much religious activity and belief is influenced by the Adversary, Satan. It would be too simplistic to hold that *all* non-Christian religious phenomena are merely satanic in origin, but it would be equally naive to suggest that *none* of them are. The apostle Paul reminded his readers that the pagan sacrifices in Corinthian religion, which might have seemed quite innocent, were in fact offered to demons (1 Cor 10:20). This is a sobering warning that should caution us against undue optimism concerning non-Christian religious practices.

Both the Old and New Testaments consistently denounce as idolatry the worship of other deities and participation in the rites of other religious traditions (Ex 20:2-5; Deut 7:1-6, 25-26; Ps 115; Is 41:21-24; 44:9-20; Acts 14:15; 17:16, 23-24, 29; 1 Cor 8:4-6). Furthermore, Scripture speaks of those who are not yet saved as "spiritually blind" and under the power of the "god of this age" (2 Cor 4:4; Eph 4:17-18). Certainly Satan uses false teaching and deception to blind followers of other reli-

---

[56]Wright, "Christian and Other Religions," p. 5. Emphasis in original. The quotation within Wright's statement is from John Stott, *Christian Mission in the Modern World* (London: Falcon, 1975), p. 69.

gions, just as false beliefs can be used to oppress atheists or agnostics who profess no religious commitments.[57] But within the religious dimension, perhaps satanic distortion is most evident in the common tendency to blur the distinction between the Creator and the creature. Eve was tempted by the suggestion that she, a mere creature, could become like God (Gen 3:4-5). The tendency to blur the distinction between God and humankind—either to bring God down to our level or to deify human beings—is a common feature of religion and can be found in the polytheistic religions of the ancient world as well as in many modern-day traditions. It is especially pronounced in some Hindu traditions and Shinto, and it has become popular in the West in the New Age movement, which preaches the essential divinity of human beings. Yet this is merely an echo of Satan's deception: "You will be like God" (Gen 3:5).

A discussion of demonic influence and the religions would not be complete without some mention of the remarkable recent interest in missiology in a cluster of controversial concepts and practices associated with spiritual warfare. The 1980s and 1990s saw the proliferation of publications, seminars and special courses dealing with power evangelism, power encounters, exorcism, curses, demonic transmission, territorial spirits, spiritual mapping, strategic prayer walks and so on—all growing out of the assumption that the reason Christian missions face such stiff resistance in certain societies is failure of the church to understand spiritual realities properly and to use particular practices in combating the demonic powers.[58] According to this view, other religions are basically hostile domains of darkness and evil, controlled by demonic powers. The proper approach to other religions, then, is to claim our authority in Christ and to challenge directly the demonic powers, driving them out so that the gospel can be embraced. The issues are complex and cannot be treated here in any detail, but a few brief comments are in order.[59]

---

[57]We should not assume that idolatry is found only among non-Christian religions in non-Western cultures. Much in the modernized and secularized West can also be idolatrous, as Vinoth Ramachandra reminds us in *Gods That Fail: Modern Idolatry and Christian Mission* (Downers Grove, Ill.: InterVarsity Press, 1996).

[58]The literature here is voluminous. See, for example, Charles Kraft, *Christianity with Power: Your Worldview and Your Experience of the Supernatural* (Ann Arbor, Mich.: Servant, 1989); Charles Kraft and Mark White, eds., *Behind Enemy Lines: An Advanced Guide to Spiritual Warfare* (Ann Arbor, Mich.: Servant, 1994); Ed Murphy, *Handbook for Spiritual Warfare* (Nashville: Thomas Nelson, 1992); C. Peter Wagner, *The Third Wave of the Holy Spirit* (Ann Arbor, Mich.: Servant, 1988); C. Peter Wagner, *Warfare Prayer* (Ventura, Calif.: Regal, 1992); C. Peter Wagner, ed., *Engaging the Enemy: How to Fight and Defeat Territorial Spirits* (Ventura, Calif.: Regal, 1991); and C. Peter Wagner, ed., *Breaking Strongholds in the City: How to Use Spiritual Mapping to Make Your Prayers More Strategic* (Ventura, Calif.: Regal, 1993).

[59]For an excellent critique of the assumptions and practices associated with this emphasis, see Robert J. Priest, Thomas Campbell and Bradford A. Mullen, "Missiological Syncretism: The New Animistic Paradigm," in *Spiritual Power and Missions: Raising the Issues*, ed. Edward Rommen (Pasadena: Calif.:

We must recognize the reality of the spiritual realm, including Satan and demonic powers. A spiritual battle is being waged between the kingdom of God and the god of this age, and demonic presence and activity are part of the religions. Too often Western Christians have adopted a functional naturalism that, while theoretically acknowledging the supernatural dimension, in practice ignores it. In a seminal essay in 1982 Paul Hiebert rightly called attention to the reality of what he termed the "excluded middle"—a realm of "supernatural this-worldly beings and forces" that is widely acknowledged in non-Western societies.[60] In this realm spiritual beings and forces distinct from the natural world are nevertheless understood to be present and active within it. Whereas Western missionaries tend to ignore this dimension because of naturalistic biases, most non-Western societies assume it. However, in calling for Western missionaries to take this reality more seriously Hiebert also sounded an important warning:

> Yet we need to center our theology on God and his acts and not, as modern secularism and animism do, on human beings and their desires. We need to focus on worship and our relationship to God, and not on ways to control God for our own purposes through chants and formulas. . . . It is all too easy to make Christianity a new magic in which we as gods make God do our bidding.[61]

Hiebert's concerns are well founded, for many have observed that the recent emphasis upon techniques in spiritual warfare often looks like "Christian animism." Thus, in their important critique of this movement, Robert Priest, Thomas Campbell and Bradford Mullen state, "Many missionaries and missiologists unwittingly have internalized and are propagating animistic and magical notions of spirit power that are at odds with biblical teaching, using such notions as the basis for missiological method."[62] A responsible theology of religions must avoid falling into a kind of Christian animism or syncretism that regards the phenomena of other religions simply as manifestations of demonic activity and understands the appropriate Christian response to other religions primarily in terms of dramatic displays of power.

Radical Discontinuity: Jesus Christ

In a fascinating discussion Harvey Cox, speaking from years of experience in interreligious dialogue, chides fellow ecumenists for minimizing the figure of Jesus

---

William Carey Library, 1995), pp. 9-87. The essay is followed by two responses: Charles Kraft, "'Christian Animism' or God-Given Authority?" pp. 88-136, and Patrick Johnstone, "Biblical Intercession: Spiritual Power to Change Our World," pp. 137-63—both in the same volume.

[60]Paul Hiebert, "The Flaw of the Excluded Middle," *Missiology: An International Review* 10, no. 1 (1982): 35-47; reprinted in Paul Hiebert, *Anthropological Reflections on Missiological Issues* (Grand Rapids, Mich.: Baker, 1994), pp. 189-201.

[61]Hiebert, *Anthropological Reflections*, pp. 200-201.

[62]Priest, Campbell and Mullen, "Missiological Syncretism," pp. 11-12.

Christ in dialogue. Presuming that the question of Jesus will be too divisive, some Christian participants focus upon less controversial issues, hoping to introduce the subject of Jesus at a later stage. However, the issue of Jesus is often not broached at all or, if it is, Jesus is mentioned with some embarrassment, almost as an after-thought. But Cox correctly observes that to ignore or set aside the question of Jesus is to be less than honest in one's encounter with others.

> For the vast majority of Christians, including those most energetically engaged in dia-logue, Jesus is not merely a background figure. He is central to Christian faith. Not only do the Christian dialoguers recognize this, but so do their Muslim, Buddhist, Shinto, Hindu, and Jewish conversation partners. Wherever one starts . . . any honest dialogue between Christians and others will sooner or later—and in my experience it is usually sooner—have to deal with the figure of Jesus.[63]

Whereas some Christians are reluctant to bring up the subject of Jesus, fre-quently it is precisely this that others are most eager to discuss. Cox admits that in spite of his initial reluctance to discuss the person of Jesus too quickly, "I soon dis-covered my interlocutors wanted me to, and their bearing sometimes suggested that they did not believe they were really engaged in a brass-tacks conversation with a Christian until that happened."[64]

Interest in the person of Jesus by followers of other religions should not be sur-prising. As historian Jaroslav Pelikan remarks, "Regardless of what anyone may personally believe about him, Jesus of Nazareth has been the dominant figure in the history of Western culture for almost twenty centuries."[65] No serious discussion of the relation of Christianity to other faiths can proceed far without coming to grips with the towering figure of Jesus.[66] Sooner or later, the blunt question put by Jesus to his followers—"Who do people say I am?" (Mk 8:27)—must be confronted, for Christian faith includes, above all else, commitment to the Lordship of Jesus Christ. Nowhere are the discontinuities between Christianity and other religions more pronounced than in comparing Jesus with the great leaders of other tradi-

---

[63]Harvey Cox, *Many Mansions: A Christian's Encounter with Other Faiths* (Boston: Beacon, 1988), pp. 7-8.

[64]Ibid., pp. 8-9.

[65]Jaroslav Pelikan, *Jesus Through the Centuries: His Place in the History of Culture* (New Haven, Conn.: Yale University Press, 1985), p. 1.

[66]Few non-Christian traditions have manifested as deep an interest in Jesus, or used him so effectively for their own purposes, as the neo-Hindu movements of the nineteenth and early twentieth centuries. Thinkers such Raja Ram Mohan Roy, Sri Ramakrishna, Swami Vivekananda, Keshub Chandra Sen, Sarvepalli Radhakrishnan and Mahatma Gandhi had deep appreciation for what they saw as Jesus the moral teacher, while they rejected the orthodox Christian teachings about Jesus as distinctively divine and the only Savior. With them, Jesus becomes another Asian holy man, serenely imparting transcendental moral truths. See Arvind Sharma, ed., *Neo-Hindu Views of Christianity* (Leiden, Holland: E. J. Brill, 1988).

tions. God was present and active in Jesus in a manner paralleled nowhere else.

The importance and distinctiveness of Jesus within Christianity can be seen first in the relationship between Jesus and history. In 1960 the Protestant theologian Paul Tillich visited Japan, and in conversation with Buddhist scholars in Kyoto he asked the following question: "If some historian should make it probable that a man of the name Gautama never lived, what would be the consequence for Buddhism"? Debates over the historical Jesus were raging in the West, and it was natural to inquire about similar issues in Buddhism. However, the Buddhist scholars responded by saying that the question of the historicity of Gautama Buddha had never been an issue for Buddhism. As one scholar put it, "According to the doctrine of Buddhism, the *dharma kaya* [the body of truth] is eternal, and so it does not depend upon the historicity of Gautama."[67]

This incident graphically illustrates a major difference not only between Christianity and Buddhism but also between Christianity and most other religions as well. Whereas in the case of other religions the religious teachings can be considered on their own, independently of any particular historical figure, this is not so in Christianity. The central teachings of Hinduism, for example, are considered to be eternal truths that can be expressed in various ways, but they are not necessarily rooted in any particular historical event or person. Similarly most Buddhists would hold that, although the present teachings of Buddhism are consistent with the teaching of the historical Gautama, ultimately the truth of Buddhism is eternal and distinct from Gautama. Even in Islam, a religion that takes history very seriously, the truths revealed in the Qur'an are independent of the historical Muhammad. Although he is said to have been the greatest of the prophets and is greatly revered by Muslims, Muhammad is nevertheless regarded as merely a man to whom Allah revealed his perfect revelation, the Qur'an. Had Muhammad never existed, Allah could have spoken to another prophet.

Authentic Christian faith, in contrast, is based upon the events comprising the life, death and resurrection of Jesus of Nazareth two thousand years ago. Unlike many religions, then, Christianity is in principle falsifiable, for if it could be demonstrated that Jesus of Nazareth never really existed, the Christian faith would crumble. The apostle Paul, writing to early Christians in Corinth around A.D. 55, unambiguously stated that, if in fact Jesus was not raised from the dead, then our faith is futile and useless and we are still in our sins (1 Cor 15:14-19). Here, then, is one respect in which Jesus is distinctive and unlike other religious figures: whereas it is possible to think of Buddhist or Hindu teaching apart from the historical Gautama or Shankara, for example, or to think of the Qur'an as having been

---

[67]Robert E. Wood, "Tillich Encounters Japan," in *Japanese Religions* 2 (May 1962): 48-50.

revealed to someone other than Muhammad, it is impossible to conceive of Christian faith apart from the actual life, death and resurrection of Jesus of Nazareth in first-century Palestine.[68]

Furthermore, throughout the New Testament writings we find, amid all of the rich diversity, a consistency in portraying Jesus as much more than merely a great miracle worker or rabbi. In their own ways—sometimes quite explicitly, while at other times more implicitly—the gospels and epistles place Jesus in an unprecedented relationship of identity with Yahweh, the eternal Creator who revealed himself to the Old Testament patriarchs and prophets. Jesus has the authority to do things that only God can do, such as forgive sin (Mk 2:5-11); judge the world (Mt 19:28; 25:31-46); give life, even to the dead (Jn 5:21, 25-29; 11:17-44); and speak authoritatively for God in interpreting the purposes of the Sabbath (Mk 2:23-27). Jesus states that anyone who has seen him has seen the Father (Jn 14:9)—an audacious claim within the context of Jewish monotheism. In identifying himself with the I AM of Exodus 3:14 Jesus was understood to be identifying himself with God (Jn 8:58)—an action that incurred the wrath of those listening. We find New Testament writers affirming the preexistence of the Son and his authority over all things (Jn 1:1-2; Col 1:15-17, 19; 2:9). Paul claims that all of the "fullness" *(pleroma)* of

---

[68]In emphasizing the historicity of Jesus in this manner we confront the vexing issue of the reliability of the New Testament pictures of Jesus: Can we have confidence that the New Testament writings are at all accurate in their depiction of the life and teaching of Jesus? Few issues in contemporary theology are as controversial as New Testament interpretation. Although the distinction is somewhat simplistic, contemporary interpreters of the New Testament can be broadly divided into two categories: (1) those who, while fully aware of the various critical problems involved, nevertheless accept the New Testament documents as authentic, historically reliable material describing what Jesus said and did, and (2) those who hold that the documents are primarily the creation of the early Christian community, so that, although the documents inform us of the experiences and beliefs of the early church, the task of trying to uncover what the actual historical Jesus of Nazareth said and did is at best highly problematic. While recognizing the significant critical issues involved in New Testament interpretation, and in no way denying the important part played by the early Christian communities in shaping these documents, I see no reason for concluding that the New Testament is not a reliable source for the sayings and deeds of Jesus. For an interesting example of two very different approaches to the historicity of the New Testament see Marcus J. Borg and N. T. Wright, *The Meaning of Jesus: Two Visions* (New York: HarperCollins, 1999). Helpful discussions of the issues can be found in Donald Guthrie, *New Testament Introduction*, 4th ed. (Downers Grove, Ill.: InterVarsity Press, 1990); Colin Brown, "Historical Jesus," in *Dictionary of Jesus and the Gospels*, ed. Joel B. Green, Scot McKnight and I. Howard Marshall (Downers Grove, Ill.: InterVarsity Press, 1992), pp. 326-41; Craig Blomberg, *The Historical Reliability of the Gospels* (Downers Grove, Ill.: InterVarsity Press, 1987); Ben Witherington III, *The Jesus Quest: The Third Search for the Jew of Nazareth* (Downers Grove, Ill.: InterVarsity Press, 1995); Paul Barnett, *Jesus and the Rise of Early Christianity: A History of New Testament Times* (Downers Grove, Ill.: InterVarsity, 1999); N. T. Wright, *The New Testament and the People of God,* vol. 1 of *Christian Origins and the Question of God* (Minneapolis: Fortress, 1992); and N. T. Wright, *Jesus and the Victory of God,* vol. 2 of *Christian Origins and the Question of God* (Minneapolis: Fortress, 1996).

God is present in Jesus (Col 1:19, 2:9).

One of the more remarkable passages identifying Jesus with Yahweh, the one eternal God, is the Christological hymn in Philippians 2:5-11. Not only does this affirm Christ's preexistence and essential equality with God (verses 6-8) but also it concludes by ascribing to Jesus language used in Isaiah 45:21-23 for God:

> At the name of Jesus every knee should bow
> in heaven and on earth and under the earth,
> and every tongue confess that Jesus Christ is Lord
> to the glory of God the Father. (Phil 2:10-11)

This is a partial quotation of Isaiah 45:21-23, words there spoken by Yahweh about himself. As Chris Wright observes, the implications of this for religious pluralism are significant:

> This declaration by God comes in the most unambiguously monotheistic section of the whole Old Testament. The magnificent prophecies of Isaiah 40-55 assert again and again that Yahweh is utterly unique as the only living God in his sovereign power over all nations and all history, and in his ability to save. This early Christian hymn, therefore, by deliberately selecting a scripture from such a context and applying it to Jesus, is affirming that Jesus is as unique as Yahweh in those same respects. . . . Another interesting factor here is the context of both texts. It is actually religious pluralism. In Philippians, the uniqueness of Jesus is asserted in the midst of the religious pluralism of the Greek and Roman world of the first century AD, using the same language and terms in which the uniqueness of Yahweh himself had been asserted in the midst of the pluralistic, polytheistic environment of Babylon in the sixth century BC.[69]

The astonishing claim of the New Testament is that in Jesus of Nazareth the one eternal God has become man. "The Word became flesh and made his dwelling among us" (Jn 1:14). Understood within the context of Jewish monotheism, this is an amazing assertion, not found in other religions.[70] And it is precisely this that makes the question of Jesus so controversial in the context of pluralism. As Vinoth Ramachandra remarks:

> The controversy over Jesus concerns *who he is*. For the historic Christian claim regarding Jesus of Nazareth is that no human category, whether that of "charismatic prophet," "religious genius," "moral exemplar," or "apocalyptic visionary" can do ade-

---

[69]Wright, *What's So Unique About Jesus?* p. 79. For discussion of issues in interpreting the Christological hymn in Philippians 2, see Peter T. O'Brien, *The Epistle to the Philippians* (Grand Rapids, Mich.: Eerdmans, 1991), especially pp. 238-62.

[70]The Christian doctrine of the incarnation is sometimes compared to the Hindu notion of *avatar*. But despite some similarities, when each concept is understood within its own context, the differences are clear. See John B. Carman, *Majesty and Meekness*, chapter 10; and Norman Anderson, *Christianity and World Religions: The Challenge of Pluralism* (Downers Grove, Ill.: InterVarsity Press, 1984), pp. 58-59.

quate justice to the evidence of his words and actions. No category short of deity itself
is sufficient. It is this traditional claim—that in the human person of Jesus, God himself has come amongst us in a decisive and unrepeatable way—that constitutes an
offence to pluralist society.[71]

Thus it is not merely what Jesus taught that sets him apart from other religious
leaders; it is who he is. It is not simply that Jesus has discovered the way and the
truth, and that if we follow his teachings we too can find the way for ourselves. No,
it is because of who he is and what he has done for us on the cross that he is himself the Way, the Truth and the Life (Jn 14:6). The truth of Jesus' teachings cannot
be separated from the grounding of this truth in the person of Christ as the incarnate Word of God.

It is sometimes said that the exclusivistic language of the New Testament that
speaks of Jesus as the only Savior (Jn 1:14; 14:6; Acts 4:12; 1 Tim 2:5; Heb 9:12)
should not be taken literally but rather understood metaphorically as "love language," expressing the early Christians' utter devotion to Jesus as *their* Savior,
although not necessarily the Savior for everyone. Paul Knitter, for example, argues
that, since the early Christians were products of "classicist culture," they had no
alternative but to use such exclusivistic language in expressing their love for
Christ.[72] But what they meant—devotion to Christ as *their* Lord—need not be
expressed today in such exclusivistic language.

But surely this is confused. Exclusive statements about the person and work of
Jesus were no more palatable in the first century than they are today. Far from
being dictated by the surrounding culture, such statements were in fact strongly
countercultural. John Ferguson points out that the first-century Mediterranean
world was highly relativistic and syncretistic and accommodating of divergent religious beliefs and practices so long as they did not become exclusivistic.[73] It was precisely the uncompromising exclusivism of the early Christians that provoked the
antagonism of the surrounding culture. Moreover, the assumption that the same
deity could be called by different names, or could take on different forms in different cultures, was widely accepted in the first-century Mediterranean world. Had the
early Christians wished to say that Jesus was only the savior *for them,* not necessarily for all peoples, or that the divine reality they worshiped could also be responded
to appropriately under other linguistic and religious forms, they certainly had the
resources at hand to do so. Robert Wilken states, "The oldest and most enduring

---

[71]Vinoth Ramachandra, *The Recovery of Mission: Beyond the Pluralist Paradigm* (Grand Rapids,
  Mich.: Eerdmans, 1996), p. 181. Emphasis in the original.
[72]Paul F. Knitter, *No Other Name? A Critical Survey of Christian Attitudes Toward the World
  Religions* (Maryknoll, N.Y.: Orbis, 1985), pp. 182-86.
[73]John Ferguson, *Religions of the Roman Empire* (Ithaca, N.Y.: Cornell University Press, 1970),
  chapter 12.

criticism of Christianity is an appeal to religious pluralism. . . . All the ancient crit-ics of Christianity were united in affirming that there is no one way to the divine."[74]

One of the more interesting early critiques of Christianity comes from Celsus, a second-century pagan philosopher whose *Alethes Logos [True Doctrine]* is the old-est literary attack on Christianity of which we have detailed knowledge. We know the substance of Celsus's critique through the extensive refutation given it by Ori-gen in *Contra Celsum [Against Celsus]* in the mid-third century.[75] Celsus appar-ently believed in one supreme deity with a multitude of subordinate local deities that varied with culture and place. He accused Christianity of being a subversive and dangerous revolt against accepted religious practices that had served the Medi-terranean cultures well for centuries. Celsus was well aware of the cultural and religious differences among peoples, and his appeal to diversity in support of moral and religious relativism prompted Wilken to call him "a consummate multi-cultur-alist."[76] Just as one should honor distinctive social customs in various lands, claimed Celsus, so too should the local religious traditions be accepted and hon-ored. Celsus affirmed, "It makes no difference whether we call Zeus the Most High, or Zen, or Adonai, or Sabaoth, or Amoun like the Egyptians, or Papaeus like the Scythians."[77]

In his response to Celsus, Origen appealed to both logical and historical consid-erations. Like critics of relativism ever since Plato, Origen pointed out the absurdi-ties that follow from relativism: Are we to accept any and all customs as legitimate? Is it "pious," then, to offer children for human sacrifice?[78] Furthermore, argued Origen, it does matter what names we use for God, for names are not merely arbi-trary conventions that vary with place; they refer to different realities. "The proper name for God, says Origen, is 'the God of Abraham and the God of Isaac and the God of Jacob.' "[79] Origen appealed to God's distinctive self-manifestation in history as determinative for our understanding of God. The issue, then, is not simply a matter of local customs or differing religious experiences. The decisive question is whether the one true God really has revealed himself, whether God indeed "existed within the compass of that man who appeared in Judea."[80]

---

[74]Robert Wilken, *Remembering the Christian Past* (Grand Rapids, Mich.: Eerdmans, 1995), pp. 27, 42.

[75]See *Origen: Contra Celsum*, trans. Henry Chadwick (Cambridge: Cambridge University Press, 1953). I am indebted here to the fine discussion of Celsus and Origen in Wilken, *Remembering the Christian Past*, pp. 27-46. For further discussion of pagan critiques of early Christianity, see Robert L. Wilken, *The Christians as the Romans Saw Them* (New Haven, Conn.: Yale University Press, 1984).

[76]Wilken, *Remembering the Christian Past*, p. 31.

[77]*Origen: Contra Celsum*, p. 299.

[78]Ibid., p. 293.

[79]Ibid., p. 300.

[80]Quoted in Wilken, *Remembering the Christian Past*, p. 37.

If the writers of the New Testament were indeed as influenced by the prevailing assumptions of the surrounding culture as Knitter suggests, one would expect to find there, not the exclusive statements about Christ one does find, but much greater openness to alternative images and religious figures. Perhaps Jesus could have been identified with Apollo or Mithras or Asclepius. The fact that such syncretistic accommodations are absent is significant. The early Christians surely were aware of such options but rejected them as inappropriate for communicating what they wished to say about Jesus' relation to God.

In considering the distinctiveness of Jesus Christ there is no reason to disparage or ridicule other great religious leaders. We can admire the tenacity with which Muhammad, within a highly polytheistic environment, condemned idolatry and called for worship of the one Creator. Surely we must be impressed with the great compassion and sensitivity to human suffering evident in Gautama the Buddha. And one cannot help but be struck by the keen insight into human nature and interpersonal relationships found in the teachings of Confucius.

But when all is said and done, the dissimilarities between Jesus and other religious figures far outstrip any possible similarities. Jesus was a strict monotheist. The Buddha and most likely also Confucius were at best agnostic about the existence of any God(s). Certainly no other founder of a major religion ever claimed to be the eternal Creator God. Jesus located the source of the human predicament in human sin. Religious leaders such as Confucius, Mahavira, Shankara or the Buddha identified the problem with deeply rooted ignorance or various social influences. No other figure claimed to be able to forgive sin, nor does any other major religious figure call all people to believe on himself and to find salvation in his person, as does Jesus. The Buddha, Mahavira, Confucius, Muhammad and Jesus all died, but there is no reliable historical record of any of the others, apart from Jesus, being resurrected after death. To suggest, then, that Jesus and the other religious leaders are essentially in the same category is to play fast and loose with what the New Testament says about Jesus.

How, then, should we think about non-Christian religious traditions? From the preceding discussion it should be evident why a simple answer is so difficult. Religions, just like cultures, are mixed in that they reflect what God has given in creation but what has then been corrupted through sin. As such, they manifest both good and evil, truth and falsity. In so far as religious traditions manifest the capacity for religious awareness, reflection and expression—this capacity itself a gift of God's creation and revelation—they are to be affirmed. And when this capacity finds expression, by God's grace, in submission to, and worship of, the one true God, humankind fulfills the purpose for which it was created, discovering the joy and contentment that flow from this. Moreover, whatever goodness, truth and beauty there might be in non-Christian religious traditions are there because of God the Creator, the source of all goodness and truth.

Nevertheless, other religions cannot be regarded merely as incomplete but honorable human responses to God. Not only do they manifest human rebellion against God, but as Hendrik Kraemer says, "in the light of Jesus Christ and of the truth realized in Him, and having regard to their deepest and most essential meaning and purpose, the religions are 'in error.'"[81] Thus, in so far as religious traditions deviate from what is good and true, as this is made known to us in Christ Jesus, they are to be rejected as false. Kraemer is typically forthright and perceptive on this point:

> [I]n the light of "Jesus Christ, in whom the glory full of grace and truth" has been revealed and has entered the actual, historical world of men as a power acting and operating within it—and not therefore, let me repeat, in the light of Christianity—the first thing that has to be said, and said straight out, about "other" religions is that considered in this light and in regard to their deepest, most essential purport they are all in error. In this light they are all noble, but misguided and abortive, attempts to take the fundamental religious questions—namely, what is the right relationship to God; who is God; who is man; in what do his Highest Good and his true vocation and destiny consist, in time and in eternity?—and to answer them in their own terms. Magnificent as they may be and often are, they represent, in this light, a "dark excursion of the mind" into what is from our standpoint as human beings the unfathomable mystery of God and into the mystery of man and the world. These are mysteries which, so far as His purpose with and attitude towards men and the world are concerned, God *makes* known in Christ.[82]

Whatever there is of falsity, evil and injustice within the religions is due to sin and the distortion of the Adversary. And yet even here we must remember, as Augustine taught us so long ago, that evil is parasitic upon the good, so that even the errors and distortions of other religious traditions are possible only because of the positive capacities with which God created humankind, capacities that in themselves are good and reflect the Creator.[83]

Finally, regardless of whatever goodness, beauty and truth we find in other religious traditions, we must not forget that the fact of religious diversity as we know it is itself an effect of the Fall and sin. If it were not for sin, there would not be this radical pluralization of religious responses to the divine; rather, whatever the other

---

[81]Hendrik Kraemer, *Why Christianity of All Religions?* (Philadelphia: Westminster Press, 1962), p. 97.

[82]Ibid., p. 93. Emphasis in the original.

[83]See Augustine, *Confessions* and *Enchiridion,* p. 148; *Enchiridion,* pp. 342-45; and *Basic Writings of Saint Augustine*, ed. Whitney J. Oates (New York: Random House, 1948), 1:432-33, 437.

differences among human beings in terms of ethnicity and culture, all humankind
would be united in proper worship of the one God. The Christian cannot, then,
simply accept the plurality of religious ways as part of the diversity of God's creation, for even when considered in the most positive light possible, the fact of multiple religions represents a distortion of God's intention for his creation.

Witness in Pluralistic Contexts

Witness to Jesus Christ as the one Lord and Savior for all humankind has been an
integral part of Christian faith throughout the centuries and grows out of the recognition of the truth of the gospel. Although the gospel was no more acceptable in
the first century than it is today, the apostle Paul's passion for evangelism rested
upon his conviction that it "is the power of God for the salvation of everyone who
believes" (Rom 1:16). Christ's followers are to be his ambassadors, sharing the gospel with others and inviting them to be reconciled to God through Christ (2 Cor
5:20—6:2). The legitimacy and significance of Christian witness cannot be separated from considerations of the truth of certain beliefs about God, human beings
and salvation. If, for example, atheistic humanists such as Bertrand Russell are correct that there is no God and that when we die we "shall rot, and nothing of [our
egos] will survive,"[84] then world evangelization is pointless. Or if Hinduism is correct in characterizing the human predicament as *samsara,* the wearisome cycle of
deaths and rebirths, and correct in its belief that liberation from *samsara* comes
only through rigorous self-discipline and control of one's mental faculties, then
preaching salvation in Jesus is useless. But if in fact, as the Bible claims, the fundamental cause of our predicament is human rebellion against a holy and righteous
God, and if the only remedy for this ailment is to be found in the salvation available
through Jesus Christ, then communication of the good news of salvation through
Jesus is not only a legitimate option but an inescapable imperative. As Paul put it,
"Woe to me if I do not preach the gospel!" (1 Cor 9:16).

Increasingly, the contexts within which Christian witness is to be carried out
will be religiously diverse societies in which the ideology of pluralism reigns. This
presents both challenges and opportunities for the church. It is easy to focus just
upon the challenges, but we dare not ignore the opportunities. The remarkable
resurgence of interest in religion and spirituality today presents opportunities for a
thoughtful, responsible invitation to consider the claims of Jesus. Moreover, there
is today considerable anxiety about the future of our increasingly fragmented societies. The engine driving the juggernaut of pluralism often is a quite legitimate
concern about how best to deal with radical diversity. The strong push for an undis-

---

[84]Bertrand Russell, "What I Believe," in *Why I Am Not a Christian* (New York: Allen & Unwin,
    1957), p. 54.

ciplined tolerance that refuses to make negative judgments about other traditions is undoubtedly excessive, but it is based upon an appropriate concern about the implications of deeply rooted religious diversity in society. Can Christians, Jews, Hindus, Muslims, Buddhists, Mormons, Wiccans, Baha'is and New Agers all live together without resorting to violence or abusing the rights of religious minorities? Frankly, the history of religion is not reassuring.

The issues are likely to become increasingly complex and controversial in societies marked not only by ongoing pluralization but also by political commitments to protect diversity of belief and practice. But it is within this context that the church should seize the opportunity and lead the way, demonstrating how to be both deeply committed to one's own beliefs and also appropriately tolerant and accepting of diversity. What is needed is commitment to both truth and justice—a gracious yet firm insistence upon Jesus Christ as the one Lord for all and a concern for justice that actively protects the rights of religious others to believe and practice as they do.[85] How tragic it is that, whether justified or not, Christians are the ones perceived today as intolerant and bigoted. The church must demonstrate through its actions, not merely its words, that we do accept ethnic and cultural diversity, that we are committed to justice for all and that we will support the rights of other religious communities to live and practice in our midst. But at the same time we cannot abandon our commitment to Jesus Christ as the one Lord and Savior for all humankind. So even as we accept Hindus and Buddhists and New Agers as fellow human beings created in God's image, we must urge them also to be reconciled to God by accepting Jesus Christ as their Lord and Savior.

In concluding these reflections on theology of religions we can do no better than to quote rather extensively from the distinguished theologian and missionary statesman Stephen Neill:

> [The Christian faith] claims for itself that it is the only form of faith for men; by its own claim to truth it casts the shadow of falsehood, or at least of imperfect truth, on every other system. This Christian claim is naturally offensive to the adherents of every other religious system. It is almost as offensive to modern man, brought up in the atmosphere of relativism, in which tolerance is regarded as the highest of the virtues. But we must not suppose that this claim to universal validity is something that can quietly be removed from the Gospel without changing it into something entirely different from what it is. . . . [Christian faith] maintains that in Jesus the one thing that needed to happen has happened in such a way that it need never happen again in the same way. The universe has been reconciled to its God. Through the perfect obedi-

---

[85]See S. D. Gaede, *When Tolerance Is No Virtue: Political Correctness, Multiculturalism, and the Future of Truth and Justice* (Downers Grove, Ill.: InterVarsity Press, 1993); and Richard J. Mouw, *Uncommon Decency: Christian Civility in an Uncivil World* (Downers Grove, Ill.: InterVarsity Press, 1992).

ence of one man a new and permanent relationship has been established between God and the whole human race. The bridge has been built. There is room on it for all the needed traffic in both directions, from God to man and from man to God. Why look for any other? . . . Making such claims, Christians are bound to affirm that all men need the Gospel. For the human sickness there is one specific remedy, and this is it. There is no other. Therefore the Gospel must be proclaimed to the ends of the earth and to the end of time.[86]

[86]Stephen Neill, *Christian Faith and Other Faiths: The Christian Dialogue with Other Religions* (New York: Oxford University Press, 1961), pp. 16-17.

Selected Bibliography

Abe, Masao. *Zen and Western Thought.* Edited by William R. LaFleur. Honolulu: University of Hawaii Press, 1985.

Abraham, William J. "The Epistemological Significance of the Inner Witness of the Holy Spirit." *Faith and Philosophy* 7, no. 4 (1990): 434-50.

Allen, Diogenes. *Christian Belief in a Postmodern World.* Louisville: Westminster John Knox, 1989.

Alston, William P. *Perceiving God: The Epistemology of Religious Experience.* Ithaca, N.Y.: Cornell University Press, 1991.

———. *A Realist Conception of Truth.* Ithaca, N.Y.: Cornell University Press, 1996.

Anderson, Gerald H. "American Protestants in Pursuit of Mission: 1886–1986." *International Bulletin of Missionary Research* 12 (July 1988): 98-118.

———. "Theology of Religions and Missiology: A Time of Testing." In *The Good News of the Kingdom: Mission Theology for the Third Millennium.* Edited by Charles Van Engen, Dean S. Gilliland and Paul Pierson. Maryknoll, N.Y.: Orbis, 1993.

Anderson, Gerald H., and Thomas F. Stransky, eds. *Christ's Lordship and Religious Pluralism.* Maryknoll, N.Y.: Orbis, 1981.

Anderson, Norman. *Christianity and World Religions: The Challenge of Pluralism.* Downers Grove, Ill.: InterVarsity Press, 1984.

Aslan, Adnan. *Religious Pluralism in Christian and Islamic Philosophy: The Thought of John Hick and Seyyed Hossein Nasr.* Richmond, England: Curzon, 1998.

Baird, Robert D. *Category Formation and the History of Religions.* The Hague: Mouton, 1971.

Barber, Benjamin. *Jihad vs. McWorld: How Globalization and Tribalism Are Reshaping the World.* New York: Ballantine, 1996.

Basinger, David. "Plantinga, Pluralism and Justified Religious Belief." *Faith and Philosophy* 8, no. 1 (1991): 67-80.

———. "Religious Diversity: Where Exclusivists Often Go Wrong." *International Journal for Philosophy of Religion* 47 (February 2000): 43-55.

Baumer, Franklin L. *Modern European Thought: Continuity and Change in Ideas,*

1600–1950. New York: Macmillan, 1977.

———. *Religion and the Rise of Scepticism*. New York: Harcourt Brace, 1960.

Bavinck, Johan Herman. *The Church Between Temple and Mosque: A Study of the Relationship Between the Christian Faith and Other Religions*. Grand Rapids, Mich.: Eerdmans, 1966.

Berger, Peter. *A Far Glory: The Quest for Faith in an Age of Credulity*. New York: Anchor, 1992.

———. *The Heretical Imperative: Contemporary Possibilities of Religious Affirmation*. New York: Doubleday, 1979.

———. *The Sacred Canopy: Elements of a Sociological Theory of Religion*. New York: Anchor, 1967.

———, ed. *The Desecularization of the World: Resurgent Religion and World Politics*. Grand Rapids, Mich.: Eerdmans, 1999.

Berger, Peter, Brigitte Berger and Hansfried Kellner. *The Homeless Mind: Modernization and Consciousness*. New York: Vintage, 1973.

Beyer, Peter. *Religion and Globalization*. Thousand Oaks, Calif.: Sage, 1994.

Blauw, Johannes. "The Biblical View of Man in His Religion." In *The Theology of the Christian Mission*. Edited by Gerald H. Anderson. New York: McGraw-Hill, 1961.

Bosch, David. *Transforming Mission: Paradigm Shifts in Theology of Mission*. Maryknoll, N.Y.: Orbis, 1991.

Braaten, Carl E. *No Other Gospel! Christianity Among the World's Religions*. Minneapolis: Fortress, 1992.

Bruce, Steve. *Religion in the Modern World: From Cathedrals to Cults*. New York: Oxford University Press, 1996.

Bruce, Steve, ed. *Religion and Modernization: Sociologists and Historians Debate the Secularization Thesis*. Oxford: Clarendon, 1982.

Burnyeat, Myles, ed. *The Skeptical Tradition*. Berkeley: University of California Press, 1983.

Cahoone, Lawrence, ed. *From Modernism to Postmodernism: An Anthology*. Oxford: Blackwell, 1996.

Carman, John B. *Majesty and Meekness: A Comparative Study of Contrast and Harmony in the Concept of God*. Grand Rapids, Mich.: Eerdmans, 1994.

Carpenter, Joel A., and Wilbert R. Shenk, eds. *Earthen Vessels: American Evangelicals and Foreign Missions, 1880–1980*. Grand Rapids, Mich.: Eerdmans, 1990.

Carson, D. A. *The Gagging of God: Christianity Confronts Pluralism*. Grand Rapids, Mich.: Zondervan, 1996.

Cassirer, Ernst. *The Philosophy of the Enlightenment*. Princeton, N.J.: Princeton University Press, 1951.

Chadwick, Owen. *The Secularization of the European Mind in the Nineteenth Century.* Cambridge: Cambridge University Press, 1975.

Christian, William A. *Doctrines of Religious Communities: A Philosophical Study.* New Haven, Conn.: Yale University Press, 1987.

———. *Oppositions of Religious Doctrines: A Study in the Logic of Dialogue Among Religions.* London: Macmillan, 1972.

Clark, David. *Dialogical Apologetics: A Person-Centered Approach to Christian Defense.* Grand Rapids, Mich.: Baker, 1993.

Clarke, Andrew D., and Bruce W. Winter, eds. *One God, One Lord: Christianity in a World of Religious Pluralism.* 2nd ed. Grand Rapids, Mich.: Baker, 1992.

Clarke, J. J. *Oriental Enlightenment: The Encounter Between Asian and Western Thought.* London: Routledge, 1997.

Clendenin, Daniel. *Many Gods, Many Lords: Christianity Encounters World Religions.* Grand Rapids, Mich.: Baker, 1995.

———. "The Only Way." *Christianity Today,* January 12, 1998, pp. 34-40.

Compson, Jane. "The Dalai Lama and the World Religions: A False Friend?" *Religious Studies* 32 (June 1996): 271-79.

Covell, Ralph. *Confucius, the Buddha, and Christ: A History of the Gospel in Chinese.* Maryknoll, N.Y.: Orbis, 1986.

———. "Jesus Christ and the World Religions: Current Evangelical Viewpoints." In *The Good News of the Kingdom: Mission Theology for the Third Millennium.* Edited by Charles Van Engen, Dean S. Gilliland and Paul Pierson. Maryknoll, N.Y.: Orbis, 1993.

Cowan, Steven B., ed. *Five Views on Apologetics.* Grand Rapids, Mich.: Zondervan, 2000.

Coward, Harold, ed. *Hindu-Christian Dialogue: Perspectives and Encounters.* Maryknoll, N.Y.: Orbis, 1989.

Cracknell, Kenneth. *Justice, Courtesy and Love: Theologians and Missionaries Encountering World Religions, 1846-1914.* London: Epworth, 1995.

Cragg, Gerald. *Reason and Authority in the Eighteenth Century.* Cambridge: Cambridge University Press, 1964.

Cragg, Kenneth. *The Call of the Minaret.* 3rd ed. Oxford: Oneworld, 2000.

———. *The Christ and the Faiths.* Philadelphia: Westminster Press, 1986.

———. *Sandals at the Mosque: Christian Presence Amid Islam.* New York: Oxford University Press, 1959.

Crockett, William V., and James Sigountos, eds. *Through No Fault of Their Own? The Fate of Those Who Have Never Heard.* Grand Rapids, Mich.: Baker, 1991.

Dallmayr, Fred. *Beyond Orientalism: Essays on Cross-Cultural Encounter.* Albany: State University of New York Press, 1996.

Davis, Caroline Franks. *The Evidential Force of Religious Experience.* Oxford: Clarendon, 1989.

D'Costa, Gavin. *The Meeting of Religions and the Trinity.* Maryknoll, N.Y.: Orbis, 2000.

———. *Theology and Religious Pluralism: The Challenge of Other Religions.* Oxford: Blackwell, 1986.

———. "Whose Objectivity? Which Neutrality? The Doomed Quest for a Neutral Vantage Point from Which to Judge Religions." *Religious Studies* 29 (1993): 79-95.

———, ed. *Christian Uniqueness Reconsidered: The Myth of a Pluralistic Theology of Religions.* Maryknoll, N.Y.: Orbis, 1990.

Dean, Thomas, editor. *Religious Pluralism and Truth: Essays on Cross-Cultural Philosophy of Religion.* Albany: State University of New York Press, 1995.

Demarest, Bruce. *General Revelation: Historical Views and Contemporary Issues.* Grand Rapids, Mich.: Zondervan, 1982.

Deutsch, Eliot, ed. *Culture and Modernity: East-West Philosophic Perspectives.* Honolulu: University of Hawaii Press, 1991.

Dewick, Edward Chisholm. *The Christian Attitude Toward Other Religions.* Cambridge: Cambridge University Press, 1953.

Drummond, Richard Henry. *Toward a New Age in Christian Theology.* Maryknoll, N.Y.: Orbis, 1985.

Dulles, Avery. *A History of Apologetics.* Philadelphia: Westminster Press, 1971.

Dupuis, Jacques. *Toward a Christian Theology of Religious Pluralism.* Maryknoll, N.Y.: Orbis, 1997.

Elison, George. *Deus Destroyed: The Image of Christianity in Early Modern Japan.* Cambridge, Mass.: Harvard University Press, 1973.

Ellwood, Robert S. *Alternative Altars: Unconventional and Eastern Spirituality in America.* Chicago: University of Chicago Press, 1979.

Erickson, Millard. "Hope for Those Who Haven't Heard? Yes, But . . ." *Evangelical Missions Quarterly* 11 (April 1975): 122-26.

———. *How Shall They Be Saved? The Destiny of Those Who Do Not Hear of Jesus.* Grand Rapids, Mich.: Baker, 1996.

Evans, C. Stephen. *The Historical Christ and the Jesus of Faith: The Incarnational Narratives as History.* Oxford: Clarendon, 1996.

Farquhar, J. N. *The Crown of Hinduism.* London: Oxford University Press, 1913.

Friedman, Thomas. *The Lexus and the Olive Tree: Understanding Globalization.* New York: Farrar Straus Giroux, 1999.

Gaede, S. D. *When Tolerance Is No Virtue: Political Correctness, Multiculturalism, and the Future of Truth and Justice.* Downers Grove, Ill.: InterVarsity Press, 1993.

Gardiner, Patrick. "German Philosophy and the Rise of Relativism." *The Monist* 64 (April 1981): 138-54.

Gay, Craig. *The Way of the (Modern) World: Or, Why It's Tempting to Live As If God Doesn't Exist.* Grand Rapids, Mich.: Eerdmans, 1998.

Gay, Peter. *The Rise of Modern Paganism.* Vol. 1 of *The Enlightenment: An Interpretation.* New York: W. W. Norton, 1966.

————. ed. *The Enlightenment: A Comprehensive Anthology.* New York: Simon & Schuster, 1973.

Geertz, Clifford. *The Interpretation of Cultures.* New York: Random House, 1973.

Giddens, Anthony. *The Consequences of Modernity.* Stanford, Calif.: Stanford University Press, 1990.

————. *Modernity and Self-Identity: Self and Society in the Late Modern Age.* Stanford, Calif.: Stanford University Press, 1991.

Godlove, Terry F. *Religion, Interpretation, and Diversity of Belief: The Framework Model from Kant to Durkheim to Davidson.* New York: Cambridge University Press, 1989.

Green, Ronald M. *Religion and Moral Reason: A New Method for Comparative Study.* New York: Oxford University Press, 1988.

Grenz, Stanley J.. *A Primer on Postmodernity.* Grand Rapids, Mich.: Eerdmans, 1996.

Griffiths, Paul J. *An Apology for Apologetics: A Study in the Logic of Interreligious Dialogue.* Maryknoll, N.Y.: Orbis, 1991.

Griffiths, Paul J., ed. *Christianity Through Non-Christian Eyes.* Maryknoll, N.Y.: Orbis, 1990.

Gutting, Gary. *Religious Belief and Religious Skepticism.* Notre Dame, Ind.: University of Notre Dame Press, 1982.

Halbfass, Wilhelm. *India and Europe: An Essay in Understanding.* Albany: State University of New York Press, 1988.

Hamnett, Ian, ed. *Religious Pluralism and Unbelief: Studies Critical and Comparative.* London: Routledge, 1990.

Hampson, Norman. *The Enlightenment: An Evaluation of Its Assumptions, Attitudes, and Values.* Hammondsworth, England: Penguin, 1968.

Harrison, Peter. *"Religion" and the Religions in the English Enlightenment.* Cambridge: Cambridge University Press, 1990.

Harvey, David. *The Condition of Postmodernity: An Inquiry into the Origins of Cultural Change.* Cambridge, Mass.: Blackwell, 1990.

Hatch, Elvin. *Culture and Morality: The Relativity of Values in Anthropology.* New York: Columbia University Press, 1983.

Hazard, Paul. *The European Mind: 1680–1715.* London: Hollis & Carter, 1953.

————. *European Thought in the Eighteenth Century: From Montesquieu to Lessing.* New Haven, Conn.: Yale University Press, 1954.

Heelas, Paul. *The New Age Movement: The Celebration of the Self and the Sacralization of Modernity.* Oxford: Blackwell, 1996.

Heim, S. Mark. *The Depth of the Riches: A Trinitarian Theology of Religious Ends.* Grand Rapids, Mich.: Eerdmans, 2001.

————. *Salvations: Truth and Difference in Religion.* Maryknoll, N.Y.: Orbis, 1995.

Helm, Paul. *Faith and Understanding.* Grand Rapids, Mich.: Eerdmans, 1997.

Hewitt, Harold, Jr., ed. *Problems in the Philosophy of Religion: Critical Studies of the Work of John Hick.* New York: St. Martin's, 1991.

Hick, John. *Arguments for the Existence of God.* New York: Herder & Herder, 1971.

————. *A Christian Theology of Religions: The Rainbow of Faiths.* Louisville: Westminster John Knox, 1995.

————. *Death and Eternal Life.* San Francisco: Harper & Row, 1976.

————. *Disputed Questions in Theology and the Philosophy of Religion.* New Haven, Conn.: Yale University Press, 1993.

————. "The Epistemological Challenge of Religious Pluralism." *Faith and Philosophy* 14, no. 3 (1997): 277-86.

————. *Faith and Knowledge.* 2nd ed. Ithaca, N.Y.: Cornell University Press, 1966.

————. *The Fifth Dimension: An Exploration of the Spiritual Realm.* Oxford: Oneworld, 1999.

————. *God and the Universe of Faiths: Essays in the Philosophy of Religion.* New York: St. Martin's, 1973.

————. *God Has Many Names.* Philadelphia: Westminster Press, 1980.

————. "Ineffability." *Religious Studies* 36 (March 2000): 35-46.

————. *An Interpretation of Religion: Human Responses to the Transcendent.* New Haven, Conn.: Yale University Press, 1989.

————. *The Metaphor of God Incarnate: Christology in a Pluralistic Age.* Louisville: Westminster John Knox, 1993.

————. "On Grading Religions" *Religious Studies* 27, no. 4 (1981): 511-21.

————. *Philosophy of Religion.* 4th ed. Englewood Cliffs, N.J.: Prentice-Hall, 1990.

————. *Problems of Religious Pluralism.* New York: St. Martin's, 1985.

Hick, John, ed. *The Myth of God Incarnate.* Philadelphia: Westminster Press, 1977.

————. *Truth and Dialogue in World Religions: Conflicting Truth-Claims.* Philadelphia: Westminster Press, 1974.

Hick, John, and Paul F. Knitter, eds. *The Myth of Christian Uniqueness: Toward a Pluralistic Theology of Religions.* Maryknoll, N.Y.: Orbis, 1987.

Hiebert, Paul G. *Anthropological Reflections on Missiological Issues.* Grand Rapids, Mich.: Baker, 1994.

————. "Critical Issues in the Social Sciences and Their Implications for Mission Studies." *Missiology* 24 (January 1996): 65-82.

Hiebert, Paul G., R. Daniel Shaw and Tite Tiénou. *Understanding Folk Religion*. Grand Rapids, Mich.: Baker, 1999.

Hocking, William E., ed. *Re-Thinking Missions: A Laymen's Inquiry After One Hundred Years*. New York: Harper & Brothers, 1932.

Hollis, Martin, and Steven Lukes, editors. *Rationality and Relativism*. Oxford: Blackwell, 1982.

Hunsberger, George R., and Craig Van Gelder, eds. *The Church Between Gospel and Culture: The Emerging Mission in North America*. Grand Rapids, Mich.: Eerdmans, 1996.

Hunter, James Davison. *American Evangelicalism: Conservative Religion and the Quandary of Modernity*. New Brunswick, N.J.: Rutgers University Press, 1983.

————. *Evangelicalism: The Coming Generation*. Chicago: University of Chicago Press, 1987.

Hutchison, William R. *Errand to the World: American Protestant Thought and Foreign Missions*. Chicago: University of Chicago Press, 1987.

Huxley, Aldous. *The Perennial Philosophy*. London: Grafton, 1985.

Jackson, Carl T. *The Oriental Religions and American Thought: Nineteenth-Century Explorations*. Westport, Conn.: Greenwood, 1981.

Johnson, Roger A. "Natural Religion, Common Notions and the Study of Religions: Lord Herbert of Cherbury." *Religion* 24 (July 1994): 213-24.

Kellogg, Samuel H. *A Handbook of Comparative Religion*. 1899. Reprint, Philadelphia: Westminster Press, 1927.

————. *The Light of Asia and the Light of the World*. London: Macmillan, 1885.

King, Richard. *Orientalism and Religion: Postcolonial Theory, India and the "Mystic East."* New York: Routledge, 1999.

Kirk, J. Andrew, and Kevin J. Vanhoozer, eds. *To Stake a Claim: Mission and the Western Crisis of Knowledge*. Maryknoll, N.Y.: Orbis, 1999.

Kitagawa, Joseph. "The 1893 World's Parliament and Its Legacy." In *The History of Religions: Understanding Human Experience*. Atlanta: Scholar's Press, 1987.

Knitter, Paul. *Jesus and the Other Names: Christian Mission and Global Responsibility*. Maryknoll, N.Y.: Orbis, 1996.

————. *No Other Name? A Critical Survey of Christian Attitudes Toward the World Religions*. Maryknoll, N.Y.: Orbis, 1985.

————. "Roman Catholic Approaches to Other Religions: Developments and Tensions." *International Bulletin of Missionary Research* 8 (April 1984): 50-54.

Kraemer, Hendrik. *The Christian Message in a Non-Christian World*. New York: Harper & Brothers, 1938.

————. *Religion and the Christian Faith.* London: Lutterworth, 1956.

————. *Why Christianity of All Religions?* Philadelphia: Westminster Press, 1962.

Larson, Gerald James, and Eliot Deutsch, eds. *Interpreting Across Boundaries: New Essays in Comparative Philosophy.* Princeton, N.J.: Princeton University Press, 1988.

Lee, Jung H. "Problems of Religious Pluralism: A Zen Critique of John Hick's Ontological Monomorphism." *Philosophy East and West* 48, no. 3 (1998): 453-77.

Livingston, James C. *The Enlightenment and the Nineteenth Century.* Vol. 1 of *Modern Christian Thought.* 2nd ed. Upper Saddle River, N.J.: Prentice-Hall, 1997.

Lyon, David. *The Steeple's Shadow: On the Myths and Realities of Secularization.* Grand Rapids, Mich.: Eerdmans, 1985.

Lyotard, Jean-François. *The Postmodern Condition: A Report on Knowledge.* Translated by Geoff Bennington and Brian Massumi. Minneapolis: University of Minnesota Press, 1984.

Madan, T. N. "Secularism in Its Place." *The Journal of Asian Studies* 46, no. 4 (1987): 747-59.

Marshall, P. J., and Glyndwr Williams, *The Great Map of Mankind: British Perceptions of the World in the Age of Enlightenment.* London: Dent, 1982.

Mavrodes, George I. "Polytheism." In *The Rationality of Belief and the Plurality of Faith.* Edited by Thomas D. Senor. Ithaca, N.Y.: Cornell University Press, 1995.

————. "A Response to John Hick." *Faith and Philosophy* 14, no. 3 (1997): 289-94.

McDermott, Gerald R. *Can Evangelicals Learn from World Religions? Jesus, Revelation, and Religious Traditions.* Downers Grove, Ill.: InterVarsity Press, 2000.

————. *Jonathan Edwards Confronts the Gods: Christian Theology, Enlightenment Religion, and Non-Christian Faiths.* New York: Oxford University Press, 2000.

McGowan, John. *Postmodernism and Its Critics.* Ithaca, N.Y.: Cornell University Press, 1991.

McGrath, Alister. *A Passion for Truth: The Intellectual Coherence of Evangelicalism.* Downers Grove, Ill.: InterVarsity Press, 1996.

Moser, Paul K., Dwayne H. Mulder and J. D. Trout. *The Theory of Knowledge: A Thematic Introduction.* New York: Oxford University Press, 1998.

Muck, Terry C. "Evangelicals and Interreligious Dialogue." *Journal of the Evangelical Theological Society* 36, no. 4 (1993): 517-29.

————. "Is There Common Ground Among Religions?" *Journal of the Evangelical Theological Society* 40, no. 1 (1997): 99-112.

————. *The Mysterious Beyond: A Basic Guide to Studying Religion.* Grand Rapids, Mich.: Baker, 1993.

Mullen, David George, ed. *Religious Pluralism in the West: An Anthology.* Oxford: Blackwell, 1998.

Nakamura, Hajime. *Ways of Thinking of Eastern Peoples.* Translated by Philip P. Wiener. Rev. ed. Honolulu: University of Hawaii Press, 1964.

Neely, Alan. "The Parliaments of the World's Religions: 1893 and 1993." *International Bulletin of Missionary Research* 18, no. 2 (1994): 60-64.

Neill, Stephen. *Christian Faith and Other Faiths: The Christian Dialogue with Other Religions.* London: Oxford University Press, 1961.

———. *Colonialism and Christian Missions.* New York: McGraw-Hill, 1966.

———. *A History of Christian Missions.* Rev. ed. Hammondsworth, England: Penguin, 1986.

———. *The Supremacy of Jesus.* London: Hodder & Stoughton, 1984.

Netland, Harold. *Dissonant Voices: Religious Pluralism and the Question of Truth.* Grand Rapids, Mich.: Eerdmans, 1991.

———. "Professor Hick on Religious Pluralism." *Religious Studies* 22, no. 2 (1986): 249-61.

Newbigin, Lesslie. *Foolishness to the Greeks: The Gospel and Western Culture.* Grand Rapids, Mich.: Eerdmans, 1986.

———. *The Gospel in a Pluralist Society.* Grand Rapids, Mich.: Eerdmans, 1989.

———. *A Word in Season: Perspectives on Christian World Missions.* Grand Rapids, Mich.: Eerdmans, 1994.

Newman, Jay. *Foundations of Religious Tolerance.* Toronto: University of Toronto Press, 1982.

Nicholls, Bruce J., ed. *The Unique Christ in Our Pluralist World.* Grand Rapids, Mich.: Baker, 1994.

Okholm, Dennis L., and Timothy R. Phillips, eds. *Four Views on Salvation in a Pluralistic World.* Grand Rapids, Mich.: Zondervan, 1996.

Packer, J. I. "Evangelicals and the Way of Salvation." In *Evangelical Affirmations.* Edited by Kenneth S. Kantzer and Carl F. H. Henry. Grand Rapids, Mich.: Zondervan, 1990.

———. *God's Words: Studies of Key Bible Themes.* Downers Grove, Ill.: InterVarsity Press, 1981.

Pailin, David. *Attitudes to Other Religions: Comparative Religion in Seventeenth- and Eighteenth-Century Britain.* Manchester, England: Manchester University Press, 1984.

Pannenberg, Wolfhart. "The Religions from the Perspective of Christian Theology and the Self-Interpretation of Christianity in Relation to the Non-Christian Religions." *Modern Theology* 9, no. 3 (1993): 285-97.

Patterson, James Alan. "The Loss of a Protestant Missionary Consensus: Foreign Missions and the Fundamentalist-Modernist Conflict." In *Earthen Vessels: American Evangelicals and Foreign Missions, 1880–1980.* Edited by Joel A. Carpenter and Wilbert R. Shenk. Grand Rapids, Mich.: Eerdmans, 1990.

Pinnock, Clark. *A Wideness in God's Mercy: The Finality of Jesus Christ in a World of Religions.* Grand Rapids, Mich.: Zondervan, 1992.

Plantinga, Alvin. "Justification and Theism." *Faith and Philosophy* 4, no. 4 (1987): 403-26.

———. "Pluralism: A Defense of Religious Exclusivism." In *The Rationality of Belief and the Plurality of Faith.* Edited by Thomas Senor. Ithaca, N.Y.: Cornell University Press, 1995.

———. *Warranted Christian Belief.* New York: Oxford University Press, 2000.

Plantinga, Alvin, and Nicholas Wolterstorff, editors. *Faith and Rationality: Reason and Belief in God.* Notre Dame, Ind.: University of Notre Dame Press, 1983.

Plantinga, Richard J., ed. *Christianity and Plurality: Classical and Contemporary Readings.* Oxford: Blackwell, 1999.

Popkin, Richard. *The History of Scepticism from Erasmus to Spinoza.* Berkeley: University of California Press, 1979.

Preus, Samuel J. *Explaining Religion: Criticism and Theory from Bodin to Freud.* New Haven, Conn.: Yale University Press, 1987.

Priest, Robert J., Thomas Campbell and Bradford A. Mullen. "Missiological Syncretism: The New Animistic Paradigm." In *Spiritual Power and Missions: Raising the Issues.* Edited by Edward Rommen. Pasadena, Calif.: William Carey Library, 1995.

Quinn, Philip. "The Foundations of Theism Again: A Rejoinder to Plantinga." In *Rational Faith: Catholic Responses to Reformed Epistemology.* Edited by Linda Zagzebski. Notre Dame, Ind.: University of Notre Dame Press, 1993.

———. "In Search of the Foundations of Theism." *Faith and Philosophy* 2, no. 4 (1985): 469-86.

Quinn, Philip, and Kevin Meeker, eds. *The Philosophical Challenge of Religious Diversity.* New York: Oxford University Press, 2000.

Radhakrishnan, Sarvepalli. *Eastern Religions and Western Thought.* Oxford: Clarendon, 1939.

Ramachandra, Vinoth. *Faiths in Conflict? Christian Integrity in a Multicultural World.* Leicester, England: Inter-Varsity Press, 1999.

———. *The Recovery of Mission: Beyond the Pluralist Paradigm.* Grand Rapids, Mich.: Eerdmans, 1996.

Robertson, Roland. *Globalization: Social Theory and Global Culture.* Newbury Park, Calif.: Sage, 1992.

Roof, Wade Clark. *Spiritual Marketplace: Baby Boomers and the Remaking of American Religion.* Princeton, N.J.: Princeton University Press, 1999.

Rommen, Edward, and Harold Netland, eds. *Christianity and the Religions: A Bib-*

lical Theology of World Religions. Pasadena, Calif.: William Carey Library, 1995.

Rorty, Richard. *Philosophy and the Mirror of Nature.* Princeton, N.J.: Princeton University Press, 1979.

Rose, Margaret. *The Post-Modern and the Post-Industrial: A Critical Analysis.* Cambridge: Cambridge University Press, 1991.

Ross, Andrew C. *A Vision Betrayed: The Jesuits in Japan and China, 1542–1742.* Maryknoll, N.Y.: Orbis, 1994.

Rowe, William L. "Religious Pluralism." *Religious Studies* 35 (June 1999): 139-50.

Runia, Klaas. "The Gospel and Religious Pluralism." *Evangelical Review of Theology* 14 (October 1990): 362-63.

Ruokanen, Mikka. *The Catholic Doctrine on Non-Christian Religions According to the Second Vatican Council.* Leiden, Holland: E. J. Brill, 1992.

Said, Edward. *Orientalism.* New York: Vintage, 1978.

Samartha, Stanley. *One Christ, Many Religions: Toward a Revised Christology.* Maryknoll, N.Y.: Orbis, 1991.

Sampson, Philip, Vinay Samuel and Chris Sugden, eds. *Faith and Modernity.* Oxford: Regnum Lynx, 1994.

Sanders, John. *No Other Name: An Investigation into the Destiny of the Unevangelized.* Grand Rapids, Mich.: Eerdmans, 1992.

Sanders, John, ed. *What About Those Who Have Never Heard? Three Views on the Destiny of the Unevangelized.* Downers Grove, Ill.: InterVarsity Press, 1995.

Schreiter, Robert. *The New Catholicity: Theology Between the Global and the Local.* Maryknoll, N.Y.: Orbis, 1997.

Seager, Richard Hughes, ed. *The Dawn of Religious Pluralism: Voices from the World's Parliament of Religions, 1893.* La Salle, Ill.: Open Court, 1993.

Senor, Thomas, editor. *The Rationality of Belief and the Plurality of Faith.* Ithaca, N.Y.: Cornell University Press, 1995.

Sharma, Arvind. *The Philosophy of Religion and Advaita Vedanta: A Comparative Study in Religion and Reason.* University Park: Pennsylvania State University Press, 1995.

Sharma, Arvind, ed. *God, Truth and Reality: Essays in Honour of John Hick.* New York: St. Martin's, 1993.

————. *Neo-Hindu Views of Christianity.* Leiden, Holland: E. J. Brill, 1988.

Sharpe, Eric J. *Comparative Religion: A History.* 2nd ed. La Salle, Ill.: Open Court, 1986.

————. *Not to Destroy but to Fulfill: The Contribution of J. N. Farquhar to Protestant Missionary Thought in India Before 1914.* Uppsala, Sweden: Gleerup, 1965.

————. *Understanding Religion.* New York: St. Martin's, 1983.

Sheard, Robert B. *Interreligious Dialogue in the Catholic Church Since Vatican II.*

New York: Edwin Mellen, 1987.

Smart, Barry. "Modernity, Postmodernity and the Present." In *Theories of Modernity and Postmodernity*. Edited by Bryan Turner. London: Sage, 1990.

Smart, Ninian. *A Dialogue of Religions*. London: SCM Press, 1960.

———. *Doctrine and Argument in Indian Philosophy*. London: Allen & Unwin, 1964.

———. *Reasons and Faiths: An Investigation of Religious Discourse, Christian and Non-Christian*. London: Routledge & Kegan Paul, 1958.

———. *Worldviews: Crosscultural Explorations of Human Beliefs*. 2d ed. Englewood Cliffs, N.J.: Prentice-Hall, 1995.

Smith, Christian, with Michael Emerson, Sally Gallagher, Paul Kennedy and David Sikkink. *American Evangelicalism: Embattled and Thriving*. Chicago: University of Chicago Press, 1998.

Smith, Huston. *Forgotten Truth*. New York: Harper & Row, 1976.

———. "Is There a Perennial Philosophy?" *Journal of the American Academy of Religion* 55 (fall 1987): 553-66.

Smith, Wilfred Cantwell. *Faith and Belief*. Princeton, N.J.: Princeton University Press, 1979.

———. *The Meaning and End of Religion: A Revolutionary Approach to the Great Religious Traditions*. San Fransisco: Harper & Row, 1962.

———. *Religious Diversity: Essays by Wilfred Cantwell Smith*. Edited by Willard G. Oxtoby. New York: Harper & Row, 1976.

———. *Towards a World Theology*. London: Macmillan, 1981.

Speer, Robert E. *The Finality of Jesus Christ*. New York: Revell, 1933.

Sprinker, Michael, ed. *Edward Said: A Critical Reader*. Oxford: Blackwell, 1992.

Stanley, Brian. *The Bible and the Flag: Protestant Missions and British Imperialism in the Nineteenth and Twentieth Centuries*. Leicester, England: Inter-Varsity Press, 1990.

Stott, John. *The Authentic Jesus*. London: Marshall Morgan & Scott, 1985.

Stransky, Thomas F. "The Church and Other Religions." *International Bulletin of Missionary Research* 9, no. 4 (1985): 154-58.

Streng, Frederick. *Understanding Religious Life*. 3rd ed. Belmont, Calif.: Wadsworth, 1985.

Tambiah, Stanley Jeyaraja. *Magic, Science, Religion and the Scope of Rationality*. Cambridge: Cambridge University Press, 1990.

Teasdale, Wayne, and George Cairns, eds. *The Community of Religions: Voices and Images of the Parliament of the World's Religions*. New York: Continuum, 1996.

Thelle, Notto. *Buddhism and Christianity in Japan: From Conflict to Dialogue, 1854–1899*. Honolulu: University of Hawaii Press, 1987.

Tomlinson, John. *Globalization and Culture*. Chicago: University of Chicago Press, 1999.

Toulmin, Stephen. *Cosmopolis: The Hidden Agenda of Modernity*. Chicago: University of Chicago Press, 1990.

Trigg, Roger. *Rationality and Religion*. Oxford: Blackwell, 1998.

Turner, Bryan. *Orientalism, Postmodernism and Globalism*. London: Routledge, 1994.

Tweed, Thomas A., and Stephen Prothero, eds. *Asian Religions in America: A Documentary History*. New York: Oxford University Press, 1999.

Twiss, Sumner B. "The Philosophy of Religious Pluralism: A Critical Appraisal of Hick and His Critics." *The Journal of Religion* 70 (October 1990): 533-68.

Vanhoozer, Kevin J., ed. *The Trinity in a Pluralistic Age: Theological Essays on Culture and Religion*. Grand Rapids, Mich.: Eerdmans, 1997.

Vroom, Hendrick M. *Religions and the Truth: Philosophical Reflections and Perspectives*. Grand Rapids, Mich.: Eerdmans, 1989.

Wainwright, William. "Doctrinal Schemes, Metaphysics and Propositional Truth." In *Religious Pluralism and Truth: Essays on Cross-Cultural Philosophy of Religion*. Edited by Thomas Dean. Albany: State University of New York Press, 1995.

————. *Philosophy of Religion*. 2nd ed. Belmont, Calif.: Wadsworth, 1999.

————. "Wilfred Cantwell Smith on Faith and Belief." *Religious Studies* 20, no. 3 (1984): 353-66.

Ward, Keith. "Divine Ineffability." In *God, Truth and Reality: Essays in Honour of John Hick*. Edited by Arvind Sharma. New York: St. Martin's, 1993.

————. *Religion and Revelation*. Oxford: Clarendon, 1994.

Waters, Malcolm. *Globalization*. New York: Routledge, 1995.

Wells, David. *God in the Wasteland: The Reality of Truth in a World of Fading Dreams*. Grand Rapids, Mich.: Eerdmans, 1994.

————. *No Place for Truth: Or, Whatever Happened to Evangelical Theology?* Grand Rapids, Mich.: Eerdmans, 1993.

Wiebe, Donald. *Truth and Religion: Towards an Alternative Paradigm for the Study of Religion*. The Hague: Mouton, 1981.

Wilken, Robert. *Remembering the Christian Past*. Grand Rapids, Mich.: Eerdmans, 1995.

Williams, Paul, "Some Dimensions of the Recent Work of Raimundo Panikkar: A Buddhist Perspective." *Religious Studies* 27, no. 4 (1991): 511-21.

Wilson, Bryan. *Religion in Sociological Perspective*. Oxford: Oxford University Press, 1982.

Wilson, Bryan, ed. *Rationality*. Oxford: Blackwell, 1970.

Wright, Christopher J. H. "The Christian and Other Religions: The Biblical Evidence." *Themelios* 9, no. 2 (1984): 4-15.

———. *What's So Unique About Jesus?* Eastbourne, England: Monarch, 1990.

Wykstra, Stephen J. "Toward a Sensible Evidentialism: On the Notion of 'Needing Evidence.' " In *Philosophy of Religion: Selected Readings*. 3rd ed. Edited by William L. Rowe and William J. Wainwright. Fort Worth: Harcourt Brace, 1998.

Wuthnow, Robert. *After Heaven: Spirituality in America Since the 1950s*. Berkeley and Los Angeles: University of California Press, 1998.

Yandell, Keith E. *The Epistemology of Religious Experience*. Cambridge: Cambridge University Press, 1993.

———. *Philosophy of Religion: A Contemporary Introduction*. London: Routledge, 1999.

———. "Some Varieties of Religious Pluralism." *Inter-Religious Models and Criteria*. Edited by James Kellenberger. New York: St. Martin's.

Young, Richard Fox. *"Deus Unus* or *Dei Plures Sunt?* The Function of Inclusivism in the Buddhist Defense of Mongol Folk Religion Against William of Rubruck (1254)." *Journal of Ecumenical Studies* 26, no. 1 (1989): 100-35.

———. *Resistant Hinduism: Sanskrit Sources on Anti-Christian Apologetics in Early Nineteenth-Century India*. Vienna: Institut für Indologie der Universität Wien, 1981.

Young, R. F., and S. Jebanesan. *The Bible Trembled: The Hindu-Christian Controversies of Nineteenth-Century Ceylon*. Vienna: Institut für Indologie der Universität Wien, 1995.

Yates, Timothy. *Christian Mission in the Twentieth Century*. Cambridge: Cambridge University Press, 1994.

Index of Persons